HISTORY OF
WESTERN PHILOSOPHY

THE FACTS ON FILE
GUIDE TO PHILOSOPHY

History of
Western Philosophy

David Boersema
Kari Middleton

Facts On File
An Infobase Learning Company

The Facts On File Guide to Philosophy: History of Western Philosophy

Copyright © 2012 by David Boersema and Kari Middleton

Facts On File, Inc.
An imprint of Infobase Learning
132 West 31st Street
New York NY 10001

Library of Congress Cataloging-in-Publication Data
Boersema, David.
   The Facts on File guide to philosophy. History of Western philosophy /
David Boersema, Kari Middleton.
      p. cm.
   Includes bibliographical references and index.
   ISBN 978-0-8160-8158-5
   1. Philosophy—History. I. Middleton, Kari. II. Title. III. Title: History of
Western philosophy.
   B72.B66 2012
   190—dc23   2011029436

Text design by Erik Lindstrom
Composition by Julie Adams
Cover printed by Yurchak Printing, Inc., Landisville, Pa.
Book printed and bound by Yurchak Printing, Inc., Landisville, Pa.
Date printed: March 2012
Printed in the United States of America

This book is printed on acid-free paper.

Table of Contents

Part II: Modern Philosophy   117

Part III: Continental Philosophy   211

Part IV: Analytic Philosophy   317

Introduction

The Greek philosopher Socrates, who lived in the 400s B.C.E., was said to have remarked that the unexamined life is not worth living. At the end of his own life, he was found guilty of having corrupted the youth of Athens (by essentially telling them to question authority) and was sentenced to death. Many people have at least heard of Socrates, even if they cannot say much about him. Many have also heard of his student Plato, as well as Plato's student Aristotle. All three of these thinkers had an enormous influence on the history of Western culture, indeed on world culture. Far fewer—at least outside of academia—have heard of Immanuel Kant, Georg Hegel, or Ludwig Wittgenstein, even though they, too, had an important influence on Western culture. This book provides a brief overview of the history of Western philosophy, including many of the important individuals who both shaped and were shaped by our collective culture.

Especially in the United States, where there is such high value placed on practicality, there is the sense that philosophy is an abstract, subjective, essentially useless field of study. Just about every college student who has decided to major in philosophy has faced the question (often posed by dismayed or unhappy parents): Philosophy—what are you going to do with that? At the same time, we all face philosophical questions and concerns every day. Every time we vote, we are making a choice about what kind of government we want and, in the process, implicitly asking (and answering) the philosophical question: What is the proper role of the state? Every time we go to a movie and come away from it having had a pleasant or unpleasant experience, we are implicitly asking (and answering) the philosophical question: What makes a work of art good or bad? Every time we take medicine or choose to fly in an airplane, we are implicitly asking (and answering) the philosophical question: How do I know, or have good reasons to believe, that this will do what I expect it to do? Far from being abstract, subjective, or useless, philosophy is fundamental, not only to what we do with our lives, but also to who we are and who we hope to be.

As a rigorous field of study, philosophy addresses some very basic, fundamental questions: What is reality (the field of study called metaphysics), how do we know (the field of study called epistemology), and why does it matter (the field of study called axiology). Is a fetus a person, such that it has rights? This is a metaphysical question (What makes something a person?), an epistemological question (How would we know or determine this?), and an axiological question (What gives a fetus rights?). Likewise, when we ask what sorts of things should or should not be taught in public schools, we are asking these same sorts of philosophical questions (What should be taught? How should it be taught? Why should it be taught?).

The Facts On File Guide to Philosophy set is designed to provide an accessible and engaging introduction to philosophy for students. This volume outlines the history of Western philosophy, from the beginnings to the present day. Western philosophy is more than 2,500 years old. It is usually said to have begun in what is now Greece and Turkey, roughly around 600 B.C.E. with a group of thinkers who were later called the pre-Socratics (that is, coming before Socrates). While there have been some basic questions and issues that have been common throughout this long history—for instance, questions about the nature of knowledge or of ethics—philosophical thought, including what questions and issues were seen as more or less important, has changed and evolved over those two and a half millennia. Very broadly, philosophers speak of classical philosophy (600 B.C.E.–400 C.E.), medieval and Renaissance philosophy (400–1600), modern philosophy (1600–1900), and contemporary philosophy (1900 to the present). These labels, of course, are imprecise, indicating general and broad periods in which philosophical thought can be characterized.

This volume discusses the major thinkers of each of these periods and their most influential ideas.

Note that because major ideas can be important in different contexts, and because certain thinkers made important contributions in more than one area, material within the set is occasionally repeated, with the intention of providing full context for each discussion.

David Boersema
Kari Middleton

PART I

Western Philosophy, from the Greeks to the Renaissance

Introductory Discussion Questions

1. Diamonds and coal are both forms of carbon. So, if you had a diamond and a lump of coal, would you have two things or two bits of one thing? Apples and oranges are both forms of fruit. So, if you had an apple and an orange, would you have two things or two bits of one thing?
2. Do good and just people make a good and just society or does a good and just society make good people? What is justice for a person and for a society?
3. How do we know that 7+5=12? Would 7+5=12 even if no one knew it? Could 7+5 ever not equal 12?
4. Are there things that are real and actually exist other than physical things? If there are, how would we know?
5. Is being extreme about values always bad? Is it ever bad? Is looking for (and perhaps finding) some middle ground between two opposing views always good? Is it ever good?
6. Is the expression, "Ignorance is bliss" true? Or does genuine peace of mind depend upon having knowledge (and, so, greater peace of mind upon having greater knowledge)?

The Greek Miracle

The period of classical Greek philosophy refers to philosophical thought and activity roughly in the 1,000-year period from 600 B.C.E. to 400 C.E. It is usually divided into three broad parts: pre-Socratic philosophy (600–450 B.C.E.), Athenian philosophy, usually meaning the time of Socrates, Plato, and Aristotle (450–300 B.C.E.), and Hellenistic philosophy (300 B.C.E.–400 C.E.). While the term *Hellenistic* literally refers to Greek culture, philosophers often include the works of Roman philosophers up to around 400 C.E.

The pre-Socratic philosophers primarily focused their attention on issues of natural philosophy, that is, fundamental knowledge of nature, and directly wrote much less on ethics or social and political philosophy. Today, we might well think of them as early scientists as much as early philosophers. The pre-Socratics focused on four overlapping fundamental themes: (1) appearance v. reality, (2) change v. permanence, (3) accident v. essence, and (4) the many v. the one. The theme of appearance v. reality has to do with questioning whether or not the way things appear to be to us is, in fact, the way they really are. Is the real nature of trees or water or anything in the world the same as how we experience them? For example, we would say that water is composed of two gases and those gases are composed of molecules and atoms and subatomic particles. So, what we experience on an everyday basis—a wet liquid—is not what we would take to be an experience of gases or atoms. If everyday knowledge of things as we experience them is not necessarily the same thing as knowledge of things as they really are (knowledge of an underlying reality), then it is important, said the pre-Socratics, to go beyond or beneath everyday experience—that is, beyond appearances—to come to know reality. This relates directly to the second theme, namely, change v. permanence. In our everyday experience, we note that things often change, or at least they appear to change. Is there, asked the pre-Socratics, anything that is permanent, that does not change or that remains the same beneath the apparent change? This was asking whether there is a permanent substance or thing that stands under the changes we experience.

The third theme of accident and essence gets at much the same idea. Things have different properties or features. For example, a cat has physical properties, such as fur and eyes, as well as behavioral properties, such as purring and running. Some properties are said to be essential, meaning that if those properties changed or were different, then the thing itself that had those properties would be different. They are properties that are defining of what something is. Accidental properties, however, are taken as features of something that happen to be characteristics of that thing but are not necessary for that thing to be what it is. Pre-Socratic philosophers saw essential features, but not accidental features, as the underlying permanent reality of things in the world. Finally, the fourth theme, namely the many v. the one, also connects with issues of what is real and permanent and essential. The question here is: Are the things that are real (as opposed to mere appearances) made up of many basic kinds of things or are they ultimately made up of one kind of thing? At the level of appearance, the answer seems to be many kinds of things, but the question is whether at the level of what is real there are many fundamental kinds of things or just one.

The focus on this last theme in particular led to several basic schools of thought among the pre-Socratic philosophers. One school of thought is called monism, because it holds the view that all things are ultimately constituted by one kind of thing. The other school of thought is called pluralism, because it holds the view that there is more than one ultimate kind of thing that constitutes things in the world. The pre-Socratic philosophers understood things in the world to be composed of four basic elements: earth, water, air, and fire. These four elements were associated with two basic characteristics: heat and moisture. Earth was said to be cold and dry, water cold and wet, air hot and wet, fire hot and dry. The monists argued that ultimately things could be understood as being composed of one of these basic elements, while the pluralists argued that all four were necessary and no element could be accounted for in terms of any of the other three. Some pluralists even argued that there were atoms that were the ultimate building block of all things.

The second broad part of ancient Western philosophy begins with Socrates (469–399 B.C.E.). The legacy of Socrates is immense. He is said to have "brought philosophy down from the stars." This means that he focused on concerns of moral and social philosophy—for example, asking about the nature of the good life or knowledge or beauty or friendship—rather than focusing on the issues of natural philosophy that the pre-Socratics had done. Socrates was concerned with living well. He was famous for seeking wisdom and asking his fellow Athenians about basic

Socrates, his two spouses, and Alcibiades *(Painting by Reyer van Blommendael)*

concepts, such as knowledge or moral duty. What has come to be called the Socratic method was his way of asking a series of questions, with the hope of identifying the nature of these basic notions (like knowledge or moral duty). This method also pointed to the goal of having people come up with the answer to the questions on their own, rather than having the answer told to them. Although Socrates claimed he was simply seeking wisdom and, in his search, helping others seek it, he was said by others to have corrupted the youth with his teachings, and he was sentenced to death when he was 70 years old.

One of Socrates' students, Plato (427–347 B.C.E.), is considered (along with his own student, Aristotle) one of the most influential philosophers of all time. Plato's thought was wide-ranging and deep. His work was influential in the major branches of philosophy: metaphysics (the study of reality), epistemology (the study of knowledge), and axiology (the study of values). Like the pre-Socratics, Plato wanted to distinguish appearance from reality and to find what, if anything, was permanent and unchanging. But, like Socrates, he also wanted to identify the key to living well. Both of these concerns were settled for him by what he called Ideas (or Forms).

Plato argued that there are varying degrees or levels of reality, with Ideas being the most real. There are some things, such as shadows or images, that are real but fleeting, and they are real only because they are caused by something else. For example, a shadow of a person is real (there really is a shadow at times), but that shadow can go away when there is no light source to cause it. The physical person, however, still exists even when the light source goes away (for example, when the Sun goes behind a cloud). The person, Plato said, is more real than the shadow, because the person (along with the light source) causes the shadow and exists even when the shadow does not. However, there is also the Idea of Person, for Plato. The Idea of something is whatever matches the ideal definition, or core nature, of that thing. For example, even though there are no physical dinosaurs that exist today, there is the concept of dinosaur that exists. That concept, then—or, for Plato, the Idea—is even more real than physical dinosaurs. In addition, our knowledge of Ideas must come from reason, not from our physical senses (like touch, taste, etc.). This is because the physical senses can only know physical things, not ideal concepts. Reason, then, for Plato, is the highest form of knowledge. Finally, living well, living the good life, is a life that is focused on reason, since it is reason that has contact with what is most real, the Ideas. Virtue is knowledge, said Plato. When people act wrongly, he said, it is out of ignorance; they think they are doing what is right. So, to truly become good and to live well is a matter of knowledge, of knowing what is good. At the social and political level, this meant, for Plato, having the best rulers (an aristocracy), not simply popular rule (a democracy). Ideally, there could even be a Philosopher-King.

Plato's student, Aristotle (384–322 B.C.E.), had very different views from his teacher. Like Plato, Aristotle wrote on many topics and was immensely influential, not only in philosophy, but in science as well. He was so influential that during much of the later Middle Ages he was referred to simply as The Philosopher. Unlike Plato, who looked for what was permanent and unchanging, Aristotle focused on change. Change was so basic to Aristotle that his views could be summarized in the concept of teleology. The word *teleology* comes from the Greek word *telos*, which means "end" or "goal." Observing the natural world, Aristotle saw that things in the world—both nonhuman things and events in the natural world as well as human things and events in the social world—changed over time. They did not merely change, but they developed; that is, they changed in patterned ways and almost always toward some end or goal. For example, acorns became oak trees, fruit matured and ripened, flowers blossomed in the spring and not in the winter. For Aristotle, these common, natural patterns were a sign of teleology. He claimed that philosophy (including natural philosophy, or science) needed to focus on understanding the causes of these patterned changes, not on abstract Ideas.

The third broad part of ancient Western philosophy is called Hellenistic philosophy. This is because the Greek name for Greece was *Hellas*. When scholars speak of the history of Greek culture up through Aristotle, the term they use is *Hellenic*. However, when they speak of Greek and Greek-influenced culture after that time, the term they use is *Hellenistic* (Greeklike). Hellenistic philosophy, then, is philosophy after Aristotle and includes thinkers outside of the Greek city-states. There were four major philosophical traditions within Hellenistic philosophy: stoicism, Epicureanism, skepticism, and Neoplatonism.

The stoics stressed the ideal of living well, which for them meant both inner peace of mind and also good citizenship. To live well, to truly find peace of mind and social harmony, they said, one must know how the world works. Like Aristotle and some of the pre-Socratics, they saw the world as a place of change, but structured and patterned change. To be truly happy, one must know about these things, so that one can know what is within one's power to do and not to do. Humans are part of the natural world and influenced by the same laws and forces as the rest of the natural world. To know what one can (or cannot) do, one must understand nature and see one's place in it. A consequence of this belief, for the stoics, was the acceptance of the way things are, almost a determinism. As a later stoic, Epictetus (55–135 C.E.), said, "What disturbs men's minds is not events, but their judgments on events." That is, there are things that are out of our control and we need to accept them, otherwise we will not find peace of mind. Epicureanism, named after Epicurus (341–270 B.C.E.), taught very much the same views as stoicism: Being happy, living well, is a matter of peace of mind, not possessing lots of material goods or having fame, and peace of mind comes from knowing what is within one's control and what is not within one's control (so, knowing how the world works). Like both the stoics and the Epicureans, the skeptics saw peace of mind as the goal of philosophizing. The word *skeptic* comes from the Greek word *skeptikos*, which means "examiner" or "considerer." The skeptics claimed that no one can ever really know the truth about things and, so, we should suspend judgment about them; we need to become detached as much as possible and not be negatively agitated or positively excited about things (since we might always be wrong about them). Peace of mind, tranquility, is not exactly the same as indifference, but it was, for the skeptics, a matter of detachment.

Neoplatonism, as the name suggests, was a return to an emphasis on Plato, or at least on aspects of Plato's views, particularly the view that what is most real is a realm of eternal, unchanging things and truths. The most famous Neoplatonist was Plotinus. While Plotinus lived in the early Christian era and found some aspects of Plato's thought to be consistent with Christianity, he himself was not Christian and actually wrote works that were critical of Christianity. Rather than speak of God as the highest reality, he spoke of the Good as the highest reality. Rather than looking for peace of mind in detachment, like the skeptics, he argued for actively seeking and embracing the ideal Good as the only means to happiness.

Natural Philosophy

The word *philosophy* comes from two Greek words, *philo,* meaning "love" and *sophia,* meaning "wisdom." Philosophy, then, is the love of wisdom. For the Greeks, wisdom was related to, but different than, knowledge. Knowledge could be a collection of a lot of bits of information. Wisdom was not simply knowing a lot of things, but knowing first principles. By principles the Greeks meant that which underlies and connects different things. Principles are not specific, but general, perhaps even universal. That is, they refer to broad issues or facts, not simply particular things. By speaking of first principles, Greek philosophers were concerned with getting to the most basic and fundamental principles (conceptually, the first ones). The concern, then, was to understand the most basic and, at the same time, the broadest knowledge of things.

One area of this search for first principles was moral philosophy. Here the focus was on finding the first principles of living well and of moral behavior. The point was to know how to live well and to know the most basic moral principles of living well. This included what we think of as ethics, but also social and political philosophy, since people live in communities and societies. Living well, living a good life, was understood as living a life with others, so the search for first principles of moral philosophy included questions about the proper role and function of the state as well as questions about personal moral behavior.

Another area of this search for first principles was natural philosophy. Here the focus was on finding the first principles of nature, what today we would likely call laws of nature. Indeed, what we today would think of as being science is what for centuries was called natural philosophy. Those people who we think of as early scientists called themselves natural philosophers, that is, philosophers of nature. It was not until the early 1800s that the term *scientist* was coined, and, when it was, it was originally meant in a sarcastic way to talk about someone who merely collected data but did not search for first principles. Only gradually during the 1800s did the term *scientist* fully replace the term *natural philosopher.*

From the beginning of Western philosophy, starting with the pre-Socratics, natural philosophy was fundamental to Western intellectual culture. The pre-Socratics, for example, asked about what things in everyday experience were real and what things were mere appearance.

They also asked what were the basic elements out of which all things were made (and whether there were many basic elements or perhaps just one). The history of natural philosophy is essentially the history of science, until the 1800s. What led to the split between natural philosophy and the new science was that natural philosophy included the concept of final cause, meaning that things happened in nature for some purpose. Natural philosophers assumed that to understand things and events in nature they had to include the notion that there was some final purpose or goal that was part of the cause of those things and events. The new scientific view rejected this notion of final cause and claimed that natural philosophy was driven by presumed theory and philosophy rather than by the data that was observed in nature. Although this split began as early as the 1600s, it was not until the late 1800s that there was a complete and widespread split. Nonetheless, although the methods and sometimes the goals of natural philosophy and science were not always the same or consistent, the drive to discover the fundamental nature of nature was as much a part of natural philosophy as it is of science.

Elements and
the Nature of Change

Pre-Socratic Philosophy

The term *pre-Socratic philosophy* refers to the ideas of thinkers in the Mediterranean area, stretching from modern-day Italy to modern-day Turkey, roughly between 600 B.C.E. and 400 B.C.E. They are grouped together for two major reasons. First, they focused largely on the same sorts of conceptual and philosophical concerns, and, second, because Socrates had such a significant influence on subsequent philosophical thought that he is seen as a turning point between those who preceded him and those who followed him. The earliest of the pre-Socratic philosophers came from the area then known as Miletus (part of what is now western Turkey).

The pre-Socratic philosophers primarily focused their attention on issues of natural philosophy, that is, fundamental knowledge of nature, as opposed to, say, society. Today we might well think of them as early scientists as much as early philosophers. Their concerns were metaphysical (asking about what is real), epistemological (asking about how we know), and axiological (asking about what is important). In particular, their concerns were about the basic, underlying nature of the physical world, what means we can use to know about it, and why such knowledge matters.

Pre-Socratic philosophy is characterized by four overlapping fundamental themes: (1) appearance v. reality, (2) change v. permanence,

13

(3) accident v. essence, and (4) the many v. the one. The theme of appearance v. reality has to do with questioning whether the way things appear to us is, in fact, the way they really are. Is the real nature of trees or water or anything in the world the same as how we experience it? Today, we would say that water is composed of two gases and those gases are composed of molecules and atoms and subatomic particles. So, what we experience on an everyday basis—a wet liquid—is not what we would take to be an experience of gases or atoms. If everyday knowledge of things as we experience them is not necessarily the same thing as knowledge of things as they really are (knowledge of an underlying reality), then it is important, said the pre-Socratics, to go beyond or beneath everyday experience—that is, beyond appearances—to come to know reality. This relates directly to the theme of change v. permanence. In our everyday experience, we note that things often change or at least appear to change: Acorns become oak trees, kittens become cats, bananas ripen and change color and texture, things come into being and go out of existence. Is there, asked the pre-Socratics, anything that is permanent, that does not change or that remains the same beneath the apparent change? This was asking whether there is a permanent substance, or thing, that stands under the changes we experience.

The third theme of accident and essence gets at much of the same idea. Things have different properties or features. For example, a cat has physical properties, such as fur and eyes, as well as behavioral properties, such as purring and running. Some properties are said to be essential, meaning that if those properties changed or were different, then the thing itself that had those properties would be different. If a particular cat lost an ear, it would not necessarily be a different cat, but would be the same cat with one fewer ear. But if a given cat had a different set of genes, then it might well be a different cat, not the same cat that had somehow changed. Essential properties, then, are taken as properties that are defining of what something is. Accidental properties are taken as features of something that happen to be characteristic of that thing but are not necessary for that thing to be what it is. Having certain length claws can be a feature of some cat, but if those claws are trimmed it is still the same cat. Having a certain set of genes, however, can be necessary for some cat to be that particular cat. Pre-Socratic philosophers saw essential features as the underlying permanent reality of things in the world. Finally, the theme of the many v. the one also connects with issues of what is real and permanent and essential. The question here is: Are the things that are real (as opposed to mere appearances) constituted by many basic kinds of things or are they ultimately constituted by one kind of thing? At the level of appearance, the answer seems to be: many kinds of things. Cats are not the same things, or kind of things, as oak trees, and neither is the same kind of thing as water. But the question is whether at the level of what is real there are many fundamental kinds of things or just one.

The focus on this last theme in particular led to several basic schools of thought among the pre-Socratic philosophers. One school of thought is called monism, because it holds the view that all things are ultimately constituted by one kind of thing. The other school of thought is called pluralism, because it holds the view that there is more than one ultimate kind of thing that constitutes things in the world. The pre-Socratic philosophers understood things in the world to be composed of four basic elements: earth, water, air, and fire. These four elements were associated with two basic characteristics: heat and moisture. Earth was said to be cold and dry, water cold and wet, air hot and wet, and fire hot and dry. The monists argued that ultimately things could be understood as being composed of one of these basic elements, while the pluralists argued that all four were necessary and no element could be accounted for in terms of any of the other three.

Thales

Thales of Miletus is often identified as the founder of the Milesian school of natural philosophy and the first of the Western natural philosophers. His exact dates are not known, but he is said to have flourished around 580 B.C.E. Thales left no writings that are known today, and our present understanding of him is based on commentary by later Greek thinkers such as Plato and Aristotle. He is said to have engaged in a great deal of scientific investigation as well as practical application of knowledge of the natural world. For example, he is said to have predicted a solar eclipse that occurred in 585 B.C.E. and also worked as an engineer in making a river passable by diverting its waters.

A common story told about Thales is that, while speculating on the heavens and not watching where he was going, he fell into a well, much to the amusement of others and fueling the view that philosophers were impractical daydreamers. To refute this, Thales was said to predict, from his astronomical observations and inferences, an upcoming drought. Based on his predictions, he cornered the market on olive presses so that when the drought came, he made a great deal of money. This proved, he is said to have claimed, that if philosophers wanted to succeed in everyday practical ways they could, but their concerns were elsewhere.

As one of the monistic pre-Socratic philosophers, Thales is especially noted for his claim that water is the source of all things. He noted that living organisms required water (or, at least moisture) to live and that even the inanimate natural environment was formed by water, such as the creation of deltas where rivers flowed into the sea. Although we now say that this claim of water as the source of all things is false, the underlying assumptions leading to it are what are philosophically important. First, Thales identified a material substance—water—as the source of things, rather than a divine being (or beings) or some unknowable origin. Second, Thales identified this material substance as the source of things. As such, it is both the underlying cause of things and the underlying essence of things. Third, water is not merely the source of some things, but it is the source of *all* things. So, there is a unity among things that exist, regardless of how different they appear to be. Finally, it is a single substance, water, that is the source of all things. By identifying one basic element of all things, Thales is classified as an advocate of monism. These assumptions of an underlying material essence and unity are what constitute much of pre-Socratic natural philosophy as well as subsequent Western philosophy and science.

Anaximander

Anaximander (610–546 B.C.E.) was said to have studied with Thales. Almost nothing is known of his life except that he lived in Miletus, which was in a region called Ionia (now western Turkey). Although he was known to have written works on philosophy, including natural philosophy, or what today we would think of as science, only a few fragments remain. He is said to have drawn one of the first maps of the world, at least of the world as he knew of it. He also claimed that the Earth was not supported by anything, but "hung freely" in space. He was said to have introduced a primitive sundial, called a *gnomon*, to Greece, which had important value in indicating hours and even measuring seasonal time changes. He also is said to have measured distances (although inaccurately) to celestial bodies such as the Sun and Moon. In addition, he was said to have argued that humans evolved (although not in the modern Darwinian sense) from animals that lived in the sea. All of these claims point to Anaximander as being seen during his lifetime as what today we would consider a scientist.

However, he is known within philosophy far more than within science. His importance in philosophy comes from his writings on monism. Monism (from the Latin word *mono,* meaning "one") is the view that there is a single basis to all things. As a natural philosopher, and following Thales, Anaximander looked for this single basis within the natural world, not in anything supernatural, such as gods. At the time, the view was that there were four fundamental kinds of material elements: earth, water, air, and fire. That is, people saw these four kinds of things as fundamental and unique. Each one was a variation on heat and moisture: Earth was seen as cold and dry, water as cold and wet, air as warm and wet, fire as warm and dry. All natural things seemed to ultimately come down to these four elements. Thales, however, had argued that really water was the single basic element. Anaximander thought that Thales must be wrong because, he argued, there is no way that something can come from its opposite; fire (being warm and dry) cannot come from water (being cold and wet). In fact, Anaximander said, none of the four elements could be more basic than any of the others. Instead, he claimed, there is a more basic single element, but it must be unlimited, or boundless. The Greek term he used was *apeiron.* Rather than being a material kind of thing, *apeiron* is more like a force or principle. We see in nature a war of opposites in which, for instance, part of the year is warm and part of the year is cold or some days are dry and some are wet. Something must account for these facts about the world, both in terms of causing them to be and in terms of explaining them. For Anaximander, this account was not limited by any one of the elements; it was the unlimited, the *apeiron.*

While it is acknowledged that Anaximander rightly saw problems with any view of monism, because of the problem of generating opposites (such as water from fire or earth from air), his claims about *apeiron* were immediately criticized as not giving a plausible account for things, but merely giving a label to them.

Anaximenes

Anaximenes, who lived around 545 B.C.E., was said to have been a student of Anaximander. Almost nothing is known of his life other than that he lived in Miletus and studied under Anaximander. None of his writings survive, and his views are known only from the commentaries of later philosophers.

Anaximenes is usually considered the third of the early Milesian natural philosophers. He focused on the basic nature of the natural, physical world and did not write anything about ethics or political philosophy. Like the two previous Milesian philosophers, Thales and Anaximander, Anaximenes was concerned about explaining the nature of the world and the things in it in terms of natural objects and processes, as opposed to explaining them in terms of supernatural objects and processes (such as gods). Thales argued that all things come from water, while Anaximander said he was wrong because nothing can come from its opposite (so, for instance, fire, which is hot and dry cannot come from water, which is cold and wet). No single element could be the one basic element, said Anaximander; instead, there must be something that is unlimited (what he called *apeiron*).

Anaximenes thought that Anaximander's notion of *apeiron* did not resolve the problem of opposites, that is how one element could be generated by another with opposite features. Rather, he said, asserting *apeiron* ignores the problem and simply offers a label to explain it away. Like Thales, then, Anaximenes thought that one of the material elements was basic and only a material explanation would suffice to resolve the problem of opposites. As a result, he offered such an explanation by saying that air was basic and the other elements were generated by air being condensed or rarefied. As air condensed, clouds could form and eventually moisture/water would be created. If this were condensed even further, silt and mud—that is, earth—would be generated. On the other hand, by rarefying air, fire would be produced. This process could be demonstrated, he claimed, by blowing air out of one's mouth. If the opening in one's lips is small (that is, the air is condensed), then the air coming out feels cool to the touch, but if one opens one's mouth wide (that is, the air is rarefied) and blows air out, then the air coming out feels warm. While this might seem simplistic, the important conceptual point, and why Anaximenes was influential, is that qualitative features of things are explained in terms of quantity, and nothing extra-material, such as gods or *apeiron,* is needed.

Heraclitus and Change

Heraclitus

Heraclitus lived around 500 B.C.E. Almost nothing is known of his life other than the fact that he lived in Ephesus, a city in Ionia (now western Turkey). He was supposedly from a royal family, and his writings indicated that he was well educated, which implies that, for that time and place, he had a privileged family background. He is said to have been very critical of much of the social and intellectual world that he knew. For example, he is said to have claimed that the famous Greek poet Homer was a fool and should have been whipped, that Pythagoras was a fraud, and that all of the adult citizens of his hometown, Ephesus, should hang themselves. Only various fragments of his writings have survived.

As a philosopher, Heraclitus is best known for two basic views: Change is the fundamental nature of things and that there is a unity of opposites. With respect to change as the fundamental nature of things, he is said to have claimed that one cannot step into the same river twice. The reason is that the river is constantly flowing and changing, so whatever made the river what it was at one point in time is different than what it is at another point in time. If there is any unity to things or unchanging permanence to anything, he claimed, it is the very process of change, not some thing or substance (such as atoms or physical objects). In some of the fragments of his writing, he speaks of fire as the basic nature of things: "This world-order did none of the gods or men

Painting of Heraclitus, an Ionian philosopher who argued for the unity of opposites and the fundamental nature of change *(Painting by Hendrick ter Brugghen)*

make, but it always was and is and shall be: an everlasting fire, kindling in measures and going out in measures." Many later commentators have said that for Heraclitus fire was a metaphor of change (because it is itself so changeable and immaterial) and, so, it represents change as the basic nature of the world.

Many of the fragments of Heraclitus's writings focus on what later philosophers called a unity of opposites. For example, Heraclitus remarked that "death makes health pleasant and good, hunger satiety, weariness rest" and "sea is the most pure and most polluted water; for fishes it is drinkable and salutary, for men it is undrinkable and deleterious." In addition, he claimed that "war is the father of all and king of all" and that people "do not apprehend that being at variance it agrees with itself; there is a back-stretched connection, as in the bow and the lyre." The point of these comments is that things must be understood in terms of how they relate to other things; so, seawater is good for some things (fish) and bad for other things (humans). Also, a stringed instrument like a lyre is possible only because of the balance and tension of opposite forces (the string pulls in one direction while the bow or frame of the lyre pulls in another). These basic notions of change and tension became important aspects of the views of many later philosophers, such as Georg W. F. Hegel, Karl Marx, Friedrich Nietzsche, Ralph Waldo Emerson, Alfred North Whitehead, and others.

Anaxagoras

Anaxagoras (500–428 B.C.E.) was born in Clazomenae, a town in Ionia (now western Turkey). He is said to have come from a wealthy and privileged family, but he renounced that wealth to become a philosopher. He traveled to Athens as a young man and stayed for 30 years. He eventually left and returned to Ionia because he was charged with heresy, that is, views that contradicted the religious beliefs of the time. Among these heretical views were that the Sun is a fiery rock and that the Moon is Earth, meaning that the Moon is composed of the same kind of stuff as Earth. In broader terms, his views were seen as heretical because they spoke of heavenly and celestial bodies as just material objects. Later, when Socrates was also charged with crimes by some citizens of Athens, they claimed he taught these same views (and he mocked the Athenians, saying they confused him with Anaxagoras).

Anaxagoras was a pluralist. Pluralism is the view that the world is made up of a plurality, more than one kind of thing. Anaxagoras claimed that things were composed of the four classical Greek elements: earth, water, air, and fire. Everyday objects, he said, were just various combinations or mixtures of these four elements. This view was not unique to Anaxagoras; for example, Empedocles made the same claim. Everyday objects, such as trees and rocks, are different simply because they have different combinations or proportions of the basic elements in them. For example, some objects, such as metals, will melt when they are heated to a high enough temperature, while other objects, such as trees, do not melt, but ignite and burn. For Anaxagoras, this meant that metals have a greater proportion of water in them than do trees. Although this might seem like a simplistic, or simply mistaken, view to people today, what was important and influential about Anaxagoras's view is that it offered a simple, natural (not supernatural) explanation for changes and variations in things. Also, it pointed to the notion of potentiality, which became a very important component of the views of Aristotle and many other philosophers. Potentiality is the notion that things have a potential, or cause of change, within themselves. For example, an acorn is a potential oak tree. As an acorn matures and changes and ultimately becomes an oak tree, it is said that its potential (to be an oak tree) becomes realized. Aristotle (and others) saw the notion of potentiality in the views of Anaxagoras, even though he did not speak of that himself.

Besides the notion of potentiality, Anaxagoras spoke of a force, or motion, to account for change. He called this *nous,* which is usually translated as "mind," but Anaxagoras did not mean mind in the sense that there was some conscious, thoughtful intellect that caused things to happen or to change. Rather, by nous, he meant a purposive, nonrandom force, much like potentiality is nonrandom (acorns do not randomly become oak trees; it seems natural and by purpose that they do). This notion of *nous,* or purposive change, was influential later as being reconceived as final cause.

Empedocles

Very little is known of the life of Empedocles (484–424 B.C.E.) other than the fact that he lived in a Greek colony in Sicily (southern Italy). He is said to have come from a wealthy, distinguished family. During and after his life, many stories (often conflicting) were told of his exploits, including that he threw himself into a volcano.

Empedocles is considered one of the pre-Socratic pluralists, as opposed to monists. He claimed that the four elements (earth, water, air, fire) were each different in kind from the other three and that each kind was eternal and indestructible. Everyday objects were the result of various combinations of these elements and that besides these four kinds of elements there were two forces that acted on them. He called these two forces Love and Strife. In effect, the two forces were forces of attraction

Image of Empedocles from the *Nuremberg Chronicle*

(Love) and separation (Strife). Empedocles did not call Love and Strife forces, but motions. The point is that they were the cause of change. Change came about because of the interplay between Love and Strife. For instance, when something comes to be (say, some organism is born), this is a case of Love being dominant; when something disintegrates or dies off, this is a case of Strife being dominant. The history of the world, the fact that things change, is due to the ebb and flow of these two forces or motions. While this sounds simplistic to people today, Empedocles held a view that is actually quite modern: Things and events in the world are the result of their nature (what kinds of things they are) and because of fundamental forces that act on them. He even made remarks that sound like a simple version of evolution, for example, that different forms of beings came together by chance (by the interplay of Love and Strife) and some of those beings could not survive, while others could. He also commented that some features of different kinds of creatures—for example, hair, feathers, and scales—were the same, meaning that they came about as a result of forces and ended up being useful for those creatures. His views are said to have been influential on the thought of Aristotle.

Changelessness
and Mathematics

Pythagoras

Most people know of Pythagoras (571–497 B.C.E.) because of the Pythagorean theorem. He was also an important and influential pre-Socratic philosopher. Little is known definitely about his life, though many claims have been made about it. It is known that he came from Samos, a small island off the coast of Ionia (now western Turkey). He is said to have met, as a young man, the philosophers Thales and Anaximander and been influenced by them to study philosophy. He traveled to southern Italy and formed a school there, which became well known during his lifetime. This school was said to be religious, even mystical, in nature and did not survive very long after Pythagoras's death.

In the context of philosophy, Pythagoras is usually called a monist, meaning that he thought that all things ultimately were made up of one basic kind of thing. While other monists, such as Thales, spoke of the one basic kind of thing as a material, physical kind, Pythagoras identified number as the basic nature of things. Number (and proportion) was the key, uniting feature of reality. This view was the basis for his well-known work in mathematics. In terms of his work in mathematics, he is credited with having identified square numbers (where, literally, numbers of objects could be shaped into a square; for example, :: is a square made up of objects two by two). He is also credited with having

Bust of Pythagoras from
the Vatican Museum

identified irrational numbers, such as $\sqrt{2}$, in which the number cannot be written as a ratio of two other numbers (such as ½ or ¾). The mathematical work of Pythagoras and his students was fundamental to establishing a quantitative understanding of music, for example, demonstrating a mathematical relationship between octaves, musical fifths, fourths, etc.

Pythagoras saw number as the unity and unifying force of all things. For example, he claimed that 10 is a perfect number. This is because it is the sum of the first four numbers (1+2+3+4=10). These four numbers represented what the Greeks believed were the four basic elements of the natural world (earth, water, air, and fire). So, there was a natural connection between these numbers and the basic makeup of the world. In addition, humans had 10 fingers, showing, for Pythagoras, a natural relationship between the nature of the world and people. (For him, it was not by accident that humans had 10 fingers and that we used a 10-base numerical system.) A result of this view was that Pythagoras saw a fundamental and universal harmony in nature, where harmony was understood to have a mathematical basis. He is often credited with speaking of a harmony of the spheres, meaning that this harmony was part of the very structure of the universe.

Pythagoras's emphasis on number and proportion and underlying unity of things was influential on Plato's philosophy. However, the mystical and often secretive nature of his views and of the school he founded led some people to be suspicious and distrustful of him and his students, resulting finally in the closing of his school after his death.

Parmenides (fl. 580 B.C.E.)

Parmenides, who lived around 580 B.C.E., was a pre-Socratic philosopher who greatly influenced Plato. Very little is known of the life of Parmenides other than that he was from Elea, a Greek colony in southern Italy, and that when he was quite old he visited Athens and met Socrates, who was a young man at the time. Plato later wrote a book called *Parmenides* about this meeting.

Parmenides is famous for proposing and defending the view that there is a dramatic difference between the world of appearances and everyday experience, on the one hand, and the world of truth and reality, on the other. In itself, this is not unique or strange. For example, everyday experience seems to suggest that the Earth is stationary and that the planets and stars orbit the Earth. (It does not feel like the Earth is moving!) Also, modern science tells us that things in the world are in reality quite unlike how we normally think of them. For instance, everyday objects are made of atoms, which themselves are mostly empty space; but everyday objects do not seem like empty space to us. Likewise, the behavior of objects is very different for things traveling at extremely high speeds (approaching the speed of light) or for subatomic objects than the behavior of objects of everyday experience.

Parmenides' views were not strange, then, simply because he claimed that reality was different than appearances, but because he claimed that reality is One, that Being was the one underlying permanent reality. What he said was that "whatever is, is and whatever is not, is not." This sounds obscure and puzzling, but what he was getting at is that anything we can think of or speak about must exist. We cannot even think of or speak of nonbeing, because to think or speak of something is to think or speak of some "thing." There must be something, even if it is not a material thing that is being referred to even when we deny that it exists; otherwise, for Parmenides, what we say is simply nonsense. For example, if we say that "Santa Claus does not exist," the name *Santa Claus* must refer to something or other, otherwise what we say would literally be nonsense; it would be as meaningless as saying that "Blah Blah does not exist." So, whatever is, is (and whatever is not, is not).

Change, for Parmenides, is an illusion, merely appearance. In fact, it is impossible, even inconceivable, he argued, because for change to be possible, there must be something that is not, that is, something changes into something else that currently it is not. For instance, to say that something changed—say, an apple changed from green to red as it ripened—would be meaningful only if what it changed into could *be* (otherwise, it would be like saying that an apple changed from green to blah blah). So, green must be (exist). If it does, then it *is,* and since whatever is, is, then it is just what is real.

In addition, whatever is—whatever exists—must be uncreated (otherwise, there was a time when a thing was nothing) and indestructible (otherwise, there will come a time when a thing is nothing). Likewise, Being is One, since if two separate things existed, both would Be, but they would both be Being, which is one unity. So, all change and motion is mere appearance, not actual reality.

One of Parmenides' students, Zeno of Elea, famously defended his teacher's views with a series of paradoxes, or puzzles, that were intended to show that opposition to Parmenides' views led to contradictions. His greatest influence, however, was on Plato, who not only strongly defended the role and importance of reason over everyday experience, but also proposed his enormously influential view of Ideas, or aspects of eternal, unchanging reality. Other philosophers rejected the views of Parmenides, saying that he confused different conceptions of "is" or being. One notion of being is called the "is of identity"—such as saying, "Two is the square root of four"—in which case "two" and "the square root of four" are just different ways to refer to the same thing. Another notion of being is called the "is of predication" (or of having some feature)—such as saying, "This giraffe is tall"—in which case, "giraffe" and "tall" are not just different ways to refer to the same thing; they refer to different things.

Zeno of Elea

Zeno of Elea, who lived around 465 B.C.E., was a student of Parmenides, one of the most important pre-Socratic philosophers. Almost nothing is known of his personal life other than his having been said to have come from Elea, a Greek colony in southern Italy. Plato wrote that Zeno accompanied Parmenides to Athens, where they are said to have met Socrates, who was a young man at the time (probably sometime in the 450s B.C.E.).

Zeno is famous for having formulated various paradoxes, or puzzles, that were meant to show that the views of his teacher, Parmenides, were correct. In particular, Zeno's paradoxes attempted to show that if some-one assumed that Parmenides' views were wrong, then that person would end up in a paradox or a contradiction. The views that Parmenides put forward were that all of reality is One, that what is real is eternal and unchanging. All change and motion, then, is simply appearance and illusion. This view is so counter to common sense and everyday experience that many people, of course, rejected it. Zeno, however, offered several paradoxes intended to demonstrate that these commonsense beliefs were mistaken.

Zeno's paradoxes are broadly of two types: arguments against motion and arguments against plurality (that is, that reality is not One, but made up of many things). One argument against the possibility of motion is called the stadium argument. This argument says that in order for someone to move from one end of a stadium to the other, that person must cover an infinite number of points, but this cannot be done. In

In this fresco from the Library of El Escorial, Zeno of Elea shows a group of youths the doors to Truth and Falsehood.

other words, between point A (at one end of the stadium) and point Z (at the other end), there is a certain distance. However, in order to get from point A to point Z, a person must get at least halfway across the stadium (say, to point B). But to get to point B, a person must get at least halfway to that point, call it point C. Likewise, before getting to point C, a person must get halfway to it, that is, to a point D. This will go on forever; that is, in order to move from any point to any other point, there are an infinite number of points in between and the distance between any two points at all will be some amount of distance, however small it is.

A . . . . . D . . . . . C . . . . B . . . . Z

So, before a person can even move away from point A, that person will have to cover an infinite number of points before getting to any other point. In effect, then, said Zeno, in order to move at all, one must move an infinite distance, but this is impossible, so one cannot move at all. A related version of this paradox is often called the paradox of Achilles and the tortoise. In this version, Achilles is supposed to try to catch a tortoise that is a certain distance ahead of him and moving away from him. During the time it takes Achilles to reach where the tortoise is, the tortoise has moved a certain distance (even though Achilles is faster than the tortoise). When Achilles travels to where the tortoise has moved, the tortoise has now moved a little farther on. But, as with the case of the stadium, no matter how far Achilles moves in order to catch the tortoise, there are always an infinite number of points between them, and, so, Achilles can never catch the tortoise.

Another paradox that was meant to show that motion is impossible is called the paradox of the flying arrow. At any instant in time, Zeno claimed, an arrow occupies an exact set of points in space. Common sense says that an arrow that is shot into the air is in motion (it is flying). At any given instant of time, however, there is no motion, or movement through space; things are where they are at that instant (much like a photograph seems to freeze motion in time). However, time is just a collection of instants. So, for any and every given instant, an arrow is not moving (it occupies just an exact set of points in space). So, there is zero motion at any instant in time. But to add up a collection of zeroes—that is, a collection of instants in time—is still to come up with zero. Motion, then, is only apparent, not real.

Another paradox that was meant to show that reality is One and not made up of many things was similar to the paradoxes of motion, but does not involve movement. This paradox said that if something exists, it must take up a certain amount of space (however small). But if there are (at least) two different things, then each must take up some amount of space and each must occupy separate space from the other (otherwise, they would not be two different things). So, if there are (at least) two different things, then there must be some amount of space between them (however small). However, that space between those two things must itself, then, exist, since, if it did not exist, there would be no space between the two things (that is, there would be just one thing). So, if there are two things, there must also be space between them, which is to say there must be at least three things that exist. However, then, there must be some space between each of those three things in order for them to be three separate things that exist. If there is any such space (however small), this means there is a fourth thing that exists (namely, the space between the other three things). This will go on infinitely, since between any two separate things, there must be some space (that is, an additional thing that exists). The result, then, for Zeno, was that if there is more than One (thing), there must necessarily be an infinite number of things.

Although Zeno's paradoxes seem to many people to be just conceptual trickery, they actually pointed to some important philosophical issues. For example, they speak to the issue of the relationship between everyday experience and reality. Although everyday experience tells us that things are in motion, everyday experience also seems to tell us that the Earth does not move; it certainly looks like the Sun and planets and stars move, but we do not feel the Earth move on its axis. Modern physics tells us that physical reality is quite contrary to common sense at the level of the atom or at extremely high velocities, such as the speed of light. Along those lines, Zeno's paradoxes speak to the relationship between reason and experience, that is, how we know the way things really are. Again, everyday experience does not always match what our theories and rigorous experiments tell us about the world. As with other paradoxes, Zeno's paradoxes point to conceptual complexities that challenge our commonsense views and often make us look more carefully at assumptions that we make.

Greek Atomism

Leucippus and Democritus

Leucippus, who lived around 440 B.C.E., and Democritus (460–370 B.C.E.) were pre-Socratic philosophers. Almost nothing at all is known about the life of Leucippus. He is said to have come from Miletus, a town in Ionia (now western Turkey), but even that is not certain. The life of his student, Democritus, is better known. He came from Abdera, a town in Thrace (now northeastern Greece). His family was very wealthy and he traveled widely throughout his life. Because the views of these two thinkers are so closely connected and also because only one sentence from the writings of Leucippus is known today, they are almost always spoken of together. (The one sentence of Leucippus that is known is: "Nothing happens at random; whatever comes about is by rational necessity.")

Leucippus and Democritus are said to be the founders of the school of atomism. The word *atom* comes from the Greek word *tome,* meaning "to cut," and the prefix *a,* meaning "not" or any form of negation. An atom, then, is something that cannot be cut, or divided into smaller units. This is not the same conception of atom that is held today. Rather, the conception of atom for Leucippus and Democritus was of some basic component of reality that is truly the most basic (that is, it is not composed of anything more basic). This is not a notion that resulted from experimentation or scientific theory, but is more conceptual in nature. Everyday things are composed of more basic kinds of things.

Painting of Democritus,
one of the founders of
the school of atomism
(*Antoine Coypel*)

That fact of things being made up of simpler components either goes on forever or there is something—whatever it is—that is the most basic thing. Whatever that kind of thing is, it is an atom; it cannot be further decomposed or cut.

Leucippus and Democritus did not say what atoms were like (and certainly did not think of them in the terms of modern science), other than to say that they had some size, shape, position, and movement. Everyday things, such as trees and rocks and turtles, are different from each other because of the differences in the shape, arrangements, and position of the atoms that make them up. For example, A and N have different shapes, while AN and NA have different arrangements, and Z and N have different positions, or orientations. (Of course, they were not referring to letters, but these letters illustrate the notions of different shape, arrangement, and position.) They argued that atoms have tiny hooks that allow them to connect with one another, so everyday things are made up of many of these tiny atoms. When things disintegrate or die off, it is because the atoms somehow become unhooked. They did not explain why this happens, other than to say that atoms move about space and sometimes swerve, resulting in different atoms hooking up to other atoms.

While their view of atomism was influential among some later thinkers, for example, Lucretius (96–55 B.C.E.) and stoicism, many people rejected it because they found it to be a form of atheism; God/gods simply had no role in this view of the world. It was not until the beginning of the 20th century that atoms, as they are conceived today, were finally accepted as the basic components of matter.

Sophists and Socrates

Sophists

Sophist was a name given to individuals, particularly in ancient Greece, who traveled around and claimed they could teach people to live well. The word *sophist* comes from the Greek word *sophia,* meaning "wisdom." (The word *philosophy* comes from *sophia* and also the Greek word *philo,* meaning "love"; so, *philosophy* means "love of wisdom.") The sophists were not an organized group or school, but individuals who were, in effect, professional teachers. They often distinguished their efforts from the prevailing teachings of those thinkers who came to be known as pre-Socratic philosophers. The pre-Socratic philosophers had focused their concerns on natural philosophy, or wisdom about nature (what today might be seen as science). The kinds of questions that the pre-Socratics addressed were about the fundamental nature of the world, such as whether all things came from one basic kind of thing, or what, if anything, is permanent in the world and, if things change, what causes change. Later commentators claimed that the sophists humanized philosophy, by focusing their teachings not on issues about natural philosophy, but on issues related to concerns of people for living well (issues about morality and social and political philosophy).

Two individuals in particular have stood out over the years as prominent sophists: Protagoras and Gorgias. Protagoras came from the city of Abdera, in Thrace (now northeastern Greece). The exact dates of his life are unknown but later scholars estimate he was born around 485 B.C.E. He is known to have taught in Athens and to have become an important figure there, even helping to formulate many laws in Athens during the reign of Pericles. Gorgias came from Leontini, a Greek colony on the island of Sicily (in southern Italy). He, too, is said to have been born around 485 B.C.E. and is said to have lived for 100 years. Like Protagoras, he is known to have traveled to Athens and become quite prominent there. Both men became wealthy as a result of their teaching; they usually charged large fees to their students, who were children of wealthy families.

Protagoras and Gorgias, as well as other sophists, claimed that living well was a matter of context. There is no truth that is universal, they said, and, therefore, no single way of life that is good for everyone. Contrary to the views of many people at the time, they argued that no one is naturally good or bad, better or worse than anyone else. An important skill in living well, they said, was knowledge of rhetoric, or the art of persuasion. Being able to speak well and convincingly was crucial. Practical knowledge, not theoretical knowledge, is what matters, they argued. Learning and knowledge are important because of what people can do with it, such as meeting their needs and coming to good decisions. Theoretical knowledge of the nature of things, even of ethical principles, does not matter unless and until there are practical consequences of such knowledge. Because conditions in which people find themselves vary and change, the knowledge that matters is the knowledge of dealing with those variations and changes. As a result, truth—at least, truth that matters—is relative.

Although the sophists were quite popular and influential with some people, they were scorned and met with hostility by others. Some of the leading figures in Athenian society were critical of the sophists because their teachings seemed to challenge the social status quo. That is, by saying that no one is naturally good or bad, better or worse than anyone else, the sophists seemed to be challenging the aristocrats and upper levels of Athenian society, who believed that some people were indeed better than others. What appeared to be democratic teachings or sentiments, then, were unsettling to some Athenians. At the same time, people who thought of themselves as democratic and who opposed what they saw as the somewhat rigid social structures in Athenian society often saw the sophists as beholden to the wealthy aristocrats, since it was these people who paid their fees and, in effect, gave them their comfortable lifestyles.

In addition, many Athenians thought that the sophists were heretical, that they taught forms of atheism. Protagoras, for example, had claimed: "As for the gods, I have no way of knowing either that they exist or that they do not exist; nor, if they exist, of what form they are." (Later, when Socrates was charged with corrupting the youth of Athens, his accusers identified him as a sophist and teacher of atheism.)

Others—and especially famous among these are Socrates and Plato—said that the sophists were both wrong and even harmful for teaching that truth is relative and that theoretical knowledge is not important. Protagoras, for example, famously wrote, "Man is the measure of all things: of things that are, that they are; of things that are not, that they are not." These critics claimed that truth is not relative and it is not subjective; claiming otherwise leads not simply to false beliefs, but also to the view that anyone could justify any action on the basis that there is no objective truth to the matter. If it is true for me, or for my group or community, that someone who is different is inferior, then—if the sophists are correct, said Plato—there is no basis for criticizing such a view or preventing them from acting on such a view (for example, enslaving that inferior person). These critics also found fault with the sophists' emphasis on rhetoric, claiming that artful persuasion does not really help people live well if it relies on gimmicks and plays on fears and false beliefs of people (exactly the sort of thing that politicians constantly do, said Plato). Rhetoric and seeking influence, without a commitment to real knowledge and truth, said Plato, is not a trustworthy guide to living well. Because of the influence of Plato in his criticisms of the sophists, their reputation was greatly tarnished for centuries. The word *sophistry* even came to mean (and still does) false or deceitful speech and arguments. Nonetheless, some of the views held by sophists have been restated and embraced by later philosophers. For example, Kierkegaard adopted the view that truth is subjective, and pragmatism, as a school of thought, especially in America, has advocated the notion that knowledge matters only to the extent that it has practical consequences and benefits.

Socrates

Socrates (469–399 B.C.E.) was one of the most important and influential philosophers of all time, although he did not write any philosophical works. Along with his student, Plato (and Plato's student, Aristotle), Socrates is generally seen as having shaped Western philosophical thought. He lived most of his life in Athens. His family was not wealthy, but not poor either. As a young man, he is said to have worked as a stonemason (like his father). His mother was a midwife (someone who helps other women prepare for and deliver their babies). Socrates is known to have served in the Athenian military, especially in its wars with Sparta. During Socrates' life, Athens underwent significant political unrest, particularly after the conflicts with Sparta. Athenian democracy was overthrown for a period, though later restored a few years before Socrates' death. Some commentators have claimed that Socrates himself was critical of Athenian democracy, at least of the regime that he knew, and was accepting of—perhaps even endorsing—the overthrow of democracy, and this, in part, led to his execution when he was 70 years old.

Socrates became known during his life, and is famous today, because he spent much of his adult life not working in a normal job or occupation but in questioning his fellow citizens about life and philosophical issues. Although he was married and had three sons, he and his wife both had inherited enough money from their respective parents so that Socrates felt he did not need to work a normal job. In his daily wanderings throughout the city, Socrates is said to have engaged other citizens often in philosophical debates, frequently demonstrating—at least to some—that those people had confused or false beliefs. Plato later referred to Socrates as a gadfly, someone who irritated others, even though that was not his intent. Like a gadfly, however, Socrates forced people to stop their usual, mundane affairs and focus on his questions and cross-examinations. Socrates himself at times said that, like his mother, he was a midwife, and what he was helping to deliver was truth. At other times, he claimed that all he was doing was seeking truth himself and asking those who were said, either by themselves or by others, to know things. He never meant to teach anyone anything, he often said, because he himself did not know anything; he was ignorant and was looking for answers. However, in the context of his questioning and cross-examining of others, he always seemed to show that they, too, did not really know what they were said to know. One legend, during Socrates' lifetime, was that the oracle of Delphi claimed that

Socrates takes poison while his followers mourn in *The Death of Socrates*. *(Painting by Jacques-Louis David)*

Socrates was the wisest man. When told of this, Socrates is said to have replied that the only meaning he could get from this remark is that, while all people are ignorant, including himself, he at least knew that he was ignorant, whereas others did not know that they were ignorant. Whether because of his reputed antidemocratic views or because he irritated important people or for some other reason, late in life Socrates was put on trial for corrupting the youth of Athens by teaching false doctrines. At the age of 70, he was put on trial, found guilty, and executed (by having to drink poison).

Although Socrates did not write any philosophical works, there were several of his contemporaries who wrote about him. The most famous was his student, Plato, who wrote many works in dialogue form, written much like the script of plays in which the remarks and conversations of different characters are written down. Another Greek writer, Xenophon, also wrote various Socratic dialogues. In addition, the Greek playwright Aristophanes wrote satires (the most famous being *The Clouds*), in which he made fun of Socrates or at least the public perception of Socrates.

From Plato's dialogues, in particular, the style of Socrates' philoso-phizing and the content of some of his views became known. His style is now called the Socratic method. This method was a matter of posing a question, usually of the form: "What is X?" where X might be knowl-edge or beauty or virtue or some basic concept. For example, in Plato's dialogue called *Euthyphro* (named after one of the other characters in the work), Socrates asks, "What is piety (or moral duty)?" In another dialogue, *Meno,* he asks, "What is knowledge?" The Socratic method begins with some such question because someone claims to know this concept or at least acts as if he knows it. Socrates would say that he was lucky to have met such a wise person, since he (Socrates) did not know what piety (or knowledge, etc.) is and this wise person could teach him. The person usually then gives an example or two of the concept (for example, piety is prosecuting wrongdoers or doing what is loved by the gods). Socrates then shows that this answer does not fully satisfy him either because it just gives an example and does not explain how it is an example of the concept or shows that this definition fails (perhaps by including things that do not seem to fit the concept or perhaps by being self-contradictory). The result, after various attempts to provide a good definition of the concept in question, is that the person Socrates questions appears not to know what he was said to have known. This is sometimes referred to as the negative aspect of the Socratic method, the dispelling of what people thought they knew but are shown not to have known. There is also what is sometimes referred to as the positive aspect of the Socratic method, an aspect in which someone comes to know something, not by being told outright, but by being skillfully questioned and coming to see the answer himself. For example, in *Meno,* a young slave boy who has never learned geometry solves a geometrical problem by being asked various leading questions that help him come up with the answer on his own.

As part of the Socratic method, often Socrates would use analogy to get people either to see that their views were confused or to lead them to a better definition or conception of what they were investigating. For example, in questioning whether or not virtue could be taught, Socrates asks if we wanted someone to be a good physician, would we send that person to physicians? (That person, Anytus, says, yes.) Socrates goes on: To be a good shoemaker, send that person to shoemakers? And to be a good musician, send that person to musicians? And so on. The point of this sort of argument by analogy is to help the person being questioned to see that there is some underlying principle that is what really matters (in this case: to learn something, people need to be taught by experts, so to learn virtue, they must be taught by experts of virtue).

Many commentators have claimed that the Socratic method, at least as it was used by Socrates, really reveals a Socratic irony. Irony is sometimes seen as a pretense of ignorance even when someone is not ignorant or the expression of something other than—and often the opposite of—the real meaning of what is said. Many commentators have remarked that Socrates did not, in fact, think that these people he questioned really knew what they claimed to know and that his whole point in questioning them was to show them (and others) that they did not know what they said they knew. Although he repeatedly said that he did not know the answers to his own questions but believed that these prominent citizens did know—which was why he was questioning them—in the course of his questioning, he often appeared to be leading them, in debate style, to confused and contradictory conclusions. When, at the end of such questioning, being shown to look foolish, these people were sometimes angry or resentful, Socrates expressed dismay or surprise. Some commentators have said that this was irony on Socrates' part, while other commentators have said that his dismay and surprise was genuine.

In addition to the Socratic method and Socratic irony, there are aspects of Socrates' views that some people see as paradoxes. For example, during his trial, he remarked that, while the laws of Athens were important to him, they were not as important as the truth or moral laws or even his inner voice or conscience (what was called his *daimon*). However, while he was in jail, awaiting his execution, some people suggested to him that they could instead get him exiled, and his reply was that he should obey the laws of Athens, even when they seemed to harm him.

While Socrates claimed to know nothing, there are several aspects of his philosophical endeavors that seem to point to beliefs that he held. One is that virtue is knowledge. Among those people who chronicled his life, a constant and common theme was that Socrates believed that no one does what he or she believes is wrong, so when they do commit a wrong act, it must be out of ignorance; they simply do not realize that it is wrong. Knowing what is right or good, then, will lead us to doing what is right or good; ignorance, not evil intention or sin, is the problem of people behaving badly. Along with this belief is Socrates' view that what is good is objective; there really are virtues and vices, good things and bad things, right actions and wrong actions. These things are objective and not a matter of convention or subjective opinion. In addition, Socrates seems certainly to have thought that people have a soul and it is immortal. At one point he remarked that philosophy is like training for death; the point is that what matters is not the good of the moment or what is pleasing to the body, but what is truly good for the soul. Physical enjoyment and happiness are fine, he said, but they are not what really matter in the long run. While in jail and awaiting execution, he was said to be upbeat and content, saying that he was not afraid to die, since he (his soul) was not really going to die.

The legacy of Socrates is immense. Unlike his predecessors, he focused on concerns of moral and social philosophy—for example, asking about the nature of the good life or knowledge or beauty or friendship—rather than natural philosophy. Some of the content of his views, such as virtue is knowledge or the objectivity of truth and goodness, are views that Plato and many other philosophers accepted and embellished. An underlying aspect of the Socratic method became a foundation for most later philosophy, namely, that important philosophical concepts have an essence, or core nature. That is, by asking, "What is X?" (for instance, "What is knowledge?"), Socrates seemed to assume that there was some basic core nature of things that are X and that, by conceptual analysis, we could discover the necessary and sufficient conditions for what it is to be X. So, we could come to discover what knowledge is—not merely particular examples of knowledge, but the very nature of knowledge—and we could do this by analyzing the concept. This search for conceptual clarity was fundamental to Socrates, because clear thinking for him was the path to right action and to living well. This attitude and sentiment has informed philosophy ever since.

Plato

Plato (427–347 B.C.E.) was a Greek philosopher who is today considered one of the two most influential Western philosophers of all time, along with his student Aristotle. The 20th-century philosopher/physicist Alfred North Whitehead remarked that all of Western philosophy is simply a series of footnotes to Plato. Plato was born into a prominent and wealthy family in Athens. Some commentators have said that his real name was Aristocles and that "Plato" was a nickname, from the Greek word *platonos,* meaning "broad" or "flat," because he was a large person; other commentators have denied this. He lived during the time of the wars between Athens and Sparta. As a young man he became a student of Socrates and, in fact, much of what is known today about Socrates comes from the writings of Plato. When Socrates was put on trial by the citizens of Athens and then executed, Plato saw this as a sign of weakness of democracy, and his later writings on political philosophy reflect his concerns about the best form of government, which he saw as aristocracy (or rule of the best, from the Greek word *aristos,* meaning "best"). During much of his young adult life, Plato traveled, particularly to Sicily (southern Italy) and Egypt. After returning home to Athens, at the age of 40, he founded a school, which he called the Academy. It was at the Academy that Aristotle became Plato's student. Late in his life, Plato was invited to return to Sicily to help set up a government based on his own political philosophy, but the effort failed and Plato returned home to live out his life.

In metaphysics, Plato argued that there are varying degrees of reality; in epistemology, he argued that reason is superior to experience;

Copy of the marble head of Plato, sculpted by Silanion ca. 370 *(Photograph by Marie-Lan Nguyen; used under a Creative Commons license)*

in axiology, he argued that the good life comes from knowledge. All of these issues are illustrated in his famous "Allegory of the Cave" and in his doctrine of Forms.

"Allegory of the Cave"

The allegory of the cave is a story written by Plato that appears in Book VII of his most famous work, *The Republic*. In just a few pages, it captures the main themes of Plato's philosophical views and has been one of the most renowned and cited statements in all of Western philosophy. An allegory is a moral fable or parable; it is a fictional story meant to express and illustrate some basic human experience and lesson.

In the allegory of the cave, Plato has the reader imagine a cave in which people live their entire lives. Indeed, generations of people live there. They cannot see the entrance to the outside world and believe that the cave is all there is to the world. They are chained in such a way that they always face toward a wall in the back of the cave. (How they could live—move around, eat, have children, etc.—is not important; it is the moral message that matters in the allegory.) Behind the people, where they cannot see it, is a fire that illuminates the cave. Between the fire and the people is a sort of roadway where other people can move along. As they do so, the fire behind them casts shadows on the back wall of the cave. The people who are chained and looking at the wall see the shadows that are cast on the wall, but do not know about the roadway or people moving along it. All of their experiences are always and only of the shadows that appear on the wall in front of them.

Imagine, Plato said, that one day one of these chained people manages to get free and he gets up and starts to move around. When he looks behind him he sees the roadway and the fire. He comes to realize that all of his experiences prior to that moment were only of shadows on the wall, not of real things. He then proceeds to see the things that cause the shadows (that is, the things moving along the roadway) and understands that the shadows are like those things, but only shadows of them. As he proceeds even farther up the cave, he finally starts to see the diffused light from the entrance of the cave, light that is caused by the sunlight outside. Eventually, he comes to the actual entrance of the cave and looks outside. He sees real things, like trees and natural sunlight. At first, the direct sunlight is too bright for him and hurts his eyes. Slowly, however, he gets used to the sunlight and sees the outside world.

Imagine further, Plato said, that having made this discovery, the man is excited and wants to go back to tell all the other people who are still chained inside the cave. Because his eyes now have become accustomed to natural sunlight, when he goes back into the cave it is dark and he has trouble seeing in the darkness, trouble he had never had before when he lived his life in the cave. Eventually, with some difficulty, he goes back to where the others are and tells them what he had discovered and that what they think is real and have experienced all their lives as real are just shadows, at best mere imitations of real things. Their response is that they think he is crazy.

This allegory, said Plato, is the experience of the philosopher. Having come to encounter and understand things that are often quite unfamiliar and even contrary to everyday experience, the philosopher seems to other people to be crazy or strange or, at the very best, impractical, perhaps even dangerous.

The allegory also illuminates some basic aspects of Plato's views. On one hand, Plato thought that there were different levels of reality. Some things and kinds of things are more real than others. Shadows are real (they are not imaginary), but they are less real than the things that cause them. For example, there might be a shadow of a tree that is caused by sunlight behind a tree. If a cloud suddenly blocks the sunlight, the shadow of the tree will disappear, but the tree itself does not disappear. The shadow of the tree ceases to exist, but the physical tree continues to exist. For Plato, this is to say that the shadow is real, but the physical tree is even more real. But, for Plato, there is a level of reality beyond that of physical, everyday things. We can have the concept of tree even if there is no physical tree. Or, we can have the concept of circle even if there is no actual perfect circle in the world (or the concept of negative numbers, even if there do not exist any actual negative numbers). The concept, then, can exist even if there are no actual instances of that concept that exist. These concepts Plato called Ideas (or Forms), and they are the highest level of reality.

Besides levels of reality, there are levels of awareness or thinking for Plato. On one level, there are just images or illusions (like the shadowy images of things on the wall). These are one level of awareness, but they are like mere sensations. Beyond images, there are beliefs, thoughts with content. Of course, beliefs can be false; that is, we can have beliefs that turn out simply to be wrong. For example, we might believe that Abraham Lincoln lived in the 1700s or that apes have tails like monkeys. Beliefs are greater than images or sensations, but they are less than knowledge. Knowing involves true beliefs (which means that they connect with facts). However, we might have a true belief, but only because we just happen to guess something correctly. For example, we might believe there is life on some distant planet, not because we have any evidence for this, but just because we like the thought that it might be true. If it turns out to be true, then we have a true belief, but it was just a lucky guess. So, real knowledge, for Plato, is true belief with justification for that belief.

The allegory of the cave, then, was a way for Plato to try to get people to see life as being like emerging from living in a cave to discovering things as they really are, with different levels of reality and different levels of awareness. Philosophical education is life's slow but steady emergence out of the cave of ignorance into the light of knowledge.

As previously noted, Plato claimed that there are different levels of reality. Shadows are real, but they are not as real as the objects they are shadows of. For instance, a shadow of a dog is real. However, if a cloud comes by and blocks the sun, causing the shadow to go away, the dog does not disappear. The dog's shadow is real, but the actual, physical dog is even more real; it exists even when the shadow does not. For Plato, while actual dogs are real, they are not as real as the concept of Dog (what he called the Idea or Form of Dog). For example, if we had a concept of Dog, that concept could exist even if all the actual, physical dogs died off. (We have the concept of Dinosaur even though there are no actual dinosaurs.) Just as an actual dog is more real than a shadow dog, so the concept or Idea of Dog is even more real than actual dogs. For Plato, there are degrees of reality, and what is most real is not the everyday objects of common experience; instead, Ideas are the most real things. Plato further claimed that the Ideas are like ideal, perfect objects and actual, physical individuals are like imperfect copies of these ideal Ideas. For instance, we normally think of and experience many different breeds of dogs as well as individual dogs. All of these dogs have lots of features that are particular. That is, one dog might be black, while another is brown; one dog is large, while another is small. But for them all to be dogs there must be something they have in common (or some set of things they have in common) that makes them dogs. There must be some set of features or conditions that things have in order for them to be dogs rather than cats or trees. Those features are the essence of Dog and what constitute the Idea of Dog.

With respect to epistemology (knowledge), Plato argued that our senses, like smell, taste, sight, etc., give us knowledge only of those less real things such as shadows or physical individual objects. What is most real—Ideas—is not known by the senses, but by reason. Whereas the senses give us information about the physical world and are connected to the body (bodily senses), reason gives us information about Ideas and is connected with the soul. For Plato, the bodily senses could only know physical facts, not facts about Ideas. We can come to know Ideas, but it takes effort, said Plato. As a result, knowledge of Ideas must be gained in a thoughtful way. For example, we naturally come to know physical things and relationships between them (such as knowing different individual dogs and the fact that one is larger or darker than another). But there are also abstract objects, such as numbers and mathematical relationships. Our knowledge of these is not by bodily senses; we never see or smell or taste numbers, much less objects like square roots. Of course, we see, say, two dogs and two other dogs and then claim that we know that we see four dogs. But, the dogs are just instances; they are not the numbers themselves. (We could come to know that 2+2=4 even if we did not see those four dogs.) Knowledge of mathematics, then, for Plato, is not the result of bodily senses, but the result of reason and it is the soul, not the body, that reasons. Ultimately, the soul can come to know Ideas, but, for Plato, this must mean that the soul is distinct from and superior to the body.

One of the basic questions that Plato investigated was What is knowledge? The people in the cave, he said, do not have knowledge, only beliefs. Obviously, believing something, no matter how firmly or confidently one believes it, is not the same thing as knowing it; we can have false beliefs. No matter how strongly someone believes that the Sun is only 50 miles in diameter, that person does not know that it is. So, for Plato, knowledge is not belief. In addition, it is not the same thing as true belief, because we might have a true belief, but have it simply from a lucky guess. For example, on a multiple choice question on an exam, someone might believe that the correct answer to the question is option B, but not really know that that is the correct answer. If it turns out that it is correct, then that person had a true belief, but not knowledge (just a good guess or a good hunch). For Plato, then, knowledge is true belief that has justification for it. Plato's conception of knowledge—as justified true belief—shaped the study of epistemology for centuries.

With respect to axiology (values), Plato's claims about the soul knowing the Ideas have an immediate implication about education. If the person who leaves the cave rushes out into the sunlight, having been in the darkness of the cave, he would be blinded by the sudden bright light; the blinding sensation would even be painful. Instead, it would be better for that person to leave the cave gradually and become acclimated to the bright light. Likewise, Plato said, people need to be educated gradually to see the Ideas. Only after having studied everyday, common objects (say, through science) and then having studied abstract objects, such as mathematics, is a person ready to study philosophy (the discipline for studying Ideas) fruitfully. At his Academy, then, Plato had a structured curriculum and required students to study observational science before mathematics and then only later could

Painting of Plato's symposium from 1873 *(Painting by Anselm Feuerbach)*

ide exactly the
is that matches
even different kir.
e trees have leaves
eaves that do not; son
do not; some grow in cer
etheless, said Plato, for the
eatures that they all share in.
be trees. The correct definitio
mon, and unique features of tre
he ideal form of trees (which is why
tead of *Idea*).
ality, with Ideas being the highest
rticular and fleeting. For instance,
e sunlight. The shadow is certainly
behind a cloud or sets, the shadow
ysical tree that cast that shadow is
Plato, than the shadow, since the
when the Sun goes behind a cloud
ore real than the shadow of a tree,
n the physical tree, said Plato. This
ven if that tree dies or is cut down.
ent away, the Idea of Tree would
can exist even though there are no
Plato, there can be Ideas of things
is the Idea of Circle, even if there
rld. Also, there are Ideas of things
piece of paper is white, the word
s with trees or anything else, there
hite and, for Plato, there must be
definition. Beyond merely match-
Ideas cause the physical, everyday
hysical, everyday instances cause
st as the shadow of a tree could not
ng and causing the shadow (along
claimed, the physical tree must be
ee. More broadly, his point is that

they study philosophy. Otherwise, he thought, if they tried to study philosophy before they were ready, they would find it painful and would reject it.

The writings of Plato are in dialogue form, much like the scripts of plays, with the conversation of different characters laid out. His early writings are said to be accounts of the life and teachings of Socrates. These early works include *Meno, Apology, Crito, Phaedo,* and others. His later writings had the same style, with Socrates as the main character, but scholars claim that these writings portray Plato's own beliefs and views, not those of the real Socrates. These works include *The Republic, The Symposium, Theaetetus, Timeaus, Laws,* and others. During much of the Middle Ages, the only complete work of Plato's that was known to European thinkers was *Timaeus,* but during the Renaissance there was a revival in interest and knowledge of Plato's other works, which by then had been rediscovered and, subsequently, became enormously influential throughout Western culture.

Justice

Plato's most famous work, *The Republic,* is about the nature of justice. In this book, he raised the question, What is justice? He argued that living well is the soul's function and that to fulfill this function requires justice. To live well, to do the right thing, he said, requires knowledge of what is true and real—that is, knowledge of the Ideas. Justice, however, is a matter both of the individual and of society in general (as Plato put it: the soul and the state). In each case, justice is a matter of balance and harmony among the parts of the soul or state. The soul, he said, was like a chariot driver trying to steer two horses. One horse is spirit and the other horse is reason. So, our bodily senses (spirit) move us in one direction, while our reason moves us in another. The harmonious soul brings these into balance and steers the right course; this is what a just person is.

Plato claimed that we can think of justice as applying to individual people and also to a society, or state, collectively. That is, we speak of an individual as being just (or unjust) and a state as being like an enlarged individual (so we can speak of a state also as being just or unjust). In either case, justice is a matter of the harmony of the different parts of something. With individuals, he said, there are different parts of the

Fragments of Plato's *Republic* appear in the Papiro Oxyrhynchus.

soul (which, for him, meant the person). In some respects, people want whatever they think will please them, but, in addition, people also feel the need to be fair and do the right thing. A just person is someone who balances his various urges, responsibilities, etc. In the same way, a society or state is made up of various parts—workers, soldiers, and administrators, etc. A just state, said Plato, is one in which there is a balance and harmony among these various groups. In particular, each group needs to fulfill its appropriate function or role. For example, soldiers need to protect the state from those who might harm it, while workers need to provide the goods and services that are needed by people. Administrators, or rulers, need to govern well. He called these administrators guardians, because their role is guarding the well-being of the state. The best state, then, is one in which each group performs its appropriate role (and does not try to do the job of another group) and those people who are best suited for the duties of a particular group are in fact part of that group. In other words, those people who are best at producing things should be workers, while those who are best at protecting should be soldiers, and those who are best at guiding should be guardians/rulers.

Who would be best at ruling? For Plato, it is philosophers. The reason for this is because philosophers are those who are concerned

correct definition of *tree* would inc
of Tree, then, for Plato, is whatever
tures. Of course, different trees, a
different features. For example, s
the autumn, while other trees hav
light colored bark, while other tre
of soil, while others do not, etc. N
to all be trees, there must be som
mon—otherwise, they would not
tree provides just those essential,
In effect, such a definition provid
the term *Form* is sometimes used

For Plato, there were levels c
level. Some things that are real ar
a tree might cast a shadow if it is
real; it exists. However, if the Sun
goes away; it no longer exists. Th
also real, in fact, it is more real,
physical tree continues to exist e
or sets. Just as the physical tree
the Idea of Tree is even more rea
is because the Idea of Tree can e
In fact, even if all trees someh
still exist, like the Idea of Dino
dinosaurs anymore. In addition
that are abstract. For example,
are no true, perfect circles in th
such as white. If someone says
white must refer to something.
must be some correct definitic
some Idea of White that match
ing a definition, Plato claimed
instances of them, much like
the shadows of themselves. Tha
exist without that physical tre
with some light source), so, too
caused and the cause is the Id

lower levels of reality are caused by corresponding higher levels of reality. As well, Ideas can exist independently of the particular instances of them existing. That is, the Idea of Circle can exist even if no true circles exist in everyday experience and the Idea of Tree can exist even if no trees existed. Plato's Doctrine of Ideas was a fundamental part of his views that, while everyday experience seems to show that things are constantly changing, there is an underlying permanent reality (the reality of Ideas).

This Doctrine of Ideas has been immensely influential in philosophical thought ever since Plato, but it has been critiqued ever since Plato put it down on paper. In fact, he himself raised some questions and doubts about this view in some of his own later writings. For example, he asked whether there is an Idea of Hair and an Idea of Dirt, etc. Plato had earlier identified Ideas with what is ideal and incorruptible and good, so Ideas of Hair and Dirt (and any other unpleasant notions) seemed questionable. In addition, Plato's student, Aristotle, said that there must be an infinite series of levels of Ideas. This is because if there is an Idea for any concept, that is, for anything that can be defined, then there would be, say, an Idea of Maple, as well as an Idea of Tree, as well as an Idea of Living Thing, as well as an Idea of Thing That Can Be Defined, etc. Furthermore, said Aristotle, just because we have words or terms that can be defined, it does not necessarily follow that there must exist something that matches those definitions. For instance, we could define "unicorn," but that does not mean that, therefore, there must be actual unicorns or an Idea of Unicorn. Some words or terms (and their definitions) are only about imaginary things. Other philosophers have rejected the view that things must have essences. Many philosophers, however, have defended the underlying notion of Ideas and related conceptions of ideal, unchanging things that are real (a view often today called Platonism).

Doctrine of Opposites

The doctrine or opposites refers to aspects of one of Plato's arguments, that of the immortality of the soul. This doctrine is expressed especially in Plato's work called *Phaedo* (Phaedo is the name of one of the characters in this book). The background event of this book is that Socrates has been condemned to die by the citizens of Athens. While he is waiting in prison, he engages in a discussion with Phaedo (and others) about a number of philosophical topics, including whether there is a soul and, if so, whether or not it is immortal. One of the characters in the book, Cebes, questions Socrates whether the soul is immortal. In answering Cebes, Socrates puts forth the doctrine of opposites.

Socrates begins by asking whether things come from their opposites, for example, beauty from ugliness or justice from injustice. He suggests some analogies to make the point. For instance, he says, "If something smaller comes to be, it will come from something larger before, which becomes smaller." Likewise, "the weaker comes to be from the stronger, and the swifter from the slower." Also, "if something worse comes to be, does it not come from the better, and the more just from the more unjust?" The point that Socrates is trying to make is that for us to say that something has become, say, smaller, then it had to have been larger before; that is, it is now smaller than it was before, which means that it must have been larger earlier, or else it could not have become smaller. Something can only become smaller if it used to be larger than it has now become. Likewise, this is true for stronger/weaker, swifter/slower, more just/more unjust, etc.; indeed, it is true for any pair of comparisons. But, of course, smaller is the opposite of larger and stronger is the opposite of weaker, etc. So it must be the case that things come from their opposites.

Now, says Socrates, death is the opposite of life (and dying is the opposite of living). Since things come to be from their opposites, obviously something must be living in order for it to die; nonliving things cannot die. But, Socrates continues, this same point must be true also in reverse; that is, life must come from somewhere, namely, its opposite (death). In addition, says Socrates, things (or features of things) are not destroyed when their opposite approaches. For example, as something becomes smaller, largeness is not destroyed, rather it (largeness) goes away; it departs. Opposites do not themselves become their own opposites; that is, largeness does not become smallness, although a large thing becomes smaller. So, says Socrates, when death approaches, life is not destroyed, but merely departs, which is to say, a soul (life) departs the body but is not destroyed.

While many religious-minded philosophers have found this argument and the doctrine of opposites convincing, many others have not.

Critics have said that while it is true that it might make sense to speak of the doctrine of opposites as being relevant to comparative pairs (such as larger/smaller), it is not relevant to other things or features. For instance, while becoming lighter presupposes having been darker before, light does not presuppose or necessarily come from dark or blue does not have to come from not blue. Such critics have claimed that whether or not it makes sense to speak of an immortal soul, the doctrine of opposites is not an adequate basis.

Aristotle

Aristotle (384–322 B.C.E.) was a Greek philosopher who is today considered one of the two most influential Western philosophers of all time with Plato. He was so influential that during the later Middle Ages he was simply referred to as The Philosopher, and it is practically impossible to overstate his impact on philosophy and also science over the centuries. Aristotle was born in Stagira, in Macedonia (now northern Greece). His father was the court physician to the King of Macedonia. At the age of 18 he entered Plato's school in Athens, The Academy, and stayed for almost 20 years. After Plato's death, he returned to Macedonia and became the tutor for a young prince who later came to be known as Alexander the Great. At the age of 40, Aristotle returned to Athens and founded his own school, The Lyceum, where he taught until 323 B.C.E., when Alexander died. Because Aristotle was associated with Alexander, who many Athenians saw as a foreign conqueror, Aristotle left Athens that year, saying he did not want the Athenians to sin twice against philosophy (a reference to the trial and execution of Socrates, who had been condemned to death by Athenians in 399 B.C.E.). Aristotle died the following year.

Aristotle is said to have written many works in the style of Plato, namely, dialogues (with the form like the script of a play, with various characters engaged in conversation about some philosophical topic); however, these have been lost. The vast store of writings that remain today of Aristotle's work are actually compilations of notes he and some of his students wrote. They range over practically all areas of philosophy, including natural philosophy (or science). Aristotle's writings

Illustration of Aristotle from the *Nuremberg Chronicle*

and thinking were very systematic. He often wrote on classifying and categorizing subjects before then analyzing them. For example, with respect to knowledge, broadly speaking, he claimed that there were three fundamental kinds of knowledge: theoria, praxis, techné. Theoria is theoretical knowledge, with the goal of theoretical understanding. For Aristotle, this type of knowledge included mathematics and physics, but also theology (the study of God). Praxis is practical knowledge, with the goal of practical action and conduct. For Aristotle, this type of knowledge included ethics, economics, even social and political philosophy. Techné is technical knowledge, with the goal of making or producing something. For Aristotle, this type of knowledge included art and rhetoric; while we might think this focused on the sorts of things that today we would consider technology, it even more had to do with the notion of technique (in various fields, not just technology). A major aspect of this division of different types of knowledge was that Aristotle was more concerned with describing and explaining the many kinds of things (in this case knowledge) that there are rather than looking for one underlying essence of things. Whereas Plato had focused on discovering and identifying the core features of whatever he studied, Aristotle was more comfortable with looking at the many kinds and variations of those things he studied, without assuming that there were some core features to them.

Plato famously asked, What is knowledge? and answered by saying that there is a single kind of thing that knowledge is. There are all sorts of cases in which we claim to have knowledge. For example, I know my name; I know that 2+2=4; I know that the Sun is larger than the Earth; I know I am awake right now; I know George Washington was once president of the United States. Plato said that if these cases are all truly cases of knowledge, then they must have something in common in order for them to be knowledge. In addition, things that I do not know (that is, cases where I do not have knowledge, but, perhaps an opinion or just a belief) must lack something in order for them not to be knowledge. For Plato, the core essence of knowledge was justified true belief. That is, for him, knowledge was a true belief that had some justification to back it up. Aristotle, however, did not assume or look for some core essence to all cases of knowledge. Rather, he said that what counts as knowledge depends in part on the goal of inquiry. In other words, what we count as a case of knowledge depends in part, at least, on what we want to know and why we want to know it. Sometimes we want a basic theoretical understanding of how and why things are the way they are (such as a scientific theory); this is theoria. Other times we want more of a practical application of information in order to solve some problem or give us a way to get along in the world (such as building a bridge); this is praxis. Yet other times we want some technique for accomplishing some goal or creating something, but it is not necessarily a practical application of information (such as crafting a moving speech or song); this is techné. These different kinds of knowledge are similar to, though not exactly the same as, today's notions of knowledge that something is the case (like knowing that cats are mammals) and knowledge how to do something (like knowing how to ride a bike).

A fundamental and crucial aspect of Aristotle's thought was the notion of teleology. The word *teleology* comes from the Greek word *telos,* meaning "end" or "goal." Unlike Plato, who argued for levels of reality, with those things that are permanent and unchanging as being the most real—what are called Platonic Forms—Aristotle stressed the notion of change and variability of things. Much of Aristotle's understanding of the world generally and of particular things and events in the world is teleological. This means that he saw things as naturally undergoing change, and change toward some end or goal. He often spoke of this in terms of potentiality and actuality. For example, an acorn, he said, is potentially an oak tree. It will naturally undergo change during its lifetime and that change will be toward the goal of becoming an oak tree. When it finally reaches that goal and becomes an actual oak tree, we can say that its potential has been actualized. Aristotle, who avidly studied biology, said this change or movement toward some end or goal was fundamental to understanding things in the world. In a word, he saw the world as teleological.

Along the lines of this teleological perspective, Aristotle wrote on the nature of change (or, as he sometimes called it, motion) and on the causes of change. His writings on this issue were extremely influential in philosophy as well as in science. Aristotle claimed that when something happens, there is always a cause for it. His understanding of cause, however, is different than what we usually think of it today; it is teleological. Nothing merely happens, for Aristotle; there is always some end or goal. In nature, that is to be understood in terms of things having potentiality and changing toward their actuality. Aristotle observed that in nature things do not simply happen randomly; acorns become oak trees, kittens grow up to be cats (not oak trees); bodies form scars over wounds; fingers grow a certain length and then stop. There appear to be natural ends or goals throughout nature. For Aristotle, change is the way of the world, but it is not random, isolated change; it is purposive, teleological change.

Related to this basic view of teleology (or purposive change), Aristotle placed great importance on the notion of function. We could never understand, for example, what a heart or lung is simply by describing what it looks like or how much it weighs. We can only understand it in terms of its function, and function is itself teleological, for Aristotle. That is, if something functions, or has a function, that is always toward some end or goal. The function of the heart is to circulate blood (to help maintain an organism). But, for Aristotle, function is not just a scientific concept. He also saw function as basic to understanding ethics and politics. When we speak of, say, a good knife, what we mean by saying it is good is that it fulfills its proper function, which, in the case of a knife, is to cut well. When we speak of a good lake, what we mean by saying it is good is that it fulfills its function of either supporting fish or providing drinkable water for people or for being beautiful or for being useful for recreation or whatever. But the point is that a lake is good to the extent that it fulfills its function(s). Aristotle took this notion of something being good in terms of function and argued that the good of something depends upon the nature of what that thing is. So, a good knife is not the same thing as a good lake or a good horse, because these things are different kinds of things and they have different functions. Humans, he argued, are in essence rational animals. That is, what distinguishes humans from other things is our capacity to think rationally. (This does not mean that we think or act rationally all the time, but it is our defining characteristic, for Aristotle.) Since this is what defines humans, that is, what distinguishes us from other things, the function of humans is to act rationally. To fulfill our function as humans is to act in accordance with right reason (i.e., rationally). Ethics, then, is the study of what are the principles of acting in accordance with right reason. For Aristotle, this involved two parts: proper action and right reason.

In terms of proper action, Aristotle argued for what is known as the doctrine of the mean. Mean here means "middle point." That is, he argued for moderation. For example, he said that a virtue, such as courage, is a mean between two excesses. Those two excesses are (1) too little bravery (that is, cowardice) and (2) too much bravery (that is, foolhardiness). Or, the proper feeling and action with respect to, say, shame is modesty, which is the mean between the excesses of bashfulness and shamelessness.

In terms of right reason, Aristotle famously systematized the study of logic. He formulated syllogisms as the basic conception of arguments and laid out the principles of logical analysis. His work on syllogisms was the basis for all later studies of logic and was fundamental to formal education up to today. If he had written nothing else, he would be renowned today for this single accomplishment.

While Aristotle's basic view of the world was teleological, and this reflected his strong emphasis on change and function, he also was very influential in terms of his views about physics. He claimed that there were two basic spheres in the universe. One sphere he called the terrestrial sphere and the other he called the celestial sphere. The terrestrial sphere included the Earth up to the Moon, the celestial sphere, the Moon and onto the rest of the heavens. Aristotle observed that on the Earth, things moved either naturally or unnaturally (what he called violently). Natural motion depended upon the nature of the thing that was moving. Heavy objects naturally fell to the ground, while light objects either fell much more slowly or, in the case of, say, a balloon rose into the sky. Aristotle argued that things moved naturally depending upon their nature, where their nature was a function of the four classical elements: earth, water, air, and fire (see pre-Socratic philosophy). Heavy things tended to fall to the ground, for Aristotle, because that is their natural place. Being made up primarily of the element earth, they would seek their natural place in the world. Light objects, on the other hand, would seek their natural place, which might be to rise if they were made up of air or fire. Unnatural (or violent) motion was when things moved contrary to their natural motion. For example, if someone threw a rock into the air, being made of earth, it would seek its natural place on the ground. Having been thrown, while it was moving upward, its motion would be unnatural, but, because of its nature, it would seek to return to the ground and, so, it would slow down and eventually fall back to the ground. All of this discussion was about the terrestrial sphere, where things come into existence and go out of existence. The celestial sphere, however, for Aristotle, was a place of perfection. In the heavens (not the religious sense of heaven, but where the planets and stars are), things are incorruptible or eternal. Aristotle claimed that heavenly objects must be made up of some fifth element (the later Latin word was *quintessence,* meaning "fifth essence"), because if they were made up of any of the four terrestrial elements, they would seek their natural place and fall into the terrestrial sphere. So, they are composed of something incorruptible and they move only by natural motion, which, he said, was circular; this is why they move in circular orbits around the Earth (which he thought was stationary and at the center of the universe). Although today we say that Aristotle's views about physics were wrong, they were the basic conception of the physical world for many centuries.

Aristotle also wrote very influential works on politics, art and drama, psychology, and a number of other topics. Because of the breadth of his writings, he probably had more influence on later thought even than Plato, but together they are acknowledged as having immeasurably shaped Western thought.

Syllogism

The term *syllogism* comes from the Greek word *logos,* meaning "word" and the Greek prefix *syl,* meaning "together." A syllogism is a basic form of argument and the formal study of syllogisms is most often traced back to the writings of Aristotle in the fourth century B.C.E. The study of syllogisms was treated as the full subject of logic from Aristotle's time up to the end of the 19th century, when it was fit into a larger discipline and seen as being correct, but limited in scope.

Syllogisms are based on a subject/predicate view of language. This view holds that sentences contain a subject and something that is said about that subject (that is, a predicate). For instance, in the sentence, "Whales are mammals," the word *whales* is the subject and the phrase *are mammals* is the predicate. Some sentences do not have a subject/predicate form and, therefore, they are not treated within the study of syllogisms. For instance, the command "Shut the door!" does not have a predicate that says something about a subject. Although there might be an implied subject in this case (namely, whoever is being commanded), there is still nothing being said about that subject.

The technical term for sentences that fall within the study of syllogisms is *categorical propositions.* This means that they are sentences

An 1811 painting of Aristotle *(Painting by Francesco Hayez)*

that can be either true or false; they supposedly describe the world. Any sentence that can be either true or false is said to have a truth-value, where the value is either true or it is false. For example, the sentence "Whales are mammals" supposedly states a fact, and in fact it does, so its truth value is "true." The sentence "Whales are dogs" also has the form of stating a fact, but in this case the sentence is false and its truth-value is "false." However, the sentence "Shut the door" cannot be either true or false; it has no truth-value.

Every categorical proposition has four components. One component is the subject and another is the predicate. These two components each refer to some class of things. For example, in the sentence "Whales are mammals" the subject term *(whales)* refers to the class of whales and the predicate term *(mammals)* refers to the class of mammals. The other two components of categorical propositions are the quantifier and the copula. The quantifier is simply some word or phrase that modifies the subject and indicates whether the subject term refers to its entire class of things or just part of that class. For example, in "All cows have lungs," the word *all* is the quantifier and it indicates that the subject term *(cows)* refers in this case to the entire class of cows. On the other hand, in "Some fish have lungs" the word *some* is the quantifier and it indicates that the subject term *(fish)* refers in this case only to part of the entire class of fish. For the sake of convenience, quantifiers are said to be either universal, meaning that the subject term refers to its entire class of things, or particular, meaning that the subject term refers to only part of its class of things. Finally, the copula is simply some form of the verb to be. A copula is said to be either affirmative, meaning that the predicate does apply to the subject, or negative, meaning that the predicate does not apply to the subject. For instance, "Whales are mammals" contains an affirmative copula, but "Some dogs are not black" contains a negative copula.

Given the four components of any categorical proposition (namely, the quantifier, subject, copula, and predicate), there are four basic forms of categorical proposition that are possible. These forms are: (1) universal affirmative, or any sentence of the form "All A are B"; (2) universal negative, or any sentence of the form "All A are not B" (also sometimes written "No A are B"; (3) particular affirmative, or any sentence of the form "Some A are B"; and (4) particular negative, or any sentence of the form "Some A are not B."

Syllogisms are argument patterns that contain only categorical propositions. Standard form syllogisms contain exactly three categorical propositions. Those three categorical propositions are two premises and a conclusion. A premise is the evidence or warrant that is said to support the conclusion and the conclusion of a syllogism is said to follow from the premises. For example, in the syllogism "All humans are mortal" and "Socrates is human" therefore "Socrates is mortal," the first two sentences are the premises and the third sentence is the conclusion. Every standard form syllogism contains exactly two premises and a conclusion.

Each of the three sentences in a syllogism is a categorical proposition and each categorical proposition can be one of four possible forms. For example, one syllogism might be of this pattern: All A are B, All B are C, therefore All A are C. Another syllogism might be: All A are B, No B are C, therefore All A are C. Yet another syllogism might be: Some A are not B, All B are C, therefore Some A are C. As a result, there are 64 different patterns of syllogisms that result from various combinations of categorical propositions. Finally, for each of these patterns, there are four different ways that the two premises can be constructed. For instance, "All A are B" is a universal affirmative form and the sentence "All B are A" is also a universal affirmative form, but they are different sentences. Because each of the 64 different patterns of syllogisms can be put into four different combinations, there turn out to be 256 possible syllogisms. Syllogistic logic is the analysis of which of those 256 possible syllogisms are in fact valid, which is to say which of those syllogisms have a conclusion that actually follows from the premises.

Form and Matter

Form and matter are two fundamental concepts in metaphysics. In particular, they relate to what kinds of things there are in the world and the nature of those things. For example, in our everyday experience we encounter many different kinds of things: cats, trees, water, clouds, oxygen, etc. Some things we think of as objects (such as cats and trees), but other things we think of as events (such as a party or a hurricane or a toothache). Those things we think of as objects have various features or characteristics. For instance, a cat has legs and fur, while a tree has leaves and bark, a cloud is puffy, and water flows. Philosophers sometimes call these features or characteristics properties. The things that have those attributes are sometimes referred to as substances. So, flowing or being puffy or having leaves are all properties of certain substances (in this case, water, clouds, and trees, respectively).

A long-standing philosophical debate centers on how to understand substances and properties. This debates goes as far back as Plato and

Aristotle (in fact, even farther back, but they focused attention on it). Plato argued that words referred to things. So, when we say, *Some dogs are black,* the words are meaningful and they refer to something. For instance, *dog* refers to a particular kind of object and *black* also refers to a particular kind of object. For Plato, they do not refer simply to actual physical objects that we encounter everyday. Instead, *dog* refers to an Idea (or Form). Ideas, for Plato, were whatever matches the ideal definition of some word. Since there are lots of different kinds of dogs that we encounter, there must be something they all have in common to be dogs (and there must be something that non-dogs lack for them not to be dogs). In other words, there must be some essence to being a dog. So, for Plato, *dog* really refers to whatever that essence is. The same was true, for Plato, for the word *black*. That is, he claimed that there must also be a Idea of Black, or something—some substance—that matches the essence of black.

Aristotle disagreed. He claimed that *black* refers not to a substance, or thing, but to a property. For Aristotle, a substance is a thing and he speaks of two sorts of substances: primary substance and secondary

Plato speaks with his student Aristotle in this marble panel from the bell tower of Florence. *(Sculpture by Luca della Robbia)*

substance. A primary substance is a concrete, specific individual thing, while a secondary substance is a more general kind of thing. So, for him, *dog* does not refer to a primary substance, but "Lassie" or "Fido" (that is, the name of some specific dog) does. *Dog* refers to a secondary substance.

For Aristotle, everyday objects are made up of both matter and form. The matter is the physical makeup of objects. The form is the structure that the matter has such that the particular substance is what it is. As an example, one could have a pile of wood (matter) and with that wood one could make, say, a specific table. But, one could take that same pile of wood (matter) and make, say, a specific desk. Each of those two specific things is a different primary substance; that is, they are two distinct individual things. For Aristotle, a given table is certain matter (those pieces of wood) structured into a certain form (the form or structure of that specific table). If that same matter (those pieces of wood) are structured into a different form, then the substance we have would be a different (primary) substance; it would be that specific desk rather than that specific table. The general point, for Aristotle, is that every substance must have both form and matter. A specific table is not simply a pile of wood; rather it is wood in a particular structured form. For Aristotle, there can be no matter without form and no form without matter. That is to say, for Aristotle, all matter has some structure or other (so there is no formless matter) and all form has matter; that is, there cannot exist a substance that is merely a structure with no physical components (so there is no matterless form). Plato was wrong, then, he said, to think that there could exist some Idea of Dog or Idea of Black (or Idea of anything), if that meant some ideal, nonmaterial structure. Plato, he said, confused substances with properties. For Aristotle, Plato's Ideas really just refer to the (ideal) properties of substances.

Cause

Aristotle analyzed the concept of cause. He argued that a full account of cause involved four components or, as some commentators on Aristotle say, four types of causes. They are: (1) material cause, (2) formal cause, (3) efficient cause, and (4) final cause. All four, for Aristotle, were necessary to fully understand cause, that is, how something (or some event or state of affairs) comes to be. For example, we see a tree (as a natural creation) or a statue (as a human creation) and wonder how it came to exist. The four causes were Aristotle's way of explaining how something comes to be. In effect, the four causes are answers to four separate but related questions. A material cause answers the question: *from* what does something come to be? A formal cause answers the question: *into* what does something come to be? This sounds odd to us today, but his point was that the same material(s) could have brought about or caused some other thing to happen (or come to be). For instance, a pile of wood could be used to make a desk or the same pile of wood could be used to make a table. For Aristotle, things are not simply things; that is, they are not simply collections of material or matter. Things always have some form or structure. Things are structured (or formed) matter. Understanding how something happens (or comes to be) involves understanding matter in its form. An efficient cause answers the question: *By* what does something come to be? This is the sense of cause that today we usually think of; what events or actions took place that resulted in this thing happening (or coming to be). A final cause answers the question: *For* what does something come to be?

Starting with the example of a statue, the point of these four causes can be seen. First, a statue is made out of some material (for instance, bronze or stone). So, part of the explanation for how this statue came to be is the material from which it is made. If it had been made out of other material, it would be a different statue; much like a given person is made out of a particular grouping of DNA. What caused this statue, then, is explained in part by its material cause.

However, that very same material might have been shaped into a different statue. Any material thing, said Aristotle, always has some particular form or structure. That particular form or structure is part of the explanation for what that thing is. So, to explain this particular statue, it is not enough to only speak of the material cause; one must also speak of the formal cause, that is, the form into which those materials are fashioned.

An efficient cause is the notion that most people today think of as the (or a) cause of something. For Aristotle, an efficient cause is that by which something comes to be. In the case of a statue, it is by the work of the sculptor, who takes material and manipulates it into a particular form. The actions of the sculptor are the efficient cause of a given statue.

For Aristotle, there is also the final cause. The final cause is the purpose or end or goal that is met by the coming to be of something. In the case of a particular statue, the purpose might be to honor someone or some event. In the case of a tree or any natural thing (including any natural event or process), the purpose might be to promote the survival of some organism or the overall ecological balance of some natural system. The view that things are to be explained in terms of purposes or goals is called teleology (from the Greek word, *telos,* meaning "end" or "purpose"). Much of the apparent controversy between science and religion, even today, is over the issue of whether teleological explanations, or final causes, of natural things are meaningful.

Eudaimonia

The Greek term *eudaimonia* is usually translated as happiness, or flourishing. The term comes from the Greek word *eu,* meaning "good," and *daimon,* meaning "spirit." Literally, then, eudaimonia means the state of having a good spirit, as in a guardian spirit. Less literally, eudaimonia is the state of living or doing well—of flourishing or being happy. In ancient philosophy, eudaimonia was considered to be the ultimate goal and the ultimate good in human life. So eudaimonia is the state of living the good life for humans (it does not apply to non-human animals or inanimate things). Although eudaimonia involves happiness, here happiness does not mean a short-lived feeling (the way a person might feel, for instance, during a pleasant evening spent with friends). Rather, happiness has to do with the way one lives one's life as a whole. Moreover, eudaimonia is objective; it is not based on a person's individual preferences. Rather, the idea of eudaimonia is that there is a way of living that is good for all humans. This does not mean that everyone must behave exactly the same way in order to live well and be happy—that everyone must pursue sports as a hobby, for instance. It does mean, however, at least for the Greeks, that there are certain components of human flourishing and human happiness that are objective, that apply to every person's flourishing and happiness. Many ancient philosophers believed that living virtuously was one component of eudaimonia. On this view, it was not possible for a person to flourish and be happy unless she lived virtuously. It is usually thought that Socrates believed that living virtuously was sufficient for eudaimonia, that nothing else was needed. This was also the view of Plato and the later stoic philosophers. Aristotle, in contrast, claimed that although virtue was a necessary component of eudaimonia, it was not sufficient; that is, something more than virtue was required. In particular, Aristotle believed that some material goods were necessary to achieve eudaimonia. One could not, according to Aristotle, live a life of eudaimonia while living in abject poverty. Ancient philosophers also often connected eudaimonia with the use of reason. For instance, Plato and Aristotle argued that a life of eudaimonia is a life lived in accordance with reason. Because Aristotle believed that the function, or purpose, of humans is to reason, he regarded eudaimonia as fulfilling the human function in an excellent way. The stoics, who believed that the universe was ordered in a rational way that is ultimately for the best, thought eudaimonia required living "in agreement with nature." In contemporary philosophy, eudaimonia has received renewed attention in virtue ethics.

Doctrine of the Mean

In Western philosophy, the doctrine of the mean is most closely associated with Aristotle's writings on ethics. Along with many other philosophers, Aristotle focused on living well. This usually was framed as virtue, or excellence (the Greek term was *areté*). This focus on virtue is not the same thing as a focus on principles of ethics, such as respecting rights or determining the best action on the basis of the principle of the greatest good for the greatest number. Rather, the focus is on being a good person, on developing and exercising virtues.

Aristotle's teacher, Plato (and Plato's teacher, Socrates), had said that virtue is knowledge. This view included the notion that no one does what one truly believes is wrong. If someone does what is wrong, one must have simply been mistaken or ignorant. Aristotle, however, claimed that there are both virtues of intellect and virtues of character. It is not enough to know the good or to know the right thing to do, but one must also act on it. The study of ethics, then, is to become good. That would include knowing the good, so virtues of intellect are important.

Fundamental to Aristotle's views of virtues of character is what is called the doctrine of the mean. The word *mean* means "middle point." For example, mathematicians talk about the mean number of a set of numbers. (For example, 7 is the mean of the set 1,4,7,10,13). The emphasis is on moderation, finding a middle point, or moderate action, among different possible actions. Aristotle claimed that virtue involved the mean action among a set of actions connected to some feeling. For example, courage is the mean between two excesses: cowardice and foolhardiness. Modesty is the mean between bashfulness and shamelessness.

While virtue is the mean, what counts as an appropriate mean will vary depending upon contexts. For instance, what might be a rash or foolhardy action for someone might be a courageous action for someone who has relevant training or experience (such as a firefighter trying to save someone in a burning building). Or, less dramatic, what might be a moderate amount of food to eat could be different for a young child as opposed to a full-grown adult. Nonetheless, for Aristotle, given any relevant context and circumstances, moderation is the appropriate action.

Catharsis

Another area with respect to values that Aristotle wrote about was aesthetic value (rather than moral value). Aesthetic value has to do with values associated with art. For example, one might say that a certain movie was good, not because it had a virtuous message, but because the acting was convincing or the storyline was compelling. In the context of aesthetic value, Aristotle is especially known for his notion of catharsis. *Catharsis* is a Greek term meaning purging or purification. Aristotle linked catharsis with tragic drama (plays that are tragedies). By the very concept of tragedies in the literary sense, terrible things happen in tragedies. People commit horrific acts, such as murder and incest. People suffer, sometimes unjustly. People die, often innocent people. Yet in Aristotle's time, as well as in our own, people choose to watch tragic dramas. It seems we choose to watch them because we enjoy them. But how can there be enjoyment in watching terrible—even though fictional—things unfold? In his book *Poetics,* Aristotle suggests that one reason that tragic drama appeals to us is that, by watching tragedies, we can undergo a catharsis of negative emotions such as fear and pity. That is, viewing tragedies allows us

Early Islamic portrayal
of Aristotle teaching a
student

to rid ourselves of these emotions, and in this way viewing tragedies brings a certain relief and cleansing. On another interpretation, viewing tragedies allows emotions such as fear and pity to be purified; on this reading of Aristotle, tragedy does not allow us to rid ourselves of these emotions, but it makes these emotions purer than they were. In either case, according to Aristotle, viewing tragedies is beneficial; it has a positive effect.

As it is controversial how Aristotle thought catharsis actually worked, it is also controversial whether Aristotle believed that catharsis was the main purpose of tragedy. However, Aristotle's comments on tragedy and catharsis are often considered in contrast with (and perhaps as a reply to) Plato's view of drama. Plato criticized drama for inciting negative emotions and thereby having a bad effect on society; Aristotle's comments on tragedy run counter to this view.

Although Aristotle focused on viewing tragic plays, it is possible to apply his comments about catharsis to experiencing art in general—for example, reading works of tragic fiction or poetry, listening to music, or viewing paintings. That is, perhaps experiencing other art forms could have a cathartic effect, purging the person of negative emotions and providing a sort of cleansing. Yet it is not obvious that experiencing art, including tragic drama, always provides catharsis. Perhaps it depends in part on the emotions (or lack thereof) a person brings to the experience of art in the first place. Perhaps, also, experiencing art might strengthen a person's negative emotions rather than purging (or purifying) them. A very sad person who watched a tragic movie, for instance, might walk away feeling worse than ever. However, the possibility of such cases does not mean that no one ever experiences a genuine catharsis through art.

Hellenistic Philosophy

While Socrates, Plato, and Aristotle are commonly recognized as the foundations of Western philosophical thought, there were important and influential thinkers and schools of thought following them. The several centuries after Alexander the Great's conquest of Greek city-states and much of the surrounding world are often referred to as Hellenistic, indicating that this is distinguished from the earlier Hellenic period. For philosophers, the Hellenistic period includes not only philosophers who lived in Greece during the several hundred years after Aristotle (and Alexander), but also those in Rome in the first two or three centuries of the common era. So, very broadly speaking, Hellenistic philosophy covers the time between 300 B.C.E. and 400 C.E. (Some scholars put the ending date as 529 C.E., when Plato's Academy was officially shut down.) Although today Hellenistic philosophy is seen as less significant than that of Socrates, Plato, and Aristotle, that has not always been the case. During the European Renaissance of the 17th and 18th centuries, the thought of Hellenistic philosophers such as Epicurus and Lucretius was considered major. Within Hellenistic philosophy, four schools of thought in particular were prominent: stoicism, Epicureanism, skepticism, and Neoplatonism.

Stoicism

The term *stoicism* comes from the Greek word *stoa,* meaning "porch." This term became associated with a particular school of philosophy because the philosopher Zeno of Citium (335–263 B.C.E.) delivered lectures in Athens at a public "porch." (Zeno of Citium was not the same person as Zeno of Elea, the earlier pre-Socratic philosopher who was a follower of Parmenides.) Very little is known of the life of Zeno other than that he was from the island of Cyprus and came to Athens as a young man, where he learned of Socrates and admired what he saw as Socrates' strength of character. Only a few fragments of his writings remain.

Zeno was less concerned with academic philosophy—meaning questions that seemed to focus on analyzing concepts such as knowledge or virtue—and was more concerned with practical philosophy, that is, philosophy for life. The primary emphasis was on living well; to the extent that knowledge was necessary toward the goal of living well, it was important, but only to that extent. Today stoic means being unperturbed, even unemotional. This is because the goal of stoic philosophy was to attain peace of mind as the means for living well.

Zeno argued that we are citizens of the world, not merely of an individual community or country. The term *cosmopolitan* is meant to capture this notion (*cosmos* means "world" or "universe" and *polis* refers to community). For Zeno, regardless of what particular community or country we live in and under what social laws we are governed, as citizens of the world, we are first and foremost governed by natural laws. For that reason, we need to understand those natural laws. Indeed, without that, we will not live well. What he taught, then, covered three broad topics: physics (or the study of the natural world), logic, and ethics. These topics essentially dealt with the questions of How are things by nature?, What attitude should we adopt towards them?, and What results from such attitudes? In terms of physics, Zeno held a materialist view, which means that the world is composed of physical, material things. Unlike what is usually seen as modern materialism, however, Zeno did not deny the existence of God. However, God, too, for Zeno, was understood as part of the material world (not above or beyond it). With respect to logic, Zeno held to what is today called an empiricist view. This means that all knowledge comes from physical sensations. In ways that very much foreshadow philosophers in the 1600s, Zeno claimed that knowledge is the result of physical impressions that are caused by material objects in the world and all knowledge must come from and be based on these impressions and sensations.

Finally, in terms of ethics, living well is a matter of living in accordance with nature. Right action is action that reflects natural laws. Human laws, if they are meant to help people live together well, need to be consistent with natural laws (or, at least, not inconsistent with them). Living poorly, and failing to attain peace of mind, is the result of acting contrary to natural laws. As a later stoic philosopher, Epictetus (50–130 C.E.) said, "Do not seek to have events happen as you want them to, but instead want them to happen as they do happen, and your life will go well." This is a version of the modern saying of having the knowledge of what things you cannot change, the courage to change things that you can, and the wisdom to know the difference. As a result of this view that living well means living in accordance with nature, Zeno claimed that no things are good or bad in themselves; good or bad is a matter of our relationship to things. A good relationship is one in which we understand the nature of things and act accordingly (that is, not wanting things to be what/how they are not). For instance, as (again) Epictetus remarked, "If you are fond of a jug, say 'I am fond of a jug!' For when it is broken you will not be upset." This is because it is the nature of jugs that they (can) break. On the other hand, Epictetus went on to say, "If you kiss your child or your wife, say that you are kissing a human being; for when it dies you will not be upset." Again, it is the nature of living beings to die. Knowing that, and genuinely accepting that fact (and natural law), one should not be upset when someone dies, as if it were possible that he or she might not die. It is our judgments and responses to things and events that are in our control, not the things or events themselves. These responses, especially emotions, he claimed, disturb calmness and the balance of reason.

Epicureanism

Where stoicism saw people as citizens of the world, the school of thought founded by the Greek philosopher Epicurus (341–270 B.C.E.) was very much individualistic. Epicurus was born on the island of Samos, which at the time was a colony of Athens. He went to Athens during the very year that Aristotle left Athens (323 B.C.E.). With the death of Aristotle's former student, Alexander the Great, the following year, there was considerable social and political turmoil. Many later commentators have remarked that this turmoil might have played a role in Epicurus seeing public life as upsetting the tranquility of individuals' lives. The result was that Epicurus left Athens and moved to Asia Minor (now western Turkey) and became influenced by the philosophy of the atomists there. Years later, he returned to Athens and set up his school at what came to be called "The Garden," to distinguish it from "The Porch" that was associated with the stoics.

There were a number of similarities between the views of the stoics and those of Epicurus. Both were materialist, meaning that they saw the world as composed of material, physical things and events. Both were empiricist, meaning that knowledge is based only on sensations. In a sense, we bump into the world. Both saw the goal of philosophy as helping us to live well and saw living well as having peace of mind. However, as noted above, Epicurus was not concerned with social and political matters. His emphasis was on individuals finding peace of mind and that society was nothing more than a collection of individuals.

One result of Epicurus's endorsement of atomism was that he saw the soul as mortal. What we call the soul was, for him, not some thing separate from our bodies, but was particular kinds of atoms associated with the functioning of a person. When a person dies, those atoms disperse just as do the atoms that make up a person's body.

The main focus of Epicurus's teachings was on attaining peace of mind and that the goal of action was to seek pleasure and happiness. For this reason, his views are said to be hedonistic (from the Greek word, *hedon,* meaning "pleasure"). Indeed, today, when people use the term *epicure,* they refer to someone who seeks pleasure, usually physical pleasures. For Epicurus, however, there were various kinds of pleasures and different levels of pleasures. True pleasure and happiness, for Epicurus, was actually quite the opposite of what today is taken as epicurean. For Epicurus, true pleasure and happiness come from wisdom, not merely physical pleasures.

Epicurus spoke of pleasures that are (1) natural and necessary, such as consuming food, (2) natural but not necessary, such as having sex, and (3) not natural (or necessary), such as having expensive clothes. The last group—the pleasures that are not natural (or necessary)—is one that he labeled as vain. (Saying that these are not natural did not mean that they were unnatural, or contrary to nature, but simply that they were not required by nature.) Given that there are different types of pleasures, Epicurus offered what he saw as a fourfold remedy

Bust of Epicurus at the Louvre *(Photograph by Eric Gaba)*

to avoiding pain. This included meditation on the nature of things in order to achieve peace of mind. Much like the stoics, Epicurus argued that we face aggravations and frustrations (that is, a lack of tranquility) when we want things to be different than they are. So, a necessary part of attaining peace of mind is to be able to understand the nature of things so we can judge them and respond to them appropriately. (If we got upset every time it rained, we would be in for a difficult time, since rain is natural and there is nothing we can do to stop it!) As part of meditating on the nature of things—and the second of his fourfold remedy—Epicurus said we should not fear death. Death is, after all, a part of nature. Third, he argued that simplicity and frugality are the basis of a healthy and happy life. We will not be happy, he claimed, by constantly trying to acquire the latest products or have the biggest house, etc. Put plainly, for Epicurus, a simple life is a happy life. Finally, he said that repose of mind comes from following these basic practices and values. So, quite the opposite of merely seeking physical pleasures, Epicurus stated that living pleasantly required living prudently and honorably and justly, but, likewise, living prudently and honorably and justly required living pleasantly. So, seeking genuine, true pleasure is the proper goal for people, but genuine, true pleasure for people is a matter of being virtuous. This view was revived centuries later by the 19th-century British philosopher John Stuart Mill as part of what came to be known as utilitarianism.

Skepticism

In a broad sense, skepticism is the attitude of critical inquiry: It is a willingness to question beliefs and claims, even when they seem obvious and fundamental, and to examine them closely on their merits rather than simply accepting them at face value. In this sense, skepticism is at the heart of philosophy, perhaps best captured by the famous remark by the Greek philosopher Socrates that the unexamined life is not worth living. To examine one's life requires examining what one does, which in turn requires the examination of one's beliefs, for how we act often depends on what we believe; and to examine one's beliefs is to subject them to critical inquiry. A skeptic in this spirit is an investigator, continually investigating the meaning and basis of claims to knowledge and truth, examining whether we know what we claim to know or whether we have adequate grounds for what we claim to know.

This kind of skepticism is closely associated with the skepticism of classical Greece, and indeed the word *skeptic* derives from the Greek word *sképtesthai,* meaning "to investigate." Traditionally, classical skepticism is divided between two schools of thought: Pyrrhonian skepticism and Academic skepticism. Pyrrhonian skepticism takes Pyrrho of Elis (ca. 365–270 B.C.E.) as its founder. Pyrrho himself wrote nothing and what we know of him and his views today comes mainly from the writings of Sextus Empiricus (ca. second century), who wrote several hundred years after Pyrrho's death. Academic skepticism is associated with the Academy, the school founded by Plato, when the Academy came to be led by skeptics such as Arcesilaus (ca. 315–240 B.C.E.) and Carneades (214–129 B.C.E.). It is often thought that Academic skeptics denied that knowledge was possible, whereas Pyrrhonian skeptics claimed neither that knowledge was possible nor that knowledge was not possible; they simply withheld judgment.

Pyrrhonian skeptics clearly emphasized the suspension of judgment. To suspend judgment is neither to accept a claim nor to reject it; it is to refrain from making a judgment about the truth or falsity of the claim at all. To illustrate, consider a judgment in a criminal case. Suppose that someone, accused of stealing from her employer, says she had no motive to do so and that she and her employer were on good terms; suppose, further, that both claims seem plausible. But now suppose that property belonging to the employer was found in the employee's home. Pressed for an explanation, the defendant claims someone is trying to frame her. There is no clear evidence of framing, although at least one person had the means of doing so and was on bad terms with the defendant. Faced with all these facts, a jury might choose to acquit the defendant. Jury members might regard the evidence as insufficient to show either that she is innocent or that she is guilty. In short, the jury might well suspend judgment on the question of whether the accused actually stole the property, believing neither that she did nor that she did not. The skeptics take this attitude of suspension of judgment beyond a few individual cases; for them, it is very often, perhaps always, reasonable to suspend judgment. Skeptics thought that one ought to suspend judgment about all manner of claims—about what is the right thing to do, for example, and claims about the nature of reality. They directed their skeptical attacks against the claims of Epicureanism and stoicism, in particular, popular schools of thought during their time. For the skeptics, there was no reason for preferring an Epicurean or stoic claim over an opposite claim; so, one ought neither to believe nor disbelieve the claims in question.

The goal of Pyrrhonian skepticism was to attain peace of mind by suspending judgment. To see why suspending judgment might lead to such inner tranquility, consider what might happen when someone does not suspend judgment. Suppose, for instance, someone believes that reconciliation with an estranged friend is necessary for a good life. If she fails to reconcile, she will feel distress and worry. If, however, she neither believes that reconciliation is necessary for a good life nor that it is not, these worries will not plague her. Similarly, if she has no beliefs about what future events would be good or bad, she will not fret about

Illustration of Plotinus from the *Nuremberg Chronicle*

the future, fearful of some outcomes and desirous of others. Having made no judgment about what would be a good or bad outcome, she will be able to accept whatever happens with equanimity. As the Pyrrhonian skeptics saw it, the suspension of judgment is a way of achieving inner tranquility.

Neoplatonism

As the term suggests, *Neoplatonism* is a new version or interpretation of the thought and views of Plato. The term itself was coined many centuries after the Neoplatonists themselves lived. They thought of themselves simply as Platonists, that is, as people who, broadly speaking, followed basic beliefs of Plato. As a school of thought, Neoplatonism was generally spiritual, often even mystical, in focus. The major Neoplatonist was Plotinus (204–270 C.E.), who was said to have been born in Egypt. Almost nothing is known of his early life, but it is known that as a young man he went to Alexandria and studied philosophy. Later, in his late 30s, he moved to Rome, where he taught until the end of his life.

The gist of Plotinus's thought was compiled after his death by his most famous follower, Porphyry (233–305 C.E.), into six groups of nine essays each. Taken from the Greek word for "nine," these writings came to be known as *The Enneads.* In these writings, Plotinus tried to spell out his views on the nature of reality and philosophy. Philosophy, he said, awakened people to their divine and spiritual nature, and this came about, he said, much as Plato had argued, by looking beyond the material world of everyday experience to what is universal and eternal. However, he said, reality is ineffable, that is, inexpressible. Any effort to describe what it is would be limited and limiting. Nonetheless, Plotinus tried. What is real, he claimed, or most real, is the One (also spoken of as the Good). We cannot say what it is, because, again, any statement of what it is would imply some limit. We can say *that* it is, but not *what* it is. At best, we might be able to suggest what it is not: it is not limited, it is not contained in something else, it is not knowable or expressible, etc. In spite of the ineffability of the One, Plotinus claimed that it is the ground of all being and all value and that it is positive (meaning that nothing negative or bad pertains to it). He said this because he took goodness not to be the same as something being good. "Good" is a feature of things (such as a good book or a good person). Goodness, on the other hand, for Plotinus was not a feature or quality of anything; it simply was the Good. All that we can speak of in terms of reality are what Plotinus said are emanations from the Good. By emanations he meant they are an overflow of the Good, much as light emanates from the sun. What emanates from the Good is what he called *Nous,* or Intellect. It is Being and it is related to the Good much as a circle is related to its center. A second emanation is what he called World-Soul, or principle of life. This is akin to Aristotle's notion of form and matter. All things, for Aristotle, are composed of matter in some form or other. For instance, a collection of pieces of wood could be configured into the form of a bookcase or into a different form of a table. For Aristotle, there was no matter that did not have some form or other and also no form that was not composed of some matter. For Plotinus, the World-Soul is like matter, where Nous is like form. Finally, the material world of everyday experience flows out of these more basic emanations.

There were aspects of Plotinus's thought that were amenable to early Christianity. For example, there is the sense that the Good (or God) is reality and that everything comes from the Good (or God). There is the sense that what is spiritual and divine is the most important and it is not to be equated with what is material. However, there were aspects of Christianity that Plotinus did not accept. He did not see Jesus as being God (or the Good). In addition, he did not agree with many Christians that the material world was somehow bad or even evil. The material world of everyday experience was still, for him, something that comes from the Good, so it cannot be bad.

While Neoplatonism was quite different in content and focus from other schools of thought of Hellenistic philosophy—especially, for example, the atomism of Epicurus—it did share the value of seeking peace of mind and living well. Nonetheless, the emphasis on spiritual and mystical claims made it stand out against these other schools of thought, but also made it more palatable to the emerging force of Christianity.

Medieval and Renaissance Philosophy

Medieval Philosophy

Medieval philosophy refers to the philosophy of the Middle Ages, roughly the years 400–1400. This 1,000-year stretch of time included many of the most important and influential thinkers of Western philosophy: Augustine (354–430), Boethius (480–526), Ibn Sina, also known as Avicenna (980–1037), Anselm (1033–1109), Peter Abelard (1079–1142), Al-Ghazali (1058–1111), Moses Maimonides (1135–1204), Thomas Aquinas (1225–74), and William of Ockham (1285–1347), among many others. While many people speak of the Middle Ages as the Dark Ages—meaning that there was little knowledge or progress during this time—this is inaccurate and few historians or scholars today use that term. In addition, the late Middle Ages (roughly, the years 1100–1400) were considerably different philosophically than the early Middle Ages. This is because of the reintroduction in the West of many classical philosophical works that had been unavailable for centuries. That is, much of earlier classical philosophical works, such as those of Plato and Aristotle, had been relatively unknown to people in Europe, although they were thoroughly studied and critiqued in the lands of what is now called the Middle East. Following the breakup of the Roman Empire, most of classical Greek learning had gone east to the Middle East and had, in effect, been lost to European culture. Only centuries later, beginning roughly around the 12th century, did those classical works begin to be translated into Latin and become available to European scholars.

In some respects, medieval philosophy was a continuation of earlier classical philosophy and in some respects it was not. Although the specific works of classical philosophy were relatively unknown to medieval scholars, their broad, general views were the basis for medieval thought. For example, the general notion that the world was teleological—fundamental to Aristotle's understanding—was assumed during the Middle Ages. Likewise, the basic classical notions of natural philosophy (or science) carried over into and throughout the Middle Ages, such as the view that there were two spheres that made up the universe, the terrestrial sphere and the celestial sphere. The classical conception of things in the world being constituted by matter and form, along with both essential and accidental features, was taken as a given for medieval philosophers. Also, much as the classical philosophers, medieval philosophers saw matters of ethics and morality in terms of virtues and eudaimonia, and held an assumption of moral realism (that is, that good and bad were objective features of things and actions).

Probably the most fundamental way in which medieval philosophy was different from earlier classical philosophy was that the former was influenced heavily by Christianity. Metaphysical questions about the nature of God took on great importance for medieval philosophers, as did questions about the relationship between faith and reason and the understanding of human nature (particularly in terms of questions about a human soul). In addition, philosophical approaches to addressing ethical and moral issues were different for medieval philosophers. For instance, new virtues (sometimes called theological virtues), such as faith, hope, and charity, became basic to medieval ethics, as opposed to classical virtues of courage, temperance, and reason.

With the reintroduction of much classical philosophy to the West in the 1100s, medieval philosophers faced and embraced the challenge of reconciling classical thought with contemporary Christian doctrine and practice. In many ways, this challenge dominated medieval philosophy during the final centuries of the Middle Ages.

The Problem of Universals

In the area of metaphysics, one of the most debated and discussed topics during the Middle Ages was the issue of universals. Universals, as opposed to particulars, are said to be those things that are general in nature. While there might be many instances of, say, white patches, white itself (or whiteness) is said to be a universal. Universal terms, then, are said to refer to those universal things, rather than to the particular instances of that universal. So, the word *white*, then, refers not simply to some particular patch(es) of white, but to the universal abstract object that is whiteness. Philosophers have held various views about what they call the problem of universals. Some believe that universal terms really do refer to universal abstract objects, and this view is often called realism. Others deny that universals exist; they claim that only particular, concrete objects actually exist and, for the sake of convenience, we use universal terms. These are merely empty names that do not really refer to anything (other than, perhaps, the collection of all of those particular things that have that feature or characteristic that the universal term denotes; for example, *white* does not refer to some universal abstract object, but—if it refers at all—to all the white particulars in the world). This view is usually called nominalism. Finally, some philosophers say that universal terms do refer, but not to some abstract objects out there in the world; rather, they refer to concepts in our minds. This view is seen as a midway point between realism and nominalism; it is usually called conceptualism.

One important figure in the debates over universals was William of Ockham (1280–1349), a medieval philosopher and theologian who today is mostly known for his rejection of metaphysical realism. William is believed to have been born in the town of Ockham, near London. He studied at Oxford University and was ordained in 1306. Because of his empiricist views, he met with disfavor from some of his teachers and other clerics, eventually being summoned before Pope John XXII to defend himself against charges of heresy. After several years of house arrest, he fled to Bavaria (now Germany), where he wrote a number of works that were critical of the hierarchy of the Catholic Church. He was believed to have died of the Black Plague.

William is now best known for what is called Ockham's razor. Ockham's razor is a reference to the principle that explanations should be as simple as possible, but not too simple! (Today we often hear the expression KISS, or Keep It Simple, Stupid!) In Ockham's own writings he frequently remarked that "plurality is not to be posited without necessity" and "what can be explained by the assumption of fewer things is vainly explained by the assumption of more things." So, there are two ways that this has been understood. One way is in terms of what is real. In this case, Ockham's razor is said to suggest that one should not assume the existence of things unless their assumption is necessary (or, at least reasonable). We might be able to explain noises in the attic by claiming that there are goblins up there who are stomping around, but we could probably explain those noises without assuming the existence of goblins. The second, and related, way that Ockham's razor has been understood is more explicitly about explaining (and not about what things there are to be explained). So, even if the noises in the attic are made by, say, squirrels and not by goblins, we should explain this by claiming that the squirrels are looking for food or shelter, not that they are having a dance party.

With respect to the issue of universals, William rejected them outright. His view is often referred to as nominalism (from the Latin word *nomina,* meaning "name"). For William, universal terms such as *white* or *dog* referred not to some independently existing real object, but rather they were convenient names that we use to speak about particular objects, such as white patches or different individual dogs. We notice similarities and resemblances between various particular individual things and, because of this noticing as well as for our convenience, we label them under the same name. So, for William, if there are four dogs in a room, there are only four objects in that room, not five (four particular dogs plus the form or essence of Dog).

The reason we speak of universals, said William, is that we recognize, or perhaps formulate, similarities between objects that we encounter and we then form concepts based on those similarities. If universal terms refer to anything at all, they could only refer to these concepts. (This is one reason that some philosophers have claimed that William actually held a view called conceptualism, not a hard-core view of nominalism.) Our knowledge comes from bumping into the world, so to speak, and forming concepts out of our perceptions of things. Not only is there no reason to think that universals actually exist and are real, but also, for William, there is reason to think that they do not exist and are not real. In a word, he thought that realism about universals was incoherent; it is a view that contradicts itself. This is because, he said, metaphysical realism must claim that a universal is both one thing and many things at the same time. For example, the universal term *humanity* must refer to one thing, what is common to all humans, but must also refer to many things because it is a property of each and every human. This, he claimed, was to say that humanity is both one thing and many things at the same time, which he found incoherent.

Another important figure in the debates of universals was Peter Abelard (1079–1142), a medieval philosopher and theologian who rejected the view of metaphysical realism. Today he is best known for his famous and troubled love affair with a woman named Heloise, whose family was irate over the situation and ended up attacking and castrating Abelard. To philosophers, however, he was a rigorous and complex thinker. Abelard was born in the town of Pallet (in what is now France). He studied under a number of well-known thinkers as a student, but his combative personality led to strained relationships with most of them. As he challenged the views of his teachers and some standard claims of the Catholic Church, he became ever more caught up in controversy. During his life a number of his writings were officially condemned by the church and for a while he was excommunicated.

With respect to the issue of metaphysical universals, Abelard rejected them. He argued that the universality of a universal term, such as *white*, was simply that it could be truly spoken of with regard to many individual things. In other words, the term *white* could be applied to many different things: this white piece of paper, that white cloud, that other white shirt, etc. So, the universality of white was not, for Abelard, because the term refers to some additional thing that exists (namely, whiteness), but the universality of white was simply that it correctly applied to many things. Nonetheless, for Abelard, although universals themselves are not real, it is a common feature of real things (that is, real particular individuals) that accounts for and justifies the application of that universal term to them. That is, white correctly, or truly, applies to some things (and not to others), but not because there is some thing—whiteness—that is real and, in some sense or other, causes the whiteness in particular white things. As he put it, there is not common cause; there is common conception.

This notion of conception was important for Abelard. If universal terms refer to anything, it is a concept, not some independent abstract object. This view—that what a universal term refers to is a concept—is today called conceptualism. (Some scholars have claimed that Abelard was more of a nominalist than a conceptualist, meaning that he denied that universal terms referred to anything, even to concepts.) In laying out his view, Abelard spoke of the power of abstraction. Abstraction is our ability to focus on one aspect of something while ignoring other aspects of it. For example, we can look at a rug and just focus on its shape, while ignoring its color. (Perhaps we wonder if it will fit well in a particular room and we do not care about its color.) Universals, he said, were, in effect, the products of this ability to abstract. Although what actually exists, for Abelard, is, say a particular piece of paper, we can ignore some of its features and just focus on, say, its color. We can do this with other pieces of paper, with the result that by mentally abstracting the color away from all of the other features of different pieces of paper, we have the concept of a given color, say, white. But, for Abelard, this is only an abstract concept, not a real thing out in the world independent of our abstraction. The concepts, or at least our conceptions, are real, and they might very well be the result of experiencing real features of things (that is, different pieces of paper really are white), but concepts can also reflect certain interests that we have as opposed to other interests. For example, there might be something common between a dog and a table (they have legs) or between a bird and a rocket and a balloon (they all fly, in some sense). We can even have concepts of imaginary things that do not exist (such as unicorns or elves). The point, again, is that, for Abelard, universal terms do not presuppose the existence of universal objects.

Aquinas's Proofs of God's Existence

Because of the importance of Christianity for medieval philosophers, one issue that arose was that of the nature of the relationship between humans and God. This included, for philosophers at least, the issue of the relationship between faith and reason. One topic connected to this issue was not simply believing that God exists and has a particular nature, but knowing, or at least reasoning about, God's existence and nature. As a result, a number of medieval philosophers offered various proofs for God's existence. Among the most famous of these were given by Thomas Aquinas (1225–74), who was especially concerned with reconciling Aristotle's classical views with Christian doctrine.

Aristotle had argued that God was the Unmoved Mover. For him, the concept of motion was similar to the concept of change. Things, for him, are moved in the sense that they change in some way or other; that is, they move from one state of being to another state of being. For instance, a person might move in the sense of walking across a room, and, so, change position in that room. Another sense of motion, or change, for Aristotle, would be a piece of fruit ripening. Over the course of time, it changes from one state of being to another, as it ripens. Aristotle would have spoken of this as the fruit being in motion, even though the motion was in terms of maturing, not in terms of its location in space.

For Aristotle, all things in the natural world move (or change). However, there must be some cause(s) for any change. As we trace back a series of causes to account for any motion, Aristotle claimed that eventually we must get back to some first starting point, something that is itself not moved. This unmoved mover, he said, is God.

Drawing on Aristotle's writings, Aquinas offered five proofs (or five ways of proving) God's existence. One way is often called the proof from motion. It is simply Aristotle's argument of the unmoved mover. A second way, for Aquinas, was a closely related argument that he called the proof from efficient cause. It is essentially the same point, that for any effect, there must be some efficient cause—call it C—that is, something that brought about that effect. But, then, there must have been an efficient cause—call it D—for C, and another efficient cause—call it E—for D, and so on. Aquinas said that this cannot go on back infinitely; there must be a first cause (or uncaused cause), namely, God.

Aquinas's third way of proving God's existence is from the notions of possibility and necessity. In nature, he said, we find things that exist, but they might not have existed. It is possible that George Washington might never have been born, say, if his parents had never met. George Washington's existence, then, was not necessary; that is, he did not necessarily exist. Aquinas claimed that this is true of all things in the natural world; if they exist, they might not have. To say that they exist, but do not necessarily exist, is to say that they exist contingently (which, again, simply means that they happen to exist, but not necessarily). Since all things in the natural world exist contingently, for Aquinas, there must have been some point back in time when nothing existed (because nothing *must* exist necessarily). However, if there was ever a moment in time when nothing existed, then there would still be nothing existing, since you can't get something from nothing! But, said Aquinas, this is false; things do exist! That means that there must be something that exists necessarily, namely God.

His fourth proof of God's existence is called the proof of gradation. This refers to the notion that things can have comparable qualities, or grades. For example, one person might be tall, but another person is taller, or one rock is heavy and another rock is heavier. Things can have more or less of some quality or feature (such as more or less height or weight). However, said Aquinas, to speak of gradations presupposes some standard by which to determine whether or not something has more or less of that quality or feature. Since people can be more or less good, he claimed that there must be a standard of goodness, or perfection. That is, there must be the thing that is the most good, or most perfect, namely, God.

Finally, Aquinas's fifth way was what he called the governance of the world. This is his notion that the universe is orderly, not chaotic. There must be some cause for this orderliness and that cause is God. This is often spoken of as the design argument, because it says that the universe shows such orderliness and complexity that it must be designed, not random, and the designer is God.

Renaissance Philosophy

Most historians speak of the European Renaissance as the time between the mid-1400s and the mid-1600s. It is also the time that has been called the Scientific Revolution. Among the important philosophers of the time were Marsillo Ficino (1433–99), Giovanni Pico della Mirandola (1463–94), Desiderius Erasmus (1466–1536), Michel de Montaigne (1533–92), and Francis Bacon (1561–1626). Even better known today, this time included some of the most famous people in the history of science, such as Nicolas Copernicus (1473–1543), Johannes Kepler (1571–1630), and Galileo Galilei (1564–1642). During this time there were tremendous social and cultural changes. This was the period of the "discovery" of the New World and the rise of global exploration and colonialism. The influence and authority of the Catholic Church were questioned and challenged by the rise of nation-states in Europe and also by theologians such as Martin Luther (1483–1546). At the same time, new technologies were emerging, such as the printing press that made information more accessible to more people.

A major change at this time was the emergence of a mechanical view of the world. That is, more and more there came to be the view that the world was like an enormous, complex mechanism that operated by definite precise causes and laws. As part of this mechanical picture of the world, the traditional Aristotelian view of final cause was, in large part, dropped. (Final cause was the notion that things must be explained in terms of some purpose or goal or end; things happen for a reason, for some potential goal to be realized.) Scientists began more and more to speak of proximate causes, meaning mechanical, physical causes that could be measured and tested, while setting aside ultimate causes, meaning purposes or goals or even God. Since only proximate causes could be measured and tested, they would be the focus of scientific inquiry and explanation. Along with this new focus on proximate causes, scientists placed more emphasis on inductive reasoning, that is, on beginning with particular information and generalizing from that information as they gathered more information. This, they said, was how to "read the book of nature" rather than assuming that knowledge must be deduced from principles that were assumed to be true (which is what they claimed was the long-standing view derived from Aristotle).

Francis Bacon was particularly critical of the Aristotelian world-view. He was highly critical of earlier methods of inquiry and advocated a new method for acquiring knowledge. It had been common for philosophers to make use of syllogisms, a special form of logical argument. An example of a syllogism is: "All men are mortal. Socrates is a man. Therefore, Socrates is mortal." Syllogisms proceed deductively; that is, the conclusion is intended to follow logically, not empirically, from the reasons (premises) given for that conclusion. Put another way, the premises lead to the conclusion simply as a matter of logic, not because the natural world behaves one way rather than another or because there is some phenomenon in nature on which the conclusion is based. For example, in the previous example, the conclusion that Socrates is mortal follows logically from the premises that Socrates is a man and that all men are mortal. So, *if* the premises are true, then the conclusion must be true also. But the conclusion follows from the premises as a matter of logic, not because of the way the natural world is. To see this, consider the syllogism: All men are immortal. Socrates is a man. Therefore, Socrates is immortal. It is false, of course, that all men are immortal, and in fact because no man is immortal, the conclusion of this syllogism (that Socrates is immortal) is false as well. However, the conclusion does follow logically from the premises (it just happens to be the case that one of those premises, that all men are immortal, is false).

Bacon charged that the use of syllogisms in philosophy, especially in natural philosophy (or science) hindered the progress of learning about the world for the reason that, too often, thinkers drew general conclusions on the basis of just a few observations and then proceeded to use those general observations in syllogisms to draw more conclusions. But a general conclusion on the basis of just a small number of observations of the natural world is not likely to be a very strong conclusion; for example, the general conclusion that all swans are white is not a very strong conclusion if it is based on observing just a handful of white swans. It would not be surprising if such general statements turned out to be false. In that case, however, using such statements in syllogisms would likely lead to false conclusions (just as, in the example above, the premise that all men are immortal helps lead to the false conclusion that Socrates is immortal). Natural philosophy, Bacon thought, had relied too little on actual observations of the actual world.

Bacon specifically identified four other problems that weaken methods of inquiry; he dubbed these problems the Four Idols. The Idols of the Tribe are flaws in human perception and reasoning; our senses sometimes deceive us, and sometimes our understanding distorts what is real (we misconstrue the nature of what is real or true). The Idols of the Cave are a person's individual biases and limited perspective. These can occur as a result of what a person is taught, a person's personality, or a person's circumstances. A person who spends most of her life living in a lush landscape, for instance, will have a different perspective regarding plant life than someone who has spent most of his life living in a desert landscape. The mistake would come in assuming that one's own perspective is the only and best perspective, or put another way, that one's own experience is uniquely authoritative. The third kind of idols are the Idols of the Marketplace, which are the concepts and words people use in conversation and communication with each other. Of course, there is nothing wrong with many concepts and words. But, Bacon thought, because sometimes concepts and language are vague, misleading, or even refer to nothing, mistakes in inquiry can arise as a result. For instance (though this is not Bacon's example), it was once thought there must be a special substance called phlogiston, and scientists spent time and energy discussing and attempting to examine the nature of phlogiston. But it turned out there was no such substance; the word *phlogiston* did not refer to anything at all. Finally, the Idols of the Theater are the dogmatic beliefs associated with philosophical theories in particular (the phrase Idols of the *Theater* suggests that various philosophical theories are fictional, like plays).

A good method of inquiry would avoid these Idols. In addition, Bacon had something positive to say about how a good method of inquiry would proceed (not just what it should avoid), describing his preferred method in some detail. Inquiry, he thought, should involve a new kind of induction. Induction, roughly, is the drawing of general conclusions on the basis of individual observations; drawing the conclusion that all crows are black after observing many individual black crows is an example of induction. However, Bacon thought it was a mistake to investigate the world simply by adding up a lot of individual observations. Of course, making individual observations was necessary, and it was necessary to make a lot of them; Bacon criticized earlier ways of science for relying on too few individual observations. Merely making individual observations, however, for Bacon was not enough. To investigate some phenomenon in nature one should not merely observe many instances of that phenomenon and see under what conditions it occurred, but also make many observations of cases in which the phenomenon in question did *not* occur and note the conditions in those cases as well. In addition, according to Bacon, one should observe the circumstances under which the phenomenon occurs in greater degrees and when it occurs in lesser degrees. On the basis of such data, one should try to determine the essential nature of the phenomenon in question (to test one's hypothesis about that nature, it might be necessary to experiment). For instance, a Baconian investigation of lightning would involve the observation and documentation of when lightning occurred, when it did not occur, the degrees to which lightning occurred (are there just a few lightning flashes in some cases and more in others?), and the circumstances of each case. Bacon's writings were very influential on subsequent philosophers and thinkers as well as on the emerging modern worldview that included scientists such as Isaac Newton (1643–1727), philosophers such as Thomas Hobbes (1588–1669), and political thinkers such as Thomas Jefferson (1743–1826).

Concluding Discussion Questions

1. How did pre-Socratic natural philosophers explain the difference between appearance and reality? How did they explain what is permanent about reality and what changes?

2. What is Plato's allegory of the cave? Is he correct that most people are like those living in the cave and that everyday experiences and beliefs are only glimmers of reality? Why did Plato think that the Idea of Tree is more real than individual, physical trees?

3. What did Plato see as the essence of justice? What did he mean by the notion of a Philosopher-King? Does his view of justice and a Philosopher-King fit with modern conceptions of democracy? How is it better or worse than modern conceptions of democracy?

4. What did Aristotle mean by teleology? How did he use this notion to explain things and events in the world? Why did he reject Plato's views about Ideas and Plato's belief that the Idea of Tree is more real than individual, physical trees?

5. What did Aristotle mean by the Doctrine of the Mean? What did he mean by eudaimonia? How are his views on ethics and happiness similar to, but also different from, Plato's views on ethics?

6. Both Socrates and the later Hellenistic philosophers focused on living well. What was similar about what they said and what was different?

Further Reading

Adler, Mortimer J. *Aristotle for Everybody*. New York: Macmillan, 1978.

Annas, Julia. *Plato: A Very Short Introduction*. Oxford: Oxford University Press, 2003.

Aristotle. *Basic Works of Aristotle*. Edited by Richard McKeon. New York: Random House, 1941.

Barnes, Jonathan. *Aristotle: A Very Short Introduction*. Oxford: Oxford University Press, 2001.

Brickhouse, Thomas C., and Nicholas D. Smith. *The Philosophy of Socrates*. Boulder, Colo.: Westview Press, 2000.

Grube, G. M. A. *Plato's Thought*. Boston: Beacon Press, 1958.

Inwood, Brad, and Lloyd P. Gerson, eds. *Hellenistic Philosophy: Introductory Readings*. 2nd ed. Indianapolis, Ind.: Hackett Publishing Company, 1996.

Jones, W. T. *The Classical Mind*. New York: Harcourt, Brace, Jovanovich, 1970.

Luce, J. V. *An Introduction to Greek Philosophy*. New York: Thames and Hudson, 1992.

O'Grady, Patricia F. *The Sophists: An Introduction*. London: Duckworth Publishers, 2008.

Osborne, C. *Presocratic Philosophy: A Very Short Introduction*. Oxford: Oxford University Press, 2004.

Plato. *Plato's Complete Works*. Edited by John M. Cooper and D. S. Hutchinson. Indianapolis, Ind.: Hackett Publishing Company, 1997.

Sharples, R. W. *Stoics, Epicureans, and Sceptics: An Introduction to Hellenistic Philosophy*. New York: Routledge, 1996.

Taylor, C. C. W. *Socrates: A Very Short Introduction*. Oxford: Oxford University Press, 2001.

Warren, J. *Presocratics: Natural Philosophers before Socrates*. Berkeley: University of California Press, 2007.

Glossary

"Allegory of the cave"   a hypothetical story written by Plato intended to show that there is a difference between appearance and reality, as well as between knowledge and mere belief. People living in a cave experience only illusions and images of what is real, but they believe that their experiences give them knowledge of what is real.

atomism   with respect to classical Greek philosophy, the view that reality is made up of innumerable objects that are the smallest possible things ("atom" comes from Greek meaning "uncuttable," that is, what cannot be composed of anything smaller).

doctrine of the mean   Aristotle's notion that right action is the mean, or middle point, between extremes, such as bravery being the middle point between cowardice and foolhardiness.

epicureanism   the views associated with Epicurus, namely, that pleasure is the proper goal of life. However, for Epicurus, the highest level of pleasure is wisdom, which comes from knowledge of the nature of the world, not mere physical, passing pleasures.

eudaimonia   Greek term meaning "living well" or "happiness" that is mostly associated with the views of Aristotle, who argued that there are two kinds of virtue, virtues of intellect (knowing what is right and good) and virtues of habit (doing what is right and good).

final cause   the purpose or goal for which some effect happens; one of four types of causes spelled out by Aristotle to explain fully the existence or occurrence of something. The other three types of cause are material cause (that from which something occurs), the formal cause (that into which something occurs), and the efficient cause (that by which something occurs).

Ideas   from the Greek term *eidos,* sometimes also translated as Forms. For Plato, Ideas are not thoughts in someone's mind, but whatever matches the correct definition of something that was being defined; they are the ideal, perfect form of whatever is being defined. For Plato, individual things (such as an individual dog) is an imperfect copy of its corresponding Idea (the Idea of Dog).

monism   with respect to classical Greek philosophy, the view held by some pre-Socratic philosophers that all reality is composed of one basic kind of element (*mono* means "one").

natural philosophy   with respect to classical Greek philosophy, the search for the basic principles of nature, as opposed to, say, moral philosophy, which was the search for the basic principles of right action and goodness. The term *natural philosophy* related to what today we think of as science (the term *scientist* did not replace the term *natural philosopher* until the 1800s).

Neoplatonism   a modern term to characterize the views of Plotinus and others who drew direct inspiration from the works of Plato, especially the emphasis on levels of reality, with everyday material things being held as less real than a more spiritual, divine realm. Although some Neoplatonist doctrines sounded akin to Christianity, the Neoplatonists rejected much of Christianity, particularly the claims that Jesus was divine.

philosopher-king   a term associated with Plato's claim that the best and wisest ruler (king) would be a philosopher, because, for him, philosophers seek true knowledge and justice.

pluralism   with respect to classical Greek philosophy, the view held by some pre-Socratic philosophers that reality is composed of more than one basic kind of element (that is, it is composed of a plurality of elements).

potentiality/actuality   the view, associated primarily with Aristotle, that things in the world have a natural goal or end; they have a natural potential to become something actual, such as an acorn is potentially an oak tree.

pre-Socratics   term used to refer to the earliest Greek philosophers who lived roughly from 600–400 B.C.E. (before Socrates). The pre-Socratics focused primarily on natural philosophy (what today we would call science) as opposed to social or moral philosophy.

skepticism   the view that questions the validity of claims to knowledge. With respect to classical Greek philosophy, the school of skepticism was associated with Pyrrho, who claimed that we must suspend judgment on the truth of any claim because we cannot have more conclusive evidence that a claim is true than that it is false.

socratic method   a term associated with the philosophizing style of Socrates, who would ask a series of questions of those who claimed to know something. In the course of such questioning, Socrates would (usually) get them to recognize their own errors or perhaps, but not always, even lead them to greater understanding.

sophist/sophistry   from the Greek word *sophia,* meaning "wisdom." The sophists were teachers for hire who claimed they could and would teach people the skills for living well. Socrates, and later Plato, opposed what he saw as the relativism and mere beliefs (as opposed to real knowledge) that was taught by sophists. Because of this opposition, and the influence of Socrates and Plato, the term *sophistry* came to be understood as false and even (intentionally) deceptive reasoning and argumentation.

stoicism   a school of thought among Hellenistic philosophers associated first with Zeno of Citium. The term comes from the Greek word *stoa,* meaning "porch," from which Zeno taught. Stoicism advocated peace of mind as the goal of life and claimed it would be attained by people understanding the nature of the world and, so, being unperturbed. Today the term *stoic* means being calm, reserved, and unemotional.

syllogism   a form of logical structure of arguments first formulated by Aristotle. A syllogism is an argument form that shows how two classes of objects are related to each other via their relation to a third class. For example, from the statements "All dogs are mammals" and "All mammals are warm-blooded" it follows that "All dogs are warm-blooded."

teleology   literally, the study of goals; this term is usually associated with the view that things and events in the world do not happen by chance, but are purposeful and goal-directed. In classical Greek philosophy, this view is most directly associated with Aristotle.

Key People

Anaxagoras (500–428 B.C.E.) *Pre-Socratic philosopher who supported the pluralist view that all things are composed of the four basic elements (earth, water, air, and fire), with different everyday objects, such as trees and dogs, being a combination of different proportions of those elements. He emphasized the notion of potentiality.*

> But before . . . things were separated off, while all things were together, there was not even any color plain; for the mixture of all things prevented it, of the moist and the dry, the hot and the cold, the bright and the dark, and of much earth in the mixture and of seeds countless in number and in no respect like one another. For none of the other things either are like one to the other. And since this is so, we must suppose that all things are in the whole . . . And since these things are so, we must suppose that there are many things of all sorts in everything that is being aggregated, seeds of all things with all sorts of shapes and colors and tastes.

> [From G. S. Kirk and J. E. Raven, eds. and trans. *The Presocratic Philosophers*. Cambridge: Cambridge University Press, 1957.]

Anaximander (610–546 B.C.E.) *Pre-Socratic philosopher who argued that no single material element could be generated from any other element; the boundless apeiron is the basic source of all things.*

The following passage is an account of Anaximander's views, given by the later Greek philosopher Simplicius.

> Of those who say that it [the basic substance] is one, moving, and infinite, Anaximander, son of Praxiades, a Milesian, the successor and pupil of Thales, said that the principle and element of existing things is the *apeiron* [indefinite], being the first to introduce this name of the material principle. He says that it is neither water nor any other of the so-called elements, but some other *apeiron* nature, from which come into being all the heavens and the worlds in them. And the source of

coming to being for existing things is that into which destruction, too, happens "according to necessity . . ."

[From G. S. Kirk and J. E. Raven, eds. and trans. *The Presocratic Philosophers.* Cambridge: Cambridge University Press, 1957.]

Anaximenes (fl. 545 B.C.E.)   *Pre-Socratic philosopher who claimed that air is the material source of all things, with other elements being generated by the quantitative change (condensation or rarefaction) of air.*

The selection below is a statement by Theophrastus, a later Greek philosopher, summarizing the views of Anaximenes.

Anaximenes, son of Eurystratus, of Miletus, a companion of Anaximander, also says that the underlying nature is one and infinite like him, but not undefined as Anaximander said but definite, for he identifies it with air; and it differs in its substantial nature by rarity and density. Being made finer it becomes fire, being made thicker it becomes wind, then cloud, then (when thickened still more) water, then earth, then stones; and the rest come into being from these.

[From G. S. Kirk and J. E. Raven, eds. and trans. *The Presocratic Philosophers.* Cambridge: Cambridge University Press, 1957.]

Aristotle (384–322 B.C.E.)   *Important philosopher who rejected much of Plato's teachings and had great influence on later philosophy and science, arguing that the world must be understood in terms of goal-directed changes.*

The selections below focus on Aristotle's basic claim that the world is teleological (that is, goal-directed), and it must be understood in terms of change going from potentiality to actuality.

Since Nature is the principle of movement and change, and it is Nature that we are studying, we must understand what "movement" is; for, if we do not know this, neither do we understand what Nature is . . . Further, movement (it is said) cannot occur except in relation to place, void, and time. Evidently, then, for these reasons and because these four things—movement, place, void, and time—are universal conditions common to all natural phenomena, we must consider each of them on the threshold of our inquiry; for the treatment of peculiar properties must come after that of properties common to all natural things.

We must begin, then, as already said, with movements in general or progress from this to that. Now, some potentialities never exist apart, but always reveal themselves as actualized; others, while they are something actually, are capable of becoming something else than they are, that is to say, have potentialities not realized at the moment; and these potentialities may concern their substantive being (what they are) or their quantity or their qualities; and so on with the other categories of existence . . .

Now, motion and change cannot exist in themselves apart from what moves and changes. For, wherever anything changes, it always changes either from one thing to another, or from one magnitude to another, or from one quality to another, or from one place to another . . . motion is the function of a movable thing, all the time that it is bringing its potentiality into act, not *qua* itself, but *qua* movable.

To illustrate what I mean by "qua" this or that. The bronze is potentially the statue, but neither to be the statue nor to move or change in any respect is the self-realizing of the bronze *qua* bronze . . .

[Aristotle. *Physics. Book III*. From *The Basic Works of Aristotle*. Edited by Richard McKeon. New York: Random House, 1941.]

Democritus (460–370 B.C.E.)   *Pre-Socratic philosopher, along with Leucippus, who is credited with formulating the view that the material world is comprised of innumerable, indivisible atoms.*

Only small fragments of the writings of Democritus exist, but other Greek philosophers spoke and wrote of him and his works. The selection below is from Aristotle's remarks on Democritus.

Leucippus and his associate Democritus hold that the elements are the full and the void; they call them being and not-being respectively.

Statue of Democritus meditating on the seat of the soul *(Sculpture by Léon-Alexandre Delhomme; photograph by Marie-Lan Nguyen)*

Being is full and solid, not-being is void and rare . . . The two together are the material causes of existing things . . . [They] say that the differences in atoms are the causes of other things . . . [Democritus] thinks that they are so small as to elude our senses, but they have all sorts of forms and shapes and differences in size. So he is already enabled from them, as from elements, to create by aggregation bulks that are perceptible to sight and the other senses.

[From G. S. Kirk and J. E. Raven, eds. and trans. *The Presocratic Philosophers.* Cambridge: Cambridge University Press, 1957.]

Empedocles (484–424 B.C.E.) *Pre-Socratic philosopher who claimed that all physical things were composed of the four basic elements and in addition were governed by two fundamental forces, Love and Strife (or attraction and repulsion).*

Only fragments of the writings of Empedocles still exist. The following passage speaks to the four basic elements and the two fundamental forces of attraction and repulsion.

> A double tale I will tell: at one time it grew to be only one from many, at another it divided again to be many from one. There is a double coming into being of moral things and a double passing away. One is brought about, and again destroyed, by the coming together of all things, the other grows up and is scattered as things are divided again. And these things never cease from continual shifting, at one time all coming together, through Love, into one, at another each borne apart from the others through Strife . . . From these things sprang all things that were and are and shall be, trees and men and women, beasts and birds and water-bred fishes, and the long-lived gods too . . .

> [From G. S. Kirk and J. E. Raven, eds. and trans. *The Presocratic Philosophers*. Cambridge: Cambridge University Press, 1957.]

Epicurus (341–270 B.C.E.) *Hellenistic philosopher who supported the view of atomism and who argued that pleasure/happiness is the goal of life and that wisdom (not mere physical pleasure) is the greatest pleasure/happiness.*

The following passage is from Epicurus's Principle Doctrines, *in which he suggests that true pleasure and happiness are connected with wisdom and virtue.*

> It is not possible to live pleasantly without living prudently and honorably and justly, nor again to live a life of prudence, honor, and justice without living pleasantly. And the man who does not possess the pleasant life, is not living prudently and honorably and justly, and the man who does not possess the virtuous life, cannot possibly live pleasantly.

> A man cannot dispel his fear about the most important matters if he does not know what is the nature of the universe but suspects

the truth of some mythical story. So that without natural science it is not possible to attain our pleasures unalloyed.

[Epicurus. *The Epicurus Reader*. Brad Inwood and Lloyd P. Gerson, trans. Indianapolis, Ind.: Hackett Publishing Company, 1994.]

Heraclitus (fl. 500 B.C.E.)   *Pre-Socratic philosopher who famously claimed that one cannot step into the same river twice and that fire was the fundamental element of reality.*

The following fragments from Heraclitus's writings illustrate his views that variation and opposition are fundamental to existence.

Sea is the most pure and most polluted water; for fishes it is drinkable and salutary, but for men it is undrinkable and deleterious.

Disease makes health pleasant and good, hunger satiety, weariness rest.

. . . there would be no musical scale unless high and low existed, nor living creatures without male and female, which are opposites.

Upon those that step into the same rivers different waters flow . . . It scatters and . . . gathers . . . it comes together and flows away . . . approaches and departs.

All things are an equal exchange for fire and fire for all things, as goods are for gold and gold for goods.

[From G. S. Kirk and J. E. Raven, eds. and trans. *The Presocratic Philosophers*. Cambridge: Cambridge University Press, 1957.]

Leucippus (fl. 440 B.C.E.)   *Pre-Socratic philosopher, along with Democritus, who is credited with formulating the view that the material world is comprised of innumerable, indivisible atoms.*

Although there is only one sentence that today is definitely attributed to Leucippus ("Nothing happens at random; whatever comes about is by rational necessity."), others wrote about the writings and teachings of Leucippus. Below is a remark quoted from Simplicius.

They (that is, Leucipus, Democritus, Epicurus) said that the first principles were infinite in number, and thought they were indivisible atoms and impassible owing to their compactness, and without any void in them; divisibility comes about because of the void in compound bodies.

[From G. S. Kirk and J. E. Raven, eds. and trans. *The Presocratic Philosophers.* Cambridge: Cambridge University Press, 1957.]

Parmenides (fl. 580 B.C.E.)   *Pre-Socratic philosopher who argued that reality is One, eternal, and unchanging; all change is mere appearance and cannot even be talked or thought about.*

The fragment below of Parmenides' writings is meant to show that any change or motion of what is real is impossible, because that would mean that there is some state of being that is not currently real.

One way only is left to be spoken of, that it *is*; and on this are full many signs that what *is* is uncreated and imperishable; for it is entire and without end. It *was* not in the past, nor *shall* it be, since it *is* now, all at once, one, continuous; for what creation will you seek for it? How and whence did it grow? . . . How could what *is* thereafter perish? And how could it come into being? For if it came into being, it is not, nor if it is going to be in the future. So coming into being is extinguished and perishing unimaginable.

[From G. S. Kirk and J. E. Raven, eds. and trans. *The Presocratic Philosophers.* Cambridge: Cambridge University Press, 1957.]

Plato (427–347 B.C.E.)   *Influential philosopher who shaped much of later Western thought and who argued that there are levels of reality, with the world of Ideas as the most real.*

The reading below is from Plato's allegory of the cave, in which he tells a story to make the point that the world of everyday experience is like a world of shadows, a world that is only a shadow of what is truly real.

Socrates: And now, I said, let me show in a figure how far our nature is enlightened or unenlightened:—Behold! human beings living in an underground cave, which has a mouth open towards the light and reaching all along the cave; here they have been from their childhood, and have their legs and necks chained so that they cannot move, and can only see before them, being prevented by the chains from turning round their heads. Above and behind them a fire is blazing at a distance, and between the fire and the prisoners there is a raised way; and you will see, if you look, a low wall built along the way, like the screen which marionette players have in front of them, over which they show the puppets.

Glaucon: I see.

Socrates: And do you see, I said, men passing along the wall carrying all sorts of vessels, and statues and figures of animals made of wood and stone and various materials, which appear over the wall? Some of them are talking, others silent.

Glaucon: You have shown me a strange image, and they are strange prisoners.

Socrates: Like ourselves, I replied; and they see only their own shadows, or the shadows of one another, which the fire throws on the opposite wall of the cave?

Glaucon: True, how could they see anything but the shadows if they were never allowed to move their heads?

Socrates: And of the objects which are being carried in like manner they would only see the shadows?

Glaucon: Yes . . .

Socrates: To them, I said, the truth would be literally nothing but the shadows of the images.

Glaucon: That is certain.

Socrates: And now look again, and see what will naturally follow if the prisoners are released and disabused of their error. At
first, when any of them is liberated and compelled suddenly to
stand up and turn his neck round and walk and look towards
the light, he will suffer sharp pains; the glare will distress him,
and he will be unable to see the realities of which in his former
state he had seen the shadows . . .

[Plato. *The Republic, Book VII.* Translated by Benjamin Jowett.]

Plotinus (204–270 C.E.)   *Neoplatonist philosopher who claimed that
all reality comes from the one (or the good) and, like Plato, that what is
most real is nonmaterial.*

Plotinus's most famous work is The Enneads. *The passage below is his
effort to speak about what is indescribable, namely,* The One.

Because what the soul seeks is The One and it would look upon the
source of all reality, namely the Good and The One, it must not
withdraw from the primal realm and sink down to the lowest realm.
Rather it must withdraw from sense objects, of the lowest existence,
and turn to those of the highest. It must free itself from all evil since
it aspires to rise to the Good. It must rise to the principle possessed
within itself; from the multiplicity that it was it must again become
one. Only thus can it contemplate the supreme principle, The One.

[From Elmer O'Brien, trans. *The Essential Plotinus.* Indianapolis, Ind.: Hackett
Publishing Company, 1964.]

Pyrrho (365–270 B.C.E.)   *Skeptical philosopher who argued that peace
of mind can be attained only by recognizing that one must always suspend judgment about the truth or falsity of anything, and, so, be detached
and unperturbed.*

*There are no writings of Pyrrho that exist today. However, the most
renowned follower of Pyrrhonic skepticism was Sextus Empiricus (ca.
160–210 C.E.) who gave a full account of this view in his work,* Outlines of
Pyrrhonism, *from which the following selection comes.*

The originating cause of Skepticism is, we say, the hope of attaining
quietude. Men of talent, who were perturbed by the contradictions
in things and in doubt as to which of the alternatives they ought to

accept, were led on to inquire what is true in things and what false, hoping by the settlement of this question to attain quietude. The main basic principle of the Skeptic system is that of opposing to every proposition an equal proposition; for we believe that as a consequence of this we end by ceasing to dogmatize.

[Sextus Empiricus. *Outlines of Pyrrhonism,* translated by R. G. Bury. Cambridge: Harvard University Press, 1933.]

Pythagoras (571–497 B.C.E.) *Pre-Socratic philosopher who argued that quantity, number, and proportion are the fundamental reality.*

No writings of Pythagoras exist, but his works and teachings were passed down by his followers, as noted in the passage below by Aristotle.

[The] Pythagoreans, as they are called, devoted themselves to mathematics; they were the first to advance this study, and having been brought up in it they thought its principles were the principles of all things. Since of these principles numbers are by nature the first, and in numbers they seemed to see many resemblances to the things that exist and come into being . . . [These] thinkers also consider that number is the principle both as matter for things and as forming their modifications and their permanent states, and hold that the elements of number are the even and the odd, and of these the

Pythagoras tunes his bells in this woodcut from the *Theorica Musicae* by Franchino Gaffurio.

former is unlimited, and the latter limited; and the 1 proceeds from both of these . . . and the whole heaven, as has been said, is numbers.

[From G. S. Kirk and J. E. Raven, eds. and trans. *The Presocratic Philosophers.* Cambridge: Cambridge University Press, 1957.]

Socrates (469–399 B.C.E.)   *Renowned citizen of Athens who claimed the unexamined life is not worth living and who engaged with his fellow citizens in the analysis of important moral concepts.*

There are no writings from Socrates, but others wrote works that purported to be reports of what he said. One of the most famous is Meno, *written by Plato. The following passage gives an example of the Socratic method, in which Socrates poses a series of questions to someone in order to answer the question, What is X? (in this case, what is virtue?).*

Socrates: . . . By the gods, Meno, be generous, and tell me what you say that virtue is; for I shall be truly delighted to find that I have been mistaken, and that you and Gorgias do really have this knowledge; although I have been just saying that I have never found anybody who had.

Meno: There will be no difficulty, Socrates, in answering your question. Let us take first the virtue of a man—he should know how to administer the state, and in the administration of it to benefit his friends and harm his enemies; and he must also be careful not to suffer harm himself. A woman's virtue, if you wish to know about that, may also be easily described: her duty is to order her house, and keep what is indoors, and obey her husband. Every age, every condition of life, young or old, male or female, bond or free, has a different virtue: there are virtues numberless, and no lack of definitions of them; for virtue is relative to the actions and ages of each of us in all that we do. And the same may be said of vice, Socrates.

Socrates: How fortunate I am, Meno! When I ask you for one virtue, you present me with a swarm of them, which are in your keeping . . . And so of the virtues, however many and differ-ent they may be, they have all a common nature which makes them virtues; and on this he who would answer the question,

"What is virtue?" would do well to have his eye fixed: Do you understand?

Meno: I am beginning to understand; but I do not as yet take hold of the question as I could wish.

Socrates: When you say, Meno, that there is one virtue of a man, another of a woman, another of a child, and so on, does this apply only to virtue, or would you say the same of health, and size, and strength? Or is the nature of health always the same, whether in man or woman?

Meno: I should say that health is the same, both in man and woman.

Socrates: And is not this true of size and strength? If a woman is strong, she will be strong by reason of the same form and of the same strength subsisting in her which there is in the man. I mean to say that strength, as strength, whether of man or woman, is the same. Is there any difference?

Meno: I think not . . .

Socrates: Then now that the sameness of all virtue has been proven, try and remember what you and Gorgias say that virtue is . . .

Meno: If you want to have one definition of them all, I know not what to say, but that virtue is the power of governing mankind.

Socrates: . . . Yet once more, fair friend; according to you, virtue is "the power of governing"; but do you not add "justly and not unjustly"?

Meno: Yes, Socrates; I agree there; for justice is virtue.

Socrates: Would you say "virtue," Meno, or "a virtue"? . . .

Meno: Quite right; and that is just what I am saying about virtue—that there are other virtues as well as justice . . .

Socrates: Yes, Meno; and again we are in the same case: in
searching after one virtue we have found many, though not in
the same way as before; but we have been unable to find the
common virtue which runs through them all.

[Plato. *Meno.* Translated by Benjamin Jowett.]

Thales (fl. 580 B.C.E.)   *Pre-Socratic philosopher often credited as the
first Western natural philosopher and who claimed water was the source
of all things.*

*No writings of Thales still exist, but later Greek philosophy knew of
his works and thoughts. Below Aristotle speaks about these.*

Most of the first philosophers thought that principles in the form of
matter were the only principles of all things: for the original source
of all existing things, that from which a thing first comes-into-being
and into which it is finally destroyed, the substance persisting but
changing in its qualities . . . Thales, the founder of this type of philosophy, says that it is water (and therefore declared that the earth is
on water), perhaps taking this supposition from seeing the nurture of
all things to be moist . . . taking the supposition both from this and
from the seeds of all things having a moist nature, water being the
natural principle of moist things.

[From G. S. Kirk and J. E. Raven, eds. and trans. *The Presocratic Philosophers.*
Cambridge: Cambridge University Press, 1957.]

Zeno of Citium (335–263 B.C.E.)   *Stoic philosopher who argued that
peace of mind is the goal of inquiry and of life; peace of mind comes from
knowing the nature of things and responding accordingly.*

*No writings of Zeno of Citium exist today. However, a later follower
of his stoical teachings, Epictetus (50–130 C.E.), captured his views in his
own writings. The selection below is from Epictetus's work,* Enchiridion.

What disturbs men's minds is not events but their judgments on
events. For instance, death is nothing dreadful, or else Socrates
would have thought it so. No, the only dreadful thing about it is

men's judgment that it is dreadful. And so when we are hindered, or disturbed, or distressed, let us never lay the blame on others, but on ourselves, that is, on our own judgments. To accuse others for one's own misfortunes is a sign of want of education; to accuse oneself shows that one's education has begun; to accuse neither oneself nor others shows that one's education is complete.

Ask not that events should happen as you will, but let your will be that events should happen as they do, and you shall have peace.

[Epictetus. *The Discourses and Manuel,* translated by P. E. Matheson. Oxford: Oxford University Press, 1916.]

Zeno of Elea (fl. 465 B.C.E.)   *Presocratic philosopher, follower of Parmenides, who proposed various paradoxes intended to show that motion and plurality of things are impossible.*

The selections below are three of Zeno's paradoxes. The first and second are intended to show that to move any distance at all, one must first move half that distance, but first half of that half, and so on, infinitely. The third is meant to show that at any moment in time, things are at rest (that is, there is zero movement), so a collection of moments is just a collection of zero movements, which is to say that there is no movement.

The first [paradox] asserts the non-existence of motion on the ground that that which is in locomotion must arrive at the half-way stage before it arrives at the goal.

The second [paradox] is the so-called Achilles, and it amounts to this, that in a race the quickest runner can never overtake the slowest, since the pursuer must first reach the point whence the pursued started, so that the slower must always hold a lead. This argument is the same in principle as that which depends on bisection [that is, the first paradox].

The third [paradox] is . . . to the effect that the flying arrow is at rest, which result follows from the assumption that time is composed of moments.

[From G. S. Kirk and J. E. Raven, eds. and trans. *The Presocratic Philosophers.* Cambridge: Cambridge University Press, 1957.]

PART II
Modern Philosophy

Introductory Discussion Questions

1. You have concepts of various things, such as the concepts of addition and subtraction, the Sun, morality, your own mind, and God. How do you think you acquired these concepts? Did you acquire them all in the same way?

2. Conclusions in mathematics seem quite certain. For example, it seems unlikely that you could ever be mistaken in thinking that five multiplied by two equals 10 (in simple arithmetic) or that triangles have three sides (in geometry). Do you think you can achieve the same level of certainty about matters outside mathematics? For instance, can you be as certain that the Earth is round or that smoking causes cancer? Can you be as certain that God exists or does not exist? Why or why not?

3. Do you think the mind is different from the body, or is it just part of the body (the brain, for example)? Why or why not?

4. Do you think it is ever morally acceptable to rebel against the government in your country, such as by refusing to obey its laws when you do not want to, or even by attempting to overthrow the government? If yes, when might such actions be morally acceptable, and why? If no, why would such actions not ever be morally acceptable?

5. Sometimes very bad things happen to people and animals who do not seem to deserve them. If God is all-powerful, all-good, and all-knowing, how can we explain the existence of such suf-

fering? Do you think such suffering shows that an all-powerful, all-knowing, and all-good God does not exist? Why or why not?

6. Do you think there are any universal moral rules—that is, moral rules that should be followed no matter what? If yes, what is an example of such a rule? If no, why not?

An Overview of
Modern Philosophy

Modern philosophy begins where the Renaissance ends, roughly in the 1500s, and continues at least until the work of the German philosopher Immanuel Kant (1724–1804) in the 18th century. The French philosopher René Descartes (1596–1650) is usually considered the father of modern philosophy. Other classical modern philosophers include Francis Bacon (1561–1626), John Locke (1632–1704), Baruch Spinoza (1632–77), Gottfried Leibniz (1646–1716), George Berkeley (1685–1753), and David Hume (1711–76).

To understand modern philosophy, it is helpful to understand its historical context. Modern philosophy overlaps with the Age of Enlightenment (also sometimes called the Age of Reason) during the 17th and 18th centuries, characterized by a general intellectual and cultural climate, primarily in Europe, during those two centuries. Historians often speak of the Scientific Revolution and the rise of modern political philosophy as major aspects of the Age of Enlightenment. Many enduring names of Western culture are from this time: Galileo Galilei and Isaac Newton (in science), John Milton and Daniel Defoe (in literature), Adam Smith and François Quesnay (in economics), Voltaire and Jean-Jacques Rousseau (in social commentary), Jonathan Edwards and John Wesley (in theology), Thomas Jefferson and Benjamin Franklin (in American politics), as well as the aforementioned influential philosophers Descartes and Kant. During the Age of Enlightenment, there occurred fundamental and long-lasting changes and developments involving all major branches of philosophy (metaphysics, epistemology, and axiology).

With respect to metaphysics (the study of fundamental concepts and aspects of reality), major philosophical changes occurred during the Age of Enlightenment. These changes were very much connected with the emergence of modern science. At the time, those people who today would be called scientists were instead called natural philosophers. The term *natural philosophy* had been used since early Greek philosophy for the study of the basic principles of nature and those who studied and practiced it were called natural philosophers (as opposed to, say, moral philosophers, who studied the basic principles of moral action). Intellectual and conceptual changes that were connected with science were partly the result of new information and what was discovered about the world and also partly the result of new assumptions and methods for investigating the world. One of those new assumptions was the rejection of what was called final cause, a concept defended by the ancient Greek philosopher Aristotle (384–322 B.C.E.). Final cause was the notion that things and events have a purpose, and to understand something fully required knowing not only how something came to be, but also why it came to be (that is, its function or purpose). Since the time of early Greek science, natural philosophers had included the notion of final cause as part of any explanation for some thing or event in nature. During the Age of Enlightenment, however, this notion was to a large extent abandoned (although not completely so). Scientists focused on what could be observed and measured and described, without necessarily making reference to any sense of purpose in what was being measured and described. For example, Newton spoke of the planets in their orbits as being the result of a balance of forces of nature (those forces being gravity, which would, say, pull the Moon into the Earth, and inertia, which would have the Moon move away from the Earth in a straight line). Describing orbits as a balance of natural forces did not require speaking of those orbits being the result of some divine purpose or arrangement (even though Newton himself did not reject God's role in the orderliness of the world).

Broadly speaking, before the Age of Enlightenment the general view of things and events in nature was teleological (from the Greek word, *telos,* meaning "goal" or "end"). This was replaced by a view that was mechanistic and materialistic, meaning that the world was seen as a vast, complex mechanism made of physical, material things, and that it was thought that the world could be explained in terms of the movements of those things. The new view was that the world was matter in motion. This view extended even to explaining human action. Accordingly, modern philosophy often tended to treat humans as part of the natural world, capable of being studied like other elements of the natural world, and in particular, some philosophers regarded the human body as a machine that moved according to physical laws. The most famous examples of this perspective are the writings of the English philosopher Thomas Hobbes and the French philosopher Julien Offray de La Mettrie (1709–51), who wrote a famous work entitled *Man a Machine.*

Other changes in metaphysics concerned views about God. One theme in the Enlightenment is *natural religion,* a form of theology (literally, the study of God) that is not concerned with direct revelation from God. Rather, the focus of natural religion was on understanding signs in nature of what is divine, for example, signs in nature of God's existence or of God's nature or even human moral nature as it relates to God. With respect to God's existence, for example, natural religion focused on the view that there is evidence in the natural world that can be demonstrated by reason—not by faith—that God exists. There were two very common sorts of natural theological arguments for God's existence. According to the cosmological argument, anything that exists had to come from somewhere or something; things cannot create themselves. So, the world as a whole (the cosmos) must have been created by something, namely, God. Given that the world exists, God must exist as well. The second common sort of natural theological argument for God's existence is often called the design argument. This argument says there is a lot of evidence for order and structure in the world. That is, there appears to be a lot of evidence that things in the natural world are designed, not random or haphazard. If they are designed, then there must be a designer, someone or something that does the designing. With respect to the design of the natural world, that designer is God. Probably the best-known version of this argument comes from the writings of William Paley, who in the 1800s proposed what is called the watchmaker argument. Paley said that if we found a watch out in the middle of a forest, we would assume that it was made by a watchmaker. The fact that it is complex and yet orderly is much more likely to be explained by it having been made by a watchmaker than it having just been assembled by nature. The complexity, yet obvious useful function, of the human eye (and many other things in nature) is much more easily explained, he said, by the assumption of a designer than by natural causes.

Besides God's existence, natural theology was also concerned with God's nature and humans' relationship with God. For example, many people have argued that events in the world are a sign of God's happiness or unhappiness with human actions. Also, many people have argued that there are lessons in nature for humans to learn about how they should act, lessons that are placed in nature by God for us to learn. For instance, some people have claimed that the industriousness of ants in their purposeful activities and in their collective work to build their colonies is a natural sign of how humans should behave.

One form of natural religion was deism, which was most prominent in the 17th and 18th centuries, particularly in England, France, and the United States. In the 17th century, Lord Herbert of Cherbury (1583–1648) founded English deism (although he himself did not use the term *deism*) when he made the following claims: that there is one supreme God who should be worshipped, that worshipping God means living virtuously, that people should repent their sins, and that in this life, as well as in the afterlife, God would reward good and punish evil. According to deism (from the Latin word, *deus,* meaning "god"), God exists, and it is through our reason alone that we know God exists. So, deists reject revelation, the giving of knowledge to people directly by God or other supernatural means. Deism is often called a natural religion, meaning that deists base their belief in God on evidence in the natural world. For example, some deists are (or were) convinced by the design argument that God exists. Beyond the emphasis on reason and the rejection of revelation, there was considerable disagreement among deists about specific religious doctrine, such as whether there is an afterlife and whether God intervenes in the course of the world. However, deists tended to reject religious authority and often opposed significant components of orthodox Christianity.

Such broad changes in perspective regarding the world and human beings raised questions about how humans and traditional religious beliefs fit into a new worldview. For example, one concern regarding natural theology was whether it ever conflicted with revealed religion and, if so, how to resolve that conflict. For example, do natural signs and evidence that the Earth is billions of years old conflict with any scriptural, revelatory information about the age of the Earth? In addition, did philosophical arguments for the existence of God truly show that God existed? Descartes, Leibniz, and Spinoza, for example, each offered arguments for the existence of God, although not arguments explicitly based on natural theology; others, such as Hume and Kant, were critical of traditional arguments for the existence of God, and Hume in particular was critical of the design argument. In addition, if physical things could be explained in scientific and mechanical terms, then, for example, do humans have souls? Do they have free will? Could humans have free will if all of their actions could be explained in scientific, materialist terms? Modern philosophers addressed all of these questions. Descartes, for example, argued for the existence of the human soul, which he characterized as a nonphysical substance that thinks, distinct from the body. This view led to the difficulty of how to understand the relation between mind and body, and in particular how mind and body could interact if they are different substances (for instance, how could a person's desire to run cause her body to move?). Other philosophers explained the nature of the soul—and the nature of reality in general—in such a way as to avoid this difficulty.

During the Age of Enlightenment, epistemology (the study of knowledge) also underwent significant changes. Much of the change was directly related to issues in metaphysics. During the 1600s, there was a general sense among philosophers that earlier views of the nature of knowledge and reality were suspect. There was a rise of questioning the very basis of knowledge, of what could be known and how it could be known. Modern philosophers wanted to know what we can know and how, and often they wanted to know what we can know with certainty, not just what we can be pretty sure about. Indeed, for many modern philosophers, one could not be said to know something unless one could be absolutely certain of its truth. Two broad perspectives emerged during this time: empiricism and rationalism. Very broadly speaking, both looked for some foundation of knowledge, some basic starting point on which all knowledge is built. For empiricism, that foundation was sensory experience, that is, experiences that come from our physical senses (such as sight and smell). A slogan was: Nothing in the intellect that is not first in the senses. This meant that all knowledge came from our senses, which itself meant matter in motion (that is, something "bumping into us" and therefore causing some sensory experience in us). For instance, knowing that there is a cat in front of me is the result of something (today we would say photons, or light particles) striking my eyes, causing a stimulation of nerves that cause my brain to respond in certain ways. Of particular concern for the empiricists and rationalists was whether there are any innate ideas (ideas people are born having). Empiricists tended to argue that there were not, and rationalists tended to argue that there were. Among the major empiricist philosophers of the time were Thomas Hobbes, John Locke, George Berkeley, and David Hume.

Empiricism in modern philosophy is often associated with skeptical worries, that is, worries regarding whether we have genuine knowledge. Locke argued that we are aware of only our own ideas, where "ideas" is understood broadly to mean whatever a person is thinking about or aware of (for example, thoughts, memories, sensations, and images). But, he thought, we are not directly aware of objects that exist independently of us. However, this raised the question of how we know our ideas accurately reflect how things really are (a question Berkeley settled by denying that physical objects exist in the first place). Also relevant regarding skepticism is the problem of induction, the problem of knowing whether nature behaves in uniform ways (for instance, that laws that held in the past—such as the law of gravity—will continue to hold in the future). This problem was famously posed by Hume, who argued that the belief that nature is uniform is not based on reason, for neither logic nor experience justifies the belief that nature is uniform; rather, people believe in the uniformity of nature just because they have gotten used to thinking that it is, based on their past experience.

The other broad epistemological perspective was rationalism. This view also looked for some foundation of knowledge, but it did not agree with the empiricists that the foundation was sensory experience. The term *rationalism* was based on the notion of reason (or rationality). Rationalists claimed that there was a natural light of reason that people had that made certain knowledge possible. Sensory experience, for instance, could not account for mathematical knowledge, they said, or for other broad, basic truths. In addition, sensory experience could not be a foundation for knowledge because sensory experience can be mistaken; we sometimes are wrong about what we think we experience (for instance, we see a stick in water that appears to be bent, when in fact it is straight). Rationalists tended to view reality as essentially rational—on this view, the world makes sense; it is reasonable. The most famous of the rationalists was Descartes. He wrote one of the most famous lines in all of philosophy: I think, therefore I am (in Latin, *cogito ergo sum*). Descartes's point was that he could question and doubt all sensory experiences without contradicting himself. For example, I might think I see a cat in front of me, but I could be mistaken. It might be some other kind of animal or it could be a hologram or it is possible that I might just be dreaming. The point is that having a sensory experience—or, thinking that I am having a sensory experience—is not a foundation for knowledge, since I might be wrong. However, said Descartes, I cannot be wrong or mistaken that I am thinking when I am thinking. Furthermore, if I am thinking, then I must exist (in order to be doing the thinking).

With respect to epistemology generally, what is important about the Age of Enlightenment is that knowledge was seen as requiring some sort of foundation and that this foundation was in the world. That is, the foundation for knowledge was not social agreement or what some authority might say. The foundation had to do with the very nature of human minds. In addition, this was individualistic. That is, again, knowledge was not a matter of social convention, but rather was part of the very nature of persons. As knowers, then, individuals were equal; everyone was subject to matter in motion (for empiricists) or to the natural light of reason (for rationalists). Much of the focus of philosophical thought, then, turned to epistemology and questions of what we could know and how we could know it (that is, the content and justification of knowledge). Philosophers have referred to this as the epistemological turn, meaning that what defined early modern philosophy (as opposed to medieval philosophy) was the primary emphasis on what and how individuals could know.

In terms of axiology (the study of values), fundamental and widespread changes and developments took place during the Age of Enlightenment. One such area was in ethics. There was a general shift in focus away from ethics understood as the development of personal virtues (such as courage or charity) and toward principles of social interaction and regulation of people's behavior based on these principles. A major aspect of this shift was the development of utilitarianism, especially in the 1700s. The root of the term *utilitarianism* is utility. The idea was that whatever action or rule of behavior led to the greatest good, or happiness—that is, that had utility in bringing out the greatest good, or happiness—was the right thing to do. This principle of action applied to everyone; it did not matter whether a person was virtuous or not. If one option led to more good than another option, then that first option was the right thing to do. This was seen as an objective and fair basis for determining correct actions and policies. Applied to social and political contexts, the principle of utility was seen as a basic component of democracy. For example, making a decision by having people vote and then counting up the votes was seen as in the spirit of utilitarianism. It did not matter whether a person was virtuous or not; that person's vote counted as much as any other person's vote. Utilitarianism, then, was seen as a fair and objective means of determining ethical decisions, both for individuals and for society at large. Utilitarians themselves were often on the forefront of social and political reforms.

At the same time that utilitarianism became enormously influential, another aspect of ethics during this time was the sense of perfectibility and progress. There was a widespread sense that the objective views about knowledge and values could and would lead to social progress and the betterment (perfectibility) of people. Many people believed that the emerging sciences were showing that the world could, at least in principle, be known. Progress in terms of knowing how the world works and how people can thrive in the world was taken for granted. Humans were pushing back the wilderness and darkness; they were enlightened and shedding light onto the world.

In politics and society generally, the Age of Enlightenment (and with it some modern philosophy) saw an emerging sense of democracy. By the late 1700s, some of the most influential political documents were drafted, including the U.S. Declaration of Independence and the Bill of Rights, as well as the French Declaration of the Rights of Man and Citizen. This was the time when the concept of individual natural rights became widespread, with political upheaval and revolutions as a result. This notion of individual natural rights, which evolved over several centuries, saw people as having rights as individuals, not only as citizens of some state, and having them on the basis of being persons (that is, having them naturally, not because they came from the government). At the same time, and in line with this view, was the view of the state of nature and what came to be called social contract theory. This was the broad political view that communities and political entities, such as the state, are not natural. Rather, the natural state for people is the state of nature. People choose to come together and form communities and political unions, such as states. In effect, they sign a social contract. So, those unions have legitimacy only because people choose them. The emphasis on individualism that occurred with respect to metaphysics and epistemology also occurred with respect to axiology, particularly with respect to ethics and political philosophy. Likewise, this was the same period in which the social and economic theory of capitalism emerged, and for many of the same reasons. A capitalist system was based on the assumption of individuals freely choosing certain actions in relation to other individuals; in effect, it was utilitarianism in the marketplace. The state was said not to have a legitimate role in regulating economic actions (again, the state was seen as having legitimacy to the extent that it was given it by the social contract of individuals).

The Age of Enlightenment is usually said to have ended toward the end of the 1700s. With respect to philosophy, this coincided with the philosophical writings of Kant. Kant departed from both the rationalist and empiricist traditions, offering an account of knowledge that incorporated elements of both. He argued for universal moral laws based on reason and the recognition of human autonomy.

Kant was also a strong defender of the Enlightenment, which he saw as concerned with the courage and freedom to reason independently, without being guided by the authority of others. His works spawned later philosophers to challenge his views and much of what was seen as Enlightenment philosophy.

Introduction to
Empiricism and Rationalism

Empiricism

Empiricism is the view that knowledge depends on experience. Experience is usually understood as sensory experience—that is, what we experience through our five senses. So, according to empiricism, in some way the source of knowledge is what we experience through the senses. Some versions of empiricism hold that *all* knowledge depends on experience; others hold that only some kinds of knowledge (such as knowledge of the empirical world) depend on experience. Empiricism is contrasted with rationalism, the view that reason is more important than experience in acquiring knowledge. In modern philosophy, Francis Bacon, John Locke, George Berkeley, and David Hume were all empiricists, and empiricism is often associated with modern philosophy. However, other philosophers have given empiricist arguments, such as Epicurus (50–130) and Thomas Aquinas (1225–74), and empiricism has remained significant in 21st-century philosophy.

There is an obvious sense in which experience seems to be necessary for knowledge insofar as if a person never existed she would have no experience of any kind and in that case no knowledge. What empiricists often emphasize, against rationalists, is that knowledge depends on experience in the sense that all of our concepts depend on sensory experience. Put another way, all of our ideas have their origin in experience.

This contrasts with the view that there are innate ideas, ideas that we are either born with or that we can acquire independently of experience. Locke argued that there were not. Rather, Locke wrote, the mind is like a blank slate. It begins empty and is metaphorically written on by experience; the mind receives information from the outside world passively, and it is only because the mind receives such information that people can acquire concepts and therefore knowledge based on these concepts. For example, a person might acquire the concepts of round and orange through experience, so knowledge that depends on these concepts (such as the knowledge that oranges are round) depends on experience. All materials for knowledge, according to Locke, are similarly dependent on experience. Some empiricists, Locke among them, believed that although we acquire all the materials for knowledge through experience alone, constructing knowledge out of those materials need not also depend on experience. For instance, consider mathematical knowledge, such as the knowledge that two plus two equals four. Perhaps one needs experience to acquire the concepts two, four, and addition. But, once having acquired those concepts, according to one empiricist view, a person does not need further experience to know that two plus two equals four. Rather, she can recognize that two plus two equals four just by thinking about it. No observation of the world is necessary.

To see how empiricism as an approach to inquiry (especially in science) contrasted with some earlier methods, it is worth considering the views of Francis Bacon (1561–1626) in particular. Born into a wealthy family, Bacon was an ambitious man who spent his professional life writing and in government service. He rose to the position of lord chancellor in the Elizabethan court before he was convicted of accepting bribes, served a four-day prison sentence, and was barred from ever serving in political office again. Bacon claimed that all knowledge was his province. He was highly critical of earlier methods of inquiry and advocated a new method for acquiring knowledge. It had been common for scientists to make use of syllogisms, a special form of logical argument. An example of a syllogism is: All men are mortal. Socrates is a man. Therefore, Socrates is mortal. Syllogisms proceed deductively; that is, the conclusion is intended to follow logically, not empirically, from the reasons (premises) given for that conclusion. Put another way, the premises lead to the conclusion simply as a matter of logic, not because the natural world behaves one way rather than another, or because there is some phenomenon in nature on which the conclusion is based. For example, in the above example, the conclusion that Socrates is mortal follows logically from the premises that Socrates is a man and that all men are mortal. So, *if* the premises are true, then the conclusion must be true also. But the conclusion follows from the premises as a matter of logic, not because of the way the natural world is. To see this, consider the syllogism: All men are immortal. Socrates is a man. Therefore, Socrates is immortal. It is false, of course, that all men are immortal, and in fact because no man is immortal, the conclusion of this syllogism (that Socrates is immortal) is false as well. However, the conclusion does follow logically from the premises (it just happens to be the case that one of those premises, that all men are immortal, is false).

Bacon charged that the use of syllogisms in science hindered the progress of science for the reason that, too often, scientists drew general conclusions on the basis of just a few observations and then proceeded to use those general observations in syllogisms to draw more conclusions. But a general conclusion on the basis of just a small number of observations of the natural world is not likely to be a very strong conclusion; for example, the general conclusion that all swans are white is not a very strong conclusion if it is based on observing just a handful of white swans. It would not be surprising if such general statements turned out to be false. In that case, however, using such statements in syllogisms would likely lead to false conclusions (just as, in the example above, the premise that all men are immortal helps lead to the false conclusion that Socrates is immortal). Science, Bacon thought, had relied too little on actual observations of the actual world.

Bacon specifically identified four other problems that weaken methods of inquiry; he dubbed these problems the Four Idols. The Idols of the Tribe are flaws in human perception and reasoning; our senses sometimes deceive us, and sometimes our understanding distorts what is real (we misconstrue the nature of what is real or true). The Idols of the Cave are a person's individual biases and limited perspective. These can occur as a result of what a person is taught, a person's personality, or a person's circumstances. A person who spends most of her life living in a lush landscape, for instance, will have a different perspective regarding plant life than someone who has spent most of his life living in a desert landscape. The mistake would come in assuming that one's own perspective is the only and best perspective, or put another way, that one's own experience is uniquely authoritative. The third kind of idols are the Idols of the Marketplace, which are the concepts and words people use in conversation and communication with each other. Of course, there is nothing wrong with many concepts and words. But, Bacon thought, because sometimes concepts and language are vague, misleading, or even refer to nothing, mistakes in inquiry can arise as a result. For instance (though this is not Bacon's example), it was once thought there must be a special substance called phlogiston, and scientists spent time and energy discussing and attempting to examine the nature of phlogiston. But it turned out there was no such substance; the word *phlogiston* did not refer to anything at all. Finally, the Idols of the Theater are the dogmatic beliefs associated with philosophical theories in particular (the phrase Idols of the Theater suggests that various philosophical theories are fictional, like plays).

A good method of inquiry would avoid these Idols. In addition, Bacon had something positive to say about how a good method of inquiry would proceed (not just what it should avoid), describing his preferred method in some detail. Inquiry, he thought, should involve a new kind of induction. Induction, roughly, is the drawing of general conclusions on the basis of individual observations; drawing the conclusion that all crows are black after observing many individual black crows is an example of induction. However, Bacon thought it was a mistake to investigate the world simply by adding up a lot of individual observations. Of course, making individual observations was necessary, and it was necessary to make a lot of them; Bacon criticized earlier ways of science for relying on too few individual observations. Merely making individual observations, however, for Bacon was not enough. To investigate some phenomenon in nature one should not merely observe many instances of that phenomenon and see under what conditions it occurred, but also make many observations of cases in which the phenomenon in question did *not* occur, and note the conditions in those cases as well. In addition, according to Bacon, one should observe the circumstances under which the phenomenon occurs in greater degrees and when it occurs in lesser degrees. On the basis of such data one should try to determine the essential nature of the phenomenon in question (to test one's hypothesis about that nature, it might be necessary to experiment). For instance, a Baconian investigation of lightning would involve the observation and documentation of when light-ning occurred, when it did not occur, the degrees to which lightning occurred (are there just a few lightning lashes in some cases and more in others?), and the circumstances of each case.

Despite Bacon's confidence in his empirical method of induction as a means for acquiring knowledge, empiricism in general has sometimes been associated with, or challenged by, skepticism. One reason for this is the common empiricist belief in modern philosophy that we do not experience directly objects that are external to us. For example, on this view, upon seeing a clock, the clock produces in us certain ideas, such as the idea of a certain color and the shapes of its two hands. What we experience are those ideas, not the clock directly. If we do not experi-ence the clock directly, how do we know that our ideas accurately reflect the clock itself? In general, if we do not actually experience external physical objects, how do we know their true nature? Indeed, how do we know they exist at all? George Berkeley tried to resolve these skeptical questions. We do have certain knowledge of the ordinary objects of experience, he argued, because these ordinary objects just are collec-tions of ideas. That is, there are no physical objects. Objects such as clocks are real, but they consist of collections of ideas (ideas of shape, color, solidity, and so on), not as physical things. We can know the clock really has a certain shape and a certain color and so on because its shape and color are just ideas; we cannot be mistaken about our own experi-ence. All that exists, Berkeley argued, are ideas and minds that have them; the ultimate cause of the ideas we experience is God.

Although Berkeley sought to put skepticism to rest, not many phi-losophers have been willing to follow his version of idealism (the view that what is real depends on the mind). Another of the classic British empiricists, David Hume, instead gave yet further grounds for skepti-cism. Consider again the notion that knowledge depends on experience. Yet there are some things we seem to know that we do not experience. For example, people believe that certain kinds of events cause certain other kinds of events—that viruses cause certain illnesses, say, and the temperature dropping to a certain point causes water to freeze. To use Hume's example, people typically believe that when one billiard ball strikes another, it causes the second ball to move. There seems to be a necessary connection between the first event (one ball striking another) and the second event (the second ball moving). Yet, Hume argued, we do not experience a necessary connection. All that we actually experience are particular events of one ball striking another and the second ball moving. We experience a constant conjunction of such events (the events happen at about the same time), but experience of each of these past conjunctions does not tell us that in the future, when one billiard ball strikes another, the second one will move. Experience tells us only what we have experienced in the past, not what will happen in the future. Nor, Hume argued, is it a logical truth that a billiard ball will always move when struck by another. All this suggests that we cannot know that in the future a billiard ball will move when struck by another. More important, it suggests that in general we cannot know that the future will be like the past. So, we cannot know that in the future viruses will cause illness or that water will freeze when the temperature drops to a certain point. Hume believed that we should continue to act as if the future will be like the past; but as an empiricist, he argued that we do so only out of habit, not out of reasoned belief. For Hume, then, empiricism is linked to skepticism. The problem of whether it is possible to know that the future will be like the past—put another way, whether nature is uniform—is known as the problem of induction, and it continues to be controversial today.

Rationalism

In philosophy, *rationalism* refers to views that hold that reason is more important in acquiring knowledge than experience. Reason is often understood as including intuition, a kind of direct awareness of a truth, an awareness through the mind in particular rather than through sense experience. René Descartes, Gottfried Leibniz, and Baruch Spinoza were all rationalists.

There are varieties of rationalism. Rationalists differ, for example, in their metaphysics and in their precise claims about what role reason plays (and does not play) in our acquisition of knowledge. Common to rationalist views is the idea that there is some significant knowledge that we can acquire more through reason than experience. One sort of knowledge that could be said to be acquired more through reason than experience is knowledge of analytic truths, truths that are true either by definition or form. For instance, the sentence *Circles are round* is true by definition and seems to be knowable just by using one's reason.

However, this is not very informative; rationalists believe that reason can deliver more significant knowledge than this, such as knowledge of the nature of reality. It has also often been thought that mathematical and logical knowledge are acquired through reason alone. One does not seem to need to investigate the world to know, say, that three is greater than two or that three times three equals nine.

In addition, on a rationalist view, there seem to be some truths that cannot be known through experience alone. For instance, it seems that we cannot know through experience alone truths about the empirical world that are universal (that is, that apply in all circumstances). Consider, for example, the law of conservation of energy, which states that the amount of energy in the universe remains constant. This is a truth that seems to be universal, and scientists treat it as such. Yet it seems to be impossible to establish its truth through experience. This is because experience always involves the particular—particular events and particular objects at particular times. One always measures energy at a particular time; one never measures energy for all times, and indeed it would be impossible for us to do so. So we do not know the law of the conservation of energy through experience alone. Similarly, to know that smoking causes cancer seems to require more than sensory experience. After all, all that scientists encounter in experience itself are particular instances of smoking causing cancer, not every possible case of smoking causing cancer. If, then, universal truths such as scientific laws are true, we seem to grasp their truth through reason rather than through experience.

Although rationalism and empiricism are associated especially with modern philosophy, there have been philosophers defending rationalist views throughout the history of philosophy. For example, in ancient philosophy, Parmenides and his follower Zeno of Elea argued that even though experience seems to tell us that objects move (bats fly, people walk, plants lean toward the sun, and so on) and change occurs in the world, both motion and change are illusions. They arrived at these conclusions through reason, treating reason rather than experience as the true guide to the nature of reality. Plato famously argued that what is most real are ideal concepts (Ideas) rather than the ordinary, physical objects we encounter in sense experience. Knowledge of these forms, in turn, required using one's reason (in particular, by studying philosophy), rather than making observations of the empirical world.

Moreover, according to Plato, all knowledge is recollection: Everything we know we know because we *remember* it, having known it once before prior to being born. So the mind itself, rather than experience, plays a crucial role in knowledge.

One central disagreement between rationalists and empiricist was whether there are innate ideas. An innate idea is a concept that is somehow in a person's mind from birth. Philosophers differed over what it meant more specifically for an idea to be innate. It would not seem to mean, for example, that innate ideas must be ideas one is conscious of even at birth. For if that were so, then it would seem that even newborn babies are fully aware of any ideas that are innate, such as the idea of God. But it seems unlikely that a newborn is conscious of the idea of God. An innate idea, then, might instead be an idea that a person is inclined to have and which she can acquire consciously through experience. Leibniz's analogy was that such ideas might be in a person's mind in the way that a sculpture is in a block of marble: with enough work, the ideas (and the sculpture) will emerge.

A classic rationalist argument is that innate ideas could not be acquired through experience and therefore must be innate instead. Descartes argued that the ideas of God, mind, and matter are innate. As an illustration, he considered a piece of wax that undergoes varies physical changes. Although it was once solid, if subjected to enough heat, the wax melts. As it melts, it changes its shape, color, and smell. Yet it is the *same* piece of wax despite the fact that it has undergone these changes. We do not know through the senses that it is the same piece of wax because, in Descartes's scenario, everything our senses tell us about the wax changes. So, it is through our reason instead that we know it is the same piece of wax. In particular, we know through our reason the substance of the wax, specifically that it is matter (for Descartes, this means it has extension; it takes up space). Leibniz thought that not only are there innate ideas, but that *all* our ideas are innate, and that there are innate principles as well, such as logical principles (an idea here is just a concept, such as the concept of God; a principle is something that is true or false, such as the principle that the denial of a contradiction must be true).

If some of our ideas are innate, then some of the materials for knowledge are innate. Put another way, some of the ideas we use for constructing knowledge are acquired independent of experience. In addition, the classic rationalists believed that the *process* for acquiring knowledge was mainly a matter of using reason than learning through sensory experience. So, not only do we start with innate ideas out of which we can construct knowledge, but also such construction itself is a process of reason rather than sensory experience. Descartes thought that reason could establish the existence of God and the existence of a physical world independent of himself. Spinoza and Leibniz each constructed complex metaphysical systems, that is, views about the nature and structure of reality. Reality, on their views, was rational, and to discover its fundamental nature it was necessary to use one's reason rather than sensory experience. In addition, ethical truths could be known through reason alone; Spinoza advocated an intellectual love of God. (None of this means that all rationalists ignored the empirical methods of science or believed science was unimportant; both Descartes and Leibniz made scientific contributions.)

A common thread in the conception of knowledge that Descartes, Leibniz, and Spinoza shared was that knowledge required certainty—unless the truth of a belief was certain, it did not count as knowledge. In this they were impressed by mathematical knowledge in particular and sought to establish certainty for their various other claims to knowledge as well.

René Descartes

René Descartes (1596–1650) is often considered the father of modern philosophy. Descartes was born in the French town of La Haye (which was later named after him) and beginning at about age 10 attended a Jesuit school, where his education included mathematics, science, and philosophy, especially the scholastic philosophy of that time. Afterward he studied law but chose not to practice it, serving instead as a volunteer gentleman soldier. In 1619, he had an idea for a philosophical method on which all knowledge could be based and had several dreams that convinced him he was meant to develop this method. After about another 10 years' travel and military service, Descartes left the military and moved to Holland, where he lived for about 20 years studying and writing. In addition to his philosophical work, Descartes worked in mathematics (where he helped develop analytic geometry), optics (where he discovered the law of refraction), anatomy, and physics. He published several books and established a reputation as an important intellectual. In 1649, Descartes traveled to Sweden to teach philosophy to the Swiss queen at her invitation. During his first winter there he caught pneumonia and died. He was 54 years old.

Central to Descartes's philosophical work was the desire for certainty. Much impressed by the certainty of mathematical truths and knowledge, Descartes sought the same level of certainty in all claims for knowledge—for example, knowledge that God exists and that there is a physical world. Descartes also formulated a specific method of inquiry: First, he resolved to be guided by reason and in particular to accept as true only ideas that are clear and distinct. Second, he believed he should

Portrait of René Descartes from the late 17th century *(Painting by Frans Hals)*

divide up the intellectual problems he faced into parts and, third, begin his inquiry with simpler matters before attempting to resolve more complex issues. Finally, he resolved to review his reasoning for errors.

With these principles in mind, Descartes began his quest for certainty with a specific method of doubt: If he had a reason for doubting anything whatsoever, Descartes thought, then he should suspend belief about it, neither believing nor disbelieving. Descartes found it was possible to doubt everything he believed that was based on his sensory experience (what he saw, heard, tasted, felt, or smelled). First, Descartes noted that the senses are sometimes deceptive; for instance, a stick placed in water looks bent, although it is straight. Second, Descartes argued that sometimes it was not even possible to tell whether he dreaming or awake. So he could not be sure, for instance, that he was actually sitting in his study feeling the heat of a fire even if it seemed to him that he was; for all he knew, he could merely be dreaming that he was. Indeed, it was possible that he could be dreaming *anything* that he seemed to experience through his senses, even that he had a body or that material objects exist. He should, therefore, suspend belief about everything based on his sensory experience. Moreover, Descartes argued that it was also possible to doubt mathematical truths. This is just because it was possible that an evil demon deceived him into thinking that his reasoning about mathematics (such as that as 2 + 2 = 4) was correct when in fact it was not.

Descartes's point was not that he was dreaming or that an actual evil demon actually deceived him. Rather, it was that these things were possible, and therefore that beliefs based on either sensory experience or reason were not certain; therefore, for Descartes, they did not yet count as knowledge. Descartes had established arguments for global skepticism, the view that there is no knowledge at all. However, Descartes then proceeded to argue that there is certain knowledge after all. For Descartes, the path to rejecting skepticism lay in the recognition that he himself existed. This, at least, he could not doubt. According to Descartes, he knew he existed because he was thinking, and in order to think he must exist (if he did not exist, he could not be thinking). This argument is known as the cogito argument, from the Latin phrase *Cogito ergo sum,* meaning "I think, therefore I am."

Using the certain knowledge that he existed as a starting point, Descartes went on to argue that he knew mathematical truths and that material objects existed. For Descartes, the key was proving that God existed, for if he could prove that God existed, then he could also prove (he thought) that he could trust his reason and therefore reject the possibility that an evil demon deceived him. Descartes's reasoning for God's existence is complex, but roughly it is: The idea of God is of a perfect being. Now God, according to Descartes's idea, must have a cause; it could not have come from nothing. Further, there must be as much perfection in the cause of that idea as there is in the idea itself. If there must be as much perfection in the cause of the idea as the idea itself, then God himself must be the cause of that idea. This is because only God could have as much perfection as the idea of God (Descartes himself could not be the cause of the idea of God, because Descartes is imperfect). Therefore, God exists.

According to Descartes, because God is good, God would not deceive Descartes. So God would not have given Descartes the capacity to reason unless reason, properly used, could lead to knowledge. So, Descartes thought, mathematical knowledge was certain after all: It is knowledge acquired through the proper use of reason. This is Descartes's answer to the evil demon argument (the argument that he could not trust his reason because an evil demon could be deceiving him). In answer to the dream argument (that he could not trust anything his senses told him because he might be dreaming), Descartes thought that he could not help believing that physical objects would exist and that God would not have made Descartes that way unless physical objects actually exist. However, there is a difficulty with this reasoning. Descartes proved the existence of God in order to prove that he can trust his own reasoning. This means he could not trust his own reasoning as he tried to prove the existence of God (after all, for all Descartes knew, an evil demon was deceiving him). But if this is the case, Descartes had no reason to believe that he could trust his own arguments for proving that God exists. The problem is that Descartes needed his reason to be trustworthy to prove that God exists, but he needed to prove that God exists in order to show that his reason is trustworthy. This circular reasoning has become known as the Cartesian circle, and it has been the subject of much discussion.

In a departure from the scholasticism in much of philosophy prior to his own work, Descartes sought to prove claims such as that God existed through human reason alone, rather than relying on divine revelation. As a rationalist, Descartes believed that knowledge is based on reason, rather than on experience with the sensory world. This included knowledge of material objects. As an example, Descartes noted that a material object such as a piece of wax changes its physical properties (for example, when it melts, its shape is very different than when it is solid). Yet, despite undergoing such changes, the wax is still the same piece of wax. What this showed, according to Descartes, is that there must be an underlying substance of the wax, something beyond its observable physical properties. In general, material objects have such substances, and they are understood through reason, not through observation of physical properties.

Descartes is also famous for his views about the nature of the mind and the body and the relation between them. According to Descartes, the body consists of matter. Matter, in turn, is just extended substance—that is, it is a sort of physical stuff that takes up space (for example, it has a certain width). Mind, on the other hand, is nonphysical substance. Mind is therefore distinct from the body. On Descartes's view, then, humans are composed of two substances—mind and body—that are distinct from each other but which are somehow unified and therefore interact (for example, when a person's mental desire to walk causes the body to walk). Descartes offered several arguments for the view that mind and body are distinct substances (a view known as substance dualism). First, he argued that because it was possible for him to conceive of his mind existing without his body, his mind must be distinct from his body. In another argument, Descartes claimed that his body is divisible (it can be divided into pieces) but that his mind was not divisible, and therefore his body and mind are distinct.

A persistent challenge for Descartes's view was how to explain how mind and body interact. This is because if mind and body are two fundamentally different kinds of substances, with one nonphysical and one physical, it is not easy to see how they can affect the other. For example, how can a mental desire cause the body to move? Descartes's own answer was that the mind and body somehow interact through the pineal gland in the human body. Many philosophers have found this answer unsatisfactory.

Thomas Hobbes

Thomas Hobbes (1588–1679) was an English philosopher best known today as an important thinker in political philosophy. He was born prematurely when his mother feared that the Spanish Armada was coming, which Hobbes later humorously suggested explained his fearful nature. His father was a somewhat disreputable vicar. Hobbes studied at Oxford and later became a tutor for the aristocratic Cavendish family, with whom he remained connected throughout his life. He corresponded with René Descartes and other noted intellectuals of his time and famously tried to square the circle. Hobbes lived during the English civil war and was sometimes forced to leave the country for his own safety, as he acquired enemies with his political views. For example, after the English king lost power, Hobbes (a royalist) fled to France, where he lived for about 10 years. In addition to his strictly philosophical writings, Hobbes worked in mathematics and physics and published works of history and translations. Although in his own time he was sometimes called an atheist, whether Hobbes believed in God is controversial.

In metaphysics (the study of the nature of reality), Hobbes was a materialist: He believed that everything that existed was material. He argued that thought, dreams, the imagination, and indeed all mental activity can be explained in materialist terms, specifically in terms of mechanical matter in motion. That is, according to Hobbes, all mental activity is a matter of material stuff moving in a mechanical way. For instance, Hobbes claimed that sensations can be explained by external material objects somehow exerting pressure on the sensory organs—a person perceives a yellow banana, for example, when the banana exerts physical pressure on the eye, and this pressure causes physical pressure in the heart and brain. Hobbes was also an empiricist, believing that all knowledge depends on experience and on sensations in particular: without sensations, we could not acquire knowledge, and indeed for Hobbes all knowledge is ultimately based on sensations.

Hobbes believed that human desires have physical causes. So, one has the desires one has because they are the result of a particular physical chain of events; in this way, one's desires are determined. No one chooses her desires because no one chooses the physical chain of events that cause them. Hobbes nonetheless believed it was possible for a person to be free. For Hobbes, freedom is not freedom to choose one's own desires, but rather freedom from opposition; it is the ability to do what one wants. Suppose, for example, that a person wants to grow a garden. She does not freely choose to have that desire, which is just the result of a physical chain of events. However, she is free with respect to that desire as long as she is able to act on it. Suppose, on the other hand, a person is not free to act on her desire to grow a garden; perhaps her landlord prevents her from using the land on which she lives, and no other land is available for her; in that case, she would not be free. But as long as she is free to act on her desire to grow a garden, she is free in that respect. Hobbes thus offers a version of compatibilism, the view that it is possible both for humans to be free and for determinism to be true.

Hobbes is most famous for his work in political philosophy. In his most important work, *The Leviathan,* Hobbes gave an account of the nature and purpose of government, describing a version of social contract theory, according to which humans agree to give up their freedom to a ruler—a sovereign, to use Hobbes's term—in order to attain physical security. To illustrate, Hobbes imagined humans living without government, in what he called the state of nature. Hobbes thought life in such a state would be very bad, famously describing it as "solitary, poor, nasty, brutish, and short." The reason that life in the state of nature would be so bad is because, first, people would naturally be concerned mainly with their own interests. They would seek their own survival and their own advantage. Second, they would compete for the same resources— for example, the same especially desirable land or food. Third, Hobbes thought that in the state of nature no one could ever truly be safe from

Frontispiece of *Leviathan* by Thomas Hobbes, published in 1651

attack, because people are about equal in their abilities (or equal enough that each person would be vulnerable). Even a very strong person, for instance, could be attacked while sleeping. So the state of nature would be a war of everyone against everyone else. There would be no cooperation, and people would constantly live in fear.

Hobbes thought that to escape the state of nature, people would need to agree to cede power to a sovereign. The sovereign would enforce laws and thus ensure the physical security of everyone under him. As Hobbes envisioned it, the sovereign would need absolute political authority. This was because, he believed, only a sovereign with absolute political authority would truly be able to enforce laws. If powers were divided between different branches of government, people would fight about the precise limits and scope of those powers. That in turn would lead to civil war, returning people to the state of nature. It was better to live under a ruler with absolute authority, Hobbes thought, than to return to a state of nature and live in constant fear of violence.

For Hobbes, then, rebellion against the sovereign is almost never justified. Yet Hobbes does seem to suggest it is justified if the sovereign no longer provides physical protection. Because the sovereign's subjects have ceded power to the sovereign for that purpose, one would seem to be justified in rebelling if the sovereign fails to protect. (One way of putting this is that it would be as if the sovereign had broken the social contract.) Hobbes wrote that people have a "right of nature" to protect themselves, a right they hold even in the state of nature, as well as under the sovereign.

Baruch Spinoza

Baruch Spinoza (also called Benedict Spinoza) (1632–77) was among the most important of modern philosophers. He was born in Amsterdam into a Jewish family and as a young man helped run his family's business. In 1656, Spinoza's synagogue excommunicated and cursed him. Although the charges against him were not specifically identified, it is thought that Spinoza's untraditional views about God and other matters—views he refused to renounce—led to his excommunication. Spinoza moved to The Hague and supported himself as a lens grinder, living modestly and seeking neither wealth nor fame. He earned enemies and disapproval from Jews as well as Christians for his philosophical beliefs, and in part out a concern for his own safety Spinoza published just two books during his lifetime, a work on Descartes and a work in which he defended freedom of thought and religion. In 1673, Heidelberg University offered him a position as a professor of philosophy, but Spinoza refused it in the belief that accepting the position might threaten his intellectual freedom. He died of consumption when he was 44. Other works by Spinoza, including his most important work, *Ethics,* were published after his death.

Spinoza was a rationalist: He believed that the ultimate source of knowledge was reason, not experience. He constructed a system of metaphysics (a view of reality) based on reason, and he believed reality itself was rational; reality, for Spinoza, was reasonable. Like Descartes, Spinoza regarded geometry as the model for knowledge. Geometry proceeds by stating definitions and axioms and drawing out their logical consequences. Spinoza sought to describe reality by following a geometric method, listing definitions and axioms and drawing conclusions from them. Spinoza used this method in part because he believed that knowledge required certainty; it was not enough merely to be pretty sure in a belief to count as knowing something, one must be absolutely certain. Spinoza regarded certainty, in turn, in terms of logical necessity: that is, a belief whose truth is certain is a belief whose truth is guaranteed by logic (its truth is logically necessary). In geometry, for example, it is logically certain that a triangle has three sides; this just follows from the definition of *triangle*. Similarly, Spinoza devised his metaphysical views on the basis of such starting points as the definitions of terms such as *substance* and *God*. According to Spinoza, a substance is what it is in itself. Another way to put the point is that a substance does not depend on anything else for its existence. In addition, Spinoza claimed, one does not need a concept other than that of the substance itself in order to understand the substance. By an attribute, Spinoza meant the essence of a substance, and he believed that substances could not share an attribute. This is because, roughly, if two substances shared the same attribute (or essence), there would not be a way to distinguish between them. Spinoza identified substance with God. To show that God exists, Spinoza gave three different arguments, one of which is a version of an argument known as the ontological argument: to conceive of God, he argued, is to conceive of a substance. But existence belongs to the nature of substance; that is, it is in the nature of substance to exist. So, God can be conceived only as existing, and therefore God exists.

Spinoza argued further that there can be only one substance and that that substance is God. The reason Spinoza thought there could be only one substance is that, according to him, substances cannot share attributes. God, Spinoza thought, has an infinite number of attributes. Any substance with an attribute, therefore, must be God (otherwise, it would share an attribute with God, which Spinoza thought was impossible). Spinoza believed, then, that all of reality consists of one infinite substance, a version of monism (the view that there is one kind of reality in the world); he called this substance God or Nature. That is, it can be accurately thought of as God, but it can also be accurately thought of as Nature, the structure of reality itself. As Spinoza understood God, God is not a being with whom it is possible to have a personal relationship, contrary to traditional conceptions of God. It would not make sense, for

Statue of Baruch Spinoza in the Netherlands *(Sculpture by Frédéric Hexamer)*

example, to try to communicate with God via prayer or seek favors from God. God is not a being at all in the sense of a being with desires (for if God has desires, that would imply that God is lacking something, a view Spinoza rejected). Nor is God appropriately thought of as the creator of the universe in the traditional sense. For Spinoza, rather than God creating a universe from which God is separate, God *is* the universe. All that is real is part of God's nature and necessarily part of God's nature.

Because God necessarily exists and God is reality, everything that is and everything that occurs is necessary. So, according to Spinoza, the universe is deterministic: everything that occurs does so necessarily as a result of specific causes.

As a monist, Spinoza rejected Descartes's idea that there are both thinking substances (minds) and extended substances (bodies), two different kinds of substances. Descartes's view had notoriously raised the question of how it was possible for such very different substances to interact (for example, how it was possible for a mind to control the movements of a body). Spinoza regarded thought (or mind) and extension (what occupies space, as physical objects do) as attributes of the one existing substance, God. Because they are both attributes of the same single substance, thought and extension are essentially the same. When we think of substance one way, we think of it as thought; when we think of it as another, we think of it as extension. But they are both attributes of the same substance. Because in Spinoza's view, mind and body are both attributes of the same substance, the question of how mind and body interact does not seem to pose a challenge for Spinoza as it does for Descartes.

Spinoza's writings on human psychology and on ethics were significant. Spinoza believed that happiness consisted in the intellectual love of God and the freedom from being controlled by one's passions. The intellectual love of God entailed an understanding of one's place in the universe and the rationality of the universe, as well as an acceptance of the necessity of everything that occurs.

Gottfried Wilhelm Leibniz

Gottfried Leibniz (1646–1716) was a widely accomplished intellectual who made contributions to mathematics, physics, linguistics, history, and other fields. In philosophy, he is known especially as a rationalist who developed a system of metaphysics (a systematic view about the nature of reality), in addition to writing on epistemology (the study of knowledge), ethics (the study of right action), the problem of evil, and free will and determinism. Leibniz was born in Germany. He taught himself Latin at an early age, read from his father's library, and earned degrees in law and philosophy. Although he was offered a position as a professor, Leibniz chose instead to work for noblemen and served variously in such capacities as an engineer, librarian, and diplomat. He also traveled, met other intellectual figures, and corresponded with many people. Of particular importance is Leibniz's invention of calculus, an invention that involved Leibniz in an international dispute over whether Leibniz or Isaac Newton was the true inventor; today scholars believe each thinker invented calculus independently of the other. He published few books in philosophy during his lifetime, and scholars understand his views partly by also considering Leibniz's other writings, such as his letters.

Like other rationalist philosophers, Leibniz regarded certainty as necessary for knowledge; that is, unless the truth of a belief was certain, the belief did not count as knowledge. Also like other rationalists, Leibniz believed that it was possible through reason, rather than the methods of science, to understand the nature of reality. According to Leibniz, the process of reasoning is based on certain principles, principles that could be assumed to be true because it made no sense for them to be false. One such principle was the principle of contradiction (sometimes called the principle of non-contradiction). According to this principle, if something implies a contradiction, then it is false, and whatever denies a contradiction must be true. For instance, the claim that green is not a color is false (it implies a contradiction), and the claim that it is *not* the case that green is not a color must be true (it denies a contradiction). Another basic principle whose truth can be assumed is the principle of sufficient reason. According to this principle, for anything that is true or for anything that is the case, there must be a sufficient reason for why it is true or why it is case. So, what is true is not true arbitrarily, and what exists does not just happen to exist. For Leibniz, then, the world is rational.

According to Leibniz, reality consists of simple substances called monads. There must be simple substances, he thought, because some things are composed of parts; these things must be composed of something, and what they are composed of are monads. A tree, for example, is composed of monads—at a fundamental level, it consists of simple substances that we cannot perceive through our senses. We cannot perceive monads through our senses because monads lack extension; they do not extend into space (so, they are not physical). Monads are simple in the sense that they cannot be divided. They are unique in the sense that no monad is just like any other monad. They are eternal in the sense that they neither can be created nor destroyed, except by God. Indeed, for Leibniz, nothing can causally affect a monad or be affected by a monad. That is, a monad does not cause anything, and what happens to a monad is not caused by anything outside the monad itself. This idea stems in part from the traditional idea that substances are independent, which Leibniz took to imply *causally* independent. Each monad has a sort of active force, a kind of life principle. A person's soul is a monad. But there are also monads throughout a person's body—for example, in a person's hands and feet. As an analogy, a fishpond can be understood as a pool with fish in it. But the fish themselves can be understood as composed of monads, each with its own life force. For Leibniz, even inorganic objects consist of monads, and because monads have a sort of life principle, all nature is full of life. However, some monads are more conscious and more rational than others.

Monads do undergo change, but they do so according to their own internal nature. A monad, Leibniz wrote, is pregnant with its future: it contains within in the potential for what will happen to it in the future. In addition, monads contain within themselves what has happened to them in the past. One might wonder, if reality consists of monads and these monads do not interact, how it is that what happens in the world seems to fit together. Consider, for example, that when a person intends to dive into a pool of water, her body moves and dives into the water.

Portrait of Gottfried Wilhelm Leibniz *(Painting by Johann Friedrich Wentzel)*

How does the person's intention correspond with the body's motion, if the soul (a monad) does not interact with the body? For that matter, if the body is itself a collection of monads, how is it that each separate monad within the body somehow acts in concert such that the body dives into the water? Leibniz's answer is that there is a preestablished harmony between monads. The soul does not cause the body to move, nor does the body cause the soul to feel a certain way. Rather, God has arranged it such that the actions of the one correspond with the other. Analogously, suppose two clocks tell the same time. Neither one causes the other to tell the time it does; they have just been set such that they tell the same time. Similarly, God has arranged it such that the actions of monads correspond with each other in harmony, although monads do not causally affect each other.

Leibniz's view that there is a preestablished harmony in nature is also the answer to the problem in philosophy of mind of how to explain the apparent interaction between the mind and the body. This problem has seemed especially difficult for philosophers such as Descartes, who held that minds and bodies are fundamentally two different kinds of substances, with mind being nonphysical and bodies being physical. The difficulty was that if such substances are truly that different it is not easy to see how one affects the other. In a commonsense view, what goes on in one's mind affects what goes on with one's body, and vice versa. The usual philosophical way of putting this is that mental events can cause bodily events and bodily events can cause mental events. For example, suppose the water in one's shower suddenly turns ice-cold. It is likely that a person would yelp in discomfort and quickly move to turn the water off. So the bodily event of the cold water striking one's skin seems to cause the mental event of the sensation of pain. Also, the mental event of a person desiring to stop the cold water seems to cause the bodily event of the person reaching for a knob in the shower.

For Leibniz, however, it is a mistake to think that mental events cause any bodily events, or that bodily events cause any mental events. Rather, mental and bodily events are parallel: They simply occur at the same time (or about the same time). But neither causes the other. Again, if two clocks are set to show the same time, then throughout the day, the clocks will show the same time: They are parallel. But neither clock causes the other clock to show a certain time. In the same way, according to Leibniz, mental events and bodily events are parallel, but neither causes the other. A person's desire to dive into a pool and the body's diving motion into the pool, for instance, are parallel, but the desire does not cause the bodily motion. It is as if the mind and the body were both set at the same time.

The view that mental events and bodily events are parallel is called parallelism. Because parallelism denies that mental events and bodily events affect each other, the view escapes the difficulty of explaining mind/body interaction. However, parallelism faces difficulties of its own. First, few philosophers believe there is an adequate explanation for why mental and bodily events would be parallel. Second, if parallelism is true, then nothing that we think, believe, feel, or want has any effect on anything we physically do; moreover, nothing that happens to our bodies has any effect on what we think or feel. Many philosophers find this too far-fetched to accept parallelism.

A Christian, Leibniz tried to provide an answer to the problem of evil, the problem of how to make sense of the existence of evil in the world if God is all-powerful, all-good, and all-knowing. If God is all these things, why would he allow evil to exist? Leibniz's answer was that God had created the best of all possible worlds. True, evil exists in the world. But that God could have created a better world than this one (the actual world) was not possible. An important element in Leibniz's reasoning is the principle of sufficient reason. According to this principle, if something is the case, then there must be a sufficient reason for why it is the case. Now it seems that God, being all-powerful, could have created a world different than ours: There were various possible worlds, and out of these possibilities, God chose to create this one. So, Leibniz reasoned, there must have been a sufficient reason for why God chose to create this world rather than another one. That reason, according to Leibniz, is that this is the best of all possible worlds. The evil that does occur in the world, Leibniz argued, is ultimately for a greater good.

John Locke

The English philosopher John Locke (1632–1704) was one of the most important and influential modern philosophers. The son of a lawyer, Locke studied at Westminster School and then at Christ Church, Oxford, where he was elected a studentship and received his degrees. He went on to study medicine and served as personal physician to the Earl of Shaftesbury, while also becoming involved in the English government and helping to write a constitution for the colony of Carolina. Eventually Locke's connection to Shaftesbury, as well as his own views in favor of the English Parliament, entangled Locke in political controversies and he moved to Holland for his own safety. There he became an adviser to William and Mary of Orange. When William and Mary became king and queen of England, Locke returned to England and served in various government positions. In addition to his strictly philosophical writings, Locke wrote on religious tolerance, economics, education, religion, and other topics, achieving a reputation as one of the foremost English intellectuals of his time. Today, his work is still widely read and respected.

Whereas René Descartes and other rationalists had emphasized mathematics as the model for acquiring knowledge, Locke was impressed by the empirical work of physicists such as Isaac Newton. At the same time, Locke believed reason was supremely important, remarking that it was "the last judge and guide" of all things. In one of his most influential works, *An Essay Concerning Human Understanding,* Locke sought to describe the capabilities of human understanding, such as what it is possible for humans to know and on what basis. Contrary to Descartes and others, Locke argued that there are no innate ideas. That is, humans are not born with any ideas already formed in their minds. Locke argued that if there were innate ideas, then it would seem that very young children would have them and show an awareness of them. But, according to Locke, they do not. So, there are no innate ideas. For Locke, it is not a good defense of innate ideas to say that young children do have innate ideas but that they have not yet developed them (so that the ideas are innate in the sense that children have the capacity to develop them). This is because, if to be an innate idea is just to be an idea that a person is capable of developing at some point, then it looks as if any idea a person ever has can be considered innate. But it seems implausible to suppose that all the ideas one ever has are innate. For instance, a person might acquire the idea of electrons in middle school and the idea of an iPod when iPods were first invented. But it would seem odd to suppose that these ideas were ever innate in one's mind.

Rather, Locke said, at birth the mind is like a white paper on which nothing is written; metaphorically, it is a blank tablet. As a tablet is blank until someone writes on it, the mind has no content until it receives content from experience (this view of mind is sometimes called the tabula rasa (blank tablet) view of mind). The source of all our ideas, according to Locke, is experience. In this sense, Locke was an empiricist: He believed that the human mind cannot form any ideas that are not based on experience (either directly or indirectly). Locke understood experience broadly. First, experience includes sensations—what we experience through our five senses, such as what we feel. Second, experience includes reflection, which Locke understood as an observation of the operations of one's own mind. For example, thinking and doubting are instances of reflection: they are operations of the mind that one can observe in oneself. From sensation and reflection, Locke argued, come all the materials for knowledge. Locke divided ideas themselves into simple ideas and complex ideas. Simple ideas are ideas that cannot be analyzed, meaning that they cannot be broken up into parts. An example of a simple idea is the idea of yellow. Complex ideas are made up of simple ideas, and Locke believed that we can construct complex ideas from simple ideas in specific ways. We can, for example, use abstraction. This is the process of forming a general idea on the basis of simple ideas. For example, suppose a person sees many different sorts of dogs: Some are shaggy, some are short-haired, some have pointed ears, some have floppy ears, and so on. From the simple ideas acquired by seeing these different dogs, it is possible to abstract away from specific details of these individual dogs, focus on what all the dogs have in common, and accordingly form the general idea of dog. This general idea of dog does not entail that every dog has pointed ears or a shaggy coat—it is an idea of dog in general rather than an idea of any specific dog (or specific type of dog).

Locke used "idea" in a specific sense to mean whatever is the object of a person's understanding—that is, whatever it is that a person is thinking about or understanding. According to Locke, we experience directly only ideas, not things themselves. So, for instance, we do not perceive a banana directly; we perceive only our idea of a banana. However, the banana causes a person to have an idea of the banana. The banana exists independently of human ideas (it does not just exist in our minds), although humans do not perceive it directly. In general, according to Locke, objects outside of ourselves cause us to experience ideas, and we experience those ideas rather than the objects themselves. In this way, we perceive only what is in our own minds, although there are real objects that exist independently.

Locke held that such objects have primary qualities and secondary qualities. A quality is just the power an object has to produce an idea in a person. For instance, to use Locke's example, a snowball has the power to produce in a person the ideas of cold and white. In other words, when someone picks up and looks at a snowball, the snowball causes her to have the idea of cold (it feels cold in her hands) and the idea of white (the snowball looks white). Primary qualities are inseparable from objects; objects always have them, as long as they exist. The primary qualities are solidity, extension (occupying space), figure (shape), motion or lack of motion, and number (whether an object is one or more than one). The shape of the snowball, for instance, is a primary quality: As long as it exists, the snowball always has the power to produce the idea of a certain shape in the perceiver, and the shape of the snowball is in the snowball itself. Of course, the shape of the snowball might change (it might get bigger or smaller), but shape itself is inseparable from the snowball: the snowball always has a certain shape, whatever that shape is.

Portrait of John Locke
(Painting by H. Garnier)

In contrast, secondary qualities are qualities that are not inseparable from objects and that are not really in objects. They include
colors, tastes, and sounds. For instance, although the snowball has the
power to produce the idea of white in someone who sees it, the color
white is not inseparable from the snowball. To see this, consider that
the snowball need not always produce the idea of white. In darkness,
the snowball might appear gray, for example, and to someone with
a medical condition such as jaundice, it will appear yellow. So color
is not actually in the snowball itself, although the snowball has the
power to produce the ideas of particular colors in people looking at
it. In Locke's terms, primary qualities more closely resemble objects
than secondary qualities do. Locke also held that secondary qualities
depend on primary qualities in the sense that an object's power to
produce ideas such as taste, color, and sound depends on the object's
primary qualities. In an indication of the interplay between what we
would today call science (but was then called natural philosophy)
and philosophy as we now understand it, the scientist Galileo also

defended the distinction between primary and secondary qualities, very much as Locke defended that distinction.

Locke also considered the issue of substance, although scholars debate precisely what he meant. Primary and secondary qualities are qualities of an object, but Locke wrote that that the qualities must belong to—or "subsist in"—something. Put another way, it is not as if qualities are free-floating by themselves; *something* must support them. What supports them is substance. But, according to Locke, it is impossible to know the substance of an object, and indeed we have no clear idea of what substance is. We can know only that it is that which supports the qualities of an object. In addition, Locke thought, we cannot truly know the real essences of things, such as the real essence of gold (though we can acquire beliefs about it that are probably true).

Locke's view of personal identity continues to be discussed today. The issue of personal identity is the issue of what makes a person *that* person. Another way of saying this is that personal identity is the issue of what the essence, or most basic features, of someone is, such that if that essence was different, the person would be different. Another term for personal identity is *the self.* So the issue of personal identity is: What is the self (or, what constitutes a person's self)? In his answer to this question, Locke noted that a person's body is not the same as a person's identity as a person. So, what makes a person the same person over time is not that her body stays the same (after all, it does not; cells of a living body are constantly being replaced). Rather, what makes a person the same person over time is that her consciousness is continuous; for example, in the present, she remembers her past. As an illustration, if Socrates' consciousness were transplanted into another person's body, and the resulting person had all of Socrates' memories, that person would be Socrates. In general, according to Locke, the core or essence of a person (what makes a person who she is) is a person's memories and thoughts. Suppose you are the same person now that you were when you were in kindergarten. This is because you have had certain experiences and you remember them. Of course, this does not mean you remember all of your experiences; of course you do not, and you are likely to remember some experiences at some time and forget some of them later. It is likely, for instance, that you remember little (if anything) of your experiences when you were just two years old. For Locke, however, what matters insofar as your personal identity is concerned is that your memories are continuous: at two, for instance, you remembered what happened to you in the days previous, and as time passed each day you remembered some of what happened to you in the recent or even distant past, even as you forgot other experiences. It is this continuity that matters for identity, that one's thoughts, memories, beliefs, sensations, and so on are continuous. If you woke up with amnesia one day, on the other hand, and remembered nothing at all, then according to Locke you would be a different person than the self who went to sleep prior to the amnesia: Though the pre-amnesia self and the post-amnesia self would have existed in the same body, they would be different people in the sense that they would be different selves.

In political philosophy, Locke's views were very influential both inside philosophy and outside it. For example, the framers of the U.S. Constitution, such as Thomas Jefferson, based that document and the Declaration of Independence in part on Locke's ideas. Locke's ideas in political philosophy fall within the tradition of what has come to be known as social contract theory. In political philosophy, social contract theory is the view that a government somehow derives its legitimacy from the consent of the people it governs; it is as though there is a contract between a legitimate government and its people. A central idea of social contract theory is that individual people are all better off cooperating than they would be if they did not do so. Social contract theorists typically view humans as rational, self-interested beings who would, therefore, actually be motivated to cooperate. (The term *social contract theory* is also used in ethics for the view that morality consists of rules that rational, self-interested people would agree upon; it is as though people agree on a contract about how they can and cannot behave, in order best to promote their own interests. This essay uses *social contract theory* to refer to a view in political philosophy.)

Locke argued in favor of democratic government in which government is legitimate only if it rules with the consent of those who are governed. To illustrate the purpose of government and the legitimacy of government (or lack thereof), Locke imagined people living in a state of nature, a state without government. The idea was that by understanding what life is like without government, it would be possible to understand why people form governments, what government is for, and, perhaps, when government is legitimate and when it is not. In his *Second Treatise of Government*, Locke suggested that humans did live in a state of nature at some point in the past, and that the heads of independent governments existed in a state of nature relative to each other (because they did not recognize a higher government ruling them all). However, the state of nature need not be understood as a description of a state in which humans actually existed in history and have since left. Rather, the state of nature is usually understood as an abstraction, an idea that is a useful tool for investigating the nature of government.

Locke saw the state of nature as a state in which everyone enjoys equality and freedom. In the state of nature, people are free to live as they wish, within the limits of natural law. According to this natural law, which Locke wrote was the law of reason, "no one ought to harm another in his life, health, liberty, or possessions." Yet Locke thought that there were "inconveniences" associated with the state of nature. These inconveniences are due mainly to the fact that not everyone would follow the natural law.

People tend to be biased in favor of themselves, Locke noted, and they are therefore likely not to view the natural law as applying to them. So people's safety and the security of their property would be threatened. To escape the inconveniences of the state of nature, then, people agree to give up their perfect freedom and form a government. The purpose of the government is to keep people safe and their property secure, and the government does this by making laws and enforcing them (through punishment). Forming a government is in the best interests of those governed because the government protects the security of the people by making and enforcing law. The government derives its legitimacy from the consent of the governed, and the government should follow the will of the majority. According to Locke, even if in actual situations people have not explicitly consented to form a government or obey it, by living within a given state, they have given *tacit* consent to that government and are therefore obligated to obey the will of the majority (on which the government is based). When a government no longer protects the people's interests—when it violates a person's natural rights—then people are justified in rebelling against the government. Unlike Thomas Hobbes, Locke thought it was a mistake to give a ruler absolute power. This is because the purpose of forming a government is to attain security. But, according to Locke, to give a ruler absolute power would be to undermine one's security, placing a subject at the mercy of the ruler, and that would defeat the purpose of forming a government in the first place. It was better to remain in the state of nature, Locke thought, where at least one had perfect freedom, than to live under a ruler with absolute power.

Jean-Jacques Rousseau

Jean-Jacques Rousseau (1712–78) was an important French thinker best known today for his work in political philosophy. He was born in Geneva but spent a considerable part of his life in Paris. The son of a watchmaker, Rousseau was apprenticed to an engraver but abandoned the apprenticeship. His success as a writer began when he wrote the winning entry in an essay contest that asked the question whether the arts and sciences had improved morality. (Rousseau's answer was that they had not.) He subsequently wrote various works on political philosophy, morality, society, education, and botany, in addition to writing operas, plays, a best-selling novel, and autobiographical works. Rousseau enjoyed friendships with important French thinkers such as Denis Diderot (1713–84) and maintained a longtime relationship with Thérèse Levasseur, whom he eventually married. Prior to the marriage, she bore him several children, whom Rousseau abandoned. He was forced to flee Paris in 1762 due to his controversial and unorthodox views about religion and lived for a time in Switzerland, as well as in England, where he quarreled with the Scottish philosopher David Hume. In 1767, Rousseau returned to France. He died in 1778.

In political philosophy, Rousseau is associated with social contract theory, according to which legitimate government is based on the agreement of the people governed (it is as if there is a contract between people and government). Other social contract theorists, such as Thomas Hobbes and John Locke, had described a theoretical state of nature, that is, a state of human existence in which people lived without

Portrait of Jean-Jacques Rousseau from 1766 *(Painting by Allan Ramsay)*

government of any kind. Hobbes had described such a state of nature as "solitary, poor, nasty, brutish, and short," on the grounds that humans would constantly compete with each other for the same resources, warring against each other but able to gain no permanent advantage over each other. Rousseau's account of the state of nature differed markedly. For Rousseau, the state of nature is solitary but happy. Although people in the state of nature cannot escape aging or the possibility of illness, there are plenty of resources to meet their basic needs, and people are well equipped to deal with dangers such as those posed by other animals. Moreover, humans in the state of nature are innocent, free from the corrupting influences of society. Such humans are noble savages. They are not exactly moral and nor are they immoral; rather, they are amoral, without morals altogether. Rousseau agreed with Hobbes that humans in the state of nature are self-interested in the sense that they are concerned with their own welfare. However, Rousseau also believed that humans naturally feel pity for the suffering of others. So, humans in the state of nature would act from an instinct for self-preservation, but their instinctive pity would prevent them from willfully and pointlessly harming others. Human capacities, according to Rousseau, are naturally good. Moreover, humans are perfectible. That is, they are not perfect now, but in principle it is possible for them to become perfect.

Of course, people do not always live in the state of nature. They begin to form communities at least in part because it is easier to accomplish some tasks in a group than individually; farming, for example, is easier if people divide the labor than if one person tries to complete all the tasks. Yet it is society, Rousseau thought, that corrupts human beings. Living in communities with other people, people develop modern traits such as the tendency to want to be better than others. Civilization leads to hypocrisy, envy, and deceit. At the same time, Rousseau thought, it was only by forming civil society that people fully develop their reason, a sense of duty, and robust moral virtues.

A central concern of Rousseau's was freedom, and his most famous remark was, "Man is born free; and everywhere he is in chains." He believed humans ought to retain their freedom even while living within political communities, under a government. For Rousseau, the way to preserve freedom while living under a government involves, first, the free and unanimous decision of every person within a political community to form that political community in the first place. All parties to a social contract, in other words, must actually and freely agree to that social contract. Second, in agreeing to form a government, Rousseau thought that each person must agree to submit to what he called the general will. The general will is a difficult concept in Rousseau's thought, and it has generated disagreement among Rousseau's interpreters. However, this much can be said: the general will is not just the collection of each person's individual will. Rather, the general will is the will of the entire political community as a whole. Whereas an individual might seek what benefits herself in particular, the general will seeks what will benefit the community as a whole. An individual might wish to make laws that will benefit herself, for example, such as tax laws that benefit her particular kind of business; the general will, however, makes laws to benefit the interests of the whole community rather than merely the interests of particular individuals (or even particular individual groups) within the community. Because the general will promotes the good of the entire community, by submitting to the general will, in Rousseau's view a person actually ensures her own freedom. This is so even if the general will causes some things to happen (such as certain laws to be passed) that an individual actually opposes.

George Berkeley

George Berkeley (1685–1753) was an empiricist philosopher best known today for his metaphysical idealism. He was born in Ireland to an English family and attended Kilkenny College and Trinity College, where he later taught. Berkeley published his most important philosophical works when he was quite young. In 1734, he became Bishop of Cloyne, in Ireland, where he acquired a reputation as the "good Bishop" for the concern he demonstrated for the health, poverty, and education of the people. Out of a concern for the education of colonists, Native Ameri-

Campanile and Graduate Memorial Building, Trinity College, Dublin, where George Berkeley taught

cans, and black people in the New World, he tried to establish a college on the island of Bermuda and lived for three years in Rhode Island as he did preparatory work for the college and waited for funding from the government. However, eventually it became clear that funding would never be forthcoming, and Berkeley returned to Ireland. He died in Oxford, where he had moved because one of his sons was to attend college there.

A devout Christian, Berkeley disliked the contemporary view of his time that the physical world operated mechanistically, as though the physical world and the physical objects within it were complex machines. He also rejected skepticism and was eager to defend belief in God and in an immaterial soul. Together with John Locke's influence, these factors shaped Berkeley's views about the nature of reality and knowledge. To understand Berkeley, it is necessary to understand Locke. According to Locke, we have no innate ideas (ideas we are somehow born with). Instead, all our ideas are ultimately based on experience. Experience, in turn, Locke understood as including not only what one experiences through the five senses, but one's awareness of the operations of one's own mind (such as thinking and remembering). Like other philosophers of his time, Locke also thought that we experience only our own ideas. "Ideas" is used here in a broad, special sense; an idea is not just a thought, as when a person trying to solve a problem suddenly says, "I have an idea!" Ideas include not only thoughts but also things such as sensations, memories, and images. When Locke wrote that we experience only our own ideas, he meant in particular that we do not experience things in the world directly. For example, a person does not see a pine tree directly. Instead, the tree produces in a person certain ideas, such as the idea of green pine needles and brown bark. What one is directly aware of are those ideas—not the tree itself. Locke also distinguished between primary and secondary qualities. Primary qualities are qualities of an object that are in the object itself— for example, the solidity of a tree really is in the tree, not just in one's mind. Secondary qualities are qualities that are not in an object itself. The scent of pine needles, for instance, is not in the tree itself, although the tree produces in a person the idea of that scent.

Berkeley agreed with Locke that all our ideas are derived from experience; moreover, for Berkeley all knowledge is based on experience. Berkeley also agreed that we experience only ideas directly.

However, Berkeley thought that Locke's claim that there are material objects that exist independently of being perceived leads to skepticism: after all, if we never experience anything but our own ideas, how do we know that our ideas in any way match up with an independently existing reality? It appears that we *cannot* know. And that suggests that what we seem to know of ordinary, existing things—that apples are red, that pine needles smell a certain way, that mountains are tall, and so on—we do not actually know at all. Berkeley rejected this conclusion. His solution was simply to deny that matter exists at all: There are no material objects, Berkeley argued. According to Berkeley, all that exists are ideas and the minds that perceive them. What we ordinarily take to be material objects are collections of ideas. A pine tree, for example, is a collection of ideas such as the color green, rough bark, and pine needles of a certain size and shape. That is *all* apparently material objects are—collections of ideas in the mind. This does not mean that sensible objects (objects perceived through the senses) are not real; it just means that their existence is mind dependent. Now the question of how it is possible to know that our ideas match up with independently existing objects does not arise. That is because there are no such independently existing objects. Moreover, knowledge of what we experience can count as genuine knowledge because we experience all that there is to experience: our ideas. The view that what is real are ideas, not material objects, is idealism. Here idealism does not mean having lofty ideals, but is the view that what is real depends on the mind (the term *idealism* comes from the word *idea*). Berkeley himself called his view immaterialism.

It might sound strange to believe that only ideas and minds exist and material objects do not. Berkeley believed, however, that his view was actually consistent with common sense because what we ordinarily talk about and have beliefs in are objects of experience. Berkeley gave specific arguments for his idealism. As noted, we experience only our ideas; sensible objects are collections of ideas. But ideas can exist only in a mind; they cannot exist independently of a mind. If they exist, therefore, they exist because they are perceived by a mind. To be, Berkeley wrote, is to be perceived (in Latin, *esse est percipi*). Berkeley also rejected the primary/secondary qualities distinction. Secondary qualities are not in the objects themselves and therefore depend on a perceiver. But, Berkeley argued, it was impossible to conceive of a sensible object without thinking of it as having secondary qualities. So, if secondary qualities depend for their existence on the perceiver, so too do primary qualities.

Our ideas do have a cause, Berkeley believed: The cause is God. To see why this is so, Berkeley noted that some of our ideas are involuntary; it is not up to us whether we have them (for instance, one cannot decide to see an apple just because one wants to). Yet they must have a cause, and for Berkeley that cause must be another mind, the mind of God. God's existence also explains why objects continue to exist even when an individual mind no longer sees them. They continue to exist because God perceives them. In general, sensible ideas are ideas in the mind of God.

In response to Berkeley, Samuel Johnson famously said, "I refute Berkeley thus," and kicked a rock. Presumably Johnson meant that his ability to kick the rock proved that the rock was physical, thus refuting Berkeley's claim that there are no physical objects. But this was not really a refutation of Berkeley. This is because Berkeley never denied that a person could kick a rock. In general, he never denied that we can act on the ordinary objects of experience or for that matter that we can be acted upon by the ordinary objects of experience (as when falling snowflakes make a person feel cold and wet). For Berkeley, the sensation of resistance that is felt when a person kicks a rock is an idea in the person's head—of course, it is real, but it is not physical in nature. Similarly, the perception of the rock moving away from oneself after being kicked is also an idea. Berkeley never denied that one could have such experiences. He just denied that these experiences are best explained by supposing such objects are physical. A person can successfully kick all the rocks she wants—but neither she nor the rock is physical. One can also ride a horse, burn oneself on a hot stove, and go hiking in the mountains. But in each case, for Berkeley, the experiences would involve ideas and collections of ideas—they would not involve matter.

Few philosophers have been willing to defend Berkeley's claim that matter does not exist. However, idealism did not disappear and is not dead. Immanuel Kant, for example, gave a different account of idealism, calling his view transcendental idealism. Kant argued that the mind organizes experience, rather than passively receiving ideas. For example, Kant argued that space does not exist absolutely and independently of the mind. Rather, we experience objects in time and in space because the mind organizes experience that way: In this way, space is something the mind itself brings to experience rather than something the mind encounters in experience. Kant's view is an idealist one in the sense that he argued that the objects of our knowledge are dependent on the mind. They are dependent on the mind in the sense that we can experience these objects only because the mind organizes experience by applying particular concepts. After Kant, among the most significant versions of idealism in philosophy are found in German idealism, in the absolute idealism expressed by F. W. J. von Schelling (1775–1854), Johann Gottlieb Fichte (1762–1814), and Georg W. F. Hegel (1770–1831). In its various forms, idealism suggests that what we know of reality seems to depend at least in part on how the mind works. Along these lines, it is difficult to make sense of the reality of anything that is wholly beyond our ability to grasp mentally.

David Hume

David Hume (1711–76) was a Scottish philosopher whose influence continues to be evident in such diverse areas as epistemology (the study of knowledge), metaphysics (the study of reality), ethics (the study of right action), and philosophy of religion. He was born in Edinburgh to a family that was relatively well off and studied at the University of Edinburgh, intended by his mother to become a lawyer. However, Hume disliked law and found philosophy more interesting. When he was in his 20s, he published *A Treatise of Human Nature,* hoping to achieve literary fame and success. The book was not successful, and Hume later revised it and published it as *Enquiry Concerning Human Understanding* and *Enquiry Concerning the Principles of Morals.* He worked in various positions (such as a secretary to a general and a tutor to a mad nobleman) but was not able to attain a position as professor of philosophy. While working as a librarian he wrote works on the history of England, finally establishing a literary reputation on the basis of these works. Although many of his contemporaries disapproved of Hume's antireligious views, he was well liked for his witty and kindly personality.

Hume was an empiricist who was influenced by philosophers John Locke and George Berkeley and who is famous for his skepticism. He believed that the mental content of the human mind consists of ideas and impressions. Impressions are more lively than ideas—that is, they are more vivid. Impressions include sensations, passions, and emotions. Ideas are copies of impressions. For instance, a person might see a brilliantly orange sunset and while she watches that sunset, she has an impression. Later, when she remembers the sunset, she has an idea of that sunset; her memory of the sunset is a faded copy of the original impression (seeing the sunset is more vivid than remembering the sunset). Ideas can be combinations of impressions, and in this way it is possible to have an idea of something one never actually encounters. For instance, a person might see mountains and the color gold, and she can combine her idea of mountain with her idea of gold to form the idea of a golden mountain, despite having never seen a golden mountain. An idea that has no basis in an impression (or combination of impressions) has no sense, according to Hume—it is meaningless. For this reason, Hume rejected metaphysical concepts that could not be traced back to impressions (a view that later influenced a 20th-century school of thought called logical positivism).

Hume's version of empiricism shaped his view of personal identity, the issue of what makes a person *that* person. You are not the same person as your friends, your teacher, or your family members; something makes you *you*. But how is that you are you? Put another way, what are the criteria for your identity, or your self? Moreover, are you the same

Portrait of David Hume
(Painting by Allan Ramsay)

person over time? For example, is the you who attended kindergarten the same you who exists now? Philosophers have addressed these questions in various ways. It is, perhaps, natural to suppose that one has a single, permanent self—that all that one experiences happens to one's same self, a unified entity. Consider what seems to be yourself as a five-year-old and yourself as a 10-year-old, or even what seems to be yourself an hour ago and what seems to be yourself at this moment. Suppose an hour ago you were hungry, and now you are not; an hour ago you were outside, and now you are inside; an hour ago you were looking at a grassy field and now you are looking at text. One view is that it is the same self—the same you—that underwent or is undergoing all these experiences. Hume, however, denied that there is such a self, a single, unified entity that undergoes different experiences but itself is the same thing throughout those experiences. It is in this sense that Hume was a skeptic about the existence of the self.

To see why Hume thought this, recall that Hume claimed that an idea that has no basis in an impression is meaningless—it is literally *of* nothing. But, according to Hume, no one has an impression of the self (in the sense of a unified, permanent entity). Whenever he was conscious of himself, Hume noted, he was conscious only of an impression—for example, a sensation of heat or a feeling of love. But he was never conscious of a single, unified self. Similarly, if an hour ago you were walking outside, you were conscious of impressions such as the sight of green grass; but now, as you read this, you are conscious of the sight of the words you are reading. If an hour ago, you were hungry, you were conscious of that feeling of hunger, but suppose now you are not. In such cases, by Hume's lights all that you are aware of is some impression or impressions, but you are never aware of some single, unified self. In general, if there is no impression of the self, the idea of self is empty; it has no meaning. In short, there seems to be no self at all. Rather, according to Hume, the self is just a bundle, or collection, of impressions, such as the feeling of fullness, the perception of text, and the memory of being outside an hour ago. There are, then, no essential features of what makes a person the *same* person. To talk about one's "self" is just a convenient way of talking about the bundle of impressions.

Perhaps most famously of all, Hume expressed skepticism about the notion of cause. Very often people believe that one event in the world causes another. For instance, kicking a soccer ball seems to cause it to move; boiling an egg seems to cause it to cook; viruses are thought to cause illnesses. There seems to be a necessary connection between such events, so that kicking a soccer ball will always cause it to move, and boiling an egg will always cause it to cook (under the appropriate conditions), and so on. So nature seems to be uniform: Certain types of events that caused certain other types of events in the past will continue to cause those other certain types of events in the future. On the basis of this belief, scientists formulate general laws, stating for instance that the freezing point of water will remain in the future what it has been in the past. However, Hume denied that the belief that events necessarily cause another (and the belief in the uniformity of nature) is based on reason. Consider when one billiard ball hits another. It looks as if the first ball's striking the other causes the second ball to move. But it is not logically necessary that the second ball will move upon being struck by the first: it is not a logical contradiction to suppose that it won't. In addition, our past experience of billiard balls also does not tell us that the ball will move in the future upon being struck. By Hume's lights, it is a mistake to argue that because the ball moved in the past when struck it will move again in the future when struck. It is a mistake because what is wanted is a justification for thinking that nature is uniform. To say that nature was uniform in the past and therefore will be uniform in the future is just to *assume* the very thing we want to prove (the uniformity of nature).

Hume's point was not that a billiard ball would not move when struck. Of course, he believed it would. His point was that the belief that there is a necessary connection between types of events (such as the event of one ball striking the other and the event of a ball moving) is not based on reason. Rather, according to Hume, our belief that one ball will move when struck by another is based on habit, or custom. We have seen one ball move when struck by another so often that we have seen a constant conjunction of events (that is, one event [the ball moving] constantly follows another [the ball being struck]). This constant conjunction gives rise to our belief that there is a necessary connection between the events. But the belief is a matter of custom, not of reason. Hume did not think there was anything wrong with this custom; in fact, he thought a belief in causes—and in general, a belief in the uniformity of nature—was necessary. It was not a good idea, he noted, to throw one-self out a window (even if one's belief that doing so would cause pain is a matter of custom, not reason). Nonetheless, Hume's reasoning has far-reaching consequences. Insofar as science is based on scientific laws and the view that nature is uniform, Hume's reasoning implies that science is based on custom rather than reason. The above problem concerning the uniformity of nature is known as the problem of induction, and Hume's writings have been very influential concerning it.

Hume also wrote about morality. Hume has sometimes been con-sidered a defender of non-cognitivism, the view that statements that express moral judgments (say, "murder is wrong") are neither true nor false; on this view, such statements just do not report on anything fac-tual. However, whether his view is really a version of non-cognitivism is controversial. Hume did regard moral judgments as subjective in the sense that, according to him, they are ultimately based on feelings rather than on reason. In particular, according to Hume, we regard some char-acter traits as virtues because we find them useful or agreeable (they give us pleasure); we judge other traits as morally wrong because we find them disagreeable (we disapprove of them, and the disapproval makes us feel uneasiness, a form of pain). For Hume, this does not mean that reason plays no role at all in moral judgments; a person might believe that capital punishment is morally acceptable because it helps deter people from committing certain kinds of crimes, for instance—so her moral judgment about capital punishment is based in part on her rea-soning about the effects of capital punishment. However, Hume thought that ultimately moral judgments are based on feelings rather than on reason. One argument Hume gave for this claim is that reason alone is not motivating, but moral judgments are. That is, reason alone does not motivate a person to act. Suppose, for instance, a person's reason tells her that lying to a friend will hurt the friend's feelings. That in itself would not motivate one to refrain from lying to her friend; motivation to act (to refrain from lying) requires what Hume called the passions, such as desires, fears, and hopes. In this instance, one might refrain from lying to one's friend out of a desire to spare the friend's feelings and the fear of causing pain. Moral judgments, however, are motivating: if one judges, for example, that lying to one's friends is wrong, in mak-ing that judgment one is motivated not to lie to friends. The moral judg-ment is motivating in a way that reason alone is not. What this shows,

Hume thought, was that moral judgments cannot be based on reason alone. Reason, he said, "is and ought to be the slave of the passions."

In addition, Hume thought, we cannot infer just from statements about what *is* the case statements about what *ought* to be the case. Consider, for instance, the fact that many people enjoy watching television. That is what *is* the case—it is just a matter of fact that many people enjoy watching television. However, just because many people enjoy watching television does not mean they *ought* to watch television. There seems to be no logical connection between the statement about what *is* the case— that many people enjoy watching television—and the moral claim that people *ought* to watch television. The general idea here is often put like this: you cannot derive an *ought* from an *is*. In other words, we cannot logically deduce what is moral or immoral just on the basis of claims about facts. Just because something *is* the case does not mean that something or another *ought* to be the case.

Although Hume believed that moral judgments are based on feelings rather than on reason, Hume did not regard moral judgments as arbitrary or groundless. Rather, he thought that there are some character traits (the natural virtues) for which people instinctively have feelings of approval or disapproval; the moral judgments of these traits are rooted in human nature itself. By nature, for instance, people disapprove of pointless, wanton cruelty. Approval of other character traits (artificial virtues, such as justice) is based more on convention or social rules. However, even in these cases, according to Hume, the approval is ultimately related to finding traits agreeable or useful. Of course, Hume was aware that people do sometimes disagree about moral matters. Sometimes such disagreements are rooted in disagreements about related empirical facts, and they can be resolved if people come to agree about those facts. In addition, people might disagree about moral matters because people sometimes have a biased view in favor of themselves or their own interests (for instance, a person might be less inclined to view cheating unfavorably if she herself stands to benefit by cheating).

Hume's writings in the philosophy of religion have also been very influential. Hume was critical of what is called the design argument (or teleological argument) for the existence of God. According to this argument, there are things in nature that are so orderly that they must have been designed; indeed, the universe as a whole is so orderly that it must have been designed. The parts of the universe are complex and seem to fit together; the orbits of the planets, for instance, theoretically could be quite different than what they are, such that they collide with each other from time to time, but they do not. In addition, features of the universe seem to work toward some function. For instance, plants store energy from the Sun in the complex process of photosynthesis in order to make food for themselves; the different parts of the plants work in complex ways in order to fulfill this function. According to the argument, such order could not have come about merely as the result of random chance; rather, the most reasonable explanation for the orderly nature of the universe is that someone (or something) designed the universe, and that someone (or something) is God. In short, the orderliness of things shows that God exists.

A famous version of this argument came from the 18th-century clergyman William Paley, who argued that nature is "more wonderfully organized than the most subtle human contrivance." Paley's famous analogy was that the world is like a watch and God is a watchmaker. Imagine, he said, that we were out in nature and we came upon a watch. The watch seems to be complex, that is, made up of many different parts; they seem to work together, that is, if any of the parts were missing, the watch would not function; they seem to be purposive, that is, they seem to work together to accomplish some goal, etc. Is it not much more likely and reasonable to assume that the watch had a watchmaker than that it just happened to come about? Similarly, Paley thought, is it not much more likely and reasonable that the universe also has a designer, rather than that it just happened to have the orderly features that it does?

Paley defended his specific universe/watch analogy after Hume's time; however, the design argument had its defenders well before Paley and during Hume's own time. Hume was not impressed by the design argument, nor by the analogies of the kind Paley offered. When a person comes upon a house, Hume noted, it is likely we will conclude that the house had a builder. This seems reasonable enough: after all, we have had much experience in witnessing, directly or indirectly, the building of houses by people. Most of us have likely seen houses in the process of being built, perhaps known people who have helped to build them, and known people who have themselves known people who built houses. Moreover, we have never known a house not to have a builder—we have never known a house simply to have sprung up, wholly formed and as if of its own accord. In Humean terms, we can say that we have experienced a constant conjunction of events: people building houses and the consequent completion of houses. (Remember, that is what it means, according to Hume, to say that one kind of event causes another: that we have experienced a constant conjunction of those kinds of events.)

So far this seems uncontroversial. The difficulty, according to Hume, lies in the attempt to extend this reasoning to the building (design and creation) of the universe. In the case of houses, long experience has taught us to correlate houses with builders. That is, we infer that humans designed and built a particular house because of past experience, but we have no such experience when it comes to the design and creation of an entire universe. If to say that one event caused another (as a human architect and builder causes the building of a house) is just to say that there is a constant conjunction of events, then there seems to be no basis on which to claim that a designer (such as God) caused the design and creation of the universe; after all, we have no experience at all of creations of universes, let alone experience of a constant conjunction of events when it comes to universes. Of course, Paley and other defenders of the design argument can concede that we have no such experience, but argue that we can reason by analogy: If a watch or a house has certain features and it is reasonable to conclude that someone designed them, and if the universe has certain features, it is reasonable to conclude that someone (God) designed the universe. Hume's point, however, is that this is not a very good analogy. This is because a house (or a watch) is quite different from a universe. A house, for instance, is quite a finite thing—compared to the universe, for the most part houses simply do not last very long. A house, compared to the universe, is also a fairly simple thing; though a modern house has plumbing and wiring systems, in addition to its simple physical structure to keep it from collapsing, it does not seem to have anywhere near the complexity of the universe, with its vast array of different kinds of things, from the functioning of cells to the creation of oceans and continents. A house seems to have a fairly simple function: to keep its inhabitants warm, safe, and dry. But it seems much more difficult to infer what the function of the entire universe might be. Given such differences between a house and a universe, Hume thought that whatever similarities exist between a house and the universe, they did not at all justify the conclusion that a universe (like a house) must have a designer. Presumably he would have made similar arguments against Paley's watch/universe analogy. An argument by analogy works only insofar as there are strong and relevant similarities between the two things being compared and an absence of relevant differences. By these criteria, in Hume's view, analogies such as the house/universe analogy were not a good one. So, they do not prove the existence of a divine designer—that is, the existence of God.

Immanuel Kant

Immanuel Kant (1724–1804) is one of a handful of towering figures in philosophy. He wrote widely on topics such as epistemology, metaphysics, ethics, aesthetics, and religion, and few philosophers have been so influential. Kant was born in Königsberg, a town in East Prussia, and lived there all his life. His parents were Lutheran Christians of a strict kind. At the University of Königsberg, Kant studied philosophy, classics, theology, and physics, working for several years as a private tutor after graduating. In 1755, he became a lecturer at the University of Königsberg, where he was paid by student fees rather than by salary. In 1770, Kant was appointed a professor at the university. He published his most important philosophical works in his 50s and 60s. Kant never married and lived a life of famously regular habits; it was said his daily walks were so punctual that other residents could set their clocks by them. He was a popular teacher and a sociable person, enjoying many friendships and said to be an excellent conversationalist. Despite the difficulty of his works, Kant achieved renown as a philosopher during his own lifetime, and his work continues to be widely read and discussed today.

In his view of knowledge, Kant can be understood as providing a synthesis of empiricism (according to which knowledge is ultimately based on experience) and rationalism (according to which reason plays a more important role in acquiring knowledge than experience). Kant considered what makes experience possible in the first place. Plainly we experience—we have sensations, see physical objects, and do things with them, for instance. But what makes this possible? Put another way, what are the conditions for the possibility of experience? In describing

183

Portrait of Immanuel
Kant in 1775 *(Painting by
J. G. Becker)*

the nature and limits of knowledge, Kant called his arguments transcendental in the sense that they transcend—go beyond—discussion of
the objects of experience by focusing on what makes experience possible
to begin with.

The key insight in Kant's reasoning is the idea that, rather than our
knowledge conforming to objects, objects conform to our knowledge.
To see what this means, consider that on an ordinary view, we experience what we do because objects in the world produce in us certain
experiences. For example, one sees a red cup because the red cup produces in us the sensation of a red cup. But suppose, Kant thought, we see
the red cup in part because the cup conforms to *how* we know: Rather
than passively perceiving the cup, the mind actively structures how we
experience the cup. It is in this sense that objects conform to our knowledge: What we know depends on how the mind structures experience.

According to Kant, that the mind structures experience is what makes experience possible in the first place. For example, we experience what we experience in time and space. But, for Kant, space and time do not absolutely exist out there independent of the mind. Rather, the mind orders experience such that we always experience what we experience in space and time. Empiricists had argued that we acquire the idea of space through experience, by encountering objects outside of ourselves. In contrast, Kant argued, that we encounter objects outside of ourselves presupposes the notion of space: if we did not have the notion of space already, we would not experience objects as outside ourselves in the first place. So the idea of space is something the mind brings to experience, rather than something we encounter in experience. Similarly, the idea of time is something the mind brings to experience, rather than encounters in experience.

That the mind structures experience in terms of space and time explains how it is possible to experience sensible objects (that is, objects perceived through the senses). In addition, Kant thought, what explains understanding and knowledge of such objects is that the mind structures experience using certain a priori concepts (concepts independent of experience). These concepts are concepts the mind actively brings to experience; it is only because the mind organizes experience by using these concepts that we can make sense of what we experience. So, without them, knowledge is not possible. Kant called these concepts categories. To show that we experience objects only through the categories, Kant again considered what is necessary for experience in the first place. It seems that we cannot experience objects as objects unless we have the concept of object. But, according to Kant, one cannot have the concept of object unless one also has the categories. In other words, the very concept of object involves certain a priori concepts. For example, the concept of object requires the concept of substance, the concept of something permanent (a cup, say, is a permanent object in the sense that it does not flicker in and out of existence even when it undergoes change; even painted blue, for instance, a once-red cup is the *same* cup, just colored differently). When we make judgments about the objects we experience, Kant argued, we do so according to certain logical forms of the mind, and we always use the categories to do so.

An important point in all this is that Kant sides neither with rationalism nor empiricism. According to Kant, it is a mistake to suppose that all knowledge is based strictly on experience. This is because knowledge requires the application of categories, and the mind itself applies the categories. So the mind does not begin as a blank tablet (as Locke argued), passively receiving information via the five senses. Empiricists were wrong to think that it does. But, Kant thought, it is also a mistake to suppose that knowledge is based on reason alone. This is because knowledge requires that judgments (which involve categories) be applied to something: specifically, the objects of experience. In other words, the concepts themselves do not provide knowledge but merely a way of structuring experience. What we have knowledge of are the objects of experience (that is, of the things we experience). So, without sense experience—without perception—the concepts are empty, for they have nothing to apply to. But without categories, sense experience is blind, because we need the categories in order to experience.

An important component of Kant's thought is that the categories apply *only* to the objects of experience. That is, they apply only to phenomena, the objects of perception—what we perceive through senses. Phenomena are contrasted with noumena, the objects of thought. Noumena are entities beyond the five senses: One can think about them, but one can never see, feel, hear, smell, or taste them. In Kant's work, noumena are things as they actually are, independently of how they are perceived, while phenomena are the appearances of things (Kant uses appearances broadly, to include all perceptions, not just what one sees). For instance, a person might perceive an orange as round, orange-colored, and tart tasting. That is how the orange appears; the perceived shape, color, and taste of the orange are phenomena. Now consider the orange independently of how it is perceived, what the orange is in itself regardless of how it looks, feels, or tastes to anyone. That is the noumenon of the orange. Because the categories apply to phenomena, Kant believed that noumena are unknowable. Put another way, it is impossible for us to have knowledge of things in themselves, independent of how we perceive them. Knowledge, then, is confined to phenomena—the appearances of things.

Kant's views also had implications for the nature of the self. What we experience seems to be unified—it fits together as one. For instance, when a person lifts a rose to her nose and smells it, she experiences as one experience the scent of the rose, the feel of the rose, and the look of the rose. According to Kant, that experience is unified is possible only because the self is unified. So, the self is not just a collection of experiences (contrary to the view of David Hume). Of particular note here is Kant's concept of the transcendental ego. *Ego* is Latin for "self," so the transcendental ego is a kind of self. It is a transcendental self in the sense that it is a necessary condition for experience. So, it is not something that we encounter in experience. Rather, the transcendental ego is what makes experience possible in the first place; in that sense it transcends (goes beyond) experience. In addition, the transcendental ego also makes knowledge possible.

Consider that experience involves many different perceptions throughout time. For example, suppose on a trip in the desert, a person sees a cactus, a lizard, and a wild burro and feels happy at one time and tired at another. When a person experiences these various perceptions, those perceptions all belong to the same self—it is the *same* self that sees the cactus at one time and the wild burro at another, feels happy at one time and tired at another. This self is the transcendental ego. We do not actually experience the transcendental ego, according to Kant; we do not even know anything about it except that it is necessary for experience and knowledge. To see why one knows nothing more of the transcendental ego, consider that one is never aware of a single permanent subject when mentally looking inward at one's self. Rather, all one is aware of is a particular perception at any given time, such as the sensation of being happy at one time and the sensation of feeling tired at another. The self that one is aware of at such times, the self one experiences upon looking inward, is the empirical self. But it is not the transcendental ego—the transcendental ego is the self that is the subject of *all* these perceptions throughout time. It is a unified self that experiences them all. Kant called the intellectual consciousness of one's unified self apperception, or the unity of apperception. It is intellectual consciousness in the sense that is thought, not experienced empirically. (The transcendental ego is also known as the transcendental subject, because it is the unified subject of experience—that is, *it* is what has experience.)

The transcendental ego makes experience (and knowledge) possible by synthesizing one's various perceptions; it organizes perceptions using the categories. This is why it is possible for us to experience objects as *objects*, rather than as a hodgepodge of sensations. For instance, one typically perceives a cactus as a cactus, not as an unconnected stream of sensations such as the color of the cactus, its size, its shape, and its needles. In general, one's sensations are connected, or unified, such that we perceive single objects.

In his book *Critique of Pure Reason,* Kant attempted to answer the question of whether synthetic a priori judgments are possible. A synthetic a priori judgment is a judgment that is knowable independent of experience (so, one can know it just by using one's reason) but whose content goes beyond the information contained in the subject of the judgment. To understand this, consider that an analytic judgment is a judgment whose content is contained in the subject of the judgment. For instance, the statement *triangles have three sides* is analytic because what it says is contained in the subject of the sentence. By contrast, a synthetic a priori judgment says something more than what is contained in the subject of the judgment. For instance, *rivers are cold* is synthetic, as it is not part of the definition of rivers that they are cold. If the judgment that rivers were cold were knowable a priori, *rivers are cold* would express a synthetic a priori judgment (in fact, however, it does not seem to be knowable a priori).

Whether synthetic a priori judgments are possible is controversial. Kant believed that they were (in particular, he thought that mathematical judgments and general statements in physics are synthetic a priori). The key to this view is Kant's claim that the mind organizes experience according to the categories. Consider, for example, the judgments in geometry. By its nature, geometry is about space. Now the possibility of experience presupposes the concept of space; so, we have the concept of space prior to experience. Geometrical judgments about space, then, are a priori. But they are also synthetic, Kant believed (roughly, they are not just a matter of definitions). So, geometrical judgments about space are synthetic a priori; given that we do make such judgments, synthetic a priori judgments are possible.

In general, Kant thought that synthetic a priori judgments are possible in mathematics and science. Another example regards the concept of cause. David Hume had famously argued that we experience no necessary connection between kinds of events (such as a connection between striking a match and the igniting of fire) and that we believe certain kinds of events follow other kinds of events because we have become accustomed to seeing those events occur at about the same time, not because we have reasoned that there is a necessary connection between those events. For instance, we commonly believe that fire produces heat, and that if fire has produced heat in the past, it will continue to produce heat in the future (that is, whenever there is fire, fire will produce heat). But such a belief, for Hume, is not based on reason but rather on our past experience that fire has been accompanied by heat. In general, Hume argued, the belief that certain kinds of events cause other kinds of events and that the future will be like the past is based simply on custom (what we have gotten used to experiencing). In contrast, Kant argued that laws of nature, including laws regarding causality, are valid; they are not simply based on custom. This is because, for Kant, the concept of causality (events causing other events) is one of the a priori categories by which the mind organizes experience. So, it is not possible *not* to understand what we experience without the concept of cause; our minds always structure experience using this concept (among others).

Although Kant believed that synthetic a priori judgments are possible in mathematics and science, Kant rejected the view that they were possible in metaphysics. Rather, according to Kant, metaphysical illusions arise when we try to apply the categories to what is beyond experience. For instance, Kant rejected traditional arguments for the existence of God. (However, Kant argued that belief in God serves an important purpose, even if God's existence cannot be proved through pure reason.)

Kant's Ethics

In ethics, Kant offered a deontological view, that is, a view focused on duty and moral law. Kant regarded morality as a matter of reason; for him, what is moral is not just a matter of personal preferences or what God commands. In addition, Kant believed that humans, because they are rational and autonomous, are uniquely valuable, and that as rational beings we can reason out what is the moral thing to do. According to Kant, the only thing that is unconditionally good is a good will. So, an action that is morally good is an action performed out of a sense of duty, rather than from what a person desires to do. For instance, keeping a promise is morally good if it is done out of duty to moral law. This does not mean that it is morally wrong to keep a promise because one wants to do so, but it does mean that such an action is not morally good in the way that keeping a promise from duty is.

Painting of *Kant and Friends at Table* from the early 20th century *(Emil Doerstling)*

But what ought one, morally, to do? Kant's answer to this is that one ought to follow the categorical imperative. A categorical imperative is an imperative (a command) that applies without exception, regardless of anyone's goals; it applies categorically. So, everyone ought to behave according to the categorical imperative. This contrasts with a hypothetical imperative, a command that depends on a person's particular goals—for instance, if one wishes to eat a banana, one should buy one at the store (the command to buy a banana at the store depends on the desire to eat a banana; without that desire or a similar one, the command does not apply). Kant believed that the moral law was a categorical imperative and, because it is based on reason and because humans are rational, autonomous beings, the moral law is a principle we can freely impose on ourselves.

Kant gave several different versions of the categorical imperative, which he believed were equivalent to each other. Perhaps his most famous version is, "Act only according to that maxim by which you can at the same time will that it should become a universal law." By maxim, Kant meant principle or rule. According to this version of the categorical imperative, one should behave only according to principles that one can rationally will that everyone should follow in similar circumstances. That is, one should act according to rules that are universalizable. Suppose, for example, someone must decide whether to promise to pay back money she knows she cannot actually repay. To see whether making such a promise is morally acceptable, she must determine what rule she would be following in making that promise. Then she must decide whether she could consistently will that everyone in similar circumstances follow that same rule. If she made a false promise, it looks as if the rule she would be following would be something like, *When you desire a loan but cannot repay it, make a false promise to repay the loan.* However, by Kant's lights, this rule is not universalizable: One cannot rationally will that everyone should follow the same rule in similar circumstances. To see why this is so, consider what would happen if everyone followed this rule. Eventually people would stop believing promises made to them about repaying loans. If people stopped believing promises, people would also stop making promises, because there would be no point in making promises if no one believed them. So if everyone followed the rule *When you desire a loan but cannot repay it, make a false promise to repay the loan,* the very practice of promise-keeping would be destroyed. This contradicts the reason for making the false promise in the first place: to take advantage of the practice of promise-keeping. For Kant, then, one cannot rationally will that everyone follow such a rule. Because the rule is not universalizable, it would be a violation of the categorical imperative to make the false promise to pay back the loan. So one has a moral duty to refrain from making a false promise, not just in this instance, but in *all* instances. Kant called duties that one always has an obligation to follow, such as the duty not to make false promises, perfect duties. Another example of a perfect duty, according to Kant, is the duty not to lie. So, for Kant, moral behavior involves universal moral rules that should not ever be broken.

Another famous version of the categorical imperative is, "Act so that you treat humanity, whether in your own person or in that of another, always as an end and never as a means only." To treat someone as an end is contrasted with treating someone as a means only, that is, only as a tool for some purpose or other. For example, to spend time with a person only for the sake of borrowing money from her, or only for one's own sexual pleasure, are instances of treating a person as a means only. Kant believed that humans are intrinsically valuable: That is, they are valuable in and of themselves, not just because they are useful for fulfilling some purpose or another. He also believed that humans are uniquely valuable because of the human capacity for rationality and autonomy. According to Kant, because humans have these traits, they have a certain dignity, and treating people as a means only wrongly ignores that dignity. To treat a person as an end, then, is to treat her as valuable in and of herself, respecting her dignity, rationality, and autonomy. This does not mean that one cannot ever morally treat a person as a means, as when one uses the services of a clerk in order to buy groceries, say; it just means that one cannot ever morally treat as a person as a means only.

One important criticism of Kant's ethics, due to Elizabeth Anscombe, is that it seems possible to describe the same action in different ways, so that the same action can be said to be following different rules. For example, making a particular false promise might be said to follow the rule, *Make a false promise when it is convenient,* but it might also be said to follow the rule, *Make a false promise when doing so will save an innocent person's life.* Whereas the first rule might not be universalizable, perhaps the second one is. This suggests that Kant's universalizability principle is not a very good guide for how one should behave morally (whether an action violates the categorical imperative depends on how the action is described, and it is not always clear how an action should be described). Another criticism is that sometimes absolute moral rules conflict, and in those cases it is not clear how one should behave.

Concluding Discussion Questions

1. When you want to move your body, you are usually able to do so. For example, when you want to run and make a decision to run, it seems that your body breaks into a run. How would Descartes explain this? How would Leibniz explain this?
2. When you strike a match against a rough surface, you expect a fire to ignite. How would David Hume explain this? How would Immanuel Kant explain this?
3. For John Locke, what does it mean to say that all knowledge is based on experience? For example, what is meant by experience? Do you think Locke is right? How would Descartes respond to Locke's claim?
4. Why did Berkeley think his view about the nature of reality was consistent with common sense?
5. What is life like in the state of nature, according to John Locke? What is it like according to Thomas Hobbes? What is it like according to Jean-Jacques Rousseau? Why would people ever choose to leave the state of nature?
6. Why do you think some people regarded Spinoza's views on God as heretical? Why might Spinoza *not* have regarded those views as heretical?

Further Reading

Ariew, Roger, and Eric Watkins. *Modern Philosophy: An Anthology of Primary Sources.* Indianapolis, Ind.: Hackett, 2009.

Berkeley, George. *Principles of Human Knowledge and Three Dialogues.* Edited by Howard Robinson. Oxford: Oxford University Press, 2009.

Descartes, René. *Meditations on First Philosophy.* Whitefish, Mont.: Kessinger Publishing, 2004.

Hobbes, Thomas. *Leviathan.* Edited by J. C. A. Gaskin. Oxford: Oxford University Press, 2009.

Hume, David. *Enquiries Concerning Human Understanding and Concerning the Principles of Morals.* Edited by L. A. Selby-Bigge and P. H. Nidditch. Oxford: Clarendon Press, 1978.

Kant, Immanuel. *Critique of Pure Reason.* Edited by Marcus Weigelt and translated by Max Muller. New York: Penguin Classics, 2008.

———. *The Groundwork of the Metaphysics of Morals.* Edited by H. J. Paton. New York: Harper Perennial Modern Classics, 2009.

Leibniz, Gottfried Wilhelm. *Philosophical Writings.* London: Everyman Paperbacks, 1995.

Locke, John. *An Essay Concerning Human Understanding.* Edited by Peter H. Nidditch. Oxford: Oxford University Press, 1975.

Scruton, Roger. *A Short History of Modern Philosophy.* London: Routledge, 2001.

Spinoza, Baruch. *The Collected Works of Spinoza.* Edited and translated by Edwin Curley. Princeton: Princeton University Press, 1985.

Thomson, Garrett. *Bacon to Kant: An Introduction to Modern Philosophy.* Lang Grove, Ill.: Waveland Press, 2001.

Glossary

analytic/synthetic   an analytic statement is a statement that is true or false either by definition or because of the structure of the statement. A synthetic statement is a statement whose truth or falsity does not depend only on definition or the structure of the statement. According to Kant, an analytic statement is a statement that says something already contained in the subject of the sentence, whereas a synthetic statement says more. For instance, *Bachelors are unmarried* is analytic because the statement just spells out information already contained in the subject of the sentence. By contrast, *Bachelors are handsome* is synthetic; it says more than what is contained in the subject.

a priori/a posteriori   a priori literally means "from the former" in Latin; describes what is known or claimed independently of sensory experience (experience via the five senses). For example, mathematical knowledge, such as knowledge that 3 + 2 = 5, is often considered a priori (it does not seem to be necessary to make observations of the world to know mathematical truths). A posteriori literally means "from the latter" in Latin; describes what is known or claimed based on sensory experience; much scientific knowledge, for instance, is considered a posteriori knowledge because it is based on observation of the natural world.

cogito ergo sum   Latin for "I think, therefore I am." The phrase is associated with René Descartes, the father of modern philosophy, who argued that he knew he existed because he was thinking. Descartes used the supposed fact of his own existence as a foundation for all his knowledge.

determinism   the view that all that occurs does so as a result of (is determined by) past events; according to determinism, given the sequence of past events, certain future events must necessarily occur as a consequence of those past events. Philosophers disagree regarding whether determinism is consistent with the possibility of free will; Thomas Hobbes argued that it is.

dualism   in philosophy of mind, the view that mind is nonphysical and the body is physical. Substance dualism holds that mind is a nonphysical substance, body is a physical substance, and that neither is reducible to the other. Property dualism holds that mind consists of, or has, nonphysical properties, and body has physical properties, and that neither mental properties nor physical properties are reducible to the other. Descartes defended substance dualism.

empiricism   the view that experience plays a more important role in acquiring knowledge than reason; experience via the five senses is often emphasized, although experience can also include experience of one's own mind. Empiricism is contrasted with rationalism.

epistemology   the philosophical study of knowledge. Topics in epistemology include the analysis of the concept of knowledge, the source of knowledge, skepticism (whether we can or do have knowledge), epistemic justification, perception, and rationality.

esse est percipi   Latin for "to be is to be perceived." The phrase is associated with George Berkeley, who argued that all that exists are minds and ideas (so, the ordinary objects of experience, such as trees and tables, depend for their existence on a perceiving mind; they are real, but they are mind-dependent).

ethics   the philosophical study of right action and moral values. Traditionally ethics is divided into three subareas: metaethics (concerning the nature of moral values and the language used to express moral judgments), normative ethics (which concerns theories about what right action is or how one ought to live), and applied ethics (which applies normative ethics to particular, practical issues, such as abortion and capital punishment).

general will   a term the French philosopher Jean-Jacques Rousseau used for the will of an entire political community; the general will promotes what will benefit the community as a whole, not just what will benefit particular individuals within a community or individual groups of people within a community.

idea   in modern philosophy, idea is often used to refer to any content of a person's mind, including thoughts, images, sensations, memories, and beliefs. Philosophers such as John Locke and George Berkeley believed that people are directly aware only of ideas, not of objects external to the people themselves.

idealism the view that reality is mind-dependent; for instance, George Berkeley defended the idealist view that all that exists are minds and ideas.

induction, problem of the problem of knowing whether the future will be like the past—for instance, that kinds of events that have caused other kinds of events in the past will continue to do so in the future; associated with David Hume in particular.

innate idea a concept that is somehow present in a person's mind from birth.

materialism the view that all that exists is made of matter (so, materialism denies the existence of nonmaterial things such as ghosts).

metaphysics the philosophical study of fundamental concepts and aspects of reality; topics in metaphysics that are prominent in modern philosophy include whether reality is composed of one fundamental kind of stuff (monism), two kinds of stuff (dualism), or multiple kinds of stuff (pluralism); whether reality is essentially physical or mental or neither; the relation between the mind and the body; and free will and determinism, among other topics.

monad according to Leibniz, the fundamental constituents of reality (everything that exists consists of monads); monads are simple, nonmaterial substances with a life-force. Monads have no effect on each other but the changes they undergo occur in harmony with the changes of other monads as a result of God arranging it that way.

monism the view that reality is composed of one fundamental kind of stuff. Spinoza, for example, argued for the monistic view that all reality consists of one substance, God or Nature.

rationalism the view that reason plays a more important role in acquiring knowledge than experience, especially experience via the five senses; contrasted with empiricism.

scholasticism a philosophical movement in the medieval era. A dominant concern of scholastic philosophy was to reconcile the teachings of Christianity with the thought of the ancient Greek philosopher

Aristotle. In the 15th century, the prominence of scholasticism gave way to modern philosophy.

social contract theory   in political philosophy, the view that a government somehow derives its legitimacy from the free and voluntary consent of the people it governs (as though there is a contract between a legitimate government and the people). In ethics, social contract theory is the view that morality consists of rules that rational, self-interested people would agree upon.

state of nature   the state of human life without government, that is, the state that people live in when they have not formed political institutions. The concept of the state of nature is associated with social contract theory, such as with the work of John Locke and Thomas Hobbes, who imagined what life would be like without government as a way of better understanding the nature and appropriate function of government.

tabula rasa   Latin for "blank tablet"; according to John Locke, at birth the mind is like a blank tablet in the sense that it has no innate ideas but instead acquires all ideas from experience.

Key People

Bacon, Francis (1561–1626) *an empiricist who argued in favor of a rigorous form of induction (the drawing of general conclusions on the basis of many individual observations) and the social nature of science.*

In the following passage, Bacon stresses a new kind of induction as a method in science. Such a method would involve noting the different individual circumstances in which a given phenomenon occurs and when it does not occur, as well as in what degrees it occurs; on the basis of such observations, Bacon thought scientists could hypothesize regarding the essential nature of the phenomenon in question.

> . . . the induction which is to be available for the discovery and demonstration of sciences and arts, must analyze nature by proper rejections and exclusions; and then, after a sufficient number of negatives, come to a conclusion on the affirmative instances . . . But in order to furnish this induction or demonstration well and duly for its work, very many things are to be provided which no mortal has yet thought of . . . and this induction must be used not only to discover axioms, but also in the formation of notions. And it is in this induction that our chief hope lies.

> [From Francis Bacon. *Novum Organum.* In *The Major Achievements of Science,* edited by A. E. E. McKenzie. Ames: Iowa State University Press, 1960.]

Berkeley, George (1685–1753) *The Irish empiricist philosopher who argued that all that exists are minds and ideas.*

In the passage below, Berkeley argues that ordinary objects (such as tables) exist but that they are nothing but ideas and therefore dependent for their existence on a perceiving mind. We experience only ideas, according to Berkeley, but ideas are mind-dependent.

> The table I write on I say exists, that is, I see and feel it; and if I were out of my study I should say it existed—meaning thereby that if I was in my study I might perceive it, or that some other

spirit actually does perceive it. There was an odor, that is, it was smelled; there was a sound, that is to say, it was heard; a color or figure, and it was perceived by sight or touch. This is all that I can understand by these and the like expressions. For as to what is said of the absolute existence of unthinking things without any relation to their being perceived, that seems perfectly unintelligible. Their *esse* is *percipi,* nor is it possible they should have any existence out of the minds or thinking things which perceive them.

It is indeed an opinion strangely prevailing amongst men that houses, mountains, rivers, and, in a word, all sensible objects have an existence, natural or real, distinct from their being perceived by the understanding. But with how great an assurance and acquiescence soever this principle may be entertained in the world, yet whoever shall find in his heart to call it in question may, if I mistake not, perceive it to involve a manifest contradiction. For what are the forementioned objects but the things we perceive by sense? And what do we perceive besides our own ideas or sensations? And is it not plainly repugnant that any one of these, or any combination of should exist unperceived?

[George Berkeley. *A Treatise Concerning the Principles of Human Knowledge* in *Works.* Edinburgh: Thomas Nelson, 1710.]

Descartes, René (1596–1650) *French philosopher often called the father of modern philosophy; Descartes reoriented the focus of philosophy to epistemology and defended a rationalist view of knowledge; he thought he could establish a foundation for all knowledge by starting with the certain knowledge that he existed.*

In the passage below, Descartes describes both his methods for acquiring knowledge and expresses his confidence in the power of human reason.

The first [method] was never to accept anything for true which I did not clearly know to be such; that is to say, carefully to avoid precipitancy and prejudice, and to comprise nothing more in my judgment than what was presented to my mind so clearly and distinctly as to exclude all ground of doubt.

The second, to divide each of the difficulties under examination into as many parts as possible, and as might be necessary for its adequate solution.

The third, to conduct my thoughts in such order that, by commencing with objects the simplest and easiest to know, I might ascend by little and little, and, as it were, step by step, to the knowledge of the more complex; assigning in thought a certain order even to those objects which in their own nature do not stand in a relation of antecedence and sequence.

At the last, in every case to make enumerations so complete, and reviews so general, that I might be assured that nothing was omitted.

The long chains of simple and easy reasonings by means of which geometers are accustomed to reach the conclusions of their most difficult demonstrations, had led me to imagine that all things, to the knowledge of which man is competent, are mutually connected in the same way, and that there is nothing so far removed from us as to be beyond our reach, or so hidden that we cannot discover it, provided only we abstain from accepting the false for the true, and always preserve in our thoughts the order necessary for the deduction of one truth from another.

[René Descartes. *The Method, Meditations and Philosophy of Descartes, translated from the Original Texts, with a new introductory Essay, Historical and Critical by John Veitch and a Special Introduction by Frank Sewall.* Washington: M. Walter Dunne, 1901. Available online. URL: http://oll.libertyfund.org/title/1698/142006. Accessed on 2010-03-31.]

Hobbes, Thomas (1588–1679)   *British, empiricist philosopher who believed people were both rational and self-interested and would agree to form a government for the sake of their own security; a materialist, Hobbes believed that all mental activity could be understood in terms of matter in motion.*

In the following passage Hobbes describes the conditions of life without government (the state of nature).

> Hereby it is manifest, that during the time men live *without* a *common power* to *keep them all* in *awe,* they are in that condition which is *called* war; and such a war, as is of every man, against every man. For war, consists not in battle only, or the act of fighting; but in a tract of time, wherein the will to contend by battle is sufficiently known: and therefore the notion of *time,* is to be considered in the nature of war; as it is in the nature of weather. For as the nature of foul weather, lies not in a shower or two of rain; but in an inclination thereto of many days together: so the nature of war, consists not in actual fighting; but in the known disposition thereto, during *all* the time there is no assurance to the contrary. *All* other time is peace.

> Whatsoever therefore is consequent to a time of war, where every man is enemy to every man; the same is consequent to the time, wherein men live without other security, than what their own strength, *and* their own invention shall furnish them withal. In such condition, there is no place for industry; because the fruit thereof is uncertain: *and* consequently no culture of the earth; no navigation, nor use of the commodities that may be imported by sea; no commodious building; no instruments of moving, *and* removing, such things as require much force; no knowledge of the face of the earth; no account of time; no arts; no letters; no society; *and* which is worst of all, continual fear, *and* danger of violent death; *and* the life of man, *solitary, poor, nasty, brutish, and short.*

[Thomas Hobbes. *The English Works of Thomas Hobbes of Malmesbury; Now First Collected and Edited by Sir William Molesworth, Bart.* London: Bohn, 1839–45). 11 vols. Vol. 3. Chapter: *CHAPTER XIII.: of the natural condition of mankind as concerning their felicity, and misery.* Available online. URL: http://oll.libertyfund.org/title/585/89842/2025612. Accessed on 2010-04-06.]

Hume, David (1711–1776)   *Scottish empiricist philosopher famous for expressing skepticism about cause/effect; he argued that we do not experience a necessary connection between cause and effect but expect one kind* *of event to follow another because we have seen those kinds of events occurring together in the past.*

In the following passage, Hume claims that we expect kinds of events to occur together (such as one billiard ball to move when struck by another, or the event of a fire's ignition to produce heat) not because we infer through our reason that there is a connection between such events, but rather because we are in the habit of experiencing those events together.

And it is certain we here advance a very intelligible proposition at least, if not a true one, when we assert that, after the constant conjunction of two objects—heat and flame, for instance, weight and solidity—we are determined by custom alone to expect the one from the appearance of the other. This hypothesis seems even the only one which explains the difficulty, why we draw, from a thousand instances, an inference which we are not able to draw from one instance, that is, in no respect, different from them. Reason is incapable of any such variation. The conclusions which it draws from considering one circle are the same which it would form upon surveying all the circles in the universe. But no man, having seen only one body move after being impelled by another, could infer that every other body will move after a like impulse. All inferences from experience, therefore, are effects of custom, not of reasoning.

Custom, then, is the great guide of human life. It is that principle alone which renders our experience useful to us, and makes us expect, for the future, a similar train of events with those which have appeared in the past. Without the influence of custom, we should be entirely ignorant of every matter of fact beyond what is immediately present to the memory and senses. We should never know how to adjust means to ends, or to employ our natural powers in the production of any effect. There would be an end at once of all action, as well as of the chief part of speculation.

[David Hume. *Enquiries Concerning the Human Understanding and Concerning the Principles of Morals by David Hume.* Edited by L. A. Selby-Bigge, M.A. 2nd ed. Oxford:

Clarendon Press, 1902. Chapter: *SECTION V.: sceptical solution of these doubts.* Available online. URL: http://oll.libertyfund.org/title/341/61956. Accessed on 2010-03-31.]

Kant, Immanuel (1724–1804)   *German philosopher who made what he called the Copernican revolution, arguing that objects conform to our knowledge, rather than knowledge conforming to objects; he believed that the mind structures experience according to certain categories, and therefore he advocated neither rationalism nor empiricism.*

Kant here relates the laws of Nature to how the mind categorizes experience; he claims that experience is possible at all because the mind structures experience according to certain concepts ("categories"). So, for example, because the mind applies the concept of cause *to experience, laws regarding causes are among the laws of Nature (we cannot experience Nature* without *such laws).*

We shall here . . . be simply concerned with experience, and the universal and *à priori* given conditions of its possibility, and thence determine Nature as the complete object of all possible experience. I think it will be understood, that I do not refer to the rules for the observation of a nature already given, which presuppose experience, or how through experience we can arrive at the laws of Nature, for these would not then be laws *à priori,* and would give no pure science of Nature; but how the conditions *à priori* of the possibility of experience are at the same time the sources from which all the universal laws of Nature must be derived.

We must first of all observe then, that, although all the judgments of experience are empirical, i.e., have their ground in the immediate perception of sense, yet on the other hand all empirical judgments are not judgments of experience, but that beyond the empirical, and beyond the given sensuous intuition generally, special conceptions must be superadded, having their origin entirely *à priori* in the pure understanding, under which every perception is primarily subsumed, and by means of which only it can be transformed into experience.

[Immanuel Kant. *Kant's Prolegomena and Metaphysical Foundations of Natural Science.* Translated with a biography and introduction by Ernest Belfort Bax. 2nd rev. ed. London: George Bell and Sons, 1891. Chapter: *THE SECOND PART OF THE MAIN TRANSCENDENTAL PROBLEM. How is pure Natural Science possible?* Available online. URL: http://oll.libertyfund.org/title/361/54872. Accessed on 2010-03-31.]

Leibniz, Wilhem Gottfried (1646–1716)   *German rationalist philosopher who believed the world consists of monads, nonphysical simple substances; he also argued that this world is the best possible of all possible worlds and therefore that everything that happens is ultimately for the best.*

Below Leibniz describes some of the fundamental characteristic of monads.

1. The Monad, of which we shall here speak, is nothing but a simple substance, which enters into compounds. By "simple" is meant "without parts." (Theod. 10.)

2. And there must be simple substances, since there are compounds; for a compound is nothing but a collection or aggregatum of simple things.

3. Now where there are no parts, there can be neither extension nor form [figure] nor divisibility. These Monads are the real atoms of nature and, in a word, the elements of things.

4. No dissolution of these elements need be feared, and there is no conceivable way in which a simple substance can be destroyed by natural means. (Theod. 89.)

5. For the same reason there is no conceivable way in which a simple substance can come into being by natural means, since it cannot be formed by the combination of parts [composition].

6. Thus it may be said that a Monad can only come into being or come to an end all at once; that is to say, it can come into being only by creation and come to an end only by annihilation, while that which is compound comes into being or comes to an end by parts.

7. Further, there is no way of explaining how a Monad can be altered in quality or internally changed by any other created thing; since it is impossible to change the place of anything in it or to conceive in it any internal motion which could be produced, directed, increased or diminished therein, although all this is possible in the case of compounds, in which there are changes among the parts. The Monads have no windows, through which anything could come in or go out. Accidents cannot separate themselves from

substances nor go about outside of them, as the "sensible species" of the Scholastics used to do. Thus neither substance nor accident can come into a Monad from outside.

[Leibniz, Gottfried Wilhelm. *The Monadology and Other Philosophical Writings*. Translated with introduction and notes by Robert Latta. London: Oxford University Press, 1898.]

Locke, John (1632–1704) *British empiricist philosopher who believed there are no innate ideas and that all concepts are derived from experience; in political philosophy, Locke advocated a democratic form of government within the context of social contract theory.*

Below, Locke succinctly describes one of his main theses: that all knowledge is ultimately based on experience, in the sense that all materials for knowledge (all ideas) are derived from experience. By experience, Locke meant experience not only of the empirical world but also experience of the workings of one's own mind.

> *All ideas come from sensation or reflection.* Let us then suppose the mind to be, as we say, white paper, void of *all* characters, without any *ideas;* how *comes* it to be furnished? Whence *comes* it by that vast store which the busy and boundless fancy of man has painted on it, with an almost endless variety? Whence has it *all* the materials of reason and knowledge? To this I answer, in one word, *from* experience; in *all* that our knowledge is founded, and *from* that it ultimately derives itself. Our observation employed either about external sensible objects, or about the internal operations of our minds, perceived and reflected on by ourselves, is that which supplies our understandings with *all* the materials of thinking. These two are the fountains of knowledge, *from* whence *all* the *ideas* we have, or can natu*rally* have, do spring.

[John Locke. *The Works of John Locke in Nine Volumes.* London: Rivington, 1824 12th ed. Vol. 1. Chapter: *CHAP. I.: Of Ideas in general, and their Origin.* Available online. URL: http://oll.libertyfund.org/title/761/80718/1923200. Accessed on 2010-03-31.]

Rousseau, Jean-Jacques (1712–1778) *French political thinker famous especially for his work* The Social Contract. *Rousseau advocated a form of government in which each person within the political community submits himself to the general will, the will of the political community as a whole.*

Illustration of Jean-Jacques Rousseau from the 1889 edition of *Grands hommes et grands faits de la Révolution française (1789–1804)* (*Illustration by H. Rousseau; engraving by E. Thomas*)

The following selection is from Rousseau's *The Social Contract* and contains some of Rousseau's most famous remarks.

> Man is born free, and everywhere he is in chains. Many a one believes himself the master of others, and yet he is a greater slave than they. How has this change come about? I do not know. What can render it legitimate? I believe that I can settle this question.

If I considered only force and the results that proceed from it, I should say that so long as a people is compelled to obey and does obey, it does well; but that, so soon as it can shake off the yoke and does shake it off, it does better; for, if men recover their freedom by virtue of the same right by which it was taken away, either they are justified in resuming it, or there was no justification for depriving them of it. But the social order is a sacred right which serves as a foundation for all others. This right, however, does not come from nature. It is therefore based on conventions. The question is to know what these conventions are . . .

. . . The problem is to find a form of association which will defend and protect with the whole common force the person and goods of each associate, and in which each, while uniting himself with all, may still obey himself alone, and remain as free as before. This is the fundamental problem of which the social contract provides the solution.

[Jean-Jacques Rousseau. *Ideal Empires and Republics. Rousseau's Social Contract, More's Utopia, Bacon's New Atlantis, Campanella's City of the Sun,* with an Introduction by Charles M. Andrews. (Washington: M. Walter Dunne, 1901). Chapter: *CHAPTER I.: Subject of the First Book.* Available online. URL: http://oll.libertyfund.org/title/2039/145421.]

Spinoza, Baruch (1632–1677)   *Dutch rationalist philosopher; Spinoza painstakingly argued for the monist view that all that exists is God or Nature, and that everything that occurs does so necessarily from the nature of God.*

Here Spinoza asserts the proposition that all that exists must exist in God, because God is the one substance; his view of God, as the text indicates, is not the traditional God of the Judeo-Christian tradition.

Prop. XV. *Whatsoever is, is in God, and without God nothing can be, or be conceived.*

Proof.—Besides God, no substance is granted or can be conceived (by Prop. xiv.), that is (by Def. iii.) nothing which is in itself and is conceived through itself. But modes (by Def. v.)

can neither be, nor be conceived without substance; wherefore they can only be in the divine nature, and can only through it be conceived. But substances and modes form the sum total of existence . . . therefore, without God nothing can be, or be conceived. *Q.E.D.*

Note.—Some assert that God, like a man, consists of body and mind, and is susceptible of passions. How far such persons have strayed from the truth is sufficiently evident from what has been said . . . all who have in anywise reflected on the divine nature deny that God has a body. Of this they find excellent proof in the fact that we understand by body a definite quantity, so long, so broad, so deep, bounded by a certain shape, and it is the height of absurdity to predicate such a thing of God, a being absolutely infinite. But meanwhile by the other reasons with which they try to prove their point, they show that they think corporeal or extended substance wholly apart from the divine nature, and say it was created by God. Wherefrom the divine nature can have been created, they are wholly ignorant; thus they clearly show, that they do not know the meaning of their own words . . . no substance can be produced or created by anything other than itself. Further . . . besides God no substance can be granted or conceived. Hence . . . extended substance is one of the infinite attributes of God.

[Benedict de Spinoza. *The Chief Works of Benedict de Spinoza.* Translated from the Latin, with an introduction by R. H. M. Elwes, vol. 2. De Intellectus Emendatione—Ethica. (Select Letters). Rev. ed. London: George Bell and Sons, 1901). Chapter: PART I.: CONCERNING GOD. Available online. URL: http://oll.libertyfund.org/title/1711/199399. Accessed on 2010-04-13.]

PART III

Continental
Philosophy

Introductory Discussion Questions

1. In what ways are you free, and in what ways are you not free? For example, is a very poor woman free in the same way (or ways) that a very wealthy man is?
2. Suppose God does not exist. Does that mean that there is no basis for morality? In general, what are our values based on? What *should* they be based on?
3. What is more real, your inner experience or the world outside of your experience?
4. Which do you think has greater influence on you, economic conditions or political conditions?
5. We interpret all kinds of things—books, movies, events, other people, etc. Do you think there are facts about the world independent of interpretation? What would make one interpretation better (or worse) than another interpretation?
6. It would seem to be a good thing to be true to yourself in the sense of living according to what you really believe is right and doing so passionately. Do you think this is sufficient for living a good life?

Introduction to Continental Philosophy

The term *continental philosophy* generally refers to the philosophy of the European continent, especially France and Germany, beginning with Immanuel Kant (1724–1804) and continuing to the present day. Continental philosophy is often contrasted with analytic philosophy, the philosophy of England and the United States, beginning roughly with the 20th century and carrying through today. Each of these terms is somewhat rough and ready; there is a wide divergence of views within both analytic philosophy and continental philosophy, and, in addition, the concerns and methods of continental and analytic philosophy somewhat overlap. However, because continental and analytic philosophy are usually contrasted, it also useful to note some of the general differences between them. A few of these are described below.

One way of understanding continental philosophy is to consider its origins, with the work of Kant. In the late 18th century, Kant effected what he called the philosophical Copernican revolution. The point of this revolution was to suppose that objects conform to our knowledge, rather than that knowledge conforms to objects. In other words, Kant argued that we do not passively receive information from the objects we experience—trees and wind and cups of tea and all the ordinary things we experience via our five senses. Rather, the mind organizes experience. For example, the mind brings to experience the concept of cause; it is this that allows us to view a fire at the end of the match as the effect of the match being struck against a rough surface, rather than as a random event, for instance. Much of continental philosophy has been shaped by Kant's revolution and responses to it; in response to Kant, for example, came the movement of German Idealism, as philosophers sought to refine, expand, and in some cases correct Kant's work.

At a broad level, Kant's Copernican revolution influenced the focus of continental philosophy on the subject of experience—that is, the thing (or self) that undergoes experiences. German Idealists construed all of reality as dependent in some way on the self, the subject of experience; phenomenologists studied pure experience and the self as the subject of experience. Existentialists considered the subject of experience in terms of how individuals actually live their lives, in concrete terms. Karl Marx (1818–83) and the critical theorists after him considered the ways in which people (again, subjects of experience) are oppressed, such as through economic, ideological, and cultural conditions. Structuralists considered the structures that govern humans and human experience, such as the self, language, and culture, and philosophers working in hermeneutics (the art and study of interpretation) used the practice of interpretation to enable us to understand ourselves better (among other things).

All of this points to other features notable in continental philosophy. Continental philosophy often focuses, not merely on theory, but on practice as well. For many continental philosophers, the intellectual claims one makes are important not only in an intellectual way, but for their relation to how one actually lives. For example, existential philosophers such as Jean-Paul Sartre (1905–80), Martin Heidegger (1889–1976), and Søren Kierkegaard (1813–55) focused on the individual person's existence. Critical theorists, influenced by Marx, emphasized the study of human societies with the aim of freeing people from what oppresses them. Phenomenologists studied pure experience; Edmund Husserl (1859–1938) did so in the hope that what people actually experience could establish a certain foundation for knowledge.

Along with this, continental philosophers have often been concerned with sociality, that is, the social aspects of human existence. For example, continental philosophers relate knowledge to power relations in human society, noting, for instance, that access to knowledge means access to power and that in this way, claims to knowledge are closely linked to power. Other philosophers, such as in postmodernism and post-structuralism, regarded the self as constituted at least by part by social relations. Put another way, the idea is that who a person is, or what makes a person *that* person, is at least partly constructed by factors such as cultural practices, values, and beliefs (identity is constructed in the sense that it is created artificially; it is not simply given, or appear fully formed at birth, say). As a simple example, a girl's identity in a society that regards females as inferior would differ importantly from a girl's identity in a society that regards females as equal to males. In contrast to this approach emphasizing sociality, analytic philosophy has often (although not always) focused on the analysis of concepts such as the self and knowledge independent of such social factors.

More than analytic philosophy, continental philosophy tends to blur distinctions between philosophy and the social sciences, philosophy and the history of philosophy, and philosophy and literary criticism. Often the concerns of analytic philosophers are very particular: for example, to give an analysis of the concept of knowledge, or right action. In contrast, continental philosophers often begin by considering a bigger picture, first viewing things as a whole rather than in terms of isolated parts. For example, Georg W. F. Hegel (1770–1831), Johann Gottlieb Fichte (1762–1814), and Friedrich Wilhelm Joseph von Schelling (1775–1854) attempted to give accounts of all of reality, incorporating everything. Other continental philosophers, such as Kierkegaard, explicitly did not attempt to systematize; rather, Kierkegaard's concern was broad in the sense of regarding how he ought to live his life.

Hegel and German Idealism

German Idealism is a school of philosophical thought prominent in Germany in the 18th and early 19th centuries. Idealism in philosophy is not the same as idealism as it is usually understood outside philosophy. In a nonphilosophical sense, idealism regards having or working toward high ideals, as when a person seeks perfect justice or beauty. However, in philosophy, idealism is the view that reality is in some way dependent on the mind. (The root of the philosophical term *idealism* is "idea," not "ideal.") Idealism is often contrasted with realism about the objects of ordinary, everyday experience (such as trees and computers), which holds that these objects are not dependent on the mind. German Idealism, then, holds that in some way reality is mind-dependent. German Idealism is associated with Romanticism, an intellectual and cultural movement that grew in part out of a response to the Enlightenment. The Enlightenment had emphasized reason, the individual, and the world as something like a complex machine, behaving mechanically according to natural laws. In response, it was more common for German Idealists and for Romantics to regard the world—and indeed, all of reality—not so much in mechanical terms but rather in organic and holistic terms, as something that grows and develops as a whole. In addition, Romantics tended to focus on emotion, passion, and lived experience rather than on abstract reason.

German Idealists include Johann Gottlieb Fichte (1762–1814), Johann Gottfried Herder (1744–1803), Friedrich Daniel Ernst Schleiermacher (1768–1834), Friedrich Wilhelm Joseph von Schelling (1775–1854), and Georg Friedrich Wilhelm Hegel (1770–1831), among others. Most central to German Idealism in its various forms is a shared intellectual heritage, specifically the ideas of the German philosopher Immanuel Kant. It was common for German Idealists to see themselves as completing, carrying forward, or in some cases correcting Kant's ideas. To understand German Idealism, then, it is necessary to understand something of Kant.

German Idealists accepted Kant's basic idea that the mind structures experience. Kant himself had called his view transcendental idealism, which is transcendental in the sense that it is concerned with what makes experience possible in the first place. It is a version of idealism in the sense that, according to it, the world of experience is mind-dependent insofar as it is (and must be) structured by the mind. However, German Idealists took issue with Kant's views in various ways. Kant contrasted phenomena, the objects of perception, with noumena, the objects of thought. Noumena are entities beyond the five senses: one can think about them, but one can never see, feel, hear, smell, or taste them. In Kant's work, noumena are things as they actually are, independently of how they are perceived, while phenomena are the appearances of things. For instance, a person might perceive an orange as round, orange-colored, and tart tasting. That is how the orange appears to one; the perceived shape, color, and taste of the orange are phenomena. Now consider the orange independently of how it is perceived, what the orange is in itself regardless of how it looks, feels, or tastes to anyone. That is the noumenon of the orange. Because the categories apply to phenomena, Kant believed that noumena are unknowable. Put another way, it is impossible for us to have knowledge of things in themselves, independent of how we perceive them. Knowledge, then, is confined to phenomena—the appearances of things.

The Idealists Fichte and Schelling rejected Kant's conception of the noumena as unknowable and also as the cause of our phenomenal experience (as the noumenon of an orange might be said to be the cause of one's experience of the orange). The notion of cause, according to Kant, applies only to phenomena; if this is the case, however, it is a mistake to claim that noumena are the causes of anything. In rejecting the notion of noumena—rejecting the notion that there is any component of reality that is unknowable and to which the categories do not apply—but retaining Kant's idea that the mind structures experience, the German

Idealists suggested that *all* of reality is mind-dependent. German Idealists also discussed the nature of the self; unsatisfied with Kant's portrayal of the transcendental ego and how the self is related to the world it experiences, the German Idealists sought to offer their own accounts. The focus of this chapter is arguably the most important of the German Idealists: Fichte, Schelling, and Hegel.

Johann Gottlieb Fichte

Johann Gottlieb Fichte (1762–1814) was born into a relatively poor family but was able to receive an education through the sponsorship of a local baron. He supported himself for a time by working as a private tutor, during the course of which he read works by Kant. Much impressed by Kant's work, Fichte arranged to meet with Kant and wrote a book called *Attempt at a Critique of All Revelation* along Kantian lines, which he was able to publish with Kant's support. Because the published version did not identify an author, it was mistakenly assumed that Kant had written the book; when it was revealed that Fichte was the

Portrait of Johann Gottlieb Fichte, published in the *Encyclopedia Americana* in 1920

author, he quickly rose to prominence and in 1794 acquired a position of professor at the University of Jena. However, sometimes he quarreled with colleagues and was perceived as too strict on students. In 1799, he was forced to resign when he was charged with atheism. He later taught at the University of Berlin. Fichte died after contracting typhoid fever from his wife, who became infected while caring for soldiers resisting Napoleon's invasion of Prussia.

Fichte saw himself as a Kantian, and indeed, because he regarded Kant as having not given a complete account of his views, he also saw himself as more of a constructor of a Kantian philosophical system than Kant himself. In his early work, *Foundations of the Entire Wissenschaftslehre* (Foundations of the Entire Science of Knowledge), Fichte considered, as Kant had, the conditions for the possibility of experience, but unlike Kant he argued that freedom is a necessary condition for the possibility of experience (without freedom, experience would not be possible). In addition, Fichte believed that Kant had not given an adequate account of the transcendental subject, understood as the subject necessary for the possibility of experience. Fichte distinguished between two philosophical approaches, the dogmatic and the idealist. The dogmatic approach begins philosophical inquiry by considering the objective world, the world as it is independent of experience and in which whatever happens, happens deterministically, the result of past events. The idealist approach begins philosophical inquiry by instead first considering the subjective, free self. Fichte thought neither approach, on purely intellectual grounds, could be shown better than the other. Which approach one takes, he wrote, depends on what kind of person one is (in general, Fichte insisted on a close relation between philosophical ideas and action). Yet he believed that the idealist approach was preferable and that the dogmatic approach could never explain ordinary experience (as he thought the idealist approach could).

At the center of philosophical inquiry, then, Fichte places the self, or what he simply called the I. Like Kant's noumena, the concept of cause does not apply to the I; so, it is free, not determined by outside events. However, he conceived of the self not as a thing, but as an activity, specifically the free activity of positing itself. The activity is free in the sense that it is not determined; it is not the effect of any cause occurring outside the I. When an I posits itself, it is aware of itself and affirms that it is itself. But, Fichte thought, an I can become aware of itself only by recognizing other things, or put another way, self-consciousness is possible only through the recognition of what is *not* oneself. Through the recognition of what is not itself, an I discovers that it is limited (this is just because if there is anything that is not itself, the I is finite—that is, limited). So, supposing that there is a world that is *not* oneself is a condition for the possibility of experience, or in other words experience is not possible unless one discovers that oneself is limited. When the I discovers that it is limited, it supposes that there is a check on itself that causes those limitations and comes to develop concepts such as space and time. In addition, out of the recognition that other beings, in addition to the I itself, are free, come ethical principles. That is, though a person is free, there are moral restrictions on how she can behave; she cannot trample on other people's freedom.

Friedrich Wilhelm Joseph von Schelling

The son of a Lutheran pastor, Friedrich Wilhelm Joseph von Schelling (1775–1854) was born in Leonberg. At the young age of 15, he studied theology at the University of Tübingen, where he met and became friends with the poet Friedrich Holderlin (1770–1843) as well as with Hegel. Schelling earned his doctorate in philosophy and later studied at Leipzig University. He worked as a private tutor for a time before beginning his academic career at various universities and in academic organizations; he received his first academic appointment, at the University of Jena, when he was just 23. His friendship with Hegel ended over what Schelling saw as a criticism by Hegel of Schelling's ideas in one of Hegel's books. Following Hegel's death, Schelling ultimately replaced Hegel as a professor at the University of Berlin.

More so than some other German Idealists, Schelling is linked to Romanticism, and he counted among his friends the German writer Johann Wolfgang von Goethe (1749–1832). Schelling's thought underwent various changes throughout his long career. His early work was influenced by Fichte in particular. Like Fichte, Schelling was concerned with human freedom and the self. However, in his philosophy of nature, Schelling sought to give nature an importance equal to that of the self. Rejecting the common Enlightenment view that the natural world consists of matter moving mechanically, Schelling instead regarded nature as an organic whole and as something that changes and develops in a purposeful way. As an analogy, Enlightenment thought viewed the natural world as rather like a complex clock, with many individual parts; Schelling regarded the natural world as something more like a tree, something alive and developing as a whole toward something in particular (as a sapling develops toward maturity). What Nature develops toward, according to Schelling, is human beings; in this way, Nature comes to consciousness. For Schelling, then, there is no sharp distinction between Nature and mind. "Nature is to be invisible mind," Schelling wrote, "mind invisible nature."

Schelling also developed what has come to be called a philosophy of identity. Kant had proposed a sharp division between the world as it is independent of the self and the self; one can never know the world in itself (the noumena). Schelling moved away from this sharp division, however, proposing that in consciousness the subject (the self that experiences) is identical with the object (what is experienced). In this, he was influenced in part by the modern philosopher Baruch Spinoza (1632–77), who had defended the view that the world consists of a single substance; for example, for Spinoza it is a mistake to suppose that the mind is a different substance than matter, including the body. Instead,

Photograph of Friedrich Wilhelm Joseph von Schelling from the early 19th century

mind and matter (including the body) are aspects of the very same substance. Viewed in one way, this substance can be considered mental; viewed in another way, this substance can be considered physical. In a somewhat similar way, Schelling argued that the self and nature share a common ground: absolute reason. Unlike Spinoza, however, who argued for a deterministic universe, Schelling believed humans are free.

Although Schelling's work often receives less attention than that given to Fichte, Schelling's influence is diverse and undeniable, affecting other philosophers in the continental tradition, such as Hegel and philosophers considered existentialists.

Georg Wilhelm Friedrich Hegel

Georg Wilhelm Friedrich Hegel (1770–1831) was born in Stuttgart, Germany. He was the son of a minor government official. Hegel studied theology at the seminary at Tübingen University, where he also became friends with Schelling and Friedrich Holderlin. Hegel earned a master's degree in theology but did not pursue the ministry. He worked as a private tutor and as a high school principal until inheriting some money from his father. He began to teach at the University of Jena, where he finished his dissertation and wrote *Phenomenology of Spirit*. Later, having lost this position in the wake of Napoleon's invasion of Prussia, he served as a newspaper editor. In 1816, he attained a position as a professor of philosophy at the University of Heidelberg, and, in 1819, accepted a position at the University of Berlin. By then, he had become famous for his philosophical work. He died of cholera in 1831. Hegel's views influenced such diverse philosophers as Jean-Paul Sartre (1905–80), Friedrich Nietzsche (1844–1900), and Karl Marx (1818–83), among others. Among his contributions to philosophy was the claim that human beings are specifically historical beings, in the sense that their thoughts, values, and beliefs are shaped by their historical circumstances.

Hegel sought to construct a complete metaphysical system—that is, a system to explain all of reality. So, this system was to explain not only physical processes in the natural world but also human cultural activities, such as philosophy and religion. Of course, Hegel did not seek to give explanations in the same way that today a scientist seeks to give explanations, such as by identifying physical causes and mechanisms or conducting experiments. Rather, Hegel thought he could explain all of reality in broad terms, by explaining its overall structure.

What all of reality shares, Hegel believed, is rationality. Specifically, according to Hegel, reality is essentially rational. So, nothing that is real can be irrational (or nonrational). Reality is identical to rationality. If reality is rational, this implies that it can be understood, as indeed Hegel thought it could be; like other German Idealists, then, Hegel broke from Kant's claim that any aspect of reality is in principle unknowable. Hegel thought there is an Absolute, or Mind (sometimes translated as Spirit). Mind, as Hegel understood it, is not a person's own individual mind—it does not consist of a person's individual memories, desires, wishes, and so on. Mind is instead all-encompassing reality; it is in this sense that Hegel's idealism is absolute, for it holds that everything real is essentially mind-dependent. Sometimes Hegel identified Absolute Mind as God. Hegel himself was a Christian, specifically a Lutheran. However, Hegel also wrote critically of Christianity and even of Jesus, and to what extent Hegel's philosophical beliefs are consistent with traditional Christianity is controversial.

History itself is the unfolding of this Absolute. In particular, it is the process of Mind coming to self-consciousness and recognizing itself as the sole reality. Hegel, who regarded freedom as among the essential features of Mind, saw this process as culminating in freedom. Perhaps Hegel's thought is best illustrated through examining human history. In human history, there have been philosophical movements, political movements, movements in art, culture, and religion, and so on. For Hegel, these various movements have not come about randomly. As one would expect if reality is rational, there is an order to what happens in the world and what has already happened; moreover, there is a progression to the world's events. So, it is not as if one idea in human history is replaced by another idea that simply happens to be different than the old idea. Instead, the new idea is more complete and captures more of truth than the old idea. In particular, this is because the new idea incorporates aspects of one idea and its opposite, to form a new idea that is superior to them both. This process of reconciling opposites to form a synthesis is called the Hegelian dialectic.

Hegel's own example of such a dialectic concerns the concepts of being, nothing, and becoming. Suppose we begin with the concept of being; as that is our starting point, we can call that the thesis. Now

Portrait of Georg Wilhelm Friedrich Hegel from 1828 *(Illustration by L. Sebbers)*

consider the opposite of being: nothing. Because it is the opposite of the thesis, nothing is the antithesis. The third movement in the dialectic is the synthesis, becoming. Becoming is a synthesis of being and nothing because it is neither being nor nothing, yet incorporates aspects of both. For example, a growing tadpole is in the process of becoming a frog. It is a tadpole, so it is something; that is to say, it exists or has being (or is an instance of being). However, it is not a frog (not yet), and in that sense it has an aspect of nothing (what does not exist). And in the process of becoming a frog it incorporates being (what exists).

Hegel thought that history progresses along such dialectical lines, by undergoing a thesis, an antithesis, and finally a synthesis—which itself forms a new thesis, to be opposed by an antithesis, until a new synthesis emerges. For example, in the history of ideas, suppose some people believed that having no government at all is the best form of human society, while others viewed an absolute dictatorship as the best form of human society. We can consider the first view the thesis, and the second the antithesis. A synthesis might be the view that a form of democratic government is the best form of human society: it incorporates (to a degree) the aspect of freedom people might enjoy in a society without government, while incorporating (to a degree) the order and stability of a society run by an absolute dictatorship. This is not Hegel's own example; it is just an illustration of how the progression of ideas in human history might work. Whatever ideas people do have, Hegel thought, and however those ideas might oppose each other, he believed it was possible for people to come to an agreement, an agreement that synthesized an original idea and its opposite.

Hegel believed that history unfolds with a progression toward greater and greater freedom. For Hegel, such freedom exists within the context of the state, which he regarded as more important than individual people living within the state. Freedom does not consist simply of the ability to do what one wants without interference. Rather, freedom is the freedom to live rationally within the context of the state, including obeying the laws of the state.

Hegel is famous for his comments on consciousness and self-consciousness, which he illustrates through a story of the master and slave (sometimes Hegel's German terms are translated as *lord* and *bondsman* instead of *master* and *slave*). According to Hegel, a person is conscious of herself only in opposition to something that is not herself. Put another way, self-consciousness arises only when one contrasts oneself with someone, or something, else. However, when two people meet, they each feel threatened by the other and therefore seek to dominate the other. Fearing death, one person eventually gives in to the other: the person who gives in is the slave, and the person who succeeds in dominating the other is the master. The slave works for the master, producing materials (food, for example).

Yet a peculiar thing occurs in the master-slave relationship. The slave becomes independent in the sense that she learns to exercise control over her environment; it is she who produces material goods, and she attains self-consciousness through exercising control over the environment. At the same time, the master becomes dependent on the slave, for without the slave, the master would not survive. Moreover, the master's self-consciousness depends on the slave in the sense that the slave must recognize the master as master, whereas the slave's self-consciousness is not similarly dependent on the master.

Hegel's description of the master and slave suggests certain ideas about the nature of freedom and society. In a relationship where one person dominates the other, neither can truly be free: the person dominated is subject to the will of the person being dominated, but the person dominating depends on the act of dominating for her own status; in that way, far from being independent, the dominating person actually depends on the person dominated. What this shows is that true freedom is not to be found in dominator/dominated relationships, and nor should such relationships form a basis for society.

Karl Marx

Karl Marx (1818–83) was one of the most influential thinkers of modern times. His writings were not only important during his lifetime, but also they shaped much of Western culture throughout the 20th century. His impact was vast in many areas, including philosophy, economics, sociology, and politics. Marx was born in Trier, Prussia (now western Germany). His family background was Jewish, but his father converted to Christianity shortly before he was born. As a student, Marx studied philosophy and law at the University of Berlin and then at the University of Jena. For years he worked as a journalist and newspaper editor, frequently criticizing his own government and other governments. In 1848, he published *The Manifesto of the Communist Party,* one of the most influential books of the modern era. After being banished from several European countries, he moved to England, where he lived in poverty, but wrote hundreds of political and social articles and editorials. In 1867, he published *Das Kapital,* an analysis of economic systems and a critique of capitalism. He continued to live in England until his death in 1883.

With respect to philosophy, Marx was heavily influenced by the German philosopher Georg W. F. Hegel. Hegel emphasized the view that the world, including both the natural world and the social world, must be understood as developing systems, not merely as a collection of things and facts. For Hegel, events in the world, and indeed the world itself, went through stages of development and this development was inevitable. This development was a movement toward what Hegel called consciousness. By this he did not mean just an everyday sense of being aware of something, but he meant that greater and greater possibilities were becoming realized. For example, in the natural world, new species and life-forms evolved, while in the social world, new forms of government and social institutions were created. Marx took this notion of development and applied it especially to human experience within society.

Marx spoke of humans as having species-being. By this term, he meant that there is something unique about humans and that distinguishes them from other species. What is unique about humans is that humans produce and create the conditions of their lives. That is, humans do not simply hunt and gather things; rather, humans manufacture and produce things. We are communal beings, said Marx, meaning that we are by our nature social beings, not hermits. As a result, there are social structures and institutions that shape how we produce and create the conditions of our lives. For example, in a rural, preindustrial culture, people lived on farms and spent most of their lives doing tasks just to stay alive, while in an urban, industrial culture, people live (largely) in cities and they produce by going to work away from their homes and they produce or create small units of some larger final product. (Almost no one today grows all his own food or weaves his own clothes or builds his own home from basic materials.) As Marx put it, who and what we are (as people) coincides with what and how we produce. In his words, "The nature of individuals thus depends on the material conditions determining their production." By this he meant that people live very differently in different economic situations and economic structures. For instance, again, in a rural, farming culture, what and how people produce will be different than what and how they produce in an urban, industrialized culture. How we understand the world and how we understand even ourselves is shaped by these economic conditions and structures.

Marx spoke of economic conditions of life as the forces of production. Forces of production involve two related aspects. The first he called the materials of production and the second he called the relations of production. The materials of production are the actual materials that go into what and how we produce. Again, in a hunting or gathering culture, those materials might be simple tools or implements to help hunt or gather or cultivate crops. In an urban, industrial culture, those materials might be factories or technological equipment. In a very

Photograph of Karl Marx

modern context, important basic materials might be information technology, such as computers. Different materials of production can and
will create different conditions for people's lives. For example, with the
creation of cars and a highway system (or some form of mass transpor-
tation), workers can travel away from their homes and go to work away
from their homes. As a result, factories and businesses can be located,
say, in a city, away from people's homes and work schedules can be set
up so that workers meet together at the factory at certain times (quite
different than, say, living on a farm or in a hunting/gathering community). Likewise, with modern information technology, people can
telecommute and still get work done collectively, but without having to
leave their homes.

The relations of production are the ways in which the materials of
production are structured. For instance, in a capitalist economic system, the materials of production (that is, the factories and technologies)
are owned by private individuals or private groups, while in a socialist
economic system, the materials of production might be owned by the
government. So, the materials of production are related to each other
and to people in different ways in different economic systems. Marx
claimed that the forces of production (that is, the materials and relations
of production) are the economic base of our lives and that they significantly shape how we see the world and how we see ourselves (or, as he
put it, they shape our consciousness and our experience). According
to Marx, for any economic base, there is an ideological superstructure
built upon it. By this he meant that people come to have beliefs and
values and that those beliefs and values are a result of living within certain economic structures. For example, a capitalist economic structure
has relations of production that are private (that is, individuals own the
factories and the businesses). As a result, Marx claimed, certain beliefs
and values arise that reflect this economic structure and that promote
this economic structure. Put another way, the moral values that arise
within a capitalist system benefit those who are in power (those who
own factories and businesses) and serve to keep powerless those who
are not in power (the ordinary workers). So, Marx said, within a capitalist system, an emphasis arises on individual priority and privacy, with
the result that people value individualism and a political, legal system
that protects individual rights and limited government (and downplays
community or responsibility to others). Briefly, then, Marx's view is

that people must produce in order to survive; in order to produce, there must be some mode of production (that is, means and organization, or materials and relations of production); social relations and patterns result from the mode of production, resulting in political, social, philosophical beliefs and values that reflect and promote that mode of production.

Even within a given economic system, Marx said, different people have different views because they experience different economic conditions in their everyday lives. So, the owners of the forces of production (what he called the bourgeoisie) are wealthy, while many workers (what he called the proletariat) are not wealthy, but often struggle to get by. Indeed, workers become alienated from their lives in the sense that they must produce to survive, but what and how they produce is determined by others. The consequence is that owners and workers are different classes and they have, in his words, different class consciousness. Marx thought that there is inevitable conflict between different economic classes and that this conflict leads to social turmoil and even revolution. In some of his writings Marx seemed to call for people to openly challenge the capitalist system and try to alter it, while in other writings Marx seemed to say that there is an inevitable series of stages of social and historical development that will result in a transformation from capitalism to socialism and finally communism. The latter view is known as dialectical materialism; its influence by Hegel is evident. However, Hegel was an idealist (he believed that reality was mind-dependent), and Marx was not. So, Marx borrowed Hegel's notion of the purposeful development of history but left out Hegel's notion that this development is a development of consciousness and that reality is mind-dependent.

Regarding religion, Marx famously described religion as the "opium of the people." Using opium can dull a person's suffering; however, it can also make a person sluggish and dull, and opium smokers are famous for spending their time dreaming opium-induced dreams. Similarly, according to Marx, religion is used by the people as a solace for their unhappy lives. Religion turns people's attention away from the alienation and unhappiness they suffer in a capitalist society and focuses their attention on illusions of an otherworldly realm. So, religion makes people more inclined to passively accept the conditions in which they live rather than seek to change them, even when those conditions are oppressive (as Marx believed they were in a capitalist society).

Not only was Marx seen as radical in his own time (although not by everyone), but during the 20th century, when his influence was the greatest, he was seen by many critics as mistaken or dangerous. He was seen by many as being mistaken because workers have not suffered within capitalism as he predicted; indeed, these critics argue, people's standards of living are the highest in capitalist societies. He was seen by many as being dangerous because his thought led to social unrest and rebellion, as well as to the oppression of many people in those political systems (such as the Soviet Union and China) that claimed to follow his teachings. Nevertheless, many of the particular social policies and practices that Marx fought for that were seen as radical have been adopted and even embraced throughout the world: free public education, child labor laws, standardized working days with an emphasis on worker safety, universal voting rights, and more.

Søren Kierkegaard

Søren Kierkegaard (1813–55) was a Danish philosopher and writer who wrote on a wide variety of topics, ranging from psychology and literary criticism to the Protestant church, in addition to his more strictly philosophical work. He is often considered the father of existentialism. Kierkegaard's father raised him with a deep sense of melancholy and religious guilt, themes that often surface in Kierkegaard's work. During college, Kierkegaard lived a life focused on food, drink, and clothes, but after his father's death, he settled down, became engaged to be married, and planned to become a Lutheran pastor. However, Kierkegaard soon broke off his engagement and dropped his studies to become a pastor, believing God had called him to a less conventional life as a writer. This belief strengthened Kierkegaard's lifelong view of himself as an outsider.

A central concern of Kierkegaard's was the human individual, and he was very critical of philosophical work that emphasized abstract, systematic thought over the individual. Kierkegaard especially faulted the work of Georg W. F. Hegel because he thought that Hegel overlooked the fact that particular individual people exist in the real world, and instead focused on abstract generalities. Kierkegaard famously wrote in his published journals that he sought an idea that was "true for him," an idea for which he himself could live and die. Kierkegaard saw the question of Christian faith—whether to believe in Christianity or not to believe—as the vital question of his life. For Kierkegaard, belief in Christianity was not a matter of reasoned argument; for example, an attempt to prove through logic that God exists is simply the wrong

Nineteenth-century painting of Søren Kierkegaard at his high desk *(Painting by Luplau Janssen)*

way to approach Christianity. There are two reasons for this. The first is that, according to Kierkegaard, there are logical reasons for thinking that Christianity is actually false: it seems absurd, for instance, that God could both be an eternal God and a mortal human (Jesus). The second reason is that, for Kierkegaard, what is crucial is not simply *that* one believes in Christianity, but *how* one believes; in particular, true Christian faith involves passionate feeling. To use Kierkegaard's term, faith involves inwardness. Because aspects of Christianity seem absurd, Kierkegaard saw faith as nonrational. Rather, faith requires a leap of faith; the person who makes such a leap passionately commits herself to Christianity, even though she is not certain that Christianity is objectively true. Because she is not sure that Christianity is objectively true, faith involves risk—she does not know whether making the leap of faith is the right choice. Yet the fact that the truth of Christianity is always uncertain is, for Kierkegaard, the very thing that makes a faithful person's commitment to Christianity passionate. This is because if one is convinced of Christianity's truth by reasoned argument, no passion is necessary; one simply believes according to the rules of logic. What this means is that the person who believes in Christianity in the right way—passionately—must always keep in mind that whether Christianity is true is uncertain, even while she continues to believe. So, for Kierkegaard, a leap of faith must be repeated throughout one's life, and in that sense Christian faith involves continuous, passionate commitment. Kierkegaard describes the decision about whether to make such a leap as filled with anxiety, or angst. At the same time, however, Kierkegaard saw the realization that one is free to make such a decision as a source of exhilaration; one can feel dizzy from freedom.

Kierkegaard's account of Christian faith points to two dominant themes of Kierkegaard's work: first, an emphasis on the individual's personal experience, and second, the belief that ideas should matter emotionally to one's life (they are not just a matter of intellectual belief). Along these lines, Kierkegaard wrote in his *Concluding Unscientific Postscript* that, "truth is subjectivity." Truth is subjectivity in the sense that it involves an individual subject's experience. Consider the belief, for example, that Jesus was God. Truth is not just a matter of whether this belief matches up to actual, historical events such as the birth of a divine Jesus. For Kierkegaard, truth has to do with *how* a person has this belief—in such a way that it matters emotionally to that person, for instance, or only in a distant, uninvolved way. So the Christianity of someone merely going through the motions of Christianity, without feeling deeply about Christianity, is less true (for Kierkegaard) than the Christianity of someone who is passionate about it. Kierkegaard's claim that truth is subjectivity is focused overwhelmingly on Christianity, as is his account of faith; he does not consider whether his view of faith would apply also, for instance, to Islam.

In two important works, Kierkegaard examined making other fundamental choices. In *Either/Or*, Kierkegaard presents a dialogue between people who represent very different ways of living: the aesthetic life, focused on personal pleasure, and the ethical life, focused on duty and ethical rules. Kierkegaard did not intend for the book to suggest that one way of life is objectively better than the other; given Kierkegaard's emphasis on individuality and subjective experience, perhaps it would seem strange if he had. However, it seems equally clear that Kierkegaard favored the ethical life in the choice between the ethical and aesthetic.

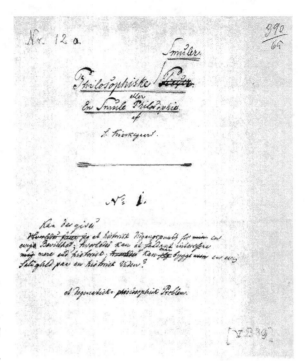

First page of the manu-
script of Søren Kierke-
gaard's *Philosophical
Fragments*

A third and yet better option regarding a way of living, for Kierkegaard, was the religious life, in which God is the focus, not either
pleasure or following ethical rules. In *Fear and Trembling*, Kierkegaard
wrote about the biblical story of Abraham, in which God asks Abraham
to kill his only son, Isaac. Kierkegaard asks, "Is there such a thing as
the teleological suspension of the ethical?" What he meant by this was
whether a person could appropriately, temporarily give up ethical rules
(such as the rule that one should not murder) for some higher purpose.
Kierkegaard's answer is yes, and specifically that Abraham does so.
Abraham suspends the rule that murder is wrong, for the sake of the
higher purpose of obeying God. Abraham's decision, by Kierkegaard's
lights, is an illustration of the religious life. However, one does not
immediately live such a life; one reaches the religious by first going
through an aesthetic stage and an ethical stage.

Friedrich Nietzsche

Few philosophers have been as influential or as widely read as the German philosopher Friedrich Nietzsche (1844–1900). Although he is associated with existentialism, Nietzsche's work ranges beyond any one area of thought. He was appointed professor of philology (that is, language and classical texts) at the University of Basel in Switzerland when he was just 24. Poor health forced him to resign in 1879, and for about the next 10 years Nietzsche lived a nomadic life in Europe, moving from place to place while he struggled with his health and continued to write. In January 1889, he went insane, collapsing on the street as he hugged a cab horse that had been beaten by its driver. He died 11 years later, without ever having recovered.

Nietzsche wrote about diverse topics, including Greek tragedy, history, music, science, religion, and truth, in addition to writing about existential concerns such as meaning and morality. By traditional philosophical standards, Nietzsche often wrote in an unconventional style, sometimes writing in aphorisms, poetry, and even stories (as in *Thus Spoke Zarathustra*) rather than constructing lengthy, systematic arguments. This has sometimes made it difficult to interpret Nietzsche, while it has made it easy to misinterpret him. Historically, one unfortunate misinterpretation was that Nietzsche's work is sympathetic to Nazism, a view that has been widely discredited (Nietzsche consistently opposed anti-Semitism). Despite Nietzsche's wide-ranging and sometimes unconventional work, key components of his thought regarding values and religion stand out.

In one of his most important books, *Thus Spoke Zarathustra,* Nietzsche's character Zarathustra famously proclaimed that God is dead, a claim Nietzsche repeated in *The Gay Science.* By this Nietzsche did not mean that God had literally died; he did not believe God literally existed in the first place. Rather, Nietzsche's point was that God had ceased to play a significant role in people's lives. In other words, although people might talk as if they believed in God and lived by God's commands, as a matter of fact belief in God made very little difference to them. Yet the death of God (in this sense) raised serious questions. Many people had once regarded God not only as the source for meaning in life, but also as the basis for morality as well. But if God does not make our lives meaningful, and if God does not tell us what is morally right and wrong, then what does? Regarding meaning, Nietzsche's answer was that meaning was to be found in *this* life and on this Earth—not in an afterlife or some other otherworldly realm. Rather than pinning one's hopes and goals on something outside our concrete lives, we can create meaning by making something of our lives in the world we actually live in.

Nietzsche emphasized creativity as one aspect of an excellent, meaningful life, and in *Thus Spoke Zarathustra,* Nietzsche described the superman (sometimes translated as the "overman"). Man, Nietzsche wrote, is something to be overcome, and the superman is the meaning of the Earth. Humanity is something to be overcome in the sense that humans can become something much better than what we are now— freer, stronger, more creative, more affirming of life. The superman is the meaning of the Earth in the sense that what can give meaning to our lives is a striving to overcome—or, in Nietzsche's phrase, a striving to *become* what we *are* in the sense of striving to realize one's potential. In addition, with the death of God, we are free to create our own values. To put the point another way, because God does not provide the basis for morality, we must decide for ourselves what is good and what is not, what is worth valuing and what is not.

Although Nietzsche believed we are free to create our own values and decide for ourselves what is good and what is not, he clearly thought that some views about what is good (and what is not) are better than others. In *On the Genealogy of Morals* and other works, Nietzsche distinguished two different kinds of morality: master morality and slave morality. Master morality is positive in the sense that it is concerned

Portrait of Friedrich Nietzsche, published in *Pan* magazine in 1899 *(Illustration by Hans Olde)*

mainly with the good, rather than being preoccupied with what it considers bad. For the master moralist, what is good has to do with creativity and excellence. Slave morality is a reaction against master morality and in that sense it is mainly negative. In particular, what motivates slave morality is resentment against the strong. Because the slave moralist fears and resents strength and excellence that it cannot (or, perhaps, does not) achieve, the slave moralist values weakness instead. Consider, for example, someone who would like to act as an individual rather than merely going along with the crowd, but who does not have the inner strength to do so; she might come to resent the person who does. Similarly, someone who cannot achieve the greatness of a first-class artist or scientist, for example, might resent people who can. Reacting against them, she prefers to keep everyone at her level. So, whereas master morality strives for excellence, slave morality prefers that everyone remain mediocre. Whereas master morality is a morality of independence and achievement, slave morality is a morality of the crowd in a negative sense, or to use Nietzsche's term, *the herd*.

Nietzsche clearly preferred master morality to slave morality. However, he believed that in a historic struggle against master morality and slave morality, slave morality had won, and he associated slave morality with Christianity in particular. For example, he viewed traditional Christian virtues such as meekness and humility as being motivated by fear rather than by a genuine sense of harmony with others. In general, Nietzsche's critique of Christian morality is based largely on the view that it is life denying rather than life affirming. To put the point another way, Nietzsche regarded Christianity as being in opposition to a life of flourishing and achievement and in favor of a meek, passive existence. One reason for this is simply Christianity's focus on otherworldly entities such as God and soul; Nietzsche believed these were illusions and that Christianity irrationally focused on them at the expense of our real lives on Earth. In addition, Nietzsche charged Christianity with being life denying by rejecting human instincts (such as sexuality) and passions. In his assessment of Christianity, Nietzsche distinguished between Jesus the person and Christianity as a body of thought and was much more critical of the latter.

Nietzsche himself emphasized a positive affirmation of life, as his idea of the eternal recurrence illustrates. According to this idea, everything that happens in the world will happen again and again, for all eternity. So, if a person spends her life as a professional poet, for example, she will repeat that career endlessly, and in general she will live every detail of her life over again exactly as she lived it once. The importance of this for Nietzsche was what such eternal recurrence means for how people should live their lives. The issue can be posed as a question: If you could live your life eternally over again exactly as you have lived it, would you choose to do so? Nietzsche believed that answering yes to this question was very difficult. That is, he believed it was very difficult to affirm one's life eternally—not merely to accept one's life, but to assent to it gladly and regard it as having such value that one would choose to live it endlessly over again. Nietzsche notes that the superman is one who would do so. In general the idea is that we should live our lives in such a way that we can say *yes* to living our lives over again, exactly as we have lived them. This includes saying *yes* not only to joy and triumph but also to suffering and tragedy—the deaths of loved ones, for example, or very serious personal disappointments. A true affirmation of life is an affirmation of eternal recurrence.

The will to power is another important component of Nietzsche's thought. Nietzsche believed that people do not merely seek to survive, they seek to flourish, and in particular they seek to maximize their power. So, according to Nietzsche, at the root of all a person's actions is the desire to increase her power—a *will* to power. For Nietzsche, the relevant sense of power here is not political power, or power over other people, which he disparaged. Rather, Nietzsche uses *power* in the sense of a person bringing her individual talents to fruition. A great poet, for instance, maximizes her power through her achievements as a poet.

In an earlier work, *The Birth of Tragedy*, Nietzsche had contrasted what he called the Apollonian impulses toward logic, restraint, and aesthetic beauty (impulses he associated with the Greek God Apollo) with the Dionysian impulse toward joy, creativity, and reckless, even destructive energy (associated with Dionysus, the Greek god of wine). It was better, he thought, for a person to lose herself wholly in neither; a superior person synthesizes the impulses of both.

Phenomenology

Contemporary philosophers sometimes use the term *phenomenology* to describe how a particular sensation feels—to talk about the phenomenology of a paper cut, for example, is to talk about the sharp pain that is characteristic of a paper cut. More commonly, however, *phenomenology* refers to a movement in philosophy (especially continental philosophy) that began in the 20th century with the work of Edmund Husserl. Phenomenology in this sense has changed over the years, with different philosophers emphasizing different topics within phenomenology and sometimes disagreeing about the nature of phenomenology itself.

The term *phenomenology* comes from the Greek word *phaino*, meaning "to appear." So in a broad sense, phenomenology is the study of how things appear to consciousness. More precisely, phenomenology is the study of consciousness and the objects of consciousness—that is, consciousness and what consciousness experiences, for example, the sight of wispy clouds on a summer day, the tart taste of a raspberry, or the experience of regarding something as beautiful. Phenomenology differs from other disciplines that study consciousness (such as psychology or cognitive science) in at least two significant ways. First, phenomenology examines consciousness and experience from a first-person perspective. So instead of studying consciousness from an outside perspective as a scientist typically does—say, by studying patterns of brain activity—phenomenologists study consciousness from the perspective of a person who is consciously experiencing, looking at what experience is like *for that person*. A second difference between phenomenology and other disciplines that study consciousness is that, whereas scientists seek to explain consciousness, phenomenologists often seek only to *describe* consciousness.

Phenomenologists typically look for underlying structures of consciousness and of experience. That is, phenomenologists want to know how consciousness and experience in general are organized. Human beings experience a great many things in the world—for instance, sights, sounds, smells, tastes, and feels of things. Yet, faced with such a stream of information, somehow we make sense of the world. Consider, for instance, the experience of being on a crowded beach. There is a smell of salt, the roar of waves, hot sand beneath one's feet, a breeze, and lots of other "stuff"—people, dogs, umbrellas, children's shovels, and so on. Instead of getting lost in all these sensations, we typically recognize the experience as being of a beach with a lot of other people and their belongings—instead of, say, an experience of a lot of foreign objects that get in one's way. For this to be possible, it seems that our consciousness and the objects of consciousness (what is experienced) must be structured in some way. Phenomenologists try to describe just how consciousness and its objects are in fact structured.

A fundamental claim in phenomenology about the structure of consciousness is that consciousness is intentional. Intentional does not mean here having an intention, as in a goal or purpose. Rather, it means that consciousness is *about* something, or put another way, consciousness is always consciousness *of*. We are never simply conscious; we are conscious *of* something or another. This does not mean that whenever we have a conscious experience there is really something "out there" that actually exists in the world: phenomenologists readily agree that sometimes we hallucinate, for example. Even while hallucinating, however, a person's consciousness is directed toward *something*. Suppose a person believes she sees a red apple on a kitchen table. Whether or not the apple actually exists, the person is having an experience of seeing a red, round piece of fruit on a table, and in that sense her experience is *about* something; it has content, it is not simply empty. According to phenomenologists, all acts of consciousness, such as seeing, remembering, and wishing, are directed toward something; they are always intentional.

Edmund Husserl (1859–1938), the founder of phenomenology, wrote about phenomenology as a method. On this conception, the phenomenological method is a way of focusing on one's experience, without assuming that the objects one experiences are independently real. To return to the red apple on the kitchen table, the phenomenologist should not assume that the apple is actually there, existing in a physical world outside her own mind. Neither should the phenomenologist assume that that apple is *not* really there. Rather, according to Husserl, the phenomenologist should suspend judgment, regarding the apple neither as real nor as unreal, "bracketing" her ordinary, everyday belief that it exists outside her mind. Husserl's term for such bracketing was *epoche*. In general, Husserl believed phenomenologists should suspend judgment about the reality of *all* objects of experience, because he believed that doing so helped a person to focus better on experience itself. By not assuming that the objects of her experience are real, a person can study experience without bias, noticing features of experience she might otherwise overlook.

In particular, Husserl believed that through the phenomenological method it was possible to intuit the essence of an object. Essences, as Husserl understood the term, are qualities shared by more than one object. An apple, for example, has qualities that only it has (such as a bruise of a particular size in a particular place). But it also has qualities it shares with other objects, such as the color red (other things are red in addition to the apple). So the color red is an essence, and it can be intuited by using the phenomenological method. Husserl called the intuition of an essence an eidetic intuition. An intuition, as Husserl and other phenomenologists used this term, is not a feeling (as when someone claims to intuit how someone else is feeling, for example). Rather, it is a kind of direct seeing with one's mind. A person literally sees, with her eyes, a red apple on the table. But she intuits (sees with her mind) the essence redness. The intuition is direct in the sense that a person simply "sees" (intuits) the essence wholly as it actually is.

Philosophers have used phenomenology to study a wide range of experiences, including the experience of time, other people, and one's own self. In addition to its influence on philosophers such as Jacques Derrida (1930–2004), phenomenology was particularly influential on existentialism. Martin Heidegger (1889–1976), for example, sought to understand the meaning of being through phenomenology; Jean-Paul Sartre (1905–80) explored consciousness and freedom; and Maurice Merleau-Ponty (1908–61) incorporated phenomenology in his philosophy of the body. In addition, phenomenology influenced social sciences such as psychology and anthropology.

Edmund Husserl

As the founder of modern phenomenology, Edmund Husserl (1859–1938) was one of the most influential philosophers of the 20th century. In addition to his influence on philosophers such as Jean-Paul Sartre, Martin Heidegger, Maurice Merleau-Ponty, Paul Ricoeur, and Jacques Derrida, Husserl's work influenced social sciences. Husserl was born into a Jewish family in the village of Prossnitz (located in modern-day Czech Republic). He studied mathematics, philosophy, physics, and astronomy, completing a Ph.D. in mathematics before turning his attention more closely to philosophy. Husserl had a long and distinguished academic career and held teaching positions at the University of Halle, the University of Göttingen, and finally the University of Freiburg before retiring in 1928. His final years were marred by the anti-Semitic policies of the German Nazi government. He died of an illness in 1938.

Influenced by a psychologist named Franz Brentano, Husserl argued that consciousness is always intentional. Intentionality is used in a special sense here; it does not have to do with having a purpose. Instead, consciousness is intentional in the sense that it is always about something: consciousness is always consciousness *of.* Another way to put the point is that our experiences always have content. For example, suppose I have the experience of seeing a black cat in my yard. Whether or not the black cat actually exists (whether or not I am hallucinating), my experience has particular content, such as the color black and the shape of a cat. That is, I experience these sensations even if I am only hallucinating and the cat does not exist—my consciousness is *of* those sensations.

Husserl also believed that it is only within experience that a division between subject (what experiences) and object (what is experienced) arises. A natural way of thinking about our experience (as when we meet people, ride bicycles, watch movies, and so on) is in terms of subjects and objects. That is, we are subjects (conscious beings) and we experience objects, things that are separate from us (bicycles, movies, and so on). Husserl believed that it is only through experience itself that we come to think of experience as divided in this way. To illustrate, suppose you are watching a very interesting movie. Completely absorbed in the movie, you ignore everything else, until some sound outside the movie (someone sneezing, say) jolts you. Then you realize again that you are sitting in a theater watching a movie. Similarly, according to Husserl, we do not *begin* experience by thinking of ourselves as a subject separate from what we experience; we are absorbed in our experiences themselves, and it is only when we stop to consider experience that a sharp separation between us and what it is that we experience occurs to us.

As Husserl developed it, phenomenology is the study of consciousness (and what consciousness experiences) from a first-person perspective and without metaphysical presuppositions. So phenomenologists study human consciousness, not from an outside perspective, but from the perspective of the conscious person herself, examining what experiences are like from an internal perspective. In addition, for Husserl, phenomenologists study consciousness without assuming that what they experience has a reality independent of the conscious person. Our normal view, of course—what Husserl called the natural attitude—is that most of the objects we see exist in a real world independent of ourselves; they do not just exist in our minds. A person reading this sentence on a screen or on a page in a book, for instance, is looking at a real, physical screen or page, according to the natural attitude. However, Husserl believed that the phenomenologist should refrain from assuming that everything she sees—and in general, everything she experiences—has a reality outside of her own experiences. She does not assume a computer screen is independently real or that anything else she experiences is independently real. Neither does she assume that it is not; she simply makes no assumption one way or the other, or put another way, she suspends judgment. Husserl called this suspension of judgment bracketing, or *epoche*.

Why bother studying consciousness, and why bother studying it in this way? For Husserl, the answer involved his belief that science, and the modern world in general, ignored our lived experiences, and that this had led to a world crisis. (Husserl lived through World War I and events that led to World War II.) Husserl was reacting against two views in particular. First, he was reacting against relativism, according to which what is true is not true absolutely, but only relative to something or another. For example, on one version of relativism, whether a scientific view is true depends on a historical period, so that a scientific view that is true in one historic period might be false in another (say, the view that the earth revolves around the sun was true in ancient times, when most people believed it, but it is false now). Second, Husserl was reacting against naturalism, the view that everything can be understood scientifically (especially in physical terms, as Husserl understand the term *naturalism*) and therefore the best way to study anything is to study it scientifically. In contrast, Husserl believed that it was a mistake to study human consciousness as though it were just another object in the world, along with bicycles and plants. According to Husserl, consciousness cannot be understood without examining our experiences as we actually live them. In addition, against relativism, Husserl sought to give knowledge an absolutely certain base. Scientific practice is fallible; it makes mistakes. Husserl wanted to base knowledge on what could *not* be mistaken, and he believed that the way to do this was through phenomenology. Scientific knowledge, according to Husserl, presupposes our lived experiences as conscious beings. Prior to doing science, there is what Husserl called the *lebenswelt*, the life-world, the world of ordinary perceptions and experience. So, it is not as if we come into the world as scientists, ready to investigate by a certain scientific method. Rather, first we are conscious beings who have experiences; even when we are doing science, we are conscious beings who have experiences and who are now doing science. So, our lived experience as conscious beings is fundamental in a way that science is not. What this implies is that, in order to attain certain knowledge of anything, we must first attend to those lived experiences as conscious beings: we must study our own consciousness. In the practice of phenomenology, we should suspend judgment—neither believing nor disbelieving in the independent reality of what we experience—because by doing so we can focus on consciousness and what appears to consciousness without biases. This in turn allows us to focus more clearly on consciousness itself.

Husserl believed that through phenomenology we can discover pure consciousness, which we cannot doubt; that is, we can be absolutely certain of pure consciousness, so pure consciousness can provide a basis for all knowledge (put another way, knowledge builds on pure consciousness as a base). In addition, Husserl argued that through the phenomenological method it is possible to intuit essences, which Husserl defined as the qualities that an object can share with other objects. For instance, a particular donkey has certain qualities. Some of these are specific to it, such as a nick on its right ear. But some qualities, such as brownness, the donkey shares with other things in the world (other objects are brown). So, brown is an essence, and through phenomenology it is possible to intuit such essences directly. In this way, the phenomenological method reveals something deep about reality.

Martin Heidegger

Martin Heidegger (1889–1976) was an influential German philosopher often considered one of the most important philosophers of existentialism; he also influenced theology, hermeneutics (the art and study of interpretation), philosophy of language, and the contemporary school of thought called deconstruction. In his youth, Heidegger planned to join the Jesuit order, but health problems (and perhaps his own reluctance) prevented him from doing so. Heidegger studied both theology and philosophy and eventually taught philosophy at the university level. In 1933, Heidegger joined the Nazi Party and gave pro-Nazi speeches while serving as a university official. These decisions later provoked an ongoing controversy about the relation between the Nazi Party and Heidegger's philosophical work.

Heidegger's work is notoriously difficult, in part because he often used words and phrases in very particular, technical ways. Because some of these terms do not translate well into English, scholars traditionally use them in Heidegger's original German. Heidegger's central philosophical question was the question of Being. By this is meant the nature of existence itself. Heidegger was not concerned so much with why individual things exist (such as rocks and planets and people) but why *anything* exists at all. That is, Heidegger sought to understand the nature of being in general, not just the natures of individual beings. In what is probably his most influential work, *Being and Time,* Heidegger approached the question of Being by examining human being, that is, the being of humans. In this study, Heidegger gave an account of how human existence itself is structured at a fundamental level; so, he gave an account of what the being of *all* humans has in common.

Heidegger's term for human being is *Dasein* (which literally means "being there"). He characterized Dasein as being that regards its own being as an issue, meaning that humans ponder their own existence (unlike the being of rocks and trees, for instance, which does not). In addition, Heidegger saw Dasein as not having a fixed nature. This is because Dasein is continually choosing, and in choosing, Dasein is not something that is static and unchanging: it creates its own nature through the process of making choices. To put this in more concrete terms, each person continually faces possibilities and can choose among these possibilities. For example, a person can choose to live or not to live; she can choose to dress like her friends or dress some other way; she can choose to spend her free time writing stories or studying math or in some other activity. Because Dasein is continually faced with such possibilities and must always choose among possibilities, Dasein is continually looking into the future. In this sense—to use language closer to Heidegger's—Dasein is continually projecting itself toward possibilities.

At the same time, Heidegger notes that people are born into a particular time and place and that they live among other people. Heidegger's phrase is that human being is being-in-the-world. This is meant to convey the idea that humans do not just live in abstraction or in isolation: We live in particular places at given times, and we live with other people. This is important in Heidegger's thought for several reasons. First, to understand a person, we must consider her in the context of her world—not her world in the scientific sense, but her world in the sense of the people she encounters, the customs and beliefs of her culture, and other factors that significantly affect her experiences. Second, facts about a person's world (such as where and when she lives) limit her possibilities. For instance, a person born in the 12th century could not choose to become a computer programmer, because at that time there were no computers. So although Dasein chooses among possibilities and in this way projects itself into the future, Dasein's possibilities are limited by facticity. Third, Heidegger describes human existence as an existence of thrownness. Metaphorically, humans are thrown into the world in the sense that we neither choose to be born nor to be born under particular circumstances in a particular time and place; we simply find ourselves existing. Because of such thrownness, Heidegger describes the world as a place that can seem strange, a place where we do not feel at home. Fourth, Dasein's identity is found in part in the identity of others. A person lives among others who, as a group, generally believe and value certain things and behave in particular ways; for example, one person's community might value regular church attendance and another person's community might not. Heidegger suggests that we can understand one aspect of who a person is by who her community is—by what her community believes, values, and does. This aspect of Dasein's identity is what Heidegger calls the they-self, and according to Heidegger, it is easy to lose one's individual identity in the they-self, just by adopting the beliefs, values, and behavior of one's community without thinking very much about it. A person lost in the they-self just goes with the flow of the group, without stopping to think that there are other possibilities open to her. (However, a person can realize that there are such possibilities through the experience of anxiety.)

Like many existentialist philosophers, Heidegger was concerned with authenticity. For Heidegger, living authentically essentially involves facing one's own death. Heidegger used the term *being-toward-death* to describe facing up to one's death in the appropriate way. Being-toward-death is not brooding about death; rather, it is living with a conscious awareness and acceptance of death. Heidegger regarded being-toward-death as positive because it allows a person to reclaim her own individuality: The realization that a person's death is hers and hers alone brings with it a realization that she is an individual. This realization, in turn, allows her to keep from getting lost in the they-self.

In his later work, Heidegger focused less on Dasein but continued to explore Being, examining Being through examinations of topics such as thinking, technology, and language.

Existentialism

Existentialism is a broad area of philosophical thought that flourished in the late 19th and early to mid-20th century. Popularized by the French philosopher Jean-Paul Sartre, it was most prominent in Europe in the 1930s–50s, and its reach extended beyond philosophy into literature and theater, such as in the works of Albert Camus, Fyodor Dostoevsky, Herman Hesse, and Samuel Beckett. Like many schools of thought, existentialism cannot be defined by listing any one set of beliefs. There is much disagreement among philosophers commonly considered existentialists; some explicitly rejected systematic theorizing and some even denied being existentialists. However, certain key themes distinguish existentialism from other movements in philosophy.

Foremost among these themes is the existentialists' focus on the human individual and the conditions of the individual's existence, such as freedom and meaning in life. Many existentialists addressed the issue of how a person should make his way in the world, broadly speaking. Along these lines, Søren Kierkegaard, often considered the father of existentialism, famously wrote in his published journal that the question for him was what to *do*—not merely what he knew, but how he should live his life. With its emphasis on the individual as he actually exists, existentialism was in part a reaction against earlier philosophical thought, such as the work of Georg W. F. Hegel and René Descartes. Hegel constructed abstract, systematic theories, which Kierkegaard viewed as overlooking real, concrete humans. Descartes emphasized that human beings are knowers, creatures of reason; existentialists tended to emphasize instead that humans are not just thinking beings, but are beings with passions,

THE JOURNALS

OF

SØREN

KIERKEGAARD

A SELECTION EDITED
AND TRANSLATED BY
ALEXANDER DRU

OXFORD UNIVERSITY PRESS
LONDON · NEW YORK · TORONTO
1938

Cover of the first English edition of *The Journals of Søren Kierkegaard*, published in 1938

concerns, and values. We wonder about our own existence, for example, and we make value judgments, considering some things good and other things not. In addition, it is not as if humans live purely independently from the hustle and bustle around us. We are beings who live in a concrete world in certain places, at certain times, and with other people. To use existential philosopher Martin Heidegger's phrase, we are being-in-the-world, and it is not possible to understand us without considering us in the context of the world we live in.

One common thread throughout existentialist writings is meaning, in the broad sense that we want our lives to matter. For atheistic existentialists, such as Friedrich Nietzsche and Jean-Paul Sartre, God does not provide meaning to our lives because God does not exist. Instead, we must create our own meaning. Nietzsche wrote about striving to be better than one is by realizing one's full potential, for example as an artist might create meaning in her life by realizing her potential as an artist. Some Christian existentialists, such as Kierkegaard and Nikolai Berdyaev, linked meaning to a person's relationship with God.

In addition, existentialist philosophers commonly view freedom as a central component of human existence—not freedom in the political sense (such as freedom of speech) but freedom in the metaphysical sense, as in the ability to freely choose for one's self how to be and what to believe. Sartre often wrote as if humans are totally free, no matter what situations they find themselves in. In Sartre's famous phrase, existence precedes essence. That is, according to Sartre, it is not as if we are born in the world with a fixed human nature. Rather, first we exist and then we create our own nature (so, our existence comes before our nature). In addition, because God does not tell us what is moral and what is not, we are free to create our values. Even a person in chains is free in these senses, and she can freely choose how to respond to her imprisonment (it is up to her whether she succumbs to despair, for instance, or makes plans to escape). Other philosophers, although agreeing that humans are free, believed that sometimes there are limiting factors. Simone de Beauvoir and Maurice Merleau-Ponty, for example, both believed that a person's historical situation can limit her freedom: a slave in a racist society, for example, is not as free as someone who is not a slave. There is a certain facticity about our lives, and this facticity can limit our freedom in certain ways. Put another way, there are certain facts about our lives, and our freedom exists within the context of those facts. No human is free to become a fish, for instance.

For many existentialists, freedom has both an unpleasant aspect and a positive aspect. Its sometimes unpleasant aspect lies in the fact that freedom is linked to responsibility. If a person is completely free, as Sartre argued, then a person is also completely responsible for who she is and what she does. In this way, freedom is a burden; we have no excuses. Moreover, Sartre argued that when a person facing a moral dilemma chooses one thing rather than another, she is choosing for everyone. That is, in deciding to do one thing rather than another, she is in effect saying that everyone in that situation should choose the same way. So freedom is a heavy responsibility; we are, wrote Sartre, "condemned to be free." Freedom is positive, however, in that we *are* free to create our own values and make of our lives what we will. We are free not merely *from* something, but free to *do* something. Many existential philosophers wrote that in various senses we create our selves, and they link a flourishing, meaningful life to acting creatively, not just in the sense of acting artistically, but also, for example, in making one's self the best person one can be. In these ways, Sartre argued that existentialism is a *positive* doctrine. Nietzsche, similarly, repeatedly wrote about joyfully affirming life in the context of living a creative life in pursuit of excellence.

Accepting one's responsibility and one's freedom are linked to living a life of authenticity, and existentialists (both Christian and atheists) emphasize the importance of living authentically. There is no one pattern of an authentic life; both a musician and a scientist, for instance, can live authentic lives. In general, to live authentically means living genuinely, without self-deception. An authentic person does not believe things and make moral choices just because others expect her to or say she should; she makes her own independent assessments and her own decisions. To put the point in Heidegger's terms, a person living an authentic life does not lose her individuality in the they-self, the group identity of the people around her. This does not necessarily mean she ignores the needs of others; Gabrel Marcel focused on love and faithfulness as crucial aspects of self-creation, for instance, and Berdyaev wrote approvingly of the possibility of a genuine community, in which each person regards the other as a free individual. Heidegger, in addition, argued that an authentic life involves being consciously aware of one's own death, not in the sense of brooding about one's death but in living with an unflinching awareness of it.

Together with the focus on individuality and self-creation, another common theme in existentialism is subjectivity. That is, existential philosophers sometimes write as if what is important is for a person to live by what *she* believes, and to create *her* values, as opposed to living by beliefs and values that apply to everyone. Kierkegaard famously wrote that truth is subjectivity. Truth is subjective, according to Kierkegaard, in the sense that *how* a person believes something is crucial, not merely whether what a person believes is objectively true. For example, Kierkegaard argued that what matters is not so much whether God actually exists as that a person believes in God passionately. At the same time, however, existentialist philosophers clearly viewed some actions as being morally better than others. For instance, Sartre argued that it was not possible for a person to be an authentic Nazi. So, although moral choices are up to the individual and nothing objectively makes one moral choice better than another, it seems that for existentialists not all moral choices are authentic.

Existentialists were also often concerned with angst, or anxiety. Angst is understood in different ways by different philosophers, but common to these understandings is that angst is a general feeling of anxiety closely related to the fundamental nature of human existence. Angst is distinct from fear in the sense that fear always has a specific object, and angst does not. That is, when a person fears, she always fears *something*—a shark, for example, or getting struck by a car. A person experiencing angst, on the other hand, does not experience angst about anything in particular; she just feels general anxiety. Sartre saw angst as arising from the responsibility that freedom involves. For Kierkegaard, a Christian, one source of angst is the dual nature of humans: because people are composed of both body and soul, there is a tension in our very identities. At the same time, because we can become aware of this tension by experiencing angst, angst can lead us to take a leap of religious faith. In this way, for Kierkegaard, angst has a positive aspect. Kierkegaard also sometimes wrote of angst as accompanying freedom, as when a person feels almost dizzy as she thinks of all her possible choices. According to Heidegger, because angst has no specific object in the world, the source of angst lies in ourselves. So in this way, the experience of angst reveals something fundamental about human existence. That is, when a person experiences angst, she examines her own existence. In so doing, she discovers her potential to make her own choices, instead of simply going along with the choices made by others.

Yet another concern in existential philosophy is absurdity. Here, absurdity is not the same thing as silliness or nonsense. Rather, absurdity is about the absence of rationality, and specifically the lack of rationality about something important—for example, religious faith, the universe, or even human existence. Kierkegaard, for instance, wrote that it was absurd that God could simultaneously be God as well as a mortal human with human qualities. Yet the claim that God is simultaneously God and human is central to Christianity, because according to Christianity, Jesus (a human) is God. Albert Camus, an atheist and existentialist writer, offered a quite different account of the absurd. For Camus, the universe is not rational. That is, it lacks meaning and any overarching order. Moreover, it is indifferent to humans in the sense that it is indifferent to human interests, values, and goals. Yet humans seek meaning. This contrast between the human desire for meaning and a meaningless universe gives rise to the absurd. Put another way, for Camus the absurd is the mismatch between humans struggling to find meaning and an indifferent universe. For Camus, the better response to the absurd is, not a Kierkegaardian leap of faith, but instead to embrace the absurd and go on living in spite of it. Camus illustrates this response in his essay "The Myth of Sisyphus." According to Greek myth, Sisyphus is condemned by the gods to roll a boulder up a mountain. Each time he has finished doing so, the boulder rolls back down the mountain, and Sisyphus must start all over again. Yet Camus says that one must imagine Sisyphus happy. Sisyphus is happy because he is consciously aware that his task is hopeless—he will always be pushing the boulder up the same mountain—but he is defiant in the sense that he continues to push the boulder up the mountain with courage and cheer. For Camus, Sisyphus symbolizes how we can respond to the absurd: by embracing the meaningless, indifferent universe and continuing to live.

Despite the diversity of views among existentialist philosophers, there have been some criticisms of existentialism broadly speaking. One criticism is that existentialists overemphasize negative aspects of human existence. Existential philosophers commonly write about the experience of anxiety, for example, or angst. Others wrote about betrayal, death, and conflict with others. Sartre, for instance, in his discussions of the Other (those who are seen as alien and strange relative to oneself, and even threatening) viewed humans as continually in conflict with each other, even during ordinary interactions. Other objections to existentialism are about an existentialist view of freedom. For example, one important criticism has been that existentialism offers a mistaken account of human freedom because it does not sufficiently acknowledge how social institutions shape our beliefs and our identities. For instance, a woman born and raised in the United States in the 21st century is likely to have a very different idea of her identity than a woman born and raised in a fundamentalist religious society where women are not allowed to attend school, drive, or vote. The first woman is liable to view herself as intellectually and politically equal to men, and she is likely to pursue some way to make a living. The second woman is likely to view herself as occupying a very different role in society and make decisions within a very different set of options; for instance, rather than considering a career, she is more likely to consider her role in society as related to her family. The idea is that our identities, our beliefs, and our values, are shaped by social forces outside ourselves in ways that existentialists fail to consider. So, according to the objection, it is not as if we are radically free to create our own nature or our own values. Further, if we are not radically free to create our own natures or our own values, we are not completely responsible for ourselves either.

Another criticism has been that existentialism does not provide criteria for making a moral decision. To use Sartre's example, suppose a young man is trying to decide whether to enlist to fight a war or to stay home and care for his widowed mother. In such a case, existentialism cannot help a young man actually decide what to do, because existentialism does not offer a specific ethics. A Christian, for example, might decide on the basis of his Christianity that he cannot fight a war in good conscience. On the other hand, someone who believes that he has a duty to fight for a just cause might choose to enlist. In contrast to these views, existentialism of Sartre's kind seems to deny that we have objective moral duties, either to fight or stay home. Although the young man, by existentialist lights, must accept his responsibility and carry out his decision with conviction, according to the objection, this does not help him decide which decision he should make in the first place (it does not seem to help just to be told to be passionate).

A related concern about existentialism is that it seems to make ethics thoroughly subjective. That is, it seems to make what is morally right and morally wrong up to each individual, leading to moral relativism. But, according to this criticism, morality is not just a matter of an individual's preferences. Just because someone prefers to torture others, for instance, does not make torturing others a morally good choice. In response to concerns such as these, Simone de Beauvoir attempted to give an existential ethic in *The Ethics of Ambiguity*, in which she argued that we should promote human freedom and fight injustice (for example, fight against racist practices and institutions).

Jean-Paul Sartre

Jean-Paul Sartre (1905–80) was a French existential philosopher, novelist, and playwright. Sartre is often credited with popularizing existentialism, particularly by offering a clear statement of atheistic existentialism in his essay "Existentialism Is a Humanism." Sartre was also a Marxist, and he was politically active throughout his life, for example, participating in the French resistance to Germany during World War II and later criticizing U.S. involvement in Vietnam. In 1964, Sartre was awarded the Nobel Prize in literature, but he refused to accept it.

Two central themes of Sartre's thought are ethics and freedom. Sartre's view of human freedom has its roots in his ontology (his view of being). According to Sartre, in a famous phrase, "existence precedes essence." With this claim, Sartre denied that there is a fixed human nature, that is, that there is an essence to human nature. Rather than coming into the world with our nature formed, we come into the world and then create ourselves in the sense of deciding what to do and what to value. In addition, Sartre's account of human freedom involves a detailed theory of human consciousness. Sartre distinguished between two kinds of being, understood roughly as two kinds of existence: being-in-itself and being-for-itself. Being-in-itself can be understood as being that is nonconscious, or as that which simply passively exists. In this category falls the being of objects such as trees and desks. In contrast, being-for-itself is being that is conscious, such as the conscious being of a human. The being of a person has both being-in-itself features and being-for-itself features. There are certain physical facts about each person that simply are, for example having a certain height, having

Photograph of Jean-Paul Sartre, published in 1983

certain parents, and living in a certain physical place. Those aspects about ourselves that are conscious, however, are being-for-itself. Reflecting upon ourselves and who we are, choosing one thing rather than another, and planning projects all illustrate being-for-itself.

When being-for-itself reflects upon itself, it views itself as an object, that is, as the object of its own reflection. But because what is reflecting is distinct from what is being reflected upon, being-for-itself is not identical with itself. So, according to Sartre, being-for-itself involves a kind of negation: in reflecting upon itself, being-for-itself inevitably denies itself, turning the subject (a conscious self) into an object (a thing viewed by a conscious self). Thus, at the heart of being-for-itself is a kind of nothingness. It is this nothingness that lies at the heart of human freedom, according to Sartre. Humans have the ability to negate, not only in the sense of self-negation as noted above, but also in the sense that we can imagine what is not the case. For example, it is possible to imagine alternative situations than the ones in which we exist, and imagine possible future situations—situations that do not now exist—as we make plans. Our freedom consists in our ability to imagine and to intend; according to Sartre, then, human freedom is absolute.

Sartre acknowledged there are limitations on one's physical freedom. A prisoner in chains is not free to leave prison, and no person is free to fly to the moon simply by flapping her arms. Freedom exists in the context of physical facts about ourselves and the world; that is, what Sartre called facticity. But the prisoner can imagine the world outside the prison walls, and the prisoner can intend to escape if given the opportunity, and in that way the prisoner is always and absolutely free.

Because humans are radically free, according to Sartre, each of us alone is responsible for who we are and what we do. It is no defense of an action merely to say that one's family, church, or society expects that action, because each of us is free to follow—or not—the teachings of one's family, church, or society. To attempt to deny one's freedom by refusing to take responsibility for one's own choices, for example, is to act in bad faith, essentially an act of self-deception. Such a life would be inauthentic. Apart from the view that one should live authentically, Sartre did not offer any particular ethical teachings, or a traditional moral theory. Moreover, for Sartre, nothing outside of ourselves provides a basis for morality.

Of special relevance here is Sartre's atheism. On one conception of morality, there are certain values and certain moral rules because those values and rules have their basis in something divine: for example, perhaps God has arranged it that murder is wrong and that it is generally a good thing to be kind. Sartre rejected the notion that there is any such divine basis for morality: for Sartre, there is no external grounding for values at all. If there are no such criteria for what is right and what is not, it might seem difficult to know what an existentialist should do in a difficult moral situation. Sartre described the case of a young man trying to decide whether to stay with his elderly mother, who depends on him, or going to war and fighting for a cause in which he believes. Seeking the advice of others is not a solution, for one chooses not only whose advice to seek but also whether to follow that advice. By Sartre's account, what would seem to make the young man's choice (whatever it is) the right choice is simply that he freely, authentically makes his choice and acts on it.

Despite the emphasis here on the individual's ability to choose and individual responsibility, Sartre also claimed that in choosing a certain action, in a certain sense, a person chooses for all people. In other words, by making a decision, a person is in effect saying that that decision would be the right decision for all others in that same situation. So, in choosing, we choose not only for ourselves but also for everyone. Because of this great responsibility, Sartre described human freedom as involving a feeling of anguish.

Sartre described a third aspect of human psychology as being-for-others. Being-for-others is the mode of existence as we are for other people. Sartre offered a famous example of a peeping Tom. While the peeping Tom is peering through a keyhole, he is completely absorbed in this activity. But if someone sees him peering through a keyhole, and the peeping Tom becomes aware of this, he then becomes aware of how he appears to the other person and feels ashamed. This is what Sartre called "the look." Through "the look" of another person, one becomes aware of how others view one, and specifically that others view one as an object, that is, as a thing in the world. Sartre's notion of "the look" of the Other led him to view relations between people as very often being in conflict. The reason for conflict, for Sartre, essentially lies in the fact that people seek to regain their own freedom and capture the freedom of others. When the peeping Tom has been discovered and experiences the look, he seeks to become a subject again (not merely the object of the Other's look), and he does so by subjecting the Other to the peeping Tom's own look. The difficulty with this is that he can capture the freedom of the Other only by acknowledging that the Other is a subject, not an object; but in viewing the Other as an object, he is treating the Other like an object and no longer as a subject.

To some scholars, Sartre's existentialism has at times been at odds with his Marxism. Traditional Marxism holds to materialism and determinism, for example, and Sartre rejected both. Similarly, in contrast to Sartre's emphasis on the individual, Marxist theory focuses on social classes, such as oppression by one social class of another. However, it is clear that in Sartre's later work, such as *Critique of Dialectical Reason,* he refined his notion of freedom to acknowledge better the social restrictions on freedom. Although humans might be free in the ontological sense above, according to Sartre, they are not always materially free. Sartre acknowledged, for example, that a prisoner given the choice of two bad options, in one sense cannot meaningfully be said to be free. For instance, the choice to be cooked in one kind of sauce rather than another is not an instance of meaningful freedom. One's material freedom is limited somewhat by the facts of one's material condition and social situation. The freedom of someone barely making a living from paycheck to paycheck is different than the freedom of the very wealthy.

Simone de Beauvoir

Simone de Beauvoir (1908–86) was a French philosopher, writer, and activist who made important contributions to feminism and to existentialism. After a teaching career, she devoted the last half of her life to writing. Her novels, like the novels of Albert Camus and Jean-Paul Sartre, explored philosophical issues, and she won a prestigious French prize for literature with her novel *The Mandarins*. A founding figure of feminism, Beauvoir was politically active in other ways as well, helping found and edit a French left-wing journal. In 1929, Beauvoir met Jean-Paul Sartre, with whom she maintained a romantic and intellectual partnership until his death in 1980, despite the fact that they never lived together. Beauvoir's work is closely related to Sartre's and has often been overshadowed by his, although she both influenced Sartre as well as departed from his views in important ways.

The Second Sex is Beauvoir's most famous and influential work. Here Beauvoir examined from an existential perspective what it is to be a human female. Although Beauvoir did not consider herself a feminist until years after the book's publication, *The Second Sex* is considered a key feminist text, in spite of criticism by both feminists and nonfeminists. Like Sartre, Beauvoir believed that there is no fixed human nature: that is, humans are not born with an unchanging nature (and nor do they acquire one after birth). Unlike Sartre, Beauvoir applied this notion explicitly to women. A person is not born a woman, Beauvoir said; she *becomes* one. So, a person does not have certain qualities (such as a desire to care for others) just because she is born with certain biological characteristics (such as having female genitalia). At the

Jean-Paul Sartre and Simone de Beauvoir at the *Monument à Balzác*

same time, Beauvoir acknowledged that men and women *are* different: although a person's biology does not determine her very nature, biological differences between men and women are real, and they matter.

Beauvoir pointed out that, although human females are not born with a fixed nature, they are raised to believe certain things and behave in certain ways. Historically, for example, women have been generally expected to have children and perform housework. Beauvoir explained society's perceptions of women in a specifically existential way: male-dominated societies view women as the Other. That is, it is not just that men regard women as different from themselves (although they do), but that they regard women as secondary. Put another way, according to Beauvoir, a male-dominated society views men as subjects in the sense that they are free beings who can engage in meaningful, creative work; but this same society views women as objects in the sense of lacking the freedom or the capacity to engage in such work. In addition, men are seen as the standard and women as deviating from that standard. In other words, women are seen not for themselves, but only for how they relate to men. Consider, for example, the claim that women are emotional. What does it mean to be emotional? It might mean that a person cries easily in public; it also might mean that a person is prone to violent anger. Perhaps women are more emotional than men in this first sense. But perhaps men are more emotional than women in the second sense (most violent crimes are committed by men). Yet the existing stereotype is that women are more emotional than men. Why? Because what it is to be emotional is seen from a male perspective; men decide what it means to be emotional, and from their perspective what it means to be emotional is not to exhibit violent anger but to be more prone to cry in public. In contrast to such strictly male perspectives, Beauvoir argued that men and women should recognize each other as free subjects, as conscious beings who can freely make choices and engage in creative, meaningful work. Women should not be seen merely as the Other, and neither should men.

Beauvoir wrote that women themselves can be partly responsible for their current status as the Other. This is because some women simply let men make decisions for them to avoid making hard decisions themselves. This suggests that it is women's own responsibility to overcome oppression: If women wish to engage in creative meaningful work in society, they should work to make that happen. However, Beauvoir also noted that sometimes a person's freedom is limited by her circumstances. For example, a person who has been raised to believe that men are smarter than women and who lives in a culture that upholds this view might have a very difficult time believing otherwise. So an oppressed person cannot always be held entirely responsible for her own oppression; some factors are outside her control.

The Ethics of Ambiguity is probably Beauvoir's second most influential work. Here Beauvoir attempted to give an existential ethics. Some people believe that what is morally right is based on God's commands, or is somehow built into the nature of reality. In contrast with such views, Beauvoir believed that nothing outside of human beings provides a basis for ethics. This raises the question of how people should make ethical decisions; on what basis *is* one action morally right and another action morally wrong? Beauvoir's answer to this question essentially involves freedom. Beauvoir believed that humans can freely choose their own values, and that each of us seek freedom. But, Beauvoir argued, we cannot will ourselves free without also willing others free, that, when we seek freedom, we necessarily seek the freedom of others. An important distinction here is between ontological freedom and political freedom. Each person is ontologically free in the sense that she is free to create her own nature and choose her own values (within some limitations). But not everyone is politically free: Some people are unjustly imprisoned or face discriminatory laws, for example. According to Beauvoir, we are responsible for taking up projects in favor of political freedom and against oppression, and these projects must involve other people.

Hermeneutics

Anyone who has ever watched a movie, listened to a song, or read a book and thought about what it meant has engaged in interpretation. One way of interpreting the movie *The Matrix*, for example, is that it is about heroism and what it takes to struggle against forces more powerful than oneself; another interpretation is that it concerns, broadly speaking, how what seems to be real or true can turn out to be deeply illusory. Or, perhaps the movie is about both or something else altogether. We also interpret events, such as the events of history or the behavior of others and of ourselves. One might, for example, after signing up for choir even though one is afraid to sing in public, wonder, "Now why did I do that?" and attempt an explanation.

But how should interpretation proceed? Suppose, for example, the people who made *The Matrix* did not intend to say anything about heroism; would that mean the movie is not, at least in part, about that? Does it matter what the makers of the movie intended? Do you need to consider the historical circumstances in which an author wrote? For instance, can you truly understand *The Diary of Anne Frank* without knowing at least some of the historical facts of the Holocaust? These are all questions related to hermeneutics, the art and study of interpretation, and one of the main areas of 20th- and early 21st-century continental philosophy. Hermeneutics involves not just the practice of interpretation, but also an examination of the principles, methods, and nature of interpretation. In addition, modern-day hermeneutics concerns not only the interpretation of written texts or works of art such as paintings and songs, but also the interpretation of human behavior and even of one's very being.

The term *hermeneutics* derives from the Greek word *hermeneia*, meaning "interpretation." Philosophers and others have engaged in hermeneutics in the broad sense of interpreting since ancient times. As an explicit discipline in and of itself, however, hermeneutics originally took shape for the purpose of interpreting the Bible. Thinkers considered how best to interpret the Bible, for example, and distinguished between different kinds of interpretation; a literal interpretation of the story of Adam and Eve and their expulsion from Eden, for example, is different than an allegorical interpretation. According to the former, Adam and Eve lived in a literal garden, ate literal forbidden fruit after Eve was tempted by an actual snake, and were thus expelled from the garden by God as punishment. On an allegorical interpretation, the story is not about an actual garden, actual fruit, an actual snake, and so on, but instead concerns (say) how the acquisition of knowledge (and corresponding loss of innocence) necessarily gives rise to the possibility of human sinfulness. Later thinkers such as Wilhelm Dilthey (1833–1911) expanded the notion of interpretation to include interpretation of humans and human behavior, and philosophers such as Martin Heidegger (1889–1976) regarded interpretation as key to understanding the nature of human being itself. So, for Heidegger, it is not just that one can (or should) interpret particular instances of human behavior but rather that the nature of human existence in general requires interpretation. Human being requires interpretation because it is not transparent to the individual herself; put another way, although a person reflects upon her being, it is not immediately obvious to her what the nature of that being is. So, she must interpret her being.

Hans-Georg Gadamer

Other key philosophers important in hermeneutics in 20th-century continental philosophy include the German philosophers Hans-Georg Gadamer (1900–2002) and Paul Ricoeur (1913–2005). Gadamer was born in Marburg, Germany. He studied philosophy and philology (the study of language and classical works) and was a student of Martin Heidegger. In 1922, he completed a dissertation on Plato, earning a doctorate in philosophy. He taught at various universities in Germany as well as in the United States of America.

Gadamer sealed his reputation as an important thinker in the hermeneutic tradition with the 1960 publication of *Truth and Method*. Among Gadamer's central claims is that understanding is necessarily conditioned by historical and linguistic circumstances. That is, first, one comes to an understanding via language: when one reads a book, for instance, one is reading sentences of a particular language, and when one has a conversation with another person, that conversation is in a language. Second, understanding is necessarily in part a product of historical circumstances in the sense that it is shaped by the historical conditions in which one lives and by what has occurred in the past. For instance, a 21st-century person's understanding of the ancient Greek poet Homer's *The Odyssey* is importantly different than an ancient Greek person's understanding of *The Odyssey*. Ancient Greeks would have known more about Greek culture, Greek city-states, and the religion and mythology of ancient Greece than the typical reader today, for example, and they would have had interests related to those things; such knowledge and interests would have influenced how they interpreted *The Odyssey*. On the other hand, a contemporary understanding of *The Odyssey* is informed not only by current circumstances but also by previous understandings of *The Odyssey* in the sense that a reader inherits understandings of *The Odyssey* from others. In school, for example, a person learns about interpretations of *The Odyssey* that have developed through time, and these interpretations were not available to readers in ancient times. In short, when a person interprets and acquires an understanding (whether it is of *The Odyssey* or some other work), her understanding involves certain ideas and beliefs she already has in mind. In one sense, these are prejudices; they are prejudgments, judgments made prior to interpreting a work in question. However, that does not necessarily make them bad, as Gadamer charged that Enlightenment thinkers had held. Rather, for Gadamer, linguistic and historical conditions are the conditions that make understanding possible in the first place. Put another way, without such conditions, one could not achieve understanding. Linguistic and historical conditions guide our understanding in the sense that they give us a place to start and help determine what in a given work we regard as new, interesting, or worth thinking about. Of course, Gadamer was aware that sometimes there are prejudices in the pejorative sense, biases that are baseless and that should be discarded. He agreed that one should look carefully at one's prejudgments or prejudices to rid oneself of those that are baseless. But it is a mistake, he thought, to suppose, that all prejudices are bad.

When a person interprets and understands, then (such as by reading a text), she brings to her reading the beliefs and ideas she already has, and at least in part these are products of linguistic and historical conditions. To use Gadamer's term, we can call those conditions for a particular person at a particular time a horizon. They constitute a horizon in the sense that they structure the space for one's ideas and beliefs, somewhat in the way a physical horizon provides a space for what one sees before the horizon. However, just as there is potentially space beyond one's immediate physical horizon (opening up the possibility for seeing new things), as when a person travels a distance, it is possible to see beyond one's immediate horizon in Gadamer's sense. One can do so by taking into account what a text, or a work, or a person might have to offer. Ideas in a book, for example, or a conversation with another person, might challenge one's own beliefs, or simply propose ideas one has never thought of. This process of bringing one's own horizon to an object of understanding together with the horizon of someone (or something) else is what Gadamer called a fusion of horizons. Through such a fusion, a person can reach a new understanding, not only of a text, but of herself and her beliefs. She might, for instance, understand better the grounds for a belief she has, or reject an old belief in favor of a new one; understanding can thus help clarify and test our prejudices. Understanding is thus, for Gadamer, not just a state of mind, but instead an experience. Moreover, understanding is ongoing; one never reaches a final understanding of *The Odyssey,* for example. Indeed, one's own horizon is never truly closed.

Paul Ricoeur

Paul Ricoeur (1913–2005) was a prominent 20th-century philosopher. He is noted for his work in phenomenology as well as in hermeneutics. Ricoeur was born in Valence, France. The death of his father in World War I left him an orphan when he was just two years old, and he was raised by his grandparents and an aunt. Drafted into the French army during World War II, Ricoeur was soon captured by German forces and spent the rest of the war a prisoner; during this time he read works by Edmund Husserl, a major influence on Ricoeur's early thought. After the war Ricoeur taught at various universities, both in Europe and in the United States. He was a prolific writer who explored topics as diverse as the meaning of life, freedom, phenomenology, interpretation, the self, ethics, theology, language, and politics; as a Christian, some of his philosophical concerns were religious (however, much of his work can be read independently of Christianity).

To understand human existence fully, Ricoeur believed, requires hermeneutics, because interpretation is basic to our existence; our lives continually involve acts of interpretation. Ricoeur regarded human action as a *text,* arguing that action has certain features characteristic of written texts. A key theme in Ricoeur's work is the self, and in his later work Ricoeur connected the sense of self to narrative. On this conception, a person makes sense of who she is by telling a story (a narrative) about herself. She singles out some features of her past, for instance, as being especially important for who she is today, and she connects these features of her past and who she is today to what she plans to do in the future. Suppose, for instance, someone is a mountain climber. She might, reflecting upon her past, think something like this: "I loved the climbing stories my uncle told when I was a girl. That is one thing that really made me want to climb. And visiting the Rocky Mountains made me even more interested." She thinks about her past in such a way that she identifies some events as the cause of her current interests and her identity as a climber; she also connects those events and her present interests with future plans, such as climbing Mt. Everest. However, our narrative identities are subject to change; that is, as our beliefs, values, and interests change we can tell ourselves a different story about our lives. In this way, our selves are not fixed and unchanging: we can understand who we are in different ways as we re-orient ourselves to different possible futures. In addition, our identities are not isolated from the identities of others: our climber's identity intersects with the identity of her uncle, for example.

Critical Theory

Critical Theory is a school of philosophical thought associated with the Institute for Social Research in Frankfurt, Germany, from the Institute's founding in 1923 to about 1970. The Institute was established initially to support Marxist thought; Karl Marx and Georg W. F. Hegel, especially Marx, were philosophical influences. The philosophical thinking associated with the Institute has come to be called the Frankfurt School. Critical theorists include Georg Lukács (1885–1971), Theodor Adorno (1903–69), Max Horkheimer (1895–1971), and Herbert Marcuse (1898–1978), as well as more contemporary philosophers such as Jürgen Habermas (1929–   ).

Although the school of Critical Theory was inspired by the work of Karl Marx, it did not adopt Marxism wholesale. Among the differences between Marx's views and those of the critical theorists was that Critical Theorists did not see it as inevitable that human society would pass from capitalism to communism. In addition, although Marx had written of oppression, he had described oppression primarily in economic terms. According to Marx, capitalist societies oppress the workers (the proletariat), although they are the ones actually producing material goods. However, critical theorists believed oppression has roots beyond the economic structures of the societies in which people live. Capitalist societies, they argued, have not just a specific economic structure, they also have a particular culture and ideology that are somewhat independent of that structure, and these can be (and are) oppressive; indeed, reason itself can be (and is) a tool of oppression. The ultimate goal of critical theory is to free people from oppression by studying human societies and the ways in which people are oppressed.

Among the most important works of Critical Theory is *Dialectic of Enlightenment,* written by Horkheimer and Adorno. Horkheimer was born in Stuttgart, Germany, into a Jewish family. He left his work in his father's business to pursue philosophy and studied psychology and philosophy; the phenomenologist Edmund Husserl was among his teachers. Horkheimer served as director of the Institute for Social Research for many years, including during a period of exile when Nazis ruled Germany. Adorno was born in Frankfurt. He studied music, psychology, and philosophy and wrote on a range of subjects, from music criticism to Marxism. Adorno went to Oxford University and then to the United States to escape Nazi persecution (his father was Jewish) but returned to Germany in 1949. After Horkheimer's death, Adorno assumed the directorship of the Institute for Social Research, a position he held until his death.

In *Dialectic of Enlightenment,* Horkheimer and Adorno were critical of what they call the "enlightenment," a term that for them refers less to a specific period in European history in the 17th and 18th centuries but instead a view that promotes instrumental reason as the sole reason. Instrumental reason, as the name suggests, is reason used as an instrument to achieve some particular end. For instance, figuring out how to make cars more fuel efficient is a use of instrumental reason, as is reasoning on the best method to sell a particular product and how to raise chickens so that they produce as many eggs as possible as quickly and cheaply as possible. Instrumental reason is utilitarian in the sense that it is concerned with the utility of reason, its use in accomplishing some task or other. Along with this theory instrumental reason comes the view of nature as something to be dominated, often via technology, and even the perspective that people too are to be controlled. What instrumental reason does not do, however, is assess the rightness of a goal itself. Perhaps some goals are worth pursuing, and others should be rejected. There seem to be good reasons, for instance, for building more energy-efficient vehicles, but it is less certain whether it is really a good goal to raise chickens so that they produce as many eggs as possible as quickly and as cheaply as possible; it is less certain because the well-being of chickens themselves tends to be overlooked in this cost-benefit calculation (that is, they are likely to suffer for the sake of efficiency). A problem with the overwhelming focus of reason as instrumental reason, then, as Horkheimer and Adorno saw it, is that it does not offer any means to critique chosen goals or its own methods. It leads instead just to passive acceptance of whatever goals there happen to be, even if this means that people suffer along the way and even if the goals themselves are not good ones. In this way, reason is oppressive. Historically, during the Enlightenment, reason had been thought to be liberating. Instead, Horkheimer and Adorno charged, it turns out to be the opposite.

Related to Horkheimer and Adorno's critique of instrumental reason is their critique of positivism. In philosophy, logical positivism refers to a cluster of views that emphasize verifiability as the criterion of meaning of claims (on one version of this view, if a claim cannot be verified at least in principle, it is literally meaningless). Horkheimer and Adorno's use of positivism is related to this specific school of thought but arguably has a broader meaning. As they saw it, positivism emphasizes the study of humans and human society using the methods of the natural sciences. This entails relying on quantitative evidence, that is, evidence that can be quantified, put in terms of numbers (for example, numerical measurements). But, as Adorno discussed in works such as *Negative Dialectics,* it also involves describing the phenomena or subject in question using general concepts and ignoring individual differences; in this way, positivistic thinking does not adequately describe reality, just because in fact not every individual is just like every other. For example, a group of people might all be classified as autistic (here, autistic is the general concept). However, the classification ignores individual differences between people; they might behave in very different ways and the source of their behavior might have rather different causes, and appropriate treatment for individuals might differ accordingly. Yet it is as if, according to the classification, each person in the group is identical to the general concept (the tendency to think in this way Adorno called identity thinking). But, in fact, they are not: Individuals, with all their particular characteristics, are not identical to general concepts.

Later critical theorists, such as Jürgen Habermas, without losing the goal of promoting freedom (emancipation), turned their attention to topics such as rationality, in particular as it relates to communication.

Jürgen Habermas

A German philosopher and sociologist, Jürgen Habermas (1929–   ) is considered to be one of the most important and influential philosophers of the 20th and early 21st centuries. His youth was spent in Germany under the Nazi regime. He attended several universities in the late 1940s and early 1950s, receiving his Ph.D. from the University of Bonn in 1954. For the next 40 years he taught at various German universities, finally retiring from teaching in 1993. During the 1980s and after, he was a permanent visiting professor at Northwestern University (near Chicago).

Habermas's writings cover a wide range of areas and issues within philosophy, but broadly they are about social and political philosophy as well as rationality and knowledge. His work is said to blend the social critique of critical theory with the approach to communication and knowledge of pragmatism. This blending became apparent in one of his early books *Knowledge and Human Interests*. In this book Habermas drew upon the work of Marx by looking at how people experience the world in their everyday lives through their work. Marx had claimed that what lay beneath people's views of the world and themselves was the economic conditions and systems in which they found themselves. Work (or productivity) is fundamental to human existence, and it shapes and influences what and how we experience the world. Habermas calls work "purposive-rational action." By this he means that it does not just happen; it is purposive, that is, we choose to do it and it is done toward achieving some goal or purpose. Also, it is not random, but rational; it requires thought and planning. However, going beyond Marx, Habermas also said that another fundamental type of structured human activity (beyond work) is communicative action (or language). If we are truly to understand what shapes and structures human activity, and, more important, if we are to help people be as free as possible, Habermas claims that we need to understand how economic control of the means of production influence us, but also how knowledge-based control of the means of communication influences us. In his book *Knowledge and Human Interests*, Habermas looks at what he called the "logic of the social sciences" and how that relates to people being controlled. While Marx had spoken of different economic classes (for example, owners of businesses vs. workers in those businesses) and of conflict between those classes as a major fact of people's lives, Habermas says that this class conflict has been largely replaced by communication-interest conflict (that is, social conflict that is the result of different kinds of knowledge and the interests and actions that go along with those different kinds of knowledge).

Jürgen Habermas speaks at the Munich School of Philosophy. *(Photograph by Wolfram Huke)*

Habermas argues that there are different kinds of knowledge and each kind is related to both interests and actions. For instance, there are instrumental (or technical) interests (that is, knowledge that serves as an instrument for controlling things in the world, such as technological knowledge that lets us build good bridges or airplanes). This knowledge is related directly to issues of work and productivity. In addition, there are practical interests (that is, knowledge concerned with practice, or interactions with other people, such as language and communication). Also, there are emancipatory interests (that is, knowledge focused on power and freedom, such as seeing how other kinds of knowledge shape our understanding of the world and ourselves). The overall point is that knowledge is never simply knowledge. Rather, what counts as knowledge and what is given the status of knowledge (as opposed to mere opinion or belief) is always related to human interests—so, it is related to values—and is related to actions and activities—so, it can be liberating or dominating. Knowledge is power and, what is taken as being knowledge is never neutral.

Given this view, Habermas focuses much of his work on what he calls communicative action. In the 1980s, he wrote what many people think of as being his most important work, *The Theory of Communicative Action*. Habermas analyzes what he refers to as the productivity of rationality, which he sees as the primary form of domination today. Again, what counts not only as knowledge but even as rationality is something that is decided and determined by those who control the means of communication. At an everyday level, we experience this concern in terms of what some people call media wars. That is, there is a lot of attention to how mass media portray events and people and how large media organizations influence not only public opinion, but also government and corporate policies and practices. Another example is the embedding of journalists with the military and whether this affects the objectivity of their coverage.

To the extent that communication is tied up with special interests, Habermas claims there can be a legitimation crisis. In particular, if and when certain interests (or the interests of certain people) try to subordinate other interests—especially via modes of communication—while at the same time promoting freedom of expression (which Habermas sees as liberating and emancipatory), then there is a crisis of legitimacy. That is, then there is an inherent conflict. Habermas thinks that such is the case in much of modern Western culture. Habermas claims to have come to his approach to social and knowledge (or communication) issues from a position influenced by the work of Karl Marx, and he also claims to ultimately be concerned with liberating and emancipating people. In his phrase, he hopes to "complete the Enlightenment Project," that is, to free people from what dominates them. To do this, he says, we must first understand what it is that holds dominion over them and to see that genuine, significant freedom involves knowledge as well as action and that being free to accomplish goals is at least as important as being free from overt control.

Structuralism

One significant school of thought in 20th-century continental philosophy is structuralism. Broadly speaking, structuralism is the view that underlying everyday things and events and experiences are fundamental structures and patterns that shape those things and events and experiences. A structure can be understood as a form or a pattern. A house can be viewed in terms of its individual rooms: a kitchen, the bedrooms, a living room, a dining room, and so on. But these parts of the house exist in virtue of a structure, the design and scaffolding of the house that organizes it and keeps it standing. A house can be arranged in some other way, but insofar as a person considers one house in particular, it is the structure of that house that enables the house to be what it is and have the parts that it has (a house with a different structure will have different kinds of parts—smaller rooms, say, or a more open floor plan). For another example, a chessboard is composed of individual squares, and one could if one liked examine each particular square. But the board also has a certain structure; they are organized in a particular way, with a precise number of squares arranged so that the board is in the shape of a square and no colors of the same square directly exist side by side. This structure is what enables one to use the board to play a game of chess as we know it; if the board were structured significantly differently, we would likely have a different game. In a somewhat similar way, according to structuralists, there are structures governing literature, language, and other aspects of human culture and society. According to structuralism, everyday things and events and experiences have their meaning only because of such underlying structures.

For example, some of those structures are economic and political. That is, we are born into social structures, such as economic systems, that already exist and that influence and give meaning to our experiences. As a school of thought, structuralism has examined a diversity of practices and phenomena; it has influenced anthropology, psychology, and literary theory.

Ferdinand de Saussure and Sigmund Freud

Structuralism takes its original inspiration from the work of the Swiss linguist and semiotician Ferdinand de Saussure (1857–1913). Saussure was born in Geneva, Switzerland, and as a student studied early languages. After attending the University of Leipzig, in Germany, he taught in Paris and later back in Geneva. After his death, his most influential book, *Course in General Linguistics,* was published in 1916 from notes and materials compiled by several of his prominent students.

Prior to Saussure, much of the study of language and languages was historical in focus. That is, linguists investigated the correlations between different languages and tried to trace the historical connections between them. While Saussure found value in such work, he stressed the view that language should be seen as a formal system, with fundamental structures and patterns. While describing and tracing the history of languages was worthwhile, he claimed, it is even more important to determine the forces that shape languages and to determine general laws about language(s).

In his writings, Saussure emphasized what he called the linguistic sign. This emphasis placed Saussure's work in the field of semiotics, or the study of signs. A sign is anything that represents something. There are natural signs, that is, signs separate from languages, such as smoke being a sign of fire or a scab or scar being a sign of an injury. These things (smoke, scars) represent something else (fire, injuries), but they are not linguistic. Saussure's concern was primarily with linguistic signs, for example, the word *horse* being a linguistic sign for an animal.

Saussure drew two distinctions about linguistic signs, both of which became fundamental for later thinkers. The first distinction was between signifiers and signifieds. A signifier is a linguistic unit (usually a word) that is used to designate something; for example, the word *tree*

Photograph of Ferdinand de Saussure *(F. Jullien Genève)*

is a signifier. A signified is what is designated. In particular, Saussure said that the signifier is a sound-image (for example, the sounds that we make when we say the word *tree* or the squiggles that we write on a piece of paper when we write the word *tree*) and the signified is the concept that is designated. An important aspect of signs, for Saussure, is that no sign has meaning in itself. There is nothing about the sounds or squiggles that we use for *tree* that has any meaning in itself; our use of these is arbitrary. The fact that languages other than English use different sounds and squiggles shows this. Signs have meaning, then, said Saussure only because of their differences with other signs. That is, *tree* has significance (in English, but not in, say, Swahili) only because we distinguish it from, say, *free* or *trek* or *true*.

The second distinction about language that Saussure discussed was the difference between what he called langue and parole. Langue is the formal, total language system and parole is the actual use of language by individual speakers. While langue is a system of structures and rules, parole is a set of activities and the two do not always match up. For example, people commonly misspeak with respect to grammar or use the wrong term or have misunderstandings about some aspects of their own language. The study of linguistic signs, then, said Saussure, must be on langue, even more than on parole. Saussure claimed that language (and signs generally) structures our experiences, often in ways that we do not see unless we focus our attention on them. His insistence that signs are structured, yet arbitrary, influenced later philosophers.

Another influence on structuralism was the psychologist Sigmund Freud (1856–1939). Freud was born in Moravia (now part of the Czech Republic) and lived much of his life in Vienna, Austria. He attended medical school in Vienna and focused his studies on physiology and physics, both of which shaped his later ideas about human psychology. He later worked in France and Germany, practicing his new science of psychoanalysis and writing both the underlying theory as well as case studies. After the Nazis took power in Germany, Freud moved to England, where he stayed until his death.

Freud claimed that there are fundamental biological and psychological structures that shape our personalities, actions, and values. Freud wrote about three interrelated aspects of persons: the organization of personality, the dynamics of personality, and the development of personality. The organization of personality included his famous notions of id, ego, and superego. The id is a term used to speak of those aspects of persons that are instinctual (and based in one's biological

Photograph of Sigmund
Freud, ca. 1900

nature). In this context, Freud spoke of the pleasure principle, that is, our basic drive to seek pleasure and avoid pain. However, there is an external world in which we exist. Another aspect of who we are, then, is what he called the ego. The ego is the region of mind connected with processing information from the world, especially as this relates to adapting to conditions in the world. In this context, Freud spoke of the reality principle. Basically, we bump into situations in the world, some pleasurable and some painful, and we cope with and respond to them. As we grow, the influence of the world on us, particularly the pains and pleasures imparted upon us by our parents (and others who shape our actions) cause the creation in us of conscience and morality. The aspects of us that are the result of such influence, Freud called the superego (that is, "above the ego"). These aspects of our selves relate to what we believe we ought to do, not simply what we want to do (or, we conceive of things such that we try to coordinate what we think we ought to do and what we want to do).

Drawing on the work of Saussure and Freud, structuralists sought to uncover the structures of various things. Claude Lévi-Strauss (1908–2009), for example, applied structuralism to anthropology, examining the structures that (he thought) governed human behavior and products, such as myths and the structure of families. Jacques Lacan (1901–81) applied structuralism to psychoanalysis. Michel Foucault (1926–84), whose work spans structuralism, as well as what is called post-structuralism, applied structuralism to human relations involving knowledge and power (for a discussion of Foucault, see next chapter). The rest of this chapter focuses on Roland Barthes (1915–80).

Roland Barthes

Roland Barthes (1915–80) was a 20th-century French philosopher and literary critic. His father died when he was only a year old, and he spent his youth with his mother first in the countryside of southern France and then in Paris. As a young man he contracted tuberculosis and spent time in a sanitorium. Later, during much of World War II, his tuberculosis returned, and he spent several years in a sanitorium. As a student, he studied at the Sorbonne, where he received degrees in literature and philology (the study of language). During his life, he taught at various universities around the world, including Johns Hopkins University in Baltimore, during the late 1970s. He died in 1980 as a result of a street accident.

Barthes was important for blending structuralism with semiotics. Semiotics is the study of signs, where a sign is anything that represents something to someone. For example, words are signs. The sounds or written squiggles that English speakers know as *dog* are signs that represent something (namely, dogs) to someone or other. Or, a stop sign is a sign; that is, it is an object that represents something (namely, a social command to behave in a certain way) to someone or other. Besides human signs, such as words or road signs, there are natural signs. For instance, smoke is a sign of fire and a scab is a sign of a wound or injury. Semiotics concerns signs broadly speaking; Barthes focused his studies largely on social and cultural signs. For example, he wrote on dress and fashion as signs of social status and expectations.

As an example of the blending of semiotics and structuralism, Barthes wrote about the significance of a particular simple magazine cover. The magazine was a French magazine called *Paris Match*. A particular cover showed a close-up picture of a young soldier and behind him was the French flag. The soldier seemed to be looking at the flag with respect. However, the picture was not as simple as it might have seemed. The soldier was a young black man who was serving in Algeria (in northern Africa), which at the time was a French colony. During the late 1950s and early 1960s, the Algerians rebelled against the French in order to become an independent country. So, this seemingly simple picture actually carried a lot of meaning in it.

Given Barthes's interest in literature and language, he argued that everyday things and events and experiences should be thought of as texts (much like books are texts). That is, magazine covers carry meaning—indeed, multiple meanings—and should be understood as needing to be interpreted, just as written books are. Barthes also saw clothes and fashion as texts. And how furniture is arranged in a room, Barthes thought, is a text. Indeed, anything that functions as a sign, or system of signs, should be thought of as a text.

Seeing everyday things and events and experiences as texts, Barthes then focused on *how* texts should be understood, and it is here that his influence was especially strong. Barthes argued that the meaning, or meanings, of texts were not the result of what some author intended or wanted. Rather, meaning is part of a whole underlying structure, because even what an author meant or intended in some text, for Barthes, is shaped and influenced by all sorts of things, including the systems of signs that the author worked with. Just as Freud had said that people sometimes act from motivations or causes that they do not themselves know or recognize, so too said Barthes, authors create from meanings that they do not themselves necessarily know or recognize. Having written a book, an author might come to discover what he was saying or trying to say.

For Barthes, not only is the meaning or meanings of texts not given to the author, but also the meaning or meanings is determined largely by readers (in fact, by the act of reading). That is, what a text means is not simply a matter of what the author says or intends, but is a matter of what is understood by readers. As a system of signs, a text does not have meaning in itself, but only in the context of a system of interpretation. Barthes was famous for speaking of "the death of the Author." By this he meant that what a text means is not determined by what an author says it means. In fact, Barthes even said that the notion of an author, meaning some person who is the source of a text's meaning, was itself a fiction. The author is the systems of signs and interpretations. This view was considered quite radical at the time and is still controversial. Nonetheless, Barthes's work was and is considered important, especially in philosophy of language and philosophy of art.

Post-structuralism, Deconstruction, and Postmodernism

Beginning in the 1970s, continental philosophy saw the rise of post-structuralism, postmodernism, and deconstruction. Each of these views was influenced by structuralism, the view that things (such as language, cultural practices, and the self) are governed by structures that give them meaning. The relationships between post-structuralism and postmodernism, postmodernism and deconstruction, and even between structuralism and post-structuralism, are matters of dispute; for example, it is not always clear where one view ends and the other begins. Some philosophers, such as Jacques Derrida (1930–2004), are considered defenders of post-structuralism, postmodernism, and deconstruction. Others, such as Roland Barthes and Michel Foucault, are considered structuralists *and*, in reference to their later work, post-structuralists.

Postmodernism has come to be a broad term used not only in philosophy but also in literary theory, art, social sciences, and even popular culture (among other areas). It is a historical movement occurring after modernism; any understanding of postmodernism, then, depends on an understanding of modernism, and there is no single, universally accepted account of precisely what post-modernism is. However, a few themes can be identified. Modern thought, as expressed during the Enlightenment, tended to focus on reason; postmodernism is more critical of reason in the sense of being critical of the view that what it is to be reasonable is purely objective. Modernism regarded the individual person as identical with her individual consciousness, or mind; in contrast, postmodernism tends to see a person's individual identity (what makes her who she is) as constructed at least in part by social factors, such as social conditions and relations. For instance, a person's identity as a worker—say, blue collar or white collar—hinges partly on the beliefs and practices of the society in which a person lives, as some occupations are considered blue collar and others are not. Modernism privileged science as a means for acquiring knowledge; postmodernism denies that there is a single correct standard for what counts as knowledge and is associated with the claim that the practice of science is not objective, but instead involves values.

Post-structuralism is a philosophical view in response to structuralism. So it is worth saying something about structuralism first. According to the Swiss linguist Ferdinand de Saussure (whose work inspired structuralist philosophers), the significance of parts in a language depends on the differences between those parts and others. For example, the word *rain* acquires its significance through its opposition to words such as *snow* and *hail*. Broadly speaking, the meaning of a word depends on its place in the system—or structure—of language as a whole; its significance does not depend on its relation to some external object (that it stands for water falling from the sky, for example). Structuralists applied this idea to things beyond language, such as texts and human behavior and the self. It was thought that one could understand a phenomenon by investigating its underlying structures. For example, the anthropologist Claude Lévi-Strauss examined structures underlying myths, looking beyond the surface differences among the many different myths worldwide to discern common patterns. Post-structuralism is especially concerned with language and interpretation, viewing not just speech and written texts as matters for interpretation, but also cultural practices, including popular culture. Post-structuralists agreed with Saussure's claim that a system, such as language or, say, the patterns of certain human behavior, can be understood in terms of structures and that meaning arises within those structures rather than through relations to objects outside the system. However, associated with post-structuralism is the view that such systems can be legitimately interpreted in many different ways.

For example, a structuralist might consider the structural or formal features of *Hamlet*, interpreting the play just on the basis of those features. For a post-structuralist, however, it is not as if there is a single system of meanings in *Hamlet*; rather, there are multiple meanings. There are multiple meanings not only of literary texts but in relation to virtually any sign or system of signs, where a sign is understood broadly to mean anything that means something to someone. So, there is no single correct account of the world, or of what counts as true, or of what counts as right action. In addition, post-structuralists have often regarded claims to knowledge, reason, and truth as being used for the purposes of acquiring or maintaining power; for example, those in power in society might define what counts as rational in a way that serves to promote their own interests and keep others subservient (opposing perspectives are dismissed as irrational).

Some post-structuralists used the method of deconstruction, the method of metaphorically taking apart something—a text such as a novel, work of philosophy, or poem, for example, or even a practice—in order to expose its hidden and underlying tensions. These tensions are often in opposition to the apparent and surface intent or meaning of that work. As a philosophical view, the main focus of deconstruction is to show that there is no central, best ground or basis or belief that is a foundation for knowing or evaluating things. The point is to deconstruct (in the sense of unweaving, not in the sense of demolishing) assumptions about what is basic or special.

Jacques Derrida

One of the foremost figures in postmodernism, post-structuralism, and deconstruction was Jacques Derrida (1930–2004), an influential 20th-century French philosopher and literary critic. He was born in Algeria at a time when it was still a French colony. His family was Jewish, and he experienced discrimination early in life, being expelled from several schools, particularly during the German occupation of France and northern Africa during the early 1940s. In the 1950s, he studied philosophy in Paris. After completing his academic degrees, he began teaching, and in the mid-1960s he published several books that made him immediately well known and controversial with many philosophers and literary theorists. From the 1970s through the 1990s, he taught at numerous universities around the world, including several in the United States (especially University of California, Irvine, where he taught one semester every year for many years). In the early 2000s, he developed cancer and died in Paris in 2004.

Derrida is best known for advocating deconstructionism. Derrida referred to deconstruction, the dismantling of any foundation for either knowing or evaluating, as his critique of the metaphysics of presence. What he meant by this was that people (and philosophers) throughout history have assumed that there are certain special notions that are the foundation(s) for everything; these foundations are assumed to be present or at the center of things. For example, some people have taken God to be at the center of everything. Other people have taken consciousness to be at the center; for example, the French philosopher René Descartes (1596–1650) famously said, "I think, therefore I am." The point of this is that what is given, what is certain, is one's own private, personal experiences. Still other people have taken the everyday natural world as the center of everything, meaning the scientific view that the natural world just is a certain way, objective and independent of human's beliefs about it. These are all examples of what Derrida called the metaphysics of presence and his deconstructive goal was to challenge this view.

Influenced by Saussure, Derrida's challenge relied on the claim that meaning depends upon differences. That is, for Derrida, we can only say what something is by saying what it is *not*. His phrase was: Difference precedes presence. This means that nothing just is a certain way; what anything is depends on being able to distinguish it from something else. For example, suppose someone said, "There is a tove in the next room." We could not say what tove is unless we had some way of identifying it, and that, for Derrida, presupposes that we have some way of distinguishing it from non-tove. In this case, we would try to think of some categories or classifications in order to figure out what is tove (and non-tove). Much like the game of "Twenty Questions," we might ask "Is tove large or small, does tove have some particular color, etc." The point is that in order to identify something, we need to be able to categorize it and that means saying what kind of thing it is *not*, just as much as what kind of thing it is. (Imagine if there were two things that seemed to be identical; we would not know how to tell if only one of them, and which one, is tove. We need, said Derrida, difference in order for there to be presence.)

By emphasizing the importance of difference, Derrida coined a term: *differance*. He meant this word to play on two different meanings. One meaning is "to differ" (that is, to recognize that there are dissimilarities). The other meaning is "to defer" (that is, to delay or postpone something). For Derrida, meaning rested on difference (as noted above) and also on deference, that is, on deferring to something. Deferring was his way of saying that what something is, and what it means, is not given at some point in time, but is something that occurs over time. What there is in the world, then, is not a matter of what we can discover (that is, what is given or present), but of what we can construct.

Derrida was famous for saying: "There is nothing beyond the text." By this he meant that things in the world are texts; that is, they must be interpreted and understood, but they are not simply given to us. However, since we can understand and interpret things and events only by their differance, that is, by differing and deferring, then things are always a matter of interpretation. We have no given facts that tell us how things must or should be interpreted or understood. For Derrida, there are no such given facts; everything is a matter of interpretation.

Many philosophers found this view to be unacceptable. They claimed that this view is wildly subjective and relative. Of course, there are facts and a real, objective world that is independent of our interpretations, they said. Some interpretations are better than others; furthermore, some interpretations are simply wrong. But, they said, under Derrida's view, we could not say that an interpretation is wrong, or, for that matter, that an interpretation is right. At times, Derrida said that this objection was exactly correct—there are no right or wrong interpretations, if right and wrong mean that there are some given facts that determine how things are. He did not see this as a problem, however. At other times, Derrida said that this objection was mistaken. His view was that there was simply no given starting point or ending point for understanding and interpretation. There is no simple given meaning to something, rather, there are meanings to it. Furthermore, what those meanings are is not settled once and for all, but flow and disseminate because of differing and deferring. So, to say that there is no fixed meaning, for Derrida, was not to say that there was no meaning; it was to say that there are many meanings.

Derrida's deconstructionism often focused on what he called marginalia, that is, things on the margins. The reason for this, he said, is by paying attention to what is on the margins, it can be easier to see what is not given or the center of attention. In much the same way of pointing out what is abnormal in order to see what is normal, we can find underlying assumptions about what is given by looking at what is simply assumed, that is, what is on the margins. Deconstruction is the use of this technique, and it is used in many fields as a means of understanding. For instance, sociologists often look at fringe groups in society to see what makes them fringe and why they are not mainstream. For Derrida, this was also how philosophy should work.

Michel Foucault

Another influential philosopher of post-structuralism and postmodernism was Michel Foucault (1926–84). Foucault was born in Poitiers, France (southwest of Paris), to a well-to-do family. He studied philosophy and psychology in school, receiving his college degree in 1952 and his Ph.D. in 1960. Following the Nazi occupation of France during World War II, he joined the French Communist Party but was never very active and eventually became disillusioned. During the late 1950s, he taught at several universities across Europe, and in the 1960s he taught in Tunisia. By the end of the 1960s, he returned to teach in France, where he remained until his death. During the 1970s and early 1980s, he was politically active while at the same time writing volumes.

Although Foucault resisted the label structuralism when it was applied to his work, Foucault's early work is often described this way. Foucault stated late in his life that the goal of much of his work had been "to create a history of the different modes by which, in our culture, human beings are made subjects." By this he meant that people were not treated as persons but as kinds of things that were the subject of social and historical forces and structures. For example, in his earlier writings of the 1960s, he wrote of how biology, economics, and language all shaped how people experienced the world and each other. For instance, following the thought of Sigmund Freud, Foucault argued that biology has a tremendous influence on how people interact and on possibilities that open up for them. Following the work of Karl Marx, Foucault claimed that one's economic conditions and situation strongly influence how one sees the world; a life of poverty is very different than a life of luxury. In addition, influenced by the writings of Saussure, Foucault said that language also is a significant force in shaping how we see and interpret the world and ourselves. These earlier thinkers had all claimed that our everyday lives and experiences were shaped by underlying structures. To truly understand people and to truly liberate them so that they can live full lives, they had all argued that we must recognize and analyze these structures. For Foucault, to really understand people and to be in a position to help them, we must see how they exist as subjects, that is, as subjects of biological and economic and linguistic conditions.

As a way of getting at people as subjects, Foucault wrote a number of important philosophical and social books that examined what he called dividing practices. For example, in an early work called *The Birth of the Clinic,* he wrote on how people came to be labeled as sick. He argued that what is seen as illness or sickness is not simply a matter of some objective medical condition. Instead, in different cultures and over different times within a single culture, sickness is understood very differently. At one point in time, for instance, sickness—or certain kinds of sickness—was understood as the result of a person being punished for living badly. What even counted as a sickness varied; for instance, being homosexual was seen as such (and, for some, still is today). The point, for Foucault, was that a person was not seen simply as a person, but, in the context of sickness as being abnormal (with health as the norm), a person was seen as a subject, that is, as a kind of person (the subject of sickness).

In another book, entitled *Madness and Civilization,* Foucault looked at how madness, or insanity, has been seen differently over time and across cultures; as he would put it, how the insane are constructed. What is seen as sane (the norm) is not, for Foucault, merely some objective fact, but is shaped and determined (that is, constructed) by different structures and values and attitudes. In another philosophical and sociological study *Discipline and Punish,* Foucault looked at how the notion of being a criminal was constructed (and differently constructed over different times). Yet another example was a series of books that Foucault wrote on the *History of Sexuality,* in which he traced the construction of what was considered normal and deviant sexual identities and practices over time and across cultures.

An important aspect of all of these kinds of subject-making (or subjectifying) forms of experience is the element of power. It is those who have power who determine and construct subjects. Although many people think of power as mostly physical or, in social settings perhaps as mostly military, for Foucault, power—especially in today's information age—is mostly knowledge. (One of his books is entitled *Knowledge/Power*.) Those who control knowledge, he said, are those with power because they shape and control what counts as legitimate constructions. It is no accident, said Foucault, that the word *discipline* means both correcting someone (such as disciplining a child) and also a form of academic knowledge (such as the discipline of philosophy or physics). In his various written works, he claimed, we could analyze forms of power as means of creating subjects and do this by looking at how those forms of power, and knowledge, identified those on the margins. So, we could find out what society (that is, those in power) means by sanity by investigating who or what counts as being insane, or what society means by legality by investigating who or what counts as being criminal, etc. Having done this, said Foucault, perhaps we would then be in a better position to resist that power if it is oppressive (or enhance that power if it is liberating). Foucault's works were very influential in the second half of the 20th century and continue to be so today.

Continental Philosophy Today

Continental philosophy has been influential not only in philosophy but also in art, social sciences, and literary theory and criticism. Yet, in opposition to analytic philosophy, it has sometimes been criticized for excessive use of jargon and simply for not being clear. Analytic philosophy self-consciously emphasizes clarity and rigor, with philosophers in the analytic tradition endeavoring to be as clear as possible about the concepts they use and the claims they make. Continental philosophers emphasize clarity less; some even explicitly refrained from making their claims as clearly as possible. Theodor Adorno (1903–69), for example, thought that his ideas were best expressed in language that was less clear, and Jacques Derrida (1930–2004) refrained from defining deconstruction, a central concern in his work, as though it cannot be adequately captured by language.

However, this need not mean continental philosophers lack rigor, but rather they are rigorous in different ways, such as (for instance) by taking account of linguistic and historical circumstances, examining easy presuppositions, and viewing humans, not necessarily as isolated individuals, but as beings whose sociality matters in important ways. For their part, continental philosophers might sometimes feel that analytic philosophy is irrelevant (one can be very clear and rigorous about something that, for nearly everyone, is not very important) or mistaken in some of its assumptions. However, there are bridges between continental and analytic philosophy; for instance, the American philosopher Richard Rorty (1931–2007) has been influenced by continental philosophy, and the German philosopher Jürgen Habermas (1929–   ) influences some analytic philosophy. As continental philosophy continues to develop today, it is varied, rich, and very much alive.

Concluding Discussion Questions

1. What does freedom mean, according to Sartre? What does it mean according to Hegel?
2. From ancient times to the 21st century, human history has been rife with conflict. How might Hegel explain this? How might Marx explain this? Do you think either is correct? Why or why not?
3. Suppose the leader of a cult forced all the cult members to commit suicide, claiming that it was God's will for the cult members to end their lives on Earth so that they could join God in heaven. Would the cult leader's actions be morally wrong? What do you think Kierkegaard would think? What would Sartre think? What would Nietzsche think?
4. According to Simone de Beauvoir, what is the relationship between women and the Other? Do you think she is right? If yes, what are some examples to illustrate her view? If not, why not?
5. How does the study of consciousness in phenomenology differ from the study of consciousness in natural science? Why might it ever be better to study consciousness in the way that a phenomenologist does instead of using the methods of natural science? Can such a phenomenological study tell us anything important about consciousness that natural science cannot?
6. On the surface, reason seems to be a positive force in the sense that it helps us figure things out and, arguably, live better lives accordingly. How might Habermas respond? How might Foucault?

Further Reading

Beauvoir, Simone de. *The Second Sex.* New York: Alfred A. Knopf, 1989.

Dudley, Will. *Understanding German Idealism.* Durham, U.K.: Acumen, 2008.

Hegel, Georg W. *Hegel: The Essential Writings.* New York: Harper Perennial, 1977.

Heidegger, Martin. *Basic Writings: Martin Heidegger.* New York: Routledge, 1993.

Husserl, Edmund, and Donn Welton. *The Essential Husserl: Basic Writings in Transcendental Phenomenology.* Bloomington: Indiana University Press, 1999.

Kant, Immanuel. *Critique of Pure Reason.* Edited by Marcus Weigelt and translated by Max Muller. New York: Penguin Classics, 2008.

Kearney, Richard, and Mara Rainwater. *The Continental Philosophy Reader.* New York: Routledge, 1996.

Kierkegaard, Søren, and Robert Bretall, eds. *A Kierkegaard Anthology.* Princeton, N.J.: Princeton University Press, 1973.

Marx, Karl. *The Portable Karl Marx.* Translated by Eugene Kamenka. New York: Penguin, 1983.

Nietzsche, Friedrich, and Walter Kaufmann, ed. and trans. *The Portable Nietzsche.* New York: Penguin Books, 1977.

Sartre, Jean-Paul. *Essays in Existentialism.* Secaucus, N.J.: Citadel, 2000.

West, David. *An Introduction to Continental Philosophy.* Cambridge, U.K.: Polity, 1996.

Glossary

absurdity   in existentialism, absurdity is about the absence of rationality, meaning, or order regarding something important, such as human existence or religious doctrine.

alienation   separation or estrangement from something of significance. Alienation can be understood as a psychological state (as a painful feeling of separation), but it can also be understood as a fundamental way of being. Alienation is a theme in existentialism; Karl Marx also claimed that in capitalist societies workers are alienated from themselves.

angst   a key concept in existentialism, often translated as anxiety; some thinkers consider angst closely related to the fundamental nature of human existence. Angst is distinct from fear in the sense that fear always has a specific object, and angst does not (it is not about anything in particular).

authenticity   a concept in existentialism; although different philosophers give different accounts of authenticity, authenticity generally involves living a life in which one accepts one freedom to choose freely one's own actions, beliefs, and values, as opposed to accepting the beliefs and values of others without ever really thinking about those values and beliefs.

bad faith   in the work of Jean-Paul Sartre, the pretense to oneself that one is not free and is therefore not responsible for one's own choices. Sartre argued that each person is entirely responsible for who he is and what he does (although he acknowledged that we are limited by physical facts; no one, for instance, is free to make himself invisible).

Being   a topic in ontology (the study of existence). Some things clearly exist and some things clearly do not. In between are things whose existence seems less clear, and what does exist seems to exist in different ways (a dandelion, for example, does not seem to exist in the same way the number five does). Studies of *being* examine such different kinds of being (kinds of existence), as well as what distinguishes what exists from what does not exist. To put the point another way, the question of being is the question "What is it to exist?"

being in itself/being for itself   in the work of Jean-Paul Sartre, a distinction between two different kinds of being, or two different kinds of existence. Being-in-itself is non-conscious being, such as the being of lamps and rocks. Being-in-itself simply *is:* it is passive. Being-for-itself is conscious being, such as the being of a human being; it is active in the sense that it reflects, chooses, imagines, and plans.

Critical Theory   a school of thought in 20th- and early 21st-century continental philosophy, influenced by Karl Marx; critical theorists agreed with Marx that economic conditions, such as in capitalist societies, are oppressive, but they argued that there are other forces of oppression as well, such as ideology, culture (including popular culture), and reason. Critical theorists subjected human society to critique with the ultimate aim of promoting freedom.

Dasein   Martin Heidegger's term for the being of the individual human; Dasein involves reflection on its own being, meaning that the being of humans ponders its own existence. Dasein does not have a permanent, fixed nature.

deconstruction   as a philosophical view, the view that there is no privileged or basic foundation or perspective; as a method, the process of metaphorically taking apart a text (understood broadly) for the purpose of exposing its underlying tensions.

dialectical materialism   the view that human history is shaped by material, economic forces that undergo predictable stages of development; usually associated with Marxism, it was seen as an account for the inevitable emergence of communism.

differance   in the work of Jacques Derrida, a term that plays on *differ* and *defer;* it describe the interplay of meaning between signs, broadly speaking; meaning arises because of the differences between signs, and meaning must be constructed; it is not simply given or present at any particular period of time (in that sense, it is deferred).

German Idealism   a school of late 18th- and early 19th-century thought in German philosophy, taking as its starting point the work of Immanuel Kant and his claim that the mind organizes experience and this organization makes experience possible. German idealists rejected Kant's notion of the noumena, real but unknowable entities. German idealists were idealists in the sense that they believed reality is mind-dependent.

hermeneutics the art and study of interpretation; hermeneutics regards the methods, principles, and nature of interpretation, from the interpretation of written texts to the interpretation of human existence. Hermeneutics has been a significant school of thought in 20th- and 21st-century continental thought.

master/slave morality Friedrich Nietzsche's distinction between morality based on resentment and fear (slave morality) and morality based on achievement and creativity (master morality); Nietzsche associated slave morality with Christianity in particular.

materialism the view that matter is all that exists.

noumena/phenomena in the work of Immanuel Kant, the distinction between that which is experienced via the five senses (the phenomena, or appearances) and that which is merely the object of thought, unexperienced and unknowable (the noumena).

Other, the a general term for those who are, or who seem to be, importantly different from ourselves and, as a consequence, seem alien, strange, and even threatening. Sartre claimed that individual humans regard other humans as the Other and, feeling threatened, respond by trying to assert themselves with respect to the Other (so, human relations necessarily involve conflict). Simone de Beauvoir argued that society views women as the Other.

phenomenology in 20th- and early 21st-century continental philosophy, the study of consciousness and the objects of consciousness; phenomenology was founded by Edmund Husserl.

postmodernism a school of thought following modernism. Postmodern is used in many, not necessarily consistent ways. Associated with postmodernism is a denial of objective standards for rationality and knowledge, the view that science involves values (it is not objective), a concern with the social aspects of concepts and human existence (including language), and a mistrust of the modern conception of progress.

post-structuralism   in 20th- and 21st-century continental thought, a school of thought following structuralism. It is associated with a focus on language, the regarding of humans and human practices as texts to be interpreted, the view that claims to knowledge and truth are closely connected to power relations, and the view that there is no privileged perspective from which to evaluate claims to knowledge or morality.

semiotics   the study of signs, where signs are understood in a broad sense to include anything that means something to someone; signs include not only linguistic signs (such as words) but signs in the natural world (for example, as smoke is a sign of fire) and signs in culture and human behavior (for example, as wearing a tie might be a sign of performing white-collar work).

structuralism   in 20th- and 21st-century continental thought, the view that language and things such as social and cultural practices and the self are governed by structures that give them meaning. The linguist Ferdinand de Saussure founded structuralism; later thinkers applied his insights to fields such as social sciences, literature, and philosophy.

superman (overman)   in the work of Friedrich Nietzsche, a person wholly and fundamentally better than human beings, for example, in creativity, independence, joyfulness, and strength in a broad sense; the superman, Nietzsche said, is as different from man as man is from an ape. The superman is the meaning of the earth, for Nietzsche, in the sense that striving to become the superman or more like the superman gives human existence meaning.

Key People

Adorno, Theodor (1903–1969)   *important German philosopher in critical theory; Adorno was critical of positivism, the enlightenment and its solely instrumental use of reason, and the tendency in thought to identify individuals with general concepts, blurring what makes individuals unique and distinct from each other.*

In this passage, from Dialectic of Enlightenment, *Adorno (with co-author Max Horkheimer) describes the Enlightenment approach to reason (instrumental reason).*

> For the Enlightenment, whatever does not conform to the rule of computation and utility is suspect. So long as it can develop undisturbed by any outward repression, there is no holding it. In the process, it treats its own ideas of human rights exactly as it does the older universals. Every spiritual resistance it encounters serves merely to increase its strength. Which means that Enlightenment still recognizes itself even in myths. Whatever myths the resistance may appeal to, by virtue of the very fact that they become arguments in the process of opposition, they acknowledge the principle of dissolvent rationality for which they reproach the Enlightenment. Enlightenment is totalitarian.

> [Horkheimer, Max, and Theodor W. Adorno. *Dialectic of Enlightenment.* London: Verso, 1979.]

Barthes, Roland (1915–1980)   *French structuralist philosopher and semiotician; Barthes applied structuralism to social and cultural signs and was famous for proclaiming the "death of the author"; the meaning of a text, according to Barthes, is not to be found in the author's intentions but rather in the reader's understanding of the text.*

In this passage, Barthes characterizes structuralism.

> . . . The goal of all structuralist activity . . . is to reconstruct an "object" in such a way as to manifest thereby the rules of functioning (the "functions") of this object. Structure is therefore actually a simula-

crum of the object, but a directed, *interested* simulacrum, since the imitated object makes something appear which remained invisible, or if one prefers, unintelligible in the natural object. Structural man takes the real, decomposes it, then recomposes it . . . between the two objects . . . of structuralist activity, there occurs something new, and what is new is nothing less than the generally intelligible . . .

[Roland Barthes. *Essais Critiques.* Translated by Richard Howard. Paris: Editions du Seuil, 1964.]

Beauvoir, Simone de (1908–1986)   *French existentialist and feminist philosopher; she is best known for her groundbreaking book* The Second Sex, *one of the founding texts of feminism. She also wrote on subjects such as existential ethics and freedom, in addition to writing novels.*

In the following passage, de Beauvoir characterizes women as the Other in relation to men.

Thus humanity is male and man defines woman not in herself but as relative to him; she is not regarded as an autonomous being . . . she is simply what man decrees; thus she is called "the sex," by which is meant that she appears essentially to the male as a sexual being. For she is sex—absolute sex, no less. She is defined and differentiated with reference to man and not he with reference to her; she is the incidental, the inessential as opposed to the essential. He is the Subject, he is the Absolute—she is the Other.

[Simone de Beauvoir. *The Second Sex.* New York: Knopf, 1953.]

Derrida, Jacques (1930–2004)   *French philosopher important in postmodernism, post-structuralism, and deconstruction.*

Derrida, in this passage, characterizes differance, a key term in his work.

. . . [a] signified concept is never present in itself, in an adequate presence that would refer only to itself. Every concept is necessarily and essentially inscribed in a chain or a system, within which it refers to another, and to other concepts, by the systematic play of differences. Such a play, then—differance—is no longer simply a concept, but the possibility of conceptuality, of the conceptual system and process and general. For the same reason, differance . . . is not what we represent to ourselves as the . . . present self-referential unity of a concept and sound.

[Jacques Derrida. *Speech and Phenomena, and Other Essays on Husserl's Theory of Signs.* Evanston, Ill.: Northwestern University Press, 1973.]

Fichte, Johann Gottlieb (1762–1814) *German Idealist philosopher who saw himself as completing Kant's system; he viewed the world as posited by the ego, or the self, and regarded freedom as a necessary condition for existence.*

In this selection, Fichte discusses the choice to approach philosophical inquiry with either idealism or dogmatism.

What sort of philosophy one chooses depends . . . on what sort of man one is; for a philosophical system is not a dead piece of furniture that we can reject or accept as we wish; it is rather a thing animated by the soul of the person who holds it. A person indolent by nature or dulled and distorted by mental servitude, learned luxury, and vanity, will never raise himself to the level of idealism. We can show the dogmatist the inadequacy . . . of his system . . . but . . . he is incapable of . . . coolly assessing a theory which he absolutely cannot endure.

[Johann Gottlieb Fichte. *The Science of Knowledge.* Edited and translated by Peter Heath and John Lachs. Cambridge: Cambridge University Press, 1982.]

Foucault, Michel (1926–1984) *French structuralist and post-structuralist philosopher whose work ranged over such diverse phenomena as power, knowledge, sexuality, and insanity; he argued that who has knowledge has power.*

Foucault here describes the relation between truth and power.

. . . truth isn't outside power, or lacking in power . . . Truth is a thing of this world: it is produced only by virtue of multiple forms of constraint . . . Each society has its regime of truth, its "general politics" of truth; that is, the types of discourse which it accepts and makes function as true; the mechanisms and instances which enable one to distinguish true and false statements, the means by which each is sanctioned; the techniques and procedures accorded value in the acquisition of truth; the status of those who are charged with saying what counts as true.

[Michel Foucault. *Power/Knowledge: Selected Interviews and Other Writings 1972–77.* Edited and translated by Colin Gordon. New York: Pantheon, 1972.]

Gadamer, Hans-Georg (1900–2002) *German philosopher whose work is especially important in 20th-century hermeneutics. Gadamer denied that interpretation involves strict rules and argued that prejudices, in the sense of prejudgments, are necessary for the possibility of understanding (which, he said, always involves linguistic and historical conditions).*

In the selection below, Gadamer characterizes prejudices.

Prejudices are not necessarily unjustified and erroneous, so that they inevitably distort the truth. In fact, the historicity of our existence entails that prejudices, in the literal sense of the word, constitute the initial directedness of our whole ability to experience. Prejudices are biases of our openness to the world. They are simply conditions whereby we experience something—whereby what we encounter says something to us. This certainly does not mean that we are enclosed within a wall of prejudices . . . instead we welcome just that guest who promises something new to our curiosity.

[Hans-Georg Gadamer. *Philosophical Hermeneutics.* Translated and edited by David E. Linge. Berkeley: University of California Press, 1976.]

Habermas, Jürgen (1929–) *German philosopher notable for his work in Critical Theory and on topics such as knowledge, rationality, and communication. In his work on communicative action, he argued that those who control the means of communication are also those who decide what counts as knowledge and what counts as rationality.*

In this passage, Habermas relates knowledge and rationality to communicative practices.

As long as the basic concepts of the philosophy of consciousness lead us to understand knowledge exclusively as knowledge of something in the objective world, rationality is assessed by how the isolated subject orients himself to representational and propositional contents

. . . By contrast, as soon as we conceive of knowledge as communicatively mediated, rationality is assessed in terms of the capacity of responsible participants in interaction to orient themselves in relation to validity claims geared to intersubjective recognition. Communicative reason finds its criteria in the argumententative procedures for directly or indirectly redeeming claims to propositional truth, normative rightness, subjective truthfulness, and aesthetic harmony.

[Jürgen Habermas. *The Philosophical Discourse of Modernity.* Cambridge, Mass.: MIT Press, 1987.]

Hegel, Georg Wilhelm Friedrich (1770–1831) *Very influential German Idealist philosopher. Hegel sought to construct a theoretical system to explain all of reality. He defended the view that history is the developmental process of Mind coming to self-consciousness and recognizing that it is reality; Hegel thought that the ultimate product of this process is freedom.*

This passage is a description by Hegel of his philosophy of history.

The only Thought which Philosophy brings with it to the contemplation of History is the simple conception of *Reason,* that Reason is the Sovereign of the World; that the history of the world, therefore, presents us with a rational process. . . . Reason . . . is Substance, as well as Infinite Power; its own Infinite Material underlying all the natural and spiritual life which it originates, as also the Infinite Form—that which sets this Material in motion . . . Reason is the substance of the Universe; viz., that by which and in which all reality has its being and subsistence . . . it is the Infinite Energy of the Universe . . .

[G. W. F. Hegel. "Introduction to the Philosophy of History." In *From Plato to Nietzsche.* Edited by Walter Kaufmann and Forrest E. Baird. Englewood Cliffs, N.J.: Prentice Hall, 1994.]

Heidegger, Martin (1889–1976) *German existential philosopher influenced by hermeneutics and phenomenology. Heidegger believed the question of Being was of fundamental importance and as a way of examining Being, he examined human being, which he called Dasein. According to Heidegger, authentic existence involves the continual projecting of oneself into the future, maintaining one's individual identity, and facing one's own death.*

In this selection, Heidegger explains what he takes to be a central feature of Dasein (human being).

Dasein is an entity which does not just occur among other entities. Rather it is ontically distinguished by the fact that, in its very Being, that Being is an issue for it . . . this is a constitutive state of Dasein's Being, and this implies that Dasein, in its Being, has a relationship towards that Being—a relationship which itself is one of Being. And this means further that there is some way in which Dasein understands itself in its Being, and that to some degree it does so explicitly. It is peculiar to this entity that with and through its Being, this Being is disclosed to it.

[Martin Heidegger. *Being and Time.* Translated by J. Macquarrie and E. Robinson. Oxford: Blackwell, 1967.]

Horkheimer, Max (1895–1971) *German philosopher important in critical theory. With Theodor Adorno, Horkheimer cowrote* Dialectic of Enlightenment, *in which they claimed that reason had become a means of oppression.*

In this passage, from Dialectic of Enlightenment, *Horkheimer and Adorno describe the Enlightenment approach to reason.*

For the Enlightenment, whatever does not conform to the rule of computation and utility is suspect. So long as it can develop undisturbed by any outward repression, there is no holding it. In the process, it treats its own ideas of human rights exactly as it does the older universals. Every spiritual resistance it encounters serves merely to increase its strength. Which means that Enlightenment still recognizes itself even in myths. Whatever myths the resistance may appeal to, by virtue of the very fact that they become arguments in the process of opposition, they acknowledge the principle of dissolvent rationality for which they reproach the Enlightenment. Enlightenment is totalitarian.

[Horkheimer, Max, and Theodor W. Adorno. *Dialectic of Enlightenment.* London: Verso, 1979.]

Husserl, Edmund (1859–1938) *German philosopher who founded phenomenology. He hoped that pure experience would provide a certain* *foundation for all knowledge and claimed that consciousness is always intentional (always of something, never empty).*

The passage below contains Husserl's characterization of consciousness.

The terminological expression . . . for designating the basic character of being as consciousness, as consciousness of something, is *intentionality*. In unreflective holding of some object or other in consciousness, we are turned or directed towards it . . . The phenomenological reversal of our gaze shows that this "being directed" is really an immanent essential feature of the respective experiences involved; they are "intentional" experiences. Consciousness of something is not an empty holding of something; every phenomenon has its own total form of intention . . . but at the same time it has a structure . . .

[Edmund Husserl. "Phenomenology." In *Encyclopaedia Britannica*, 1929.]

Kant, Immanuel (1724–1804) *German philosopher who argued that the mind organizes experience; in this way, objects conform to our mind rather than the other way around. If the mind did not structure experience, according to Kant, experience would not be possible. Kant's work in metaphysics, ethics, epistemology, and aesthetics influenced many philosophers and led to German Idealism.*

Below, Kant describes the noumena as unknowable.

Hence the pure conceptions of the understanding have no meaning whatever, when they quit the objects of experience and refer to things in themselves *(noumena)*. They serve, as it were, to spell out phenomena, that these may be able to be read as experience. The axioms arising from their relation to the world of sense, only serve our understanding for use in experience. Beyond this, are only arbitrary combinations, destitute of objective reality, and the possibility of which can neither be known *à priori,* nor their reference to objects be confirmed, or even made intelligible by an example, because all examples are borrowed from some possible experience, and consequently the objects of those conceptions are nothing but what may be met with in a possible experience.

[Immanuel Kant. *Kant's Prolegomena and Metaphysical Foundations of Natural Science.* Translated, with a biography and introduction by Ernest Belfort Bax, 2nd rev. ed. London: George Bell and Sons, 1891. Chapter: *THE SECOND PART OF THE MAIN TRANSCENDENTAL PROBLEM. How is pure Natural Science possible?* Available online. URL: http://oll.libertyfund.org/title/361/54872. Accessed on 2010-04-28.

Kierkegaard, Søren (1813–1855) *Danish philosopher considered one of the founding figures of existentialism. A Christian, Kierkegaard believed that Christianity involved a leap of faith and a passionate commitment.*

In the following passage, Kierkegaard claims that truth is subjectivity.

The objective accent falls on WHAT is said, the subjective accent on HOW it is said . . . In the ethico-religious sphere, accent is again on the "how" . . . it refers to the relationship sustained by the existing individual, in his own existence to the content of his utterance. Objectively the interest is focused merely on the thought-content, subjectively on the inwardness. At its maximum this inward "how" is the passion of the infinite, and the passion of the infinite is the truth. But the passion of the infinite is precisely subjectivity, and thus subjectivity becomes the truth.

[Søren Kierkegaard. *Concluding Unscientific Postscript.* Translated by David F. Swenson and Walter Lowrie. Princeton, N.J.: Princeton University Press, 1968.]

Marx, Karl (1818–1883) *German philosopher and political theorist. Marx was influenced by Hegel but believed that Hegel had neglected the material conditions under which people actually live. Marx advocated dialectical materialism, according to which history unfolds in a developmental way and will ultimately lead to communism.*

A short elaboration of Marx's views on moral and social values appeared in his Preface to A Contribution to the Critique of Political Economy *(1859).*

In the social production of their life, men enter into definite relations that are indispensable and independent of their will, relations of production which correspond to a definite stage of development of their material productive forces. The sum total of these relations of production constitutes the economic structure of society, the real foundation, on which rises a legal and political superstructure and to which correspond definite forms of social consciousness. The mode of production of material life conditions the social, political and intellectual life process in general. It is not the consciousness of men that determines their being, but, on the contrary, their social being that determines their consciousness. At a certain stage of their development, the material productive forces of society come in conflict with the existing relations of production . . . From forms of development of the productive forces these relations turn into their fetters. Then begins an epoch of social revolution. With the change of the economic foundation, the entire immense superstructure is more or less rapidly transformed. In considering such transformations, a distinction should always be made between the material transformation of the economic conditions of production, which can be determined with the precision of natural science, and the legal, political, religious, aesthetic or philosophic—in short, ideological forms in which men become conscious of this conflict and fight it out. Just as our opinion of an individual is not based on what he thinks of himself, so can we not judge of such a period of transformation by its own consciousness; on the contrary, this consciousness must be explained rather from the contradictions of material life, from the existing conflict between the social productive forces and the relations of production.

[Marx, Karl. *A Contribution to the Critique of Political Economy*. New York: Charles H. Kerr & Co., 1904.]

Nietzsche, Friedrich (1844–1900)   *German philosopher who wrote, often in an unconventional style, on topics ranging from aesthetics and ethics to epistemology (the study of knowledge) and the nature of reality. Nietzsche is famous for his pronouncement that God is dead. With the dead of God, Nietzsche believed humans needed to create their own values.*

In the passage below, Nietzsche claims that what is good is power, as opposed to the qualities he negatively associated with Christianity. By power, Nietzsche did not mean power over others (such as political power) but rather the flourishing of oneself, such as creativity and maximizing one's potential.

What is good? Everything that heightens the feeling of power in man, the will to power, power itself.

What is bad? Everything that is born of weakness.

What is happiness? The feeling that power is growing, that resistance is overcome. Not contentedness but more power; not peace but war; not virtue but fitness (Renaissance virtue, *virtù*, virtue that is moraline-free).

The weak and the failures shall perish: first principle of our love of man. And they shall even be given every possible assistance.

What is more harmful than any vice? Active pity for all the failures and all the weak: Christianity.

[Nietzsche, Friedrich. *The Antichrist*. Translated by H. L. Mencken. New York: Alfred Knopf, 1918.]

Sartre, Jean-Paul (1905–1980)   *French philosopher and one of the key figures of existentialism. Sartre denied that there is a fixed human nature and believed that people are free to create themselves and are thus responsible for themselves and how they live their lives.*

Sartre's essay "Existentialism Is a Humanism," from which the following passage is taken, contains perhaps the most famous characterizations of existentialism.

What do we mean by saying that existence precedes essence? We mean that man first of all exists, encounters himself, surges up in the world—and defines himself afterwards . . . there is no human nature, because there is no God to have a conception of it. Man simply is. Not that he is simply what he conceives himself to be, but he is what he wills, and as he conceives himself after already existing . . . Man is nothing but that which he makes of himself. This is the first principle of existentialism.

[Sartre, Jean-Paul. *Existentialism and Humanism*. Translated by Philip Mairet. London: Methuen, 1948.]

Saussure, Ferdinand de (1857–1913)   *Swiss linguist influential on structuralism; Saussure described language as a system in which parts have meaning because of their relations, or differences, between other parts.*

Here Saussure describes linguistic structure as the proper focus of linguistic study.

The linguist must take the study of linguistic structure as his primary concern, and relate all other manifestations of language to it . . . What, then, is linguistic structure? It is not, in our opinion, simply the same thing as language. Linguistic structure is only one part of language, even though it is an essential part. The structure of a language is a social product of our language faculty. At the same time, it is also a body of necessary conventions adopted by society to enable members of society to their language faculty.

[Saussure, Ferdinand de. *Course in General Linguistics.* London: Duckworth, 1983.]

Schelling, Friedrich Wilhelm Joseph von (1775–1854)   *German Idealist philosopher whose views changed over time; he is best known for his philosophy of nature and his "philosophy of identity," in which he identified the subject of experience (what experiences) with the object of experience (what is experienced).*

The passage below offers a brief characterization of Schelling's philosophy of nature.

So long as I myself am identical with Nature, I understand what a living nature is as well as I understand my own life; I apprehend how this universal life of Nature reveals itself in manifold forms, in progressive developments, in gradual approximations to freedom. As soon, however, as I separate myself, and with me everything ideal, from Nature, nothing remains to me but a dead object, and I cease to comprehend how a *life outside* me can be possible.

[Schelling, Friedrich Wilhelm Joseph von. "Ideas for a Philosophy of Nature." In *Texts in German Philosophy.* Translated by Peter Heath and Errol E. Harris. Cambridge: Cambridge University Press, 1989.]

PART IV
Analytic Philosophy

Introductory Discussion Questions

1. Does the name "Santa Claus" refer to anything? If not, why not? If it does, what does it refer to?
2. Are there any questions that science cannot, in principle, answer? Are there any questions that philosophy can answer?
3. What, if anything, is the primary task or purpose of philosophy?
4. Are the concepts and assumptions of everyday, ordinary language clear enough and complete enough to answer philosophical questions?
5. Is the sentence "Murder is wrong" true? Why or why not?
6. What, if anything, makes the following two sentences true (or false): "Bachelors are unmarried" and "Bachelors are unhappy."

Analytic Philosophy

Analytic philosophy is a broad area of philosophical thought and practice, mostly associated with philosophers in England and the United States in the 20th and 21st centuries. What characterizes analytic philosophy is not so much a set of shared beliefs but a way of approaching philosophy. This approach includes a focus on analysis, a style of argument that emphasizes clarity and precision. Much of 20th-century analytic philosophy concerned language, both as a subject in its own right and as a way of investigating traditional philosophical topics such as knowledge and the good. Analytic philosophy is often contrasted with continental philosophy (roughly speaking, philosophy carried out by philosophers on the European continent in the 20th and 21st centuries).

There is no single accepted account of what analysis is in the philosophical sense. At a fundamental level, however, analysis is often thought to be the examination of a thing's parts. Many analytic philosophers analyze concepts in order to understand those concepts better. For example, consider the concept of knowledge. Suppose someone claims to know that the New York Yankees won the World Series in some particular year. If the Yankees did not win the World Series that year, then the person did not *know* that the New York Yankees won (even though she might have believed it). What this suggests is that a component of knowledge is truth: knowing something involves knowing something that is *true*. If we know that knowledge involves truth, then we know that to understand what knowledge is, we should investigate truth. The primary goal of conceptual analysis is clarity: by examining the parts of a concept, we can become clearer on what that concept is.

Traditional analytic philosophy is often regarded in the context of the "linguistic turn" in philosophy, as many prominent analytic philosophers turned their attention to language. Analytic philosophers studied (and continue to study), for instance, not only knowledge and goodness, but also the words *knowledge* and *goodness*. They also studied the logical form (or structure) of sentences, as well as parts of speech such as names (*Robert Frost*, for instance) and descriptions (such as *the author of* "The Road Not Taken"). At a glance, this focus on language might seem to have little to do with serious philosophical concerns. However, philosophers studied language for at least two reasons. The first was the belief that there are interesting philosophical issues about language itself. Historically, the work of late 19th-century German philosopher Gottlob Frege (1848–1925) was influential in this respect. A second reason philosophers focused on language was the belief that it was possible to shed light on other philosophical subjects by examining language.

Bertrand Russell's (1872–1970) influential theory of descriptions was important in this respect. Russell believed that ordinary language (everyday, informal language) was flawed, vague, and potentially misleading. By putting the sentences of ordinary language into statements of formal logic, he thought, it was possible to view a sentence's logical form. Viewing the logical form of a sentence, in turn, helped philosophers better understand the meaning of those sentences and avoid potential confusions. An instance of this concerned true negative existential statements, that is, statements that accurately say that an object does not exist, such as "Pegasus does not exist." Such a statement is puzzling because, in order for "Pegasus does not exist" to be about anything (and therefore in order for the statement to be true), it seems there would have to be an object Pegasus. If there is an object Pegasus, however, then "Pegasus does not exist" is false. Yet the sentence clearly seems to be true. Some philosophers such as Alexius Meinong (1853–1920) tried to solve this puzzle by arguing that objects such as Pegasus do exist, but in a special way different than how ordinary objects exist. Pegasus, on this line of thought, *subsists*, but because Pegasus does not exist in the usual way, "Pegasus does not exist" is true.

This proposed solution left many philosophers puzzled, for it was far from clear how an object could both exist in some way and yet not exist. Russell's way of solving this puzzle was to analyze the logical forms of such sentences. Russell argued that, in the logical form of "Pegasus does not exist," the term *Pegasus* does not name an object, but instead stands for a description of an object. To analyze the truth or falsity of the sentence "Pegasus does not exist" involves analyzing the components of the description that *Pegasus* stands for. An analysis of those components shows that "Pegasus does not exist" is true. Because the truth or falsity of the sentence does not require an object "Pegasus," this eliminated a need to claim that objects such as Pegasus subsisted in some mysterious way. A close attention to the logical form of language, then, could resolve philosophical disputes.

Together with the very influential Austrian philosopher Ludwig Wittgenstein (1889–1951), Russell elaborated the relation between language and reality in the theory of Logical Atomism. According to Logical Atomism, the structure of language mirrored the structure of the world. Therefore, by analyzing the logical form of language, it was possible to learn the structure of the world itself. According to this view, there are atomic propositions expressed by very basic sentences such as, "This is red." In such a sentence, the word *this* picks out an object in the world and the word *red* picks out a quality that the object has. For each atomic proposition, there corresponds an atomic fact, in this case the fact that something is red. Such propositions are atomic in two senses: first, they cannot be analyzed into further parts; second, the structure of the world is built out of atomic facts.

In stark contrast to the formal approach of Russell and Wittgenstein was the school of ordinary language philosophy, advocated by philosophers such as J. L. Austin (1911–60) and Gilbert Ryle (1900–76). In this view, ordinary language is not something that needs to be fixed. Rather, ordinary language was therapeutic in the sense that a study of ordinary language could show philosophers, not how to *solve* certain philosophical problems, but how to *dissolve* those problems by showing that they are not genuine problems at all. We can see by the use of the word *know*, for example, that to have knowledge is not just to have an internal mental state, but to behave in certain ways. We say that a person knows how to fix a flat tire on a bike, for example, only if she can manipulate the tire in certain ways, say, by putting a patch on it. So, we do not need to look for some logical form of sentences connected to knowledge; we simply need to look carefully at how we use the concept of knowledge.

Also, Wittgenstein in his later work pointed out that language has many more uses than offering true or false descriptions of the world. Humans tell jokes, ask questions, make promises, compliment each other, and do many other things. He spoke of these many uses as being language games, and a complete understanding of language cannot focus solely on how sentences are true or false. Following these lines, philosophers such as Austin and others developed a theory of speech acts, giving an account of the different kinds of things people do with words.

The work of British philosopher G. E. Moore (1873–1958), associated with commonsense philosophy, was related to this view of ordinary language. Moore not only rejected certain conceptions of the good based on observations of how people use the word *good,* but also he rejected epistemological skepticism in favor of common sense and placed renewed emphasis on statements of ordinary language. It is common sense, for instance, that there is an external world, and that the world exists independently of whatever humans might think or believe about it. What was of philosophical interest, then, according to Moore, was not a debate about whether such propositions are true but how to understand those propositions correctly. The way to do this was through analysis of those propositions; it was important to understand what sentences such as "There are material objects" mean.

Another important school of thought in analytic philosophy is logical positivism, a view advocated by some members of what was called the Vienna Circle and popularized by A. J. Ayer (1910–89). Logical positivism represents a strain of thought in analytic philosophy that favors, and is based upon, science and that rejects traditional abstract metaphysics. On a logical positivist view, a sentence is meaningful either (1) because it is true or false by definition or (2) because it can be verified through some experience of the empirical world. Sentences that do not meet either of these criteria are meaningless. So, some logical positivists claimed that many statements about metaphysics, aesthetics, ethics, and religion are meaningless.

Among contemporary 20th-century philosophers, the American philosopher W. V. Quine (1908–2000) was crucial both to continuing the tradition of analytic philosophy as well as to critiquing it. Quine continued the traditions of analytic philosophy insofar as his work often focused on language and the relation between language and reality; like analytic philosophers before him, Quine drew lessons about ontology (the study of existence) in part from studies of both formal logic and language. Also significant is Quine's emphasis on naturalism, an approach in philosophy that carries on the tradition in analytic philosophy of valuing science. Philosophers advocating naturalism seek to explain the world in scientific terms. Quine advocated a naturalist epistemology, according to which knowledge is best understood by examining the physical or psychological processes by which humans acquire knowledge, rather than by formulating rules according to which humans ought to acquire knowledge.

However, Quine offered an important critique of analytic philosophy; he rejected the analytic/synthetic distinction. According to that distinction, statements that are analytically true are true by definition, and statements that are synthetically true are true, roughly speaking, because of empirical facts about the world. Quine argued that there is no such fundamental distinction. A body of statements that describes all of our beliefs, he said, "faces experience as a whole." What this means is that we do not evaluate the truth of a sentence just by itself, or in isolation; rather, we evaluate its truth together with every other statement we believe. Some of these statements (for example, statements regarding how grass smells) relate more closely to experience than to others, but there is no fundamental difference in kind between those statements that do and those that do not. Indeed, according to Quine, when we encounter an experience that runs counter to what we believe, it is up to us to decide which of our beliefs to modify or reject. Sometimes we choose a belief that more closely relates to experience, and sometimes we do not.

The significance this has on analytic philosophy is this: if there is no difference in kind between analytic and synthetic statements, this calls into question the very notion of analysis. This is because, according to much of analytic philosophy, the business of philosophy was to analyze language, or concepts, and it was the business of science to investigate other sorts of statements, those that are synthetic. If there is no analytic/synthetic distinction, it is much less clear what it is philosophers are supposed to analyze: philosophers might as well analyze cats as much as traditional philosophical subjects such as knowledge. Quine's own answer is that there is no rigid distinction between philosophy and science: both investigate the world.

Today, many philosophers reject this claim, continuing to believe in the analytic/synthetic distinction. Nonetheless, an explicit method of analysis today plays a less central role in Anglo-American philosophy than it once did. Analytic philosophy continues today at least in the sense that much of the philosophical work done in England and the United States continues to value precision, clarity, and an acknowledgment of how empirical science can shed light on various philosophical subjects. Although language is still a concern for many philosophers, it is less central in analytic philosophy than it was. Other main topics include philosophy of mind, philosophy of science, epistemology, metaphysics, and ethics.

Gottlob Frege

Gottlob Frege (1848–1925) was a German mathematician and philosopher often referred to as the father of modern mathematical logic and regarded as one of the founding figures of analytic philosophy. Frege came from a family of teachers, with both of his parents running a girls' school as he grew up. He attended the University of Jena as a student and then the University of Göttingen, receiving his doctorate degree from the latter in 1873. He spent his professional career as a mathematician at the University of Jena, from 1879 to 1918.

Frege shaped the history of logic and provided what is seen as the foundation of modern logic, which was to assume much importance in analytic philosophy. His work in the philosophy of language also proved highly influential. Although Frege's work is now credited as groundbreaking and the foundation of modern logic, it was almost completely ignored during his lifetime. It was only because of the efforts of two other renowned philosophers, Ludwig Wittgenstein (1889–1951) and Bertrand Russell (1872–1970), that his work came to the attention of most other philosophers and mathematicians.

Today, Frege is renowned for promoting the view of *logicism,* that is, the view that mathematics can be framed in terms of logic. Logic, he held, was the foundation of mathematics. For Frege, the basic components of mathematics, such as numbers or relations or sets, can be formulated in an axiomatic logical system and, consequently, all mathematical sentences can be formulated in terms of logical sentences. This view was endorsed by many philosophers and by some (but not all) mathematicians. Contrasted with logicism are empiricism, psychologism, and intuitionism in mathematics. In philosophy of mathematics, an empiricist view holds that the justification of mathematical truths is based on empirical experience, that is, what we experience of the empirical. According to psychologism, mathematical truths are best understood as truths about psychology; on this view, a true mathematical statement, for example, reflects a truth about how people think. And according to intuitionism, associated by philosophers such as Immanuel Kant (1724–1804), mathematics depends on a special faculty of intuition; intuition in this sense is not a hunch, or a guess that turns out to be right, but rather a kind of direct, intellectual awareness of something, such as direct awareness of an entity or a fact. Frege opposed each of these views. Mathematics, he thought was objective and does not depend on our experience of the empirical world, psychological truths, or intuition. In order to defend his own logicist view, Frege believed he needed a language other than ordinary language to formulate mathematical truths; this is because ordinary language is vague and potentially misleading. This led him to new and important developments in logic—a language that would allow him, Frege believed, to express truths more clearly and accurately than ordinary language permitted.

One of the basic developments that Frege made was to treat logic as an axiomatic system. Much like the classical Greek mathematician Euclid did for geometry, Frege set about to establish logic on the basis of certain fundamental axioms (that is, truths that were taken as given), a set of inference rules (that is, ways of deriving sentences or formulas from those axioms), and theorems (that is, derived sentences or formulas). For example, today logicians speak of certain basic logical axioms, such as the axiom of excluded middle (or, for any sentence, either it is true or false, but not both). A common rule of inference is what is called *modus ponens*. This rule says that if it is the case that a sentence P is true and also that P implies Q, then Q is true (or, one can derive Q). Another common rule of inference is called *modus tollens*. This rule says that if it is the case that a sentence Q is false and also that P implies Q, then P is false (or, one can derive, not-P). Theorems are any true sentence that can be derived from the set of axioms by using the rules of inference. For Frege, part of the importance of establishing logic as an axiomatic system was that logic could be better seen as objective and independent of people's actual reasoning. His phrase was that he wanted to "de-psychologize" logic. Logic, he claimed, involved truth, independent of whether or not people recognized that truth. Logically true sentences corresponded, for him, to real objects and facts, not simply to how people thought about things. There is a difference between implication (or what sentences follow from other sentences) and inference (or what people think follows).

Besides making the case that logic is a formal axiomatic system, Frege introduced a fundamental understanding of logical language. He expanded logic to be able to deal with not only objects or classes of objects, but also to deal with properties, or characteristics, of objects and relations between them. Aristotle's syllogisms dealt with individual objects or classes of objects. For example, the sentence "All whales are mammals" involves a subject term *(whales)* and a predicate term *(mammals)*. Frege introduced formal notation that dealt not only with such classes, but also with properties of them and relations between them. For instance, one property of whales is that they are large or that they are marine animals or that they have fins, etc. Frege showed that a logical system could show the form of sentences such as "All whales are large" or even "Plato is large." In addition, he showed that a logical system should show the form of sentences such as "All whales are larger than Plato," where *larger than* refers to a relation between things. Also, by being able to show the logical form of relations, logic can deal with sentences such as, "San Francisco is between Seattle and Los Angeles," something that syllogistic logic could not do. As part of this expanded understanding and power of logic, he introduced what is called a *quantifier*. This allows the form of sentences to be captured by logical notation that goes far beyond what traditional syllogistic logic could do. So, modern logic can formulate the following sentences: "Plato is large" is symbolized as, say: Lp (with the "L" standing for the property "is large" and the "p" standing for Plato); "All whales are large" is symbolized as, say: $(\forall x)(Wx \rightarrow Lx)$ (to be read as: "For all x, if x is a whale, then x is large"); "San Francisco is between Seattle and Los Angeles" is symbolized as, say: Bfsl (with "B" standing for the property "is between," "f" standing for San Francisco, "s" standing for Seattle, and "l" standing for Los Angeles). Frege showed that the logical forms of sentences are composed of individuals (either specific individuals such as Plato or San Francisco or variables, such as x, which could stand for unspecified individuals) as well as predicates (which included properties such as "is large" or relations such as "is larger than"). Quantifiers allow the possibility of portraying the logical form of sentences in ways that had not been possible before. Frege's system also allowed for ambiguities and lack of clarity to be resolved. For instance, the sentence, "Every boy loves some girl" can be understood in two ways. One such way is that there is one particular girl that every boy loves, so, in effect, the sentence means that every boy loves her. Another way of understanding the sentence, however, is that for each boy there is some girl (not necessarily the same girl) that is loved. Using Frege's logical notation, this ambiguity is easily clarified: the first way of understanding the sentence can be written as: $\exists x \forall y ((Gx \,\&\, By) \to Lyx)$, which would be read as: There is something, x, such that for all things, y, if x is a girl and y is a boy, then y loves x. The second way of understanding the sentence can be written as: $\forall y \exists x ((By \,\&\, Gx) \to Lyx)$.

Frege also formulated the term *truth-value* to speak of the value that a sentence could have in terms of being true or false. So, just as a mathematical sentence can turn out to be true or false depending upon the mathematical value of some variable, the truth value of a sentence will depend upon the content of some logical variable. For instance, in the mathematical sentence, $2x = 8$, the sentence will turn out to be true or false depending upon the value of x. (If the value is 4, then the sentence is true; otherwise, it is false.) The truth value of the logical sentence, Txp (meaning "x is the teacher of Plato"), depends upon the content, or value, of x. (If the content/value is Socrates, then the sentence is true; otherwise, it is false.)

In addition to his work in formal logic, Frege defended several influential ideas in the philosophy of language. For example, Frege believed that the meaning of a sentence is a function of the meaning of its parts; that is, he defended the principle of compositionality. As a simple example, "Cleo sings in the shower" has a different meaning than "Cleo sings in the classroom." Since the two sentences are composed of different words (one includes *shower,* and the other includes *classroom*), and those different words have different meanings *(shower* means something different than *classroom),* the meanings of the sentences as a whole differ. In addition, Frege advocated the idea that the meaning of a word must be considered within the context of a sentence, not independently. Precisely how this view is to be understood, as well as its relation to the principle of compositionality, are matters of debate among Frege scholars.

For many philosophers, Frege's most important development in the philosophy of language was his distinction between the sense of a linguistic term and that term's reference. The reference of a linguistic term—say, a word—is what it picks out; the sense of a term, in Frege's phrase, is the "mode of presentation," that is, how a term "presents" the object in question. For example, the planet Venus has been called the "Evening Star," for its appearance in the evening sky; it has also been called the "Morning Star," for its appearance in the morning sky. So, *Evening Star* and *Morning Star* have the same reference (the planet Venus), but they have different senses: *Evening Star* presents Venus as a celestial object that appears in the evening, and *Morning Star* presents Venus as a celestial object that appears in the morning. Similarly, the reference of the name *Mark Twain* is a certain American writer, author of books such as *The Adventures of Huckleberry Finn*. The reference of *Samuel Clemens* is the very same man (*Mark Twain* was the pen name of Samuel Clemens). However, the two names have different senses; they present the same person (Samuel Clemens) differently.

Frege believed the distinction between sense and reference helps explain why a statement such as "The Evening Star is the Morning Star" can be informative. If the terms *Evening Star* and *Morning Star* had only a reference—not senses—then it would difficult to see how this statement could tell us anything new. This is because the statement seems to be saying nothing more than that some celestial object is identical with itself—as if one were to say, "Venus is Venus." Now, "Venus is Venus" is true, no doubt, but it does not tell us anything new or interesting. Yet, "The Evening Star is the Morning Star" does say something interesting—in fact, since people did not always know that the Evening Star and the Morning Star are the very same celestial object, "The Evening Star is the Morning Star" at one point would have expressed an important discovery. How can this be, since the terms refer to the same very object? The explanation for the informativeness of the statement is that the terms *Evening Star* and *Morning Star* have different senses. So, the statement does not simply say that some celestial object is identical with itself. It says instead something to the effect that a certain celestial object that appears in the evening sky is the same celestial object as one that appears in the morning sky. This general point applies to other identity statements involving terms with the same reference. For example, for someone who does not know that Samuel Clemens used the pseudonym *Mark Twain,* or that the real name of U2 frontman is Paul David Hewson, the statements "Mark Twain is Samuel Clemens" and "Paul David Hewson is Bono" express new information. And this it seems they could not do if the relevant terms *(Mark Twain, Samuel Clemens, Paul David Hewson,* and *Bono)* had only references and no senses.

Frege believed that associated with each referring term is a sense, and that the sense determines its reference; for example, the sense of *Evening Star* has to do with a certain celestial object that appears in the evening sky. Accordingly, the reference of *Evening Star* must be a celestial object that appears in the evening sky. Moreover, according to Frege, some terms have a sense but no reference, such as *Sherlock Holmes* and *Santa Claus.* Neither Sherlock Holmes nor Santa Claus exist, so these terms fail to refer to anything; however, they have a sense (having to do with, say, being a consulting detective in one case and a gift-giving resident of the North Pole in the other). Although very influential, Frege's claims that referring terms are associated with senses and that senses determine references, later generated much controversy (see, for example, the chapter on page 383 on Saul Kripke).

G. E. Moore and
Bertrand Russell

In the 20th century, G. E. Moore and Bertrand Russell became the first true practitioners of what is commonly known as the school of analytic philosophy.

G(eorge) E(dward) Moore

Together with Russell and Ludwig Wittgenstein, G. E. Moore (1873–1958) is considered one of three philosophers of the golden age of philosophy at Cambridge University. Moore was born in London and studied classics at Dulwich College; he later studied philosophy and classics at Cambridge, where he met Russell. The two philosophers were each to influence the other, for example in their abandonment of idealism (the view that reality is essential mental). Most of Moore's professional life was spent at Cambridge; he was appointed professor there in 1925 and held that position until retiring in 1939, at which point he taught at various universities in the United States. He edited the prominent philosophical journal *Mind* for well over two decades and received the British Order of Merit. His influence in analytic philosophy was great, and his work, in areas such as perception, philosophical methodology, epistemology (the study of knowledge), and ethics (the study of right action), continues to be discussed.

In his early work, Moore critiqued and rejected idealism (the view that reality is essentially mental), carefully analyzing some common

PRINCIPIA ETHICA

BY

GEORGE EDWARD MOORE
FELLOW OF TRINITY COLLEGE, CAMBRIDGE

" Everything is what it is,
and not another thing "
BISHOP BUTLER

CAMBRIDGE
AT THE UNIVERSITY PRESS
1903

Title page of the 1903
edition of G. E. Moore's
Principia Ethica

claims made in support of idealism. He defended instead a common-sense view of the world. For example, Moore wrote that there were certain propositions that everyone knew to be true, such as that the Earth has existed for some time before oneself is born and that there are people other than oneself. These propositions, he believed, people knew with certainty; it was not merely that they felt pretty sure about them. So, against the claims of skeptics (those who cast doubt on knowledge claims), Moore defended such claims of common sense. Famously, Moore gave what he called a "proof of the external world," that is, a proof of a world that exists independently of our experience. The proof consists of holding up one's hand, with the remark, "Here is a hand," and then, holding up another hand, remarking, "Here is another one." A hand is an object external to one's own experience; so, if a person has two hands, there must be an external world. It is in this way that holding up one's two hands and pointing out that they are in fact hands is a "proof" of the external world.

Now, it seems clear that a skeptical philosopher is unlikely to accept this conclusion. A skeptic, influenced by René Descartes (1596–1650), for example, might ask, "But how do you know that those are really hands? How do you know you are not just dreaming that you have hands?" Moore's argument does not seem to reply explicitly to such skeptical worries, and indeed Moore did not regard his "proof" as a proof against skepticism. It is a proof that there is an external world, not a proof directed against skeptical arguments claiming that we have no knowledge of such a world. Indeed, Moore seemed to regard skeptical arguments as not to be taken very seriously. For Moore, it made more sense to stick to the claims of common sense than to believe skeptical claims made in a philosophical theory. We can know things with certainty, he thought, even if we do not know how we know them. By Moore's account, it is as if the philosopher's starting point is common sense. It is common sense that there are human beings in addition to oneself and that the Earth has existed for some time before oneself. What was of philosophical interest, then, according to Moore, was not a debate about whether such propositions are true but how to understand such propositions correctly. The way to do this was through analysis of those propositions. For although Moore claimed that everyone knew the meaning of claims such as, "The Earth has existed for many years past," and further that everyone knew such claims were true, Moore did not claim that everyone knew the proper *analysis* of such claims. People know what such claims mean in their ordinary sense; this does not mean that they know what such claims mean in a deeper, analytic sense, when each component of such claims is carefully considered in turn. To provide such analysis is a task of the philosopher.

Given Moore's defense of common sense, it is not surprising that Moore also defended for a time a view now known as direct realism (sometimes called naïve realism). According to this view, what we perceive when we perceive the ordinary objects of experience (cats, trees, bowls, and so on) are ordinary, physical objects, and we perceive them directly. For example, what is it one really sees when looking at an orange? One answer, given by modern philosophers such as John Locke (1632–1704), is that one sees content ("ideas," Locke would have said) produced in oneself by the orange, such as the ideas of orange and round. But one does not see the orange itself. Moore's account was that the objects of perception—what one perceives when one perceives—are sense data. Sense data are, roughly, what one immediately experiences through the senses—for example, the color red. Like other philosophers, however, Moore struggled to give an adequate account of the nature of sense data and how they related to ordinary objects (apples, people, pets, etc.). It seems to be common sense that what we perceive, at least a lot of the time, is real; so, if sense data are what we perceive, then sense data give us accurate information about reality. One view was that sense data are identical to ordinary objects; for example, perhaps sense data such as the color red, the round shape of an apple, the taste of crisp sweetness, and other such sense data are identical to an apple. However, identifying sense data with ordinary objects made it to difficult to account for the possibility of illusion. For example, a common optical illusion is that a straight stick appears bent when it is stuck in the water (the bend seems to be where the stick enters the water). Now when someone looks at such a stick, it seems clear that she sees something. But it seems equally clear that what she sees is not the stick itself—after all, what she sees is bent, and the stick itself is straight. What she sees, then, must be something else—the sense data (say, a patch of brown in a long, bent shape). If this is the case, however, then sense data are not identical with ordinary objects. Such considerations led Moore to continue to analyze the concept of perception and revise his views about the matter.

In ethics, Moore gave an influential argument known as the "open question" argument, identifying what has come to be known as the "naturalistic fallacy." A basic question in ethics is whether moral facts (assuming that such facts exist) are based on natural properties or on some other property. Here, a "natural" property can be understood as a quality that could be identified, described, and studied by the sciences, using standard scientific practice. For example, one view is that morally good actions are those actions that produce the most happiness for the people affected by that action. It is an empirical fact that some actions produce more happiness for people than other actions. To learn which actions produce the most happiness, we can research the facts about human needs and psychology, and this will help us learn that, say, giving a child regular meals will make her happier than refusing to feed her at all. So, on the view under consideration, it is a moral fact that the right thing to do in this instance is to give the child regular meals. Moreover, that moral fact is the *same* fact as the fact that giving the child regular meals will produce the most happiness for the people affected; because this fact can be identified and studied via science, it is a natural fact.

However, according to Moore's objection, the problem with this naturalist approach to moral facts is that identifying a moral fact with a natural fact always leaves an open question of whether the moral fact really is that natural fact. For instance, it always makes sense to ask, "Is the moral good really what produces the most happiness for the people concerned?" What this shows, according to Moore, is that the good cannot be identified with any natural fact; the term *good* just does not mean the same thing as any term regarding a natural fact (such as *produces happiness*). After all, if it did, then it would *not* make sense to ask, say, "Is the moral good really what produces the most happiness for the people concerned?" as *good* would just mean "what produces the most happiness for the people concerned." It would be a bit like asking, "Is a square really a geometrical object with right angles and four equal sides?" As that is all that a square is, the question makes no sense unless a person is confused about the meaning of the word *square*. But a person can know the meaning of *good*, it seems, and still meaningfully ask whether good is identical to some natural property. On the basis of such considerations, Moore held that *good* could not be defined. Although many philosophers believe that developments in philosophy of language have weakened Moore's "open argument" objection, it has remained influential.

Bertrand Russell

Bertrand Russell (1872–1970) is one of the few philosophers well known outside the field of philosophy. Russell wrote extensively about a wide range of philosophical subjects, including logic, metaphysics (the study of reality), epistemology (the study of knowledge), and ethics (the study of right action). But he was also an activist for peace and nuclear disarmament and an advocate for sexual freedom and educational and social reform. He ran for Parliament (unsuccessfully), helped establish and run an experimental school, and twice served jail time for his political activities: once for writing an article critical of the United States during World War I and once for supposedly encouraging public disobedience as he promoted the cause of nuclear disarmament. Russell's personal life was sometimes turbulent. His parents died when he was young, and he was raised by his religious and strict grandmother. In addition to having numerous love affairs, he was married four times. Although he taught at institutions such as Trinity College, Russell made his living primarily as a writer. In 1950, he received the Nobel Prize in literature.

Russell's first love in academics was mathematics. With his mentor Alfred North Whitehead (1861–1947), he coauthored the three-volume *Principia Mathematica,* a technical and influential work on mathematics and logic that was intended to demonstrate that mathematics could be reduced to logic (put another way, that all true mathematical statements could be formulated as statements in formal logic). In his later work, Russell continued to value logic, and he came to view logic as an essential tool of philosophy. Like Frege, he regarded ordinary language as vague and fraught with potential for confusion. By analyzing the logical form of ordinary language—that is, its underlying logical struc-

Photograph of Bertrand
Russell, published in 1916

ture—Russell thought that philosophical puzzles could be illuminated. As an example, consider an ordinary statement such as "Daisy does not eat ice cream" and "Santa Claus does not exist." These statements seem quite similar, so far as the grammar goes: they each seem to say something about a particular individual (Daisy in one case, Santa Claus in the other). Yet there are two apparent difficulties with treating these statements as fundamentally similar: First, it suggests that the quality of existing is like any other quality, such as the quality of eating ice cream. Yet it is not obvious that it is: after all, the quality of eating ice cream depends on existing (one cannot eat ice cream unless one exists), but not the other way around. Many philosophers deny that existence is actually a genuine quality at all (it would be odd if, asked to describe one's cow, one said, "Well, she's black and white, wears a bell, moos around supper time every night, and she exists").

The second difficulty with treating the above two statements in somewhat the same way is that it is not clear how to understand "Santa Claus does not exist." What this statement *seems* to say is that a certain person, Santa Claus, lacks existence (just as the first statement seems to say that a certain cow, Daisy, does not eat ice cream). Now if it is true that Santa Claus does not exist, then the name *Santa Claus* does not name anything. Here is the rub: if *Santa Claus* does not refer to anyone, then how can "Santa Claus does not exist" count as a meaningful sentence? After all, if *Santa Claus* refers to nothing, the sentence says of *nothing* that it does not exist. That seems nonsensical. Yet the sentence seems to be not only meaningful, but also true: it really is the case that Santa Claus does not exist. What are we to make of all this?

A statement that says, accurately, of an object that it does not exist is called a true negative existential statement. These kinds of statements are one example of how Russell thought close attention to the logical form of language could resolve philosophical puzzles. Russell thought that the logical form of such sentences is not the same as their surface grammar (the structure they appear to have at first sight). It is the surface grammar that gets us into trouble; an analysis of the logical form will get us out. By Russell's lights, the true logical form of "Santa Claus does not exist" consists of something like this: "There is one and only one person who lives at the North Pole, delivers presents every Christmas, and runs a toyshop staffed by elves." This is because the name *Santa Claus* is a disguised description—that is, it really stands for descriptions such as "the one and only person who lives at the North Pole, delivers presents every Christmas, and runs a toyshop staffed by elves." This being the case, if one wants to know whether "Santa Claus does not exist" is true, what one needs to know is whether there really is one and only one person who lives at the North Pole, delivers presents every Christmas, and runs a toyshop staffed by elves. If there is no such person who meets this description, then the sentence "Santa Claus does not exist" is true. Note that, under Russell's analysis, the meaningfulness of the statement does not depend on there existing a non-existent object (Santa Claus). This point applies to all true negative existential statements: when they are properly understood—when we recognize their logical form—they do not say of nonexistent objects that they do not exist. So, their meaningfulness does not depend on the existence of nonexistence objects. And we can truthfully utter statements such as "Santa Claus does not exist."

In general, Russell believed that all proper names in ordinary language are disguised descriptions. For example, the name *Socrates* (the name of an ancient Greek philosopher) really stands for descriptions such as "the teacher of Plato" and "the formulator of the Socratic method." Names as we ordinarily understand them are not really names at all, according to Russell, precisely because they are disguised descriptions. There are genuine names—linguistic terms that pick something out but are not disguised descriptions—but they are not ordinary names such as *Socrates, Abraham Lincoln, Daisy,* and the *Eiffel Tower.* Rather, they are terms such as *This* and *That.* These are genuine names because they are not disguised descriptions and because they pick out certain individual things, called "atoms." This brings us to Russell's view of logical atomism, a view he developed with Ludwig Wittgenstein. Russell believed that reality consists of basic, simple (that is, indivisible) constituents, such as patches of color. These constituents are atoms. They are logical atoms in the sense that they are discoverable through logic (so, they are contrasted with physical atoms, discoverable through science). In addition to atoms, Russell believed there are facts, and facts are objective (they are what they are independent of what people say or think about them). There are general facts as well as atomic facts; to defend this view, Russell reasoned that if one were to write down all the atomic facts about the world, in order to truly describe the world one would need to add the general fact that the list of atomic facts was complete. Atoms form the basis of atomic facts. Atomic facts, in their turn, are either facts concerning one simple particular with a specific quality or facts concerning individuals standing in a simple relation to each other.

As noted, Russell regarded ordinary language as riddled with lack of clarity. He thought that reality could best be described by an ideal logical language, one that was always clear. An ideal language mirrors the structure of the world: So an atomic sentence describes an atomic fact. For example, "This is white" expresses an atomic fact, the fact that some simple object (whatever is named by *This*) has the quality white. Complex facts are constructed out of atomic facts.

An important component to Russell's atomism was his empiricism, his view that experience via the five senses is the main source of knowledge. Russell famously distinguished between knowledge by acquaintance and knowledge by description. Knowledge by acquaintance is knowledge acquired via direct awareness of something. For example, consider someone looking at an orange. What she is directly aware of is a patch of color, specifically a patch of orange, so she is acquainted with this patch of color. Other examples of knowledge by acquaintance include the direct awareness of the sound of bells, the smell of strawberries, and one's own memories. In each case, one has knowledge of something or another (a sound, a scent, a memory), and one has a direct awareness of that something. A person does not need to figure out that she is aware of a particular scent, sound, color, or memory; she is aware of such things directly. Knowledge by description, by contrast, is knowledge acquired by learning descriptions associated with other things; it does not regard direct awareness of something. For instance, no one alive today ever encountered directly the ancient Greek philosopher Socrates, so no one alive today was ever acquainted (in Russell's sense) with Socrates. Yet we take ourselves to know at least some things about Socrates, such as that he was Greek and that he was a philosopher. We have certain descriptions associated with Socrates—so, our knowledge of truths about Socrates is knowledge by *description*.

What we are acquainted with, in the examples above, Russell called *sense data*—data provided by the senses, of which one is immediately aware, such as patches of color and sounds. Like Moore, Russell believed there is an external world, but he understood this world differently than an ordinary commonsense view. On a commonsense view we directly perceive ordinary external objects, such as oranges and cats and spoons. Russell thought, on the contrary, that what we have direct awareness of are sense data. So, one has direct awareness of the patch of orange color and the scent of an orange, but not of the orange itself. Rather, for Russell, the orange itself is a logical construction; it is intellectually built out of sense data such as the patch of orange color and the scent of the orange. To return to atoms, then, as complex facts are built of atomic facts, ordinary objects like oranges and trees are constructed out of atoms, such as patches of color. As an empiricist, Russell argued that knowledge by description is ultimately based on knowledge by acquaintance. So, what we know of the empirical world is ultimately based on knowledge by acquaintance.

The Early Work of
Ludwig Wittgenstein

Ludwig Wittgenstein

Ludwig Wittgenstein (1889–1951) was one of the most influential philosophers of the 20th century. His writings and teachings were so influential that philosophers speak of the "early Wittgenstein," when his work (prior to 1930) was associated very closely with the movement of logical positivism, and "late Wittgenstein," when his work (from the 1930s until his death) was fundamental to ordinary language philosophy. Wittgenstein came from a leading family in Vienna, Austria. His father was a wealthy steel industrialist and his mother and brother were renowned concert pianists. In 1908, Wittgenstein went to England and originally studied engineering, but became interested in mathematics. At Cambridge University, he met the philosopher Bertrand Russell and his interests shifted again, this time to logic and ultimately to philosophy in general. After World War I in 1921, at the urging of Russell, he published his only book that was published during his lifetime, *Tractatus Logico-Philosophicus*, a short but very complex and dense work. Believing that he had solved the fundamental problems of philosophy, he left England and taught elementary school in rural Austria. By the end of the 1920s, he became convinced that his previous philosophical views were mistaken and he returned to Cambridge in 1929. For the remaining two decades of his life, he wrote a vast amount, but published only one short essay. After his death, his writ-

Ludwig Wittgenstein's gravestone in the Ascension Parish Burial Ground *(Photograph by Andrew Dunn; used under a Creative Commons license)*

ings were edited into many books, the most important being *Philosophical Investigations,* which was published in 1953.

Throughout his writings Wittgenstein focused on language and, in particular, on how philosophical concerns and problems were associated with language. In his early work, especially *Tractatus Logico-Philosophicus,* Wittgenstein presented what came to be known as a picture view of meaning, in which language is seen as a mirror of the world. He focused on how words could be meaningful, especially how they could make contact with the world. For example, how do certain sounds or squiggles on a page (such as *cat*) mean or refer to certain things out in the world? To many people, because they use language all their lives, such a question seems silly; we just use the word *cat* to mean a certain kind of animal. However, for Wittgenstein, such a question is no sillier than asking how leaves change color or how clouds appear in the sky. Wittgenstein's answer to this question was that both language and the world had structures and those structures mirrored each other. The world, he said, was made up of facts, not just things and events. For instance, that a car is parked in someone's driveway is a fact; that is, it is a complex set of relations among various things and events, for example, relations between a car and a driveway. Facts, he said, are made up of states of affairs (the various relationships among the things and events). Finally, states of affairs themselves are made up of objects, the basic, simple things that make up the more complex, everyday things (such as cats and cars) we encounter. Language, for Wittgenstein, has a structure that is like the world's structure. Language is made up of propositions (or sentences). Propositions, then, are like facts, and, like facts, propositions are made up of simpler components, not states of affairs, but elementary propositions. For example, the sentence, "The car is in the driveway" is made up of simpler sentences such as, "There is a car," "There is a driveway," and "The car is related to the driveway in a certain way." Finally, elementary propositions are made up of names, which, for Wittgenstein, meant there was a direct link between a unit of language (a name) and a basic object in the world. One result of Wittgenstein's work on this view of language was that he developed truth tables, which are a fundamental notion of modern logic.

Wittgenstein noted that some sentences are true yet say nothing about the world; such sentences are not informative because they are necessarily true, either simply because of the meanings of the words in the statement or because of the grammar (or form) of the statement. Such sentences are called tautologies. As an example of the first kind of tautology, "Circles are round" is necessarily true because circles are round by definition; put another way, the definition of *circle* attributes to circles the quality of being round. Wittgenstein was more concerned with the second kind of tautology. As an example, the sentence "A or not A" is necessarily true because of its structure, not because of the meanings of any of the words in the sentence. In this sentence, *A* just stands for a sentence—not a specific sentence, but any arbitrary sentence (or, more precisely, for any sentence that purports to state that something is the case). For any sentence, it is the case that either that sentence describes an actual state of affairs or it does not. For instance, suppose *A* stands for "Donkeys like carrots." It is either the case that donkeys like carrots or that they do not. So, "A or not A" is true. Indeed, substitute any sentence for A, and "A or not A" is true. We can see that what makes "A or not A" tautologous is its form by noting that "A or not A" is true for any sentence no matter what sentence is substituted for *A*—that is, regardless of the definitions of the words. Although "A or not A" is certainly true, by Wittgenstein's lights it is not informative.

Tractatus
Logico-Philosophicus

By
LUDWIG   WITTGENSTEIN

With an Introduction by
BERTRAND RUSSELL, F.R.S.

NEW YORK
HARCOURT, BRACE & COMPANY, INC.
LONDON: KEGAN PAUL, TRENCH, TRUBNER & CO., LTD.
1922

Title page of the English-language edition of Ludwig Wittgenstein's *Tractatus Logico-Philosophicus,* published by Harcourt, Brace & Company in 1922

Although Wittgenstein's claims about language might sound puzzling and complex, Wittgenstein's concern was to investigate what we can meaningfully say (and know) about the world. He remarked that, "the limits of our language are the limits of our world." If language is indeed a mirror of the world, then the only things that we can say that connect up with the world are things that correspond to facts. As a result, Wittgenstein said, sentences that are not connected to facts are literally meaningless; they are literally nonsense. As a result, when we speak about values or religion or art, many of the things we say, he claimed, are literally nonsense (unless they are stating some fact about the world).

Some philosophers, especially the logical positivists, welcomed Wittgenstein's conclusions, because they wanted to rid philosophy of what they saw as empty speculation. They thought that philosophy should not be mere opinion or personal feeling. If we use language to connect to the world, then what we say needs to match up to a true description of the world. Wittgenstein himself, however, thought that the important aspects of life, such as ethics and art, were more important than descriptions about the world. However, since he had argued that language involving values was literally nonsense, he concluded that there was nothing more to say, so he withdrew from philosophy and much of society following the publication of *Tractatus Logico-Philosophicus.*

Along with philosophers such as Gottlob Frege, G. E. Moore, and Bertrand Russell, Wittgenstein helped shift the focus of philosophy to language. Through close attention to language, and notably by clearing up the confusion and lack of clarity found in ordinary language, it was possible to resolve philosophical problems.

Logical Positivism

Logical positivism, also called logical empiricism, was a philosophical movement that originated in the 1920s. It was born out of the Vienna Circle, a group of intellectuals (mathematicians, scientists, philosophers, and others) who met regularly in Vienna to share and discuss ideas. The philosophers Moritz Schlick (1882–1936), Rudolph Carnap (1891–1970), Friedrich Waismann (1896–1959), Otto Neurath (1882–1945), Carl Hempel (1905–97), and A. J. Ayer (1910–89) are all considered positivists. W. V. O. Quine (1908–2000) met with the Vienna Circle and is also associated with logical positivism; however, some of his ideas later helped undermine the movement.

The logical positivists were empiricists influenced by David Hume (1711–76). They believed that knowledge is based on sense experience (experience based on the five senses). According to the classical logical positivist program, science is the only source of knowledge about the world, and most of the claims of religion, metaphysics, ethics, and aesthetics are neither true nor false, but simply meaningless. Logic and science, the positivists observed, had advanced even as philosophers continued to discuss the same metaphysical questions without ever arriving at answers. The problem was that these metaphysical questions were nonsense, and philosophy ought to dispense with them. Instead, positivists viewed the purpose of philosophy as using logic to analyze the concepts and the claims of science. Influenced by the logical work of Gottlob Frege (1848–1925), Alfred North Whitehead (1861–1947), and Bertrand Russell (1872–1970), positivists thought that they could clarify what concepts and claims mean. Science, on this view, tells us about the world, and philosophy makes it clear precisely what science tells us.

Fundamental to logical positivism was the principle of verifiability. Positivists formulated this principle in different ways, but in each case the idea was that, according to the principle of verifiability, metaphysical claims were meaningless. On one version of the principle, sentences are meaningful only if they are either analytically true or if they are in principle verifiable through sensory experience. That is, meaningful sentences are true either because they are true in virtue of the meaning of the words (or the grammar of the sentence) or because it is, in principle, possible to verify the truth of the sentence through experience based on the five senses. For instance, the sentence "Babies are young" is analytically true because part of the definition of *babies* is that babies are young. So the sentence is meaningful. The sentence, "The cat Happy Jack has black fur" is verifiable through sense experience because in principle it is possible to see Happy Jack and his black fur. So that sentence is meaningful too. However, according to positivists, a metaphysical sentence such as "Everything that exists is One" is neither analytic nor verifiable through sense experience. So the sentence has no meaning: it is not false, it is just literally nonsense. On the basis of this reasoning, most ethical, aesthetic, and religious claims are also nonsense; it is not possible to verify, for example, the claim "The *Mona Lisa* is a good painting." Alternatively, logical positivism is associated with emotivism, the view that ethical claims express a speaker's attitude but do not express anything true or false. For instance, on this view, to say, "Cruelty is bad" is just to express one's own negative attitude about cruelty; it is not to say anything true (or false), but rather as if one were to say, "Cruelty—boo!" On this view, claims in ethics—that some action is moral or immoral, some trait good or bad, etc.—are not entirely meaningless, but their meaning is strictly emotive, or expressive. Put another way, their meaning just consists of the expression of the speaker's attitude. Similarly, when a fan at a sporting event cheers, the cheer does not say anything true or false, but it expresses the speaker's positive attitude about some turn of events in the game; that is the meaning of the cheer.

Influenced by the early work of Ludwig Wittgenstein, positivists thought the structure of language mirrored the structure of the world. As a very simple example, consider the sentence "Happy Jack is black."

It is composed of a name (*Happy Jack*) for a cat and a predicate (*black*) that identifies the color black. Corresponding to the name *Happy Jack* is a cat (Happy Jack) and corresponding to *black* is the color black, which Happy Jack is. It is as if the sentence "Happy Jack is black" mirrors the actual state of affairs that Happy Jack is black. This is a very simple and rough example, but positivists thought that any true, meaningful, nonanalytic sentence similarly mirrors a state of affairs in the world. In addition, according to positivism, any meaningful, nonanalytic sentence can be reduced to a more basic statement about sensory experience. That is, any meaningful, nonanalytic sentence can ultimately be understood as a report of experience via the five senses; these reports are called protocol sentences. For instance, "Happy Jack is happy" might be reducible to sentences that are about observing Happy Jack behave in certain ways (such as purring). According to positivists, even complex hypotheses of science—for example, those about the behavior of subatomic particles, or the movement of tectonic plates on the Earth's crust—can be reduced to protocol sentences.

However, exactly how to understand such basic reports of sensory experience was controversial among logical positivists. Some positivists argued that basic statements should be about sense data—that is, information about individual sensory experiences, such as the sensation of seeing a patch of black color when looking at Happy Jack. Other positivists rejected this view on the grounds that it made scientific claims too subjective. The concern was that scientific claims are more objective than the sense data view suggests; scientific claims should not be understood as being about individual sensations. In addition, positivists disagreed about how the principle of verifiability should apply to protocol sentences. Some positivists, such as Schlick, defended a more stringent version of the principle of verifiability and argued that some sentences about individual observations—e.g., "Here blue now" as a report of someone's seeing the color blue—are genuine reports about reality, and that their truth is certain. Other positivists, such as Neurath, did not regard the truth of any sentences, including protocol sentences, as certain. Science does not begin with such sentences, he argued. Put another way, scientific knowledge does not start as a blank slate, beginning first with protocol sentences whose truth is certain and moving on to more progressively complex hypotheses. Rather, he thought, protocol sentences are themselves hypotheses and themselves subject to confirmation, or verification, along with more complex hypotheses. Scientific inquiry, then, proceeds on the basis of some apparent truths that it might later reject in light of new observations. In a famous metaphor, Neurath likened scientific inquiry to rebuilding a ship while in the open sea. In that situation, one would have no certain, stable foundation but must use what one has while at sea; similarly, as Neurath saw it, science does not begin with the firm foundation of protocol sentences reporting sensory experience but proceeds using what information it has (including but not limited to information expressed in protocol statements) and revises as it goes along.

A persistent challenge for logical positivists was how to understand the meaningfulness of the principle of verifiability itself. Of course, they believed the principle was meaningful. Yet by its own lights it was not obvious how. After all, the principle was not verifiable by sensory experience: no observation of the empirical world would seem to verify it or not verify it. Ayer claimed that it was analytically true, but this seemed unsatisfactory. First, it was not obvious that the definition of *meaningful* involved verifiability. Second, if the verifiability principle was analytic, it was not clear how the principle could be informative. An analytic sentence such as "Babies are young" does not tell us anything new; it is just true by definition. Similarly, if the principle of verifiability were analytic, it would not seem to tell us anything new, either. In part because of concerns over how to understand the principle of verifiability, logical positivism fell out of favor by the 1960s. Quine's rejection of the analytic/synthetic distinction was also influential, casting doubt on the notion that any sentences were analytic at all. Although logical positivism as a movement is now widely considered defunct, logical positivists were very influential in analytic philosophy, as well as in specific areas such as philosophy of science and philosophy of language.

Wittgenstein and the
Philosophical Investigations

With the publication of his book *Tractatus Logico-Philosophicus,* Ludwig Wittgenstein (1889–1951) believed he had solved the problems of philosophy and left the discipline, choosing instead to teach schoolchildren for a time. By the end of the 1920s, however, Wittgenstein had changed his mind about language and about philosophy, so he returned to Cambridge to teach. During this second phase of his philosophical life (often referred to as the "late Wittgenstein"), he put forth a different view of the nature of language, made most famous in his book *Philosophical Investigations,* which was published after he died. *Philosophical Investigations* has been one of the most influential books in philosophy of the 20th century, and it continues to be read and discussed today.

Wittgenstein still believed that philosophical concerns and problems were associated with language. However, he now thought that his earlier views on language were much of the problem. During the 1930s and 1940s, he advocated a view that many people have called ordinary language philosophy. Wittgenstein now said that a major problem was thinking that language was primarily descriptive and that it mirrored the world. He claimed that we—and, for the most part, philosophers—get into conceptual problems because they take language out of context and try to force ordinary uses of language into forms that are artificial and mistaken. For example, Wittgenstein introduced the idea of family resemblance to criticize the tendency of philosophers to try to find the essence of things, often by looking for necessary and sufficient conditions. Wittgenstein's notion of family resemblance points to the similarities, while at the same time the differences, between family members. That is, in some respects individuals share certain features with their family members, but only certain features. For example, an individual might look like his mother in some ways (having a nose a certain shape, say) and like his sister in various ways (say, having similarly colored eyes and similar basic face shape). At the same time, that individual might not share other features with those family members. For instance, he might have different colored hair than his sister or different face shape than his mother. The fact is that people look like their fellow family members in some respects, but not necessarily in all respects. They resemble their family members, but are not carbon copies of them.

Now, traditionally philosophers analyzed basic concepts (or tried to identify the essence of a thing) by asking, "What is X?" where X might be truth or beauty or knowledge or friendship, etc. The typical process was to look for the essence of some concept by seeking a set of necessary and sufficient conditions that would characterize that concept. So, if we wanted to know "What is knowledge?" we might look for the features or characteristics that something would have to possess in order for it to be a case of knowledge and also what features or characteristics something would have to lack for it not to be a case of knowledge. Only those things that had all and only those particular features would then be cases of knowledge. One might suggest, as many philosophers have, that there are defining, essential features of knowledge even if we do not yet know what they are. In addition, there are reasons why we rule out certain things from being cases of knowledge—for example, mere guesses—and that points to saying that guesses do not have the necessary or sufficient features of knowledge, whatever those features might be.

However, Wittgenstein claimed that for many concepts, there is no essence and, hence, no set of necessary and sufficient conditions that they satisfy. And it might turn out that knowledge is one such concept, and in that case, it would be a mistake for epistemologists to try to formulate a set of features that characterize all and only instances of knowledge. To see how a concept might fail to have an essence (and, hence, a set of necessary and sufficient conditions it satisfies), consider all of the things that we call games. Some games, such as Monopoly or Scrabble, involve a game board and various game pieces, but that is not true of all games (for instance, playing tag). Some games involve scoring points, but not all games do (for instance, tag, again). Some games involve multiple, competing players, but not all games do (for instance, playing solitaire). It might be the case that all games involve some set of rules in order to play the game (although that might not be true); but many things besides games also involve sets of rules, so having rules does not necessarily characterize or specify the unique essence of games. There simply does not seem to be a feature that is common to *everything* that counts as a game. An analogy to help illustrate this point is to consider the nature of a rope. A rope is composed of many overlapping threads, but no single strand of thread runs through the entire length of the rope. So, there might be no single feature that runs through all cases of games, but, instead, a collection of overlapping features. That is to say, some—but not all—games involve multiple players, while other—but not all—games involve scoring points and the like. Wittgenstein's point, then, was that it is philosophically a mistake to insist that concepts (or words) must have an essence. Rather than having an essence, many basic concepts might just have a family resemblance.

One of the most famous aspects of Wittgenstein's late views on language is what he called language games. The point of language games, for Wittgenstein, is that we use language to do many things, such as giving orders, obeying orders, describing something, reporting an event, asking, thanking, cursing, greeting, joking, etc. There is simply no single function—particularly the function of describing facts in the world—that captures all that we do with language. Words are tools and we use them to do certain things, and, like tools, they are designed for various purposes. This focus on the use of language, and not merely on the structure or content of language, is often referred to as pragmatics. The focus of the pragmatics of language is on how we use language and on how the meaning of words and sentences is connected with their use. For instance, if someone says, "That is a nice hat" and he means it sincerely, that means something different than if he says it sarcastically. The words themselves—the semantics—do not change meaning, but what is meant by the use of those words differs when they are said sincerely or sarcastically. In pointing out that we use language a great many ways, Wittgenstein stressed this pragmatic nature of meaning.

In addition, precisely because language is used in so many ways, Wittgenstein urged that we not assume that the structure and content of language has some essence or is always the same. For example, when someone says, "I have a headache," that appears on the surface to have the same structure as when someone says, "I have a car." However, having a car implies that there is some object, separate from the person that is possessed by that person. This is not the case with a headache; there is not necessarily some object that a person possesses when he reports having a headache. Or, in a given situation, if someone says, "It is cold in here," that person is not reporting the weather, but perhaps asking someone else to close a window. The point is not that language means whatever someone wants it to mean, but that there is no single structure to it, even in cases where the structure appears to be like the structure of other uses of language.

Wittgenstein called these various uses of language "language games" because he insisted that using language is an activity (not merely a set of grammatical rules) and part of what he called a form of life. By "form of life," he meant that language is a natural part of human activity and can only be understood in the context of various human activities. He remarked, for example, that, "if a lion could talk, we could not understand him." The reason is that a lion's life, its natural activities and experiences of the world, are so different than a human's life that its words would not mean the same thing that they do for humans. Our uses of language, then, are like games, not meaning that they are trivial or just for fun, but are ways that we experience the world.

Wittgenstein believed that how we use language is governed by rules, somewhat in the way that games are governed by rules. In order to play a game, there must be some rules to make the game possible (imagine playing baseball without knowing how many outs a team gets or how many players a team may have). Similarly, communication via language requires that people use language in common ways, according to rules (imagine trying to have a conversation without knowing what words are supposed to mean or how to construct a grammatical sentence). Even more basic, for Wittgenstein, is that we could not even learn language without it being rule-governed, without having words retain their meaning over time and across different speakers. A consequence of this view is that there are no private languages. By saying that there are no private languages, Wittgenstein meant that there are no languages that in principle could be known only to one person (that is, privately). Of course, someone could make up a secret language or code, but that language or code would have to have some structure and rules; otherwise, it could not function. And if there were a structure and rules, it would, in principle, be knowable by others (even if no one else actually came to know the language). At its core, then, language is social.

Wittgenstein's claims are relevant not only to philosophy of language but to particular philosophical claims—for example, claims about knowledge. Just as there are rules in soccer, say, regarding how the ball can be controlled, there are rules governing uses of words like *knowledge* and *know*. Put another way, there are language games involving these terms. Wittgenstein claimed that it makes sense to claim one knows something only when what one is claiming is in doubt. Put another way, to make a claim to knowledge when no one genuinely questions the claim in question is to break one of the rules governing the use of the word *know*. To illustrate, suppose three people are sitting around a campfire when someone announces, "I know there is a campfire there." The oddity of this is that that there is a campfire likely seems obvious to all; there is no question that there is campfire, so to claim that one knows that there is seems strange. It would seem equally strange for one of our three campers to assert, "I do not know there is a campfire there." This is again because the question of there being a campfire, in ordinary circumstances, simply does not arise. Since everyone implicitly assumes that there is a campfire, both the claim to know that there is one and the claim that one does not know that there is one are odd; these claims break the rules. A way to put this point is that the ways we use the word *know* typically make sense only when there is something genuinely in question. In this scenario, that there is a campfire is not genuinely in question. Of course, there might be circumstances in which it is in question, say, if all three people believe they are possibly under the influence of some sort of hallucinatory drug; in such circumstances it might make sense to say either that one knows or does not know that there is a campfire. But in circumstances where there is no such question, it does not. These remarks apply generally to other claims to knowledge. G. E. Moore, for instance, had claimed that everyone knows that there is an external world (a world that exists outside of our own minds). By Wittgenstein's lights, however, the announcement that one knows that there is an external world is a misuse of *know,* insofar as no one genuinely doubts such claims.

Wittgenstein's emphasis on looking at how people actually use language and his insistence that philosophical problems arise when language is taken out of its normal contexts, its language games, became the rallying cry of ordinary language philosophy not only during the end of his life, but for several decades after he died.

Ordinary Language Philosophy

In the 1950s and '60s, some philosophers continued to focus on language, but with a new respect for ordinary language. Analytic philosophers such as Bertrand Russell had regarded ordinary language as unclear and misleading. Ordinary language philosophers, as these new philosophers were called, believed rather that some philosophical problems could be resolved through careful attention to ordinary language; these problems (for example, the mind-body problem) arose from misunderstanding ordinary language in the first place. So, ordinary language philosophers sometimes sought, not to solve philosophical problems, but to dissolve them—the idea was that at least some philosophical problems were never genuine problems in the first place. Ordinary language philosophers include J. L. Austin (1911–60), P. F. Strawson (1919–2006), John Wisdom (1904–93), Gilbert Ryle (1900–76), and (in his later works) Ludwig Wittgenstein (1889–1951); it was Wittgenstein who compared examining ordinary language to therapy, capable of "curing" philosophers of vexing pseudo-problems. In addition, ordinary language philosophy is characterized by an interest in ordinary language for its own sake, not merely as a means for resolving apparent philosophical problems; the many ways in which language is ordinarily used, from questions to commands to promising and making bets, were of interest to ordinary language philosophy. This shift in analytic philosophy toward a study of ordinary language is sometimes called the pragmatic turn, so-called because it directs attention toward what is called the pragmatics of language—rather roughly, the ways in which language is used, as distinct from the literal meaning of linguistic items such as words and sentences—the semantics of language. As an illustration, the sentence "I'm so pleased you could come" literally means something to the effect that a specific speaker is glad that a certain someone was able to come; this literal meaning is the semantics of the sentence. But the sentence could be used in many different ways: spoken by an employer to an employee who has arrived late to a meeting, for example, the sentence might be used sarcastically, conveying that the employee should have arrived sooner. Spoken by a host to an invited speaker, on the other hand, the sentence is more likely used to convey sincere welcome; these are the pragmatics of a sentence.

John Langshaw Austin

The British philosopher John Langshaw Austin (1911–60) is commonly considered the founding figure of ordinary language philosophy. He was born in Lancaster, England, and studied classics at Balliol College, Oxford. During World War II, he served in the British Intelligence Corps, afterward resuming his academic career at Oxford, where he was appointed White's Professor of Moral Philosophy, a position he held from 1952 to 1960. Although Austin published little while alive, he was a successful teacher and very influential in philosophy during his lifetime; his most important works, *How to Do Things with Words* and *Sense and Sensibilia*, were published posthumously. He died when he was 48 years old.

Among Austin's key contributions to philosophy was his idea that language is sometimes used to perform particular actions, or put another way that sometimes speaking is a form of doing. (His book *How to Do Things with Words* expounds this view.) Performative utterances ("performatives," for short) are such utterances, used to do things as opposed to merely reporting what is the case. As an example, when an elected representative votes in Congress on a proposed piece of legislation, the member might say, "I vote nay." In so doing, the representative is not *merely* uttering words, nor is the representative reporting a fact about the world; the representative is actually voting. That is, the representative performs an action (voting) by uttering, "I vote nay." Similarly, when someone says, "I promise to pay back the money," the speaker is making a promise; when a judge says, for instance "I sentence you to six months' probation," the judge is in fact sentencing a person to six months' probation.

Austin distinguished among locution, illocution, and perlocution. The locution of an utterance is the literal or semantic meaning of what is said—for example, the literal meaning of "With this ring, I thee wed" seems to be that, with a ring, the speaker is marrying the person spoken to. The illocution of an utterance is what a speaker intends to do in uttering the sentence in question—say, marrying the person to whom one is giving a ring. The perlocution of an utterance is the effect the utterance actually has; in this example, the marriage between a couple exchanging rings. Sometimes, as in this example, the locution, illocution, and perlocution are in harmony. However, it is possible for these different aspects of meaning to come apart. For example, after watching a bad movie, someone might say sarcastically, "That was a fabulous movie," intending to assert the very opposite of what her words literally mean. Here, the locution does not match the illocution. And as anyone who has ever had an argument knows, illocution does not always match perlocution: what we intend by our words is not always what is actually conveyed, nor does it always have the desired effect. For example, an utterance of, "You've lost a lot of weight," might be intended as a compliment but be received as an insult ("You mean I was fat before?").

Now, utterances of some sentences go wrong, so to speak, because they are false. If someone claims, "The rose in my garden grew to the moon," although the sentence is perfectly meaningful, the utterance is likely problematic, because it is almost certainly false. Austin claimed that performative utterances can go wrong, too, but in ways distinct from falsity. These typically have to do with conditions under which they are made. Not just anyone, for example, can vote in the U.S. Congress; you have to be an elected representative to do so. If a stranger burst into the Senate chamber and shouted during the formal vote, "I vote nay!" that vote would not count in the tally of votes for or against a bill. In Austin's phrase, that utterance would have been *infelicitous,* or *unhappy.* The point here is that to do some things with words, anyway, requires the speaker to hold a certain position. In addition, conventions surrounding the kind of performative utterance must be observed; for example, a Senator cannot vote on a bill whenever the Senator happens to feel like it (as when, speaking at a rally to a group of excited constituents, the Senator announces, "I vote nay!") but must wait for when the formal vote is scheduled. Moreover, conventions regarding the relevant performative utterances must exist in the first place. In the United States government, there is a convention of voting; in some nations, there are no such conventions. In a nation without voting conventions, one could not successfully vote by uttering, "I vote nay" or "I vote yea"; that utterance, too, would be infelicitous. (Similarly, in most classrooms there is typically no convention that students get to vote on how much homework they are assigned; attempts to do so are not likely to count as successful performative utterances.) Austin's work on performative utterances led to the development of speech act theory, the study of how people perform actions through language; research on speech act theory continues to the present day.

However, like many other ordinary language philosophers, Austin was also concerned with examining ordinary language not simply for its own sake but in order to examine philosophical problems. In *Sense and Sensibilia,* Austin investigated perception and the ways in which people ordinarily talk about perception (for example, with the words *looks* and *appears*). Sense perception—or, more simply, perception—is the process of becoming aware of something through the five senses (sight, hearing, touch, smell, and taste). Philosophers have traditionally been concerned with *what* we perceive: precisely what are the objects of perception? According to the naïve realist view of perception, the objects of perception are objects that we see directly and immediately, such as fence posts, trees, and birds. It is not as if we have to reason it out that there are such objects on the basis of seeing properties of those objects—for instance, it is not as if one first sees a tall green and brown shape and then figures out that one is seeing a tree. Rather, one just sees the tree itself: the perception of objects is immediate and direct in this sense.

Yet against this view is an argument based on the phenomena of illusions and hallucinations. First, consider an optical illusion—say, that an oar looks bent where it enters the water. Now insofar as you perceive something when you perceive the oar in the water, it looks as if what you perceive is something bent. But the oar is not really bent. So, contrary to the naïve realist view, what you perceive must not be the oar itself. Second, consider a hallucination, the perception of something that is not really there. Someone under the influence of drugs might hallucinate that there are green lizards on her bed, although there are no such lizards. Now the perception of seeing green lizards when there are such lizards seems indistinguishable from the perception of green lizards when there are *not* such lizards. That is, as far as the perceptual experience is concerned, one cannot tell the difference between the hallucination and the perception of actual lizards. Of course, one might know intellectually that she is hallucinating (someone might know she is under the influence of a hallucinogenic drug). But the point is that, even if you know you are hallucinating, the perception is just the same as if you were not hallucinating. This is a problem for the naïve realist view because, given that the two perceptions are indistinguishable, it appears that they are of the same nature. That is, it appears that they have the same basic characteristics. Among those basic characteristics *cannot* be that they are perceptions of the ordinary, physical objects— there *are* no such objects (lizards) in the hallucination case. So, contrary to the naïve realist view, perception is not essentially the perception of ordinary, physical objects.

One possible response to these arguments is to abandon the naïve realist view in favor of the sense data theory of perception. To return to the example of the oar that appears bent, if one perceives something bent and the oar is not bent, then it seems to follow that what one perceives is not in fact the oar itself. So, it must be something else, and according to the sense data theory, that something else is *mental* in character. In this instance the sense data consists of an oblong shape that is brown in color and bent at a certain point. *That* is the object perceived. One common understanding of sense data is that they are mental objects in the sense that they depend for their existence on the mind. This does not mean that the physical oar does not exist (or that the physical oar's existence depends on the mind). On a common sense data view, ordinary physical objects do exist. However, they are not perceived *directly*. To perceive a physical object such as an oar, one must first perceive sense data.

Austin's response to this problem of perception was not to argue that we do see objects directly, much less that we see things indirectly (via sense data). Rather, he claimed that the argument against direct perception of physical objects is confused and that close attention to ordinary language illuminates this confusion. For example, consider the word *direct*. According to Austin, the meaning of direct when it is applied to perception hinges on its opposite, indirect as applied to perception. In ordinary language, typically when people talk of indirectly perceiving something, they have something specific in mind, such as seeing a person behind oneself by looking at mirror, or watching an opera singer through binoculars. If indirect perception is perception in these and similar ways, then direct perception is perception without mirrors, binoculars, or similar devices. However, Austin claimed, the argument from illusion does not use this sense of *direct* in its claim that we do not perceive things directly; that is, in the argument, *direct* is not intended to mean free from the use of mirror, binoculars, or similar device. The problem, according to Austin, is that it is not clear what *direct* does mean in the argument. If the argument is unclear at this fundamental level, it can hardly be said to establish its conclusion. Austin's examination of the ordinary uses of *direct* and *indirect* is but one way he explored the problem of perception and the illusion argument, studying ordinary language to illuminate problems in philosophy.

Gilbert Ryle

Gilbert Ryle (1900–76) is best known today for his contributions in ordinary language philosophy and especially for his work on the concept of mind. He was born in Brighton, England, and studied at the School of Philosophy, Politics, and Economics, at Queen's College, Oxford. He taught at Christ Church, Oxford, and during World War II served in the Welsh Guards. After the war, Ryle returned to Christ Church, and he was eventually appointed Waynflete professor of metaphysical philosophy. Following G. E. Moore's editorship, from 1947 to 1971, Ryle also edited the prominent philosophy journal *Mind*.

In Ryle's most famous book, *The Concept of Mind*, he coined the term *category mistake*. Roughly, a category mistake is the mistake of regarding something as belonging to a certain category when in fact it does not. More precisely, to make a category mistake is to apply a concept to something when that concept does not actually apply to the thing in question, although the concept might apply to things that belong in a different category. For example, suppose someone asked, "What color is friendship?" This is a strange question because friendship is not the sort of thing that has a color: things like rainbows and shoes have colors, but friendship does not. Because the concept of color does not properly apply to friendship, applying the concept to friendship anyway is a category mistake. Ryle himself gave the following example. Suppose someone was given a tour of a university. She is shown offices, classrooms, athletic fields, libraries, and so on. If at the end of the tour, the visitor asked, "But where is the university?" it would be apparent that she did not understand what it means to be a university. Her mistake lies in thinking that there is anything more to the university than what she has already been shown. She would be making a category mistake by assuming that the university is something else in addition to its various structures, fields, and organization. But a university is nothing more than those sorts of things.

Category mistakes are relevant to philosophy because, according to Ryle, sometimes they give rise to apparent philosophical problems. Although these problems might appear to be genuine problems, they are not; they are just the result of category mistakes. So clearing up a category mistake could clear up a philosophical problem—not by solving the problem, but by showing there was never a real problem in the first place. In particular, Ryle believed that the mind/body problem was a result of a category mistake. The mind/body problem is the problem of how to account for the relation between the mind and the body. On the surface, one's mind might seem quite different than one's body. The mind thinks, plans, hopes, and feels. Also, the mind is aware—aware of events, other beings, and even of itself. In contrast, the body seems just to be physical stuff—it has no thoughts, awareness, feelings, or any sort of mental life at all. Yet, on this ordinary view, the mind interacts with the body: when a person wants to run, for example, her desire to run causes her body to break into a run. The view that mind and body are two fundamentally different kinds of stuff is called substance dualism, and its most famous defender is the 17th-century philosopher René Descartes. According to dualism, the mind is nonphysical, and the body is physical. But this raises the question of how a nonphysical mind can have any effect on a physical body, and vice versa. For example, it is difficult to understand how a nonphysical desire (say, a desire for sleep) could cause a person's body to move (such as by closing one's eyes).

Ryle called Cartesian dualism—dualism inspired by Descartes—a "ghost in the machine" view, and he did not intend it as a compliment. In Ryle's analogy, a nonphysical mind is the "ghost" and the machine is the "body." The idea of a ghost living inside a machine and making the machine function seems a bit silly, and Ryle's phrase "ghost in the machine" suggests that substance dualism is mistaken. According to Ryle, the mind/body problem arises from the mistake of applying the concept nonphysical to mind, as though the mind *must* be nonphysical. Put another way, dualists suppose that mental events (events such as thinking, believing, and desiring) must be nonphysical events that take place inside us. But mental events do not belong to a category of things that must be nonphysical and take place inside us. Once we stop applying the concept nonphysical to mind, the mind/body problem evaporates; on this view, it was not a real problem at all.

Rather, according to Ryle, we can understand mental events in terms of behavior. In particular, Ryle argued that we could understand words used to describe the mind and mental activity (such as the words *mind, believe,* and *feel*) in terms of how people are liable to behave in certain circumstances. For example, to say that someone believes that playing chess is fun is to say that she will agree to play chess if she is asked and that she will answer, "Yes" if asked whether playing chess is fun (among other likely behavior).

Willard Van Orman Quine

In the 20th century, few philosophers stand out more in terms of influence and philosophical contributions to analytic philosophy than the American philosopher Willard Van Orman Quine (1908–2000). He was born in Akron, Ohio, and studied mathematics and philosophy at Oberlin College. At Harvard University, he earned a Ph.D. in philosophy, writing a dissertation on Bertrand Russell and Alfred North Whitehead's book *Principia Mathematica.* Harvard was to remain the focus of Quine's academic career; he taught and researched as a Harvard faculty member for many years, including when as a traveling scholar he visited Europe and met with members of the Vienna Circle, notably Rudolf Carnap. During World War II, Quine worked in intelligence for the U.S. Navy. He made contributions to philosophy of language, analytic philosophy, epistemology, and ontology.

Although influenced by the logical positivists, Quine was also critical of the movement. Among his most important criticisms was his rejection of the analytic/synthetic distinction. Traditionally, an analytic statement is a statement thought to be true or false either by definition or by grammatical structure. A synthetic statement is statement whose truth or falsity does not depend only on definition. For example, the statement "Bachelors are unmarried" is analytic: because bachelors are unmarried according to the meaning of *bachelor,* the statement is true by definition. On the other hand, the statement "Bachelors are handsome" is synthetic. It is not part of the definition of *bachelor* that bachelors are handsome. Rather, whether the statement is true or false depends on facts about the world, specifically whether actual bachelors really are handsome. Immanuel Kant (1724–1804), who first formulated the analytic/synthetic distinction, formulated it in a slightly different way. According to Kant, an analytic statement is a statement that says something already "contained" in the subject of the sentence. For instance, the subject of the statement "Bachelors are unmarried" is *bachelors,* and *bachelors* contains the idea of being unmarried. So, the statement "Bachelors are unmarried" just spells out information already contained in *bachelors.*

Quine argued that the analytic/synthetic distinction is not a genuine distinction. Put another way, according to Quine, it is false that there are two kinds of statements, a kind whose truth or falsity depends on meaning and a kind whose truth or falsity depends on facts about the world. In his essay, Quine examines different explanations of analyticity—what makes an apparently analytic statement analytic—and rejects each of them as inadequate. For example, according to Quine, it will not do to define analyticity in terms of definitions, as in the idea that "Bachelors are unmarried" is true according to the definition of *bachelors.* Presumably to find the definition of *bachelor* one would look up the word in a dictionary. But what one would find there, Quine points out, is just a reflection of the fact that people use the word *bachelor* as being synonymous with *unmarried adult male.* But synonymy itself requires explanation. To see what analyticity is, one might look at definitions; definitions just record apparent synonymies. But in virtue of what are two terms—in this case, *bachelor* and *unmarried adult male*—synonymous? If we are to understand analyticity in terms of definitions, that seems to require an understanding of synonymy. What is needed, then, is an account of synonymy itself. But, Quine pointed out, a dictionary offers no such account: a dictionary definition does not say in virtue of what terms are synonymous, it just indicates that people treat them as synonymous. Ultimately, synonymy tends to get explained in terms of analyticity and in terms of necessity: we say, for example, that "Bachelors are unmarried" is analytic because it is necessarily true, or because *bachelors* and *adult unmarried male* are synonymous. The problem here is that analyticity itself, according to Quine, tends to get explained in terms of synonymy and necessity. This suggests that the explanations move in something like a circle, and this in turn suggests that none of these concepts—analyticity included—are really being explained, despite any appearance to the contrary. As a rather rough analogy, suppose someone explained the concept of illness by saying it was the absence of health—then, when asked for an explanation of health, said it was the absence of illness. These purported explanations do not really explain the concepts health and illness; one would be hard pressed on their basis alone to say what either health or illness consists in. According to Quine, explanations for analyticity are rather like that, hinging on concepts that themselves depend on analyticity. If analyticity cannot adequately be accounted for, Quine suggests, we are better off abandoning it—and this in fact he does.

The second dogma of Quine's essay is that of reductionism, here understood as the view that associated with each statement are statements about specific, sensory experience or experiences, to which the first statement can "reduce." For example, associated with the statement "The Pacific Ocean is salty" is specific sensory experience (that is, experience based on the five senses), such as the taste of salt in samples of the Pacific Ocean and detection of Pacific Ocean salt by scientific instruments. To say that "The Pacific Ocean is salty" can be reduced to statements about those experiences is to say that "The Pacific Ocean is salty" at bottom means nothing more than those statements about the relevant experiences. As we have seen already, this rough idea was adopted by logical positivists, who spent considerable time and effort in identifying and explaining the nature of such basic statements. The positivist view was that all knowledge was ultimately based on experience, and non-analytic statements of fact could be reduced to basic statements about experience. This was thought to be true of even the most complicated sentences, apparently removed from specific sensory experiences—say, statements about the structure of DNA or about the behavior of atomic particles. Indeed, recall that for positivists, non-analytic statement that could not be verified (at least in principle) were meaningless. Such a verification theory of meaning and reductionism are closely related. This is because to verify a statement would seem to have to do with having the specific experiences described in the basic statements to which the original statement could be reduced. For example, suppose "The Pacific Ocean is salty" can be reduced to statements about tasting salt and scientifically detecting salt in the Pacific Ocean. Then to verify that statement, one should attempt to taste salt or scientifically detect it in the Pacific Ocean.

Quine recognized the close kinship between reductionism and the verification theory of meaning, and he rejected both. In so doing, he broke definitively with key principles of the logical positivist program. The mistake of the logical positivists, Quine argued, was to suppose that each statement is verified individually, independently of other statements. But this supposition is false. Rather, statements are verified together, as a whole. Consider a commonly held belief, say, the belief expressed by the statement, "Bees pollinate flowering plants in my garden." One might suppose that one can verify this statement without regard to other statements—after all, is it not possible just to observe the behavior of bees and their effect on flowering plants in one's garden? Of course, it is possible to observe these phenomena. However, by Quine's lights, matters are more complicated than this suggests. The statement "Bees pollinate flowering plants in my garden" is closely related to many other statements, statements expressing other beliefs—for example, "Bees enter my garden," "Some plants have flowers," "Some plants use flowers to pollinate," "Some plants reproduce via pollination," or even "Bees exist." To verify "Bees pollinate flowering plants in my garden" then, is also to help verify (or not) other, related statements. Conversely, to verify (or not) these related statements is also to help verify (or not) "Bees pollinate flowering plants in my garden." If one discovered, for example, that all the bees of the world were extinct, this is evidence against both "Bees exist" and "Bees pollinate flowering plants in my garden." Even a very simple belief, say, the belief expressed by the statement, "It is snowing" is closely related to other statements, such as, "It is cold enough to snow" and "The white flakes now falling from the sky are made primarily of water"; verification of these statements proceeds together, not individually. Quine's point, then, is that no statement is ever verified in isolation. Instead, entire systems of statements are verified as a *whole*—for example, all of the statements that describe our beliefs about the world. Quine's view is a kind of holism, according to which—against the view of reductionism—a statement cannot be reduced to more basic statements about a specific experience, or experiences. We are now in a clearer position to see why Quine rejects the analytic/synthetic distinction. That distinction assumes that some sentences are individually verified in one way—say, as a matter of definition—and that other sentences are verified individually in another way (by checking facts about the world). But this assumption is false.

Quine wrote extensively about the relation between language and what exists, or language and ontology (the study of existence). He did not think that studying language would tell us what exists. He did, however, believe that it is worth examining how language *says* that something exists. Sometimes what we say seems to commit us to the view that something—some particular object, say, or a particular kind of thing—exists. This is what Quine called *ontological commitment*, and he studied how language does (and does not) carry ontological commitments. His own view was that, in what he called the web of belief—that system of statements describing our view about the world—there are no special, privileged beliefs that cannot ever be revised. If one believed that some statements are analytic, one might believe that there are such statements—for example, that one would never modify or regard as false "Circles are round," no matter what one's experiences are. Quine does acknowledge that some statements are less likely to be rejected or modified in light of experience. This is not, however, because they are analytic, or true by definition; instead, it is for pragmatic reasons. Sometimes rejecting a very a fundamental statement as false would needlessly complicate our view of the world. For this reason (probably among others), we are unlikely to reject the statement "The Earth is a physical object" or "Humans are mammals." Those statements are so fundamental that revising them (or rejecting them) would involve revising many, many more statements expressing our beliefs, introducing many complications to our web of belief. We are not likely to do this unless we have excellent reasons for doing so. Quine himself believed that all that exists are physical objects, plus classes (in logic, a kind of abstract object). However, he regarded belief in physical objects as a posit. In other words, we believe there are such objects because our best science tells us that they are, and our best science offers the most superior explanation of our experience of the world. Yet the belief is not un-revisable; it is not set in stone. In principle, it is possible that we could reject that posit—denying the existence of physical objects—if it turns out that we can best explain our experience in some other way.

As these remarks suggest, Quine was a naturalist, meaning that he believed that it was best to explain phenomena through the terms and views countenanced by science. For example, science typically does not include in its ontology the existence of a non-physical mind; instead, scientists explain mental activity and experiences (for example, thinking, perceiving, remembering, feeling, and so on) strictly in terms of physical entities and processes, notably the brain, the nervous system, and the physical processes associated with them. So it is not surprising that Quine defended a materialist view of mind, that is, a view that explains mental activity and experiences in strictly material, or physical terms (specifically, Quine held that mental states are states of the body). Quine's naturalism also led him to espouse an influential and controversial view called naturalized epistemology, according to which knowledge and how we acquire knowledge should be studied according to the methods of science. According to this view, the study of knowledge (epistemology) is properly a kind of psychology, rather than a discipline best conducted from the confines of the study or armchair, as philosophers have arguably traditionally practiced it. It is worth noting that, together with Quine's advocacy of naturalism, Quine did not see a sharp distinction between science and philosophy. Both disciplines, he believed, seek to describe the world accurately; but there is no rigid boundary between them. (This view is a consequence of Quine's rejection of the analytic/synthetic distinction; if we verify the claims in our web of belief as a whole, then it is not the case that the scientific claims are verified through individual observations while more obviously "philosophical" claims are verified by analyzing language. Rather, all claims "face"—are verified by—experience together.)

Finally, Quine wrote a great deal about philosophy of language. Among his notable claims was his thesis of the indeterminacy of translation. Quine imagined a linguist faced with the task of translating a language of which she is completely ignorant, a task called radical translation. According to Quine, all the linguist has to go on as she tries translating the language is the behavior of the native speakers. The linguist can track what the natives say and when they say it, but the linguist does not have access to the natives' beliefs or intentions. So, for Quine, behavioral evidence is the only evidence for linguistic meaning. In this sense, Quine was a behaviorist. Quine's claim was that it is possible to give different translation manuals for a language and available evidence could support all equally well, with none of them being uniquely correct. Put another way, it is possible to give different but equally good guides for translating the same language. This claim is the thesis of the indeterminacy of translation.

To illustrate, Quine imagined that *gavagai* is a word in the language the linguist is attempting to translate. The linguist tries to figure out under what sort of circumstances the native speaker utters "Gavagai" or gives an affirmative answer to the question, "Gavagai?" (perhaps by nodding, say, or using a word the linguist believes means "yes"). When a native speaker consistently utters "Gavagai," in the presence of rabbits, and seems to assent to the question "Gavagai?" when there are rabbits around, it seems reasonable to suppose that the meaning of *gavagai* has something to do with rabbits. However, for Quine, the precise meaning of *gavagai* is indeterminate. This is because how the native speakers behave—both what they say and what they do —would be consistent with various possible meanings. Put another way, the pattern of varying circumstances in which the native utters, "Gavagai" or assents to "Gavagai?" would not determine that one of these meanings rather than another is the meaning for *gavagai*. *Gavagai* could mean, simply, "rabbit." But it could also mean "undetached rabbit parts"—that is, parts of rabbits that are attached to each other (not undetached). It could even mean "rabbit stage"—that is, a particular time period (stage) of a rabbit's life. For instance, suppose the linguist points to a large rabbit and says, "Gavagai kenel," and the linguist believes that *kenel* means something like brown. The linguist could reasonably translate *gavagai* to mean "The rabbit is brown," as well as "The undetached rabbit parts are brown" or "The rabbit stage is brown." There being no single, determinate translation for *gavagai,* there is no single correct translation for *gavagai*. For Quine, this point applies to the translation manual for an entire language: Translation of another language as a whole is indeterminate.

New Developments

Analytic philosophy has grown in many directions in the latter half of the 20th century and in the beginning of the 21st. The field continues to be characterized by careful reasoning, close argumentation, and attention to clarity and detail. Analytic philosophers have applied their approach to many different problems in philosophy. Many philosophers today continue to focus on language, and the philosophy of language is alive and well. However, just as analytic philosophers before them, more recent and contemporary analytic philosophers have examined new and traditional topics in epistemology (the study of knowledge), philosophy of mind, logic, ethics (the study of right action), and other topics. Below is a description of the work of two important philosophers of the latter half of the 20th century, Donald Davidson and Nelson Goodman.

Donald Davidson

Virtually any list of the most important philosophers in analytic philosophy in the 20th century would include Donald Davidson (1917–2003). Davidson's work spanned various areas, and he is especially notable for his contributions to action theory, the study of events, philosophy of mind, and philosophy of language. Davidson was born in Massachusetts. He earned a B.A. and an M.A. in philosophy from Harvard University but interrupted his studies to serve in the U.S. Navy during World War II. He later completed his Ph.D. at Harvard University, where Quine was one of his teachers. Davidson taught at various universities, including Queen's College, Stanford University, Rockefeller

University, and the University of Chicago. In 1981, he accepted a position at the University of California, Berkeley, where he remained for the rest of his career.

According to Davidson, included in the ontological categories of the world are events. That is, particular events are among the kinds of things that are real. There are objects, of course—pencils and doors and people—but there are also events, such as the Battle of Waterloo, the World Series of 2010, and the grand opening of the World's Fair in 1986; on a more mundane level, the act of buttering toast, say, is an event (as is the act of getting up in the morning). The same event can be described in different ways. For example, the event of a cat meowing in the morning can be described as the event of a cat opening its mouth and forcing air out to create a sound, but it can also be described as the event of the cat waking up its owner in order to demand breakfast. Similarly, when someone goes snorkeling, the event can be described in terms of someone putting on a snorkeling mask and flippers and swimming in the water, but it can also be described as the event of someone looking for fish and sea turtles beneath the water. For Davidson, an action is a kind of event, specifically the kind of event that can be described in such a way that involves someone having an intention. For example, if I set an alarm clock, that event can be described as intending to get up at a specific time.

In his description of actions, Davidson made the important claim that reasons—what motivates a person to do something—can not only cause events—specifically, human behavior—but can also explain events. Indeed, for Davidson, it is possible to explain someone's action in terms of that person's reasons precisely because that reason causes the person's action. As an illustration, suppose on a hot day I wade into the ocean. How can one explain my action? By reference to my *reason* for wading into the ocean—say, for the purpose of cooling off. That, after all, is why I waded into the ocean; that was the cause of my action. Davidson noted that an action involves an attitude as well as a belief; in this case, for instance, I wanted to cool off (I had a positive attitude about doing so), and I believed that wading into the ocean would help me do so.

Now the claim that reasons can serve as both causes and explanations of human behavior might seem uncontroversial, even obvious. However, Davidson was writing in a time when behaviorist explanations of human behavior were popular, that is, explanations that made no reference to inner or mental states, including a person's feelings, attitudes, beliefs, and intentions. A common behaviorist worry was that, since no one has direct access to such mental states (no one can peer into someone else's head and view that person's intentions, for example), claims about such states were not objective or scientifically verifiable. In addition, a common belief about causes has been that, in order for something to count as a cause, it must be describable in terms of a law. For example, when one billiard ball hits another and causes it to move, what explains the movement of the second ball is Newton's laws of motion. A rough way of putting the point that causation is governed by strict laws is to say that certain kinds of events cause other kinds of events because those events are governed by strict scientific laws; in the above case, one event (one ball striking another) causes another event (the movement of the second call) because of physical laws governing motion. Yet it is not obvious that reasons, attitudes, or beliefs really fall under any laws, or put another way, that there are laws that describe and predict reasons, attitudes, or beliefs. My belief that wading into the ocean will help me cool off is certainly not obviously explained or predicted by a law, in the way that a billiard ball's motion can be explained and predicted by Newton's laws of motion.

Davidson quite agreed that reasons, attitudes, and beliefs are not governed by strict laws. Moreover, he also agreed that causation *is* governed by strict laws (such as the law of gravity). At the same time, however, Davidson held fast to his view that reasons can serve as both explanations and causes of human behavior. This brings us to Davidson's view about the nature of mind, a view called anomalous monism. With respect to anomalous monism, in addition to Davidson's claim that causation is governed by strict laws, Davidson made two basic claims: first, that some mental events interact with physical events; and, second, that there are no strict psychophysical laws (that is, strict laws governing the relation between mental events and physical events). To say that some mental events interact causally with physical events is to say that some mental events cause physical events, and physical events cause some mental events. For an illustration of the first case, think of a person's desire to answer the phone causing her to pick up the phone and answer it. For an example of the second case, think of the phone ringing as causing a person to desire to answer the phone.

Because Davidson regards causation as having to do with strict laws, if mental events cause physical events and vice versa, then they must do so according to strict, scientific laws.

We now turn to Davidson's claim that there are no strict laws governing the relation between physical events and mental events (that there are no psychophysical laws). Davidson's defense of this claim relies on his view of how people make sense of what other people are thinking, hoping, feeling, wishing, and so on. In brief, Davidson's claim is that we do so according to the principle of rationality: we try to understand another person in such a way that the person can be considered rational. Consider a person who says, "I'm just not myself today." One way of understanding this remark is to suppose that the speaker believes she is literally not herself—that she is not identical with herself. But this is contradictory; it would be strange for a person really to mean and believe that she is not the same as herself when she says, "I'm just not myself today." So, one is not likely to suppose that that is what she believes; one will cast about for a more sensible interpretation, on which the speaker appears to be more rational. One such interpretation is that the speaker means that she is behaving in ways that she normally does not, and more likely than not, that is what the speaker believes—not the contradictory belief that she is not the same as herself. What this illustrates is that when we try to make sense of what people believe, we proceed on the assumption (as much as we are able) that the speaker is rational. We avoid attributing to someone beliefs that are obviously false and beliefs that are plainly inconsistent with each other. For instance, if someone seems to believe that there is a blizzard going on, we are less likely to think that she believes she will be comfortable in shirt-sleeves if she goes outside (unless there are some rather odd circumstances that might make this latter belief rational). In short, when we attribute beliefs to others, we normally attempt to do so in such a way that the person seems rational. Similar remarks apply to how we make sense of what people desire, hope, value, and so on; for example, we are not likely to suppose simultaneously that at the same time a person hopes to sail around the world she also desires never to leave her hometown.

Making sense of mental events, then—events such as a person's beliefs, intentions, desires, and so on—requires the principle of rationality. However—and this is a key difference—making sense of physical events does not require the principle of rationality. Making sense of why the brain is active in certain ways in response to certain stimuli, for instance, does not require the principle of rationality. Rather, we understand the relations between such physical events in terms of strict, scientific laws. Davidson's claim, in other words, is that whereas we understand mentality (believing, thinking, wishing, hoping, etc.) in terms of rationality, we understand the physical world in terms of strict, scientific laws. It is this difference between the realm of the mental and the realm of the physical that, for Davidson, implies that there are no strict psychophysical laws. That is, this difference implies that there are no strict laws that govern the relation between mental events and physical events. In that sense, mental events are anomalous—unlike physical events, they cannot be explained or predicted according to strict, scientific laws.

For Davidson, this also implies that when mental events cause physical events, they must do so in virtue of some feature other than a mental property. This is because strict, scientific laws apply to physical events, not mental events. For Davidson, mental events are *identical* to physical events. One way of understanding this is that mental events, because they are physical events, have physical properties in virtue of which they can cause physical events. As an example, suppose someone's belief that the phone is ringing causes her to pick up the phone. The mental event (the belief) must have some physical property that causes the physical event (picking up the phone). For Davidson, in general, *every* individual mental event is identical to some individual physical event. That event can be described in different ways: in can be given a description in terms of mental activity, such as, "She's thinking she'd like to talk a walk in the woods." But it can also be given a description in physical terms, a description that would presumably involve describing the activity of brain cells. Davidson believed that mental events *supervene* on physical events. That is, although mental events cannot be explained just in terms of physical events (mental events are not reducible to physical events), there could be no two physical events that are exactly alike yet have different mental properties.

An important point is that, if Davidson is correct that there are no psychophysical laws, then there are no such laws that govern what a person believes, desires, hopes, intends, or so on. Not only are there no such laws, but it is also impossible to predict what a person believes, desires, hopes, or intends, etc. on the basis of physical events in a person's brain. Knowing all there is to know about the brain, on this view, will not allow us to predict that someone will want to wear orange socks, believe that there is intelligent life on other planets, or hope that a particular rock band will release another album. Moreover, knowing all the physical facts about the brain will not explain any of these mental events, either, nor any mental event. All of this, in turn, implies that humans have free will in the sense that our beliefs, desires, goals, and so on are not determined by past physical events (Davidson also thinks they are not determined by past mental events, either).

In addition to his influential work on action theory and philosophy of mind, Davidson's work was also important in the philosophy of language. As noted, Davidson believed that we explain human behavior with an assumption of rationality. Accordingly, he differed from Quine, who had discussed radical translation—the project of translating a language to which one had no prior knowledge, going on the basis of the behavior of the native speakers—to talk instead of radical *interpretation*. Davidson preferred interpretation because, he believed, making sense of a speaker's behavior (including what a speaker says) requires interpreting what a speaker believes. Quine had emphasized observing the correlations between a speaker's utterance of a word and the apparent stimulus that prompted the utterance. For example, perhaps a native speaker utters "Gavagai" only in the presence of rabbits; the presence of rabbits stimulates the utterance, and accordingly one might infer that "Gavagai" means rabbit. However, by Davidson's lights, one would make this inference only if one supposed that the native speaker believed that there really were rabbits in the vicinity in such cases (as opposed, say, to hares or marmots). Davidson argued that, when interpreting a language of which one has no prior knowledge, one must simultaneously attempt to make sense both of what the speaker believes and the meaning of what the speaker says. The way to do this, in turn, is to use what Davidson called the principle of charity: one assumes that the speaker is rational (which, in turn, entails assuming that the speaker's beliefs are often in agreement with one's own—that, say, you both believe there are rabbits about when you see them show up).

A key concern of Davidson's regarding the philosophy of language was how to understand linguistic meaning. It is apparent that sentences of language are meaningful; when a friend says, "The concert starts at seven," you know that the friend is telling you that some concert is starting at seven o'clock; you could not know this if the sentence were gibberish, or if the friend had said, "Brakish garbo blinth." But in virtue of what is language meaningful? Davidson was critical of the notion of meaning, which he found unclear. Talk of the meaning of *snow*, for example, might seem to suggest there is some entity that is the meaning of that word, but it is not clear how to make sense of that entity; for instance, it is evidently not the sort of thing one could see or touch. Davidson proposed a semantics of natural language in terms of truth conditions; that is, he explained the meaningfulness of natural language in terms of the conditions under which sentences are true. A complete theory of semantics, he thought, could tell us for every sentence the conditions under which that sentence is true. So, Davidson regarded sentences as the units of meaning (not individual words); the meaning of a sentence is its truth conditions. For example, *Owls eat mice* is true under the condition that owls eat mice; otherwise, it is not true. That condition is the meaning of *Owls eat mice*.

Nelson Goodman

Another very important analytic philosopher of the late 20th century was Nelson Goodman (1906–98). Goodman was born in Massachusetts and studied at Harvard University. While working on his Ph.D. there, he also ran an art gallery (with this experience informing his later works in the philosophy of art, for which he became well known). During World War II, he served in the U.S. Army. After the war, he returned to academia, teaching at several universities before settling in with the philosophy department at Harvard, where he taught until his retirement.

Probably Goodman's most enduring philosophical work was his introduction of the concept of "grue." He coined the word *grue* in order to raise a concern about induction as a reliable form of reasoning. Goodman's concern is often called the new riddle of induction. The original riddle of induction was raised by the 18th-century British philosopher David Hume. Hume's riddle or problem was: how can induction, or inductive inferences, be justified? The very nature of induction is that the conclusion of an argument is not guaranteed, given its premises. For example, based on past experience, we might notice a pattern of events and, as a result, we might infer that this event will happen again tomorrow. However, it is not guaranteed that it will happen tomorrow, even if it is highly probable that it will. For instance, every day for millions of years the Sun has risen in the east each morning, so we infer that tomorrow the same thing will happen. While it is highly likely that it will, there is always the (extremely remote) possibility that tonight the Earth will explode, so tomorrow the Sun will not rise in the east. Hume's question, again, was: how can induction, or inductive inferences, be justified?

Hume said that we cannot use induction itself to justify inductive inferences, as that would be arguing in a circle; it would be assuming the very thing that we are questioning, namely, the reliability of induction. On the other hand, Hume said, we cannot use deduction (in which the conclusion of an argument *is* guaranteed, given its premises) because induction is, by definition, not deductively valid. The only justification for induction, then, for Hume, was that it seemed to work much of the time. But, he said, that was a weak justification.

In the mid-1900s, Goodman raised his new riddle of induction by introducing the term, *grue*. Grue is a blend of the words, *green* and *blue*. *Grue* is defined this way: Something is *grue* just in case it is green prior to, say, January 1, 3000, and also just in case it is blue after January 1, 3000. So, for instance, someone who speaks English would say that grass is green. Someone who speaks a Gruesome language would say that grass is grue, but after January 1, 3000, that person would say that grass is not grue, but that the sky is grue. Goodman also coined the word *bleen,* as in something is bleen just in case it is blue prior to, say, January 1, 3000, and also just in case it is green after January 1, 3000. (So, to the Gruesome speaker, prior to January 1, 3000, grass is grue and after that date grass is bleen.)

Goodman suggested that we might make this example of an inductive inference: Since every emerald that has been observed in the past was green, the next emerald we observe will be green. However, one could also say that since every emerald that has been observed in the past was grue, the next emerald that we observe will be grue. Of course, we expect that the green inductive inference will be correct (because we expect that after January 1, 3000) the next emerald will, indeed, be green, but we expect the grue inductive inference will be incorrect (because we do not expect that after January 1, 3000) the next emerald will be blue.

The riddle here is that, while it appears that grue is a strange concept because it is defined by some point in time, Goodman claimed that actually, *green* could be defined in terms of *grue* and *bleen*. So, green means: something is green just in case it is grue prior to January 1, 3000, and also just in case it is bleen after that date. Goodman's point is that there is no reason to assume that green and blue are more natural than grue and bleen, since each pair of words can be defined in terms of the other pair. So, again, there is a riddle about justifying inductive inferences, since two different inferences result in this case depending upon which pair of words is taken as better. But, even if we say that one pair (green and blue) give us a better inference, the only justification seems to be that it works in this case (which lands us right back to the original riddle of induction).

Besides the concerns about grue—that is, how terms and classifications can be matched up with the world—Goodman also pointed out that a common and basic kind of expression, called counterfactuals, also led to problems, particularly because they make the distinction blurry at best between sentences that express genuine laws (of nature) and mere lawlike sentences that express accidental generalizations.

Philosophers call some sentences categoricals. This means that they purport to state a fact. For example, the sentence, "Cats are mammals" is a categorical sentence. Categorical sentences might be false, however, as in the sentence, "Cats can fly." The point is that categorical sentences (even if they turn out to be false) are of the form: S is P. Philosophers call some other sentences conditionals. These are sentences that contain some condition, or hypothetical component. For instance, the sentence, "If I sleep in too late, I will miss class" is a conditional sentence. The sentence does not state that I will sleep in too late, but, rather, states a hypothetical situation, or a condition: *if* I sleep in too late, *then* I will miss class. Conditional sentences are of the form: If S, then P.

One kind of conditional sentence is called a material conditional. This kind of conditional sentence involves a straightforward "if-then" structure, as in the sentence, "If cats are mammals, then they are warm-blooded." Another kind of conditional sentence is called a subjunctive conditional. Often in subjunctive conditionals we use words like "could" and "were," as in the sentence, "If I could flap my arms and fly, then I would be happy" or "If I were to break this window, then I would be in trouble." These are often called contrary-to-fact, or counterfactuals, by philosophers. This is because they are not factual claims. In particular, the if-part of the sentence is contrary to the facts of the world.

Philosophers have wrestled with conceptual problems about counterfactuals. One concern for philosophers is how counterfactuals relate to the notion of dispositions. Some features of things are said to be dispositions, meaning that things have a likelihood to behave in certain ways, even if they do not actually behave that way. For example, if one said that glass is fragile that means that glass is likely to break (or has the disposition to break) if it is struck and it has that disposition even if it is never struck. Counterfactuals are also related to the notion of natural laws. For instance, if one said that it is a law that metals conduct electricity, then that means that if one *were* to give an electric current to a metal, then it would conduct that current. Counterfactuals also relate to the issue of cause. For example, if one said that smoking causes lung cancer, then that means that if one *were* to smoke, then one would get lung cancer.

The reason that philosophers are concerned with counterfactuals is that they are difficult to analyze in terms of what makes them true and also in terms of how to distinguish them from other conditionals. Because by their very nature, they are contrary to facts, they are false; yet we have very good reasons for taking them to be true. So, the sentence, "If cats were birds, then they could fly" states a truth, even though it is not obvious why. For instance, if that sentence were true, would the following sentence, thereby be false: "If cats were birds, then not all birds could fly"? This difficulty of knowing how to analyze counterfactuals is important to philosophers because, as noted above, they are so basic to issues about how to understand dispositions and laws and cause.

More Recent Developments— Saul Kripke

Saul Kripke (1940–   ) has been among the most influential philosophers of 20th-century analytic philosophy, contributing especially to modal logic (logic concerning possibility and necessity), metaphysics, and philosophy of language. He was born in Bay Shore, New York, and demonstrated his intellectual talent at an early age, publishing a paper on modal logic when he was still in his teens. He later attended Harvard University, earning a bachelor's degree in mathematics. Kripke never completed an advanced academic degree, yet went on to teach and research at Harvard, Rockefeller University, and Princeton University, where he worked for many years. After retiring from Princeton, he accepted a faculty position at City University of New York Graduate Center.

In 1972, Kripke published a series of lectures called *Naming and Necessity.* It has proven to be his most influential work, introducing—or in some cases, reintroducing—important ideas in philosophy of language, necessity, and metaphysics (the study of reality). Against Frege and others, Kripke denied that the reference of a proper name (*Napoleon, George Washington,* and so on) depends in any way on senses or on descriptions associated with the name. Some philosophers, such as Bertrand Russell, had argued that names are disguised descriptions. That is, on this descriptivist view of names, a name really just stands for a description or cluster of descriptions, which give the meaning of the name. For example, the name *George Washington* stands for descriptions such as the first president of the United States, wearer of wooden dentures, and leader of American revolutionary forces. Such descriptions must apply to someone or some object uniquely; that is, as a whole, the descriptions should apply only to a single person or object. What this view seems to imply is that, in order to use a name to refer successfully to the relevant reference, one must have in mind at least some of the relevant descriptions associated with the name. For example, to use *George Washington* to refer to George Washington, a speaker must have in mind at least some of the associated descriptions to refer successfully; someone who knew nothing about George Washington could not use the name *George Washington* to refer successfully to George Washington. Kripke argued that the descriptivist view of names is mistaken. To illustrate, he gave examples in which speakers seem to use names to refer successfully when they have no descriptions or no unique descriptions associated with the name—or even when they associate a false description with a name. For example, someone who knows only that Stephen Hawking is a physicist but nothing else about him seems to be able to use the name *Stephen Hawking* to refer to Stephen Hawking; this is even though the description *is a physicist* does not uniquely pick out Stephen Hawking (it applies to other physicists). Similarly, one might associate with the name *George Washington* the description *the first president of the United States*. Now according to Kripke, even if it turns out to be false that George Washington was the first president of the United States, one could still use *George Washington* to refer to George Washington. What such scenarios illustrate, according to Kripke, is that names are not disguised descriptions after all. Reference does not depend on descriptions; reference does not depend on senses, as Frege understood them.

Kripke presented an alternative view of reference, a view known as the causal theory (Kripke himself did not claim he was presenting a theory so much as a picture of how reference works). According to this view, reference has its origins in a baptismal act, that is, an act of naming. For example, parents might name their child thus: "We give you the name *Maxfield*." The proud parents tell others about their new son; these people, hearing the parents use *Maxfield* to talk about the child, intend to refer to the same child when they use the name *Maxfield*; and others, hearing the name from them, also intend to use *Maxfield* in the same way. The reference of *Maxfield* to the child Maxfield, then, depends on two things: the initial act of naming and the passing of the name from speaker to speaker, with each speaker intending to use the name as the prior speaker used the name. This view is called the causal view because, according to it, the initial act of naming sets in motion a causal chain that enables the name to refer.

Names, Kripke argued, are rigid designators, meaning that they refer to the same person or object in all possible worlds. Kripke adopted the language of possible worlds as a way of talking about possibility and necessity. A possible world is a world different in some way than ours—for example, a world that is like the actual world except that the color of one's car is blue instead of red, or a world that is like the actual world except that Napoleon was never born. Philosophers have disagreed over how best to understand the concept of possible worlds; some have argued that possible worlds are real (there really exist different possible worlds, like ours but different in some respect or respects), and others talk about possible worlds just because it is a convenient way of talking about what is possible and what is not. This is the way it will be understood here. For example, to say that there is a possible world in which Napoleon was never born is to say that it is possible that Napoleon might never have been born, or put another way, it was not *necessary* that Napoleon be born. Of course, in the actual world, Napoleon was born, but the point is that he might not have been; it just turned out to be the case that he was.

To return to the issue of names, Kripke claimed that in all the worlds in which Napoleon (for example) existed, *Napoleon* refers to Napoleon. In some possible worlds, Napoleon existed but did rather different things than he did in the actual world; for instance, there is a possible world in which Napoleon worked as a singer instead of a head of state (again, this can just be understood as a way of saying that it is possible that Napoleon could have been a singer instead of a head of state; although in fact he did serve as head of state, it was not necessary that he did so). But in that world, however, *Napoleon* still would refer to Napoleon, the very same person. Similarly, in a possible world George Washington was not the first president of the United States; but in that world as well as this one, *George Washington* referred to George Washington, the very same person.

Because names are rigid designators, lacking senses or descriptions, this implies that some identity statements, although necessarily true, cannot be known independent of experience (a posteriori). This claim marked a break from the longstanding view that necessarily true statements can be known a priori—that is, without observation of the empirical world. As an example, consider the statement "Hesperus is Phosphorus." *Hesperus* is an ancient Greek name meaning Evening Star, referring to a celestial object that appears in the evening sky; *Phosphorous* is an ancient Greek name meaning Morning Star, referring to a celestial object that appears in the morning sky. As it happens, the planet Venus turned out to be both the Evening Star and the Morning Star; Hesperus and Phosphorus are identical, so the sentence *Hesperus is Phosphorus* is true. However, the ancient astronomers did not know at first this; rather, they discovered it on the basis of observing Hesperus and Phosphorus, and they could not have discovered it without such observations. So, *Hesperus is Phosphorus* was *not* known a priori—knowing that the statement was true required observation. At the same time, however, according to Kripke, *Hesperus is Phosphorus* is necessarily true. This is because, as the two terms refer to the same object (Venus), the statement in effect says that an object is identical with itself. And that an object is identical with itself is necessarily true (it would not be possible for an object not to be identical with itself). Kripke applied the claim that there are necessarily true, a posteriori statements to claims about kinds of things in nature (natural kinds). For example, he claimed that the sentences *water is H_2O* and *lightning is electrical discharge* are necessarily true, although they cannot be known independent of experience.

Also in metaphysics, Kripke argued for the existence of essential properties—that is, properties that are essential for the identity of a given person or thing (without that property, someone would be a different person, or a thing would be a different thing). That there are essential properties was not a new idea, going as far back as ancient philosophy. However, Kripke helped revive the claim that there are essential properties. For example, Kripke argued for the necessity of origins. That is, according to him, a person or thing's origins are an essential feature of that thing or person. It is not possible, for instance, that Napoleon could have had different biological parents than the ones he actually had (maybe other people could have raised him, but no other people could have biologically produced him). So, there is no possible world in which Napoleon had different parents. Similarly, Kripke argued for the necessity of composition: if a thing is made of a certain material, that material is an essential feature of that thing. Put another way, if it were made of a different material, it would be a different thing. For instance, a walking stick made of a certain branch of an oak tree *must* have been made of that very branch; if it were not, it would not count as the same walking stick. So, its composition is necessary: there is no possible world in which it was made of anything other than that branch of a particular oak tree. Kripke's ideas generated a great deal of discussion, disagreement, and further philosophical work that continues to the present day.

As mentioned above, Kripke is credited with having made modality once again respectable as a philosophical concern, along with some other contemporary philosophers such as David Lewis (1941–2001) and Ruth Barcan Marcus (1921–   ). Quine had argued forcefully that modality (that is, matters of necessity and possibility) were messy and vague, at best. Kripke has been seen as being instrumental in providing not only technical, logical clarity to modality, but also with applying it to other philosophical concerns, such as issues of names and rigid designators.

People often speak of things or events as being possible or as being necessary. For example, we might claim that it is possible that there is life on Jupiter; it *might be* the case that there is life on Jupiter, even if we do not know that. Similarly, we might claim that a father is necessarily older than his daughter; it *must be* the case that he is older than she is. These notions of necessity and possibility (what might be or must be) are what philosophers call modalities (modes, or ways, that something is). We often distinguish possibility and necessity not only from each other, but also from two other concepts, actuality and contingency. That is, we sometimes distinguish something as being possible from something as being actual. For instance, it was possible that Babe Ruth could have run for Governor of New York, but in actuality he did not. Likewise, while it in fact happened that Babe Ruth hit over 700 home runs, he might not have; it did not have to happen, so it was contingent (not necessary) that it happened. Philosophers also speak of sentences as being contingent (for example, *bachelors are ugly*), which means that those sentences are true sometimes, but not always, as well as other sentences being necessary (for example, *bachelors are unmarried*). In the latter case (sentences being necessary), they can be either necessarily true, such as *bachelors are unmarried* (also called tautologies) or necessarily false, such as *bachelors are married* (also called contradictions).

These notions seem common and mundane. However, a closer look at them shows that they raise a number of conceptual and philosophical issues. One such issue is that there are different kinds of necessity and possibility. For example, philosophers speak of logical possibility as opposed to physical possibility. To say that something is logically possible simply means that it does not involve a contradiction. For instance, it is logically possible that a person could jump from the Earth to the Moon, but it is not physically possible. The law of gravity is relevant to physical possibility, but not to logical possibility. However, it is logically impossible for a square to be round, but not physically impossible (at least, if we take geometrical figures to be non-physical, abstract things, so physical possibility or impossibility is irrelevant). People also speak of other kinds of possibility (or necessity), such as technological possibility (it might be logically and physically possible to fly faster than light, but it is not now technologically possible). In addition, we might speak of temporal possibility (or necessity), that is, possibility or necessity related to time and a sequence of events. Philosophers even speak of epistemic possibility (or necessity), meaning what might or must be known.

Another issue about modalities, besides the various kinds of possibility and necessity, that philosophers deal with is whether or not necessity and possibility are properly spoken of as "in the world" or only as "in language." For example, if we say that something is possible—for example, it is possible that there is life on Jupiter—does that simply mean that the sentence *there is life on Jupiter* is not a contradiction or does it mean that there is actual possible life on Jupiter? The first case could be restated as *it is possible that there is life on Jupiter.* In this case, the possibility is about the truth of the sentence, that is, that the sentence is possibly true (and not a contradiction). The second case could be restated as *It is the case that there is possibly life on Jupiter.* In this case, the possibility is about life-forms, not about the sentence. Philosophers refer to the first case as *de dicto* (from the Latin words, meaning "of language") and they refer to the second case as *de re* (from the Latin words, meaning "of things"). The reason this distinction is made is because there are conceptual questions about claiming that there are possible things, that is, that there are actually things that are possible. For instance, Quine asked: Are there more possible thin men in the doorway than possible fat men? His point was that the notion of *de re* possibility raises questions and concerns that lead philosophers astray, while *de dicto* possibility does not; however, some other philosophers, including Kripke, disagree.

Kripke has argued that matters of modality are separate from matters of knowledge and linguistic structure. Where Quine claimed that necessity and analyticity depended upon each other, Kripke has maintained that necessity is not dependent upon analyticity or on something being known a priori. So, for Kripke, if it is true that water is H_2O, then it is necessarily true and does not in any way depend upon the sentence being analytic or upon it being known a priori (in fact, it is not known a priori, but was discovered).

Pragmatist Responses to Analytic Philosophy

Relatively late in the 20th century, some philosophers working in the analytic tradition began to critique that very tradition, sometimes using the language of an earlier school of philosophical thought: pragmatism. Two such philosophers are Hilary Putnam and Richard Rorty.

Hilary Putnam

Hilary Putnam (1926–   ) has worked in such diverse areas in philosophy as epistemology (the study of knowledge), philosophy of language, ethics, and metaphysics (the study of reality). He is widely considered one of the most significant philosophers of the 20th century. Putnam was born in Chicago and completed his undergraduate studies at the University of Pennsylvania. He has taught at MIT, Northwestern University, Princeton University, and Harvard University. He is currently a professor emeritus of Harvard.

In the philosophy of language, Putnam advocated a view according to which reference of some terms does not depend on what individual speakers intend. Putnam's claim was specifically about natural kind terms, that is, terms that pick out kinds of things that occur naturally in the world—for example, *gold* picks out a metal with a certain atomic structure, and *water* picks out a fluid with certain physical properties. To illustrate, Putnam imagined a world just like our own—Twin Earth—except that the fluid that appears to be water has different prop-

Photograph of Hilary Putnam. Putnam criticized analytic philosophy and metaphysical realism with pragmatic realism. *(Used under a Creative Commons license)*

erties than water on Earth itself. Water on Earth is composed of hydrogen and oxygen; specifically, it is H_2O. Now an Earthling visiting Twin Earth might indeed, upon seeing a fluid that looks and behaves and even tastes just like water, call this fluid water, meaning to refer to that fluid on Twin Earth. But now suppose it turns out that this fluid—with Putnam, we can call it *XYZ*—is not composed of hydrogen and oxygen. Putnam's claim is that, in this case, it would be wrong to call XYZ water. *Water* refers only to the fluid that is H_2O, not to anything else. Now what is important for our purposes is that, for Putnam, this is the case even if someone who uses the word *water* does not know that water is composed of H_2O. The reference of water depends at least in part on factors external to individual speakers; no matter what a speaker might believe about the matter, the fact is that water always and only refers to H_2O (and, therefore, not to XYZ).

There is, according to Putnam, a linguistic division of labor. That is, there are some words that almost any competent speaker of a language knows the reference of; that is, most speakers know what these words pick out. But there are also words whose reference is best explained by experts in a given field. To use Putnam's example, to many speakers, beech trees and elm trees are indistinguishable. So, these speakers could not identify which trees *elm* refers to and which trees *beech* refers to. However, an arborist can likely explain in detail what makes an elm tree and what makes a beech tree a beech tree, and an arborist can identify which trees *elm* refers to and which trees *beech* refers to. Now what enables a less knowledgeable speaker to use *elm* to refer to elms—not to beeches, though they are indistinguishable by that person—is the knowledge of the arborist. The arborist and the less knowledgeable person are members of the same linguistic community, and the successful use of *elm* to refer to elms by the latter depends on the specialized knowledge of the former. This point applies to other terms, as well—for example, many people could not say precisely what makes something gold (as opposed to fool's gold), but because others can, the less knowledgeable people can use *gold* to refer only to gold. But meaning, for Putnam, is *not* a function of what any one person's beliefs or intentions are—otherwise the Earthlings who called XYZ water would be correct in doing so, since they could not distinguish between XYZ and H_2O.

Putnam is also notable for introducing to philosophy of mind the view of functionalism, the view that mental states (states such as thinking, perceiving, and feeling) should be defined in terms of their functions—in terms of what they *do*. It does not matter what mental states are made of, according to functionalism, as long as they perform certain functions. Analogously, a camera can be made of many different kinds of materials, such as plastic, metal, wood, and even paper. For something to be a camera, what matters is just that it functions a certain way (that it can take pictures), not what it is made of. Similarly, on this view, what matters for being in a mental state is to be in a state that functions in a certain way, not to be in a state made of any particular kind of stuff.

However, what makes Putnam a critic of analytic philosophy, perhaps more than anywhere else, lies in Putnam's claims in metaphysics, the study of reality. In 1976, Putnam argued against what he called metaphysical realism, characterized as the view that the world is what it is independent of however people think and believe about it. The problem with this view, as Putnam saw it, is that it implies that there is a "God's eye" view of reality, that is, a perspective independent of any interests, beliefs, and concepts. But there is no such perspective. When we view reality, it is always from some perspective or another, always with a particular set of interests, values, and concepts. Putnam did not deny that there is objectivity in the world, understood in a certain sense. For example, whatever we might think about the matter, plates on the Earth's crust move, and their motion creates earthquakes and mountains. We cannot cause the Earth to move in different ways—or not to move at all—just because we would like to do so, or just because we believe one thing rather than another. However, Putnam argued that there are different, equally correct ways of understanding the world, or in other words, there is no single correct description of reality (the American philosopher Nelson Goodman also argued for this claim). It is possible, for instance, to describe the world using different concepts or categories, and either choice could be correct. Putnam called this view internal realism, or pragmatic realism. It is realism in the sense that, according to Putnam, it admits of the ordinary person's realism; on this view, objects such as trees and ice cubes exist. But it is a pragmatic realism in the sense that we can choose to categorize the world in different ways, and our choice to use some categories or concepts rather than another might depend on our purposes and even our values. Choosing some concepts to understand experience might serve some purposes better than others, even if more than one available choice could accurately describe the world. As an example, according to some philosophical views, numbers exist as actual entities; according to others, numbers are best understood in some other way. Either choice might be correct, but we might find that one choice suits our purposes better.

As a simpler example, there are many ways we could apply the concept of pets. In Western industrialized cultures, the concept applies to cats, dogs, and birds, among other animals; it does not typically apply to alligators. Now perhaps it could apply to alligators, say, if we were interested in attempting to form some kind relationship with alligators and caring for them on a regular basis, assuming responsibility for the well-being of individual alligators. As it happens, this does not suit the interests of many people, and alligators are typically not considered pets. The point, however, is that it is not a fact about the world, strictly independently of human interests, values, and beliefs that alligators either are or are not pets. Metaphysical questions might arise within our understanding of the world; for example, if we believe that numbers exist as abstract entities, one might wonder about the status of particular numbers; but the question of whether numbers themselves exist does not arise.

In all this, Putnam rejects the fact/value distinction, long favored by logical positivists and others. The fact/value distinction is a distinction between facts and values; for example, it is a fact that sometimes people murder. That it is *wrong* for people to murder is a value judgment. Positivists had held that there is a sharp division between these; for example, on their view, facts can be empirically verified, but value statements cannot (one cannot go out in the world and make observations that would demonstrate the truth or falsity that murder is wrong). However, because Putnam held that there is more than one equally correct description of reality, and that our choice in the matter depends somewhat on our own interests and values, he rejects the fact/value distinction. What facts there are depends to some extent on our values; there is no sharp division between them. Since his defense of pragmatic realism, Putnam has revised his views, but his formulation of the view still stands as a critique of much of analytic philosophy.

Richard Rorty

One of the most prominent and controversial philosophers of the 20th century, Richard Rorty (1931–2007) began his academic career writing in the tradition of analytic philosophy. However, his 1979 book *Philosophy and the Mirror of Nature* marked his first sustained, serious critique of the field, and he never again returned to the traditional practice of analytic philosophy, though he continued to write and publish philosophical work. Rorty was born in New York City to a politically aware family acquainted with important progressive thinkers of the time. At age 15, he began to study at the University of Chicago, earning a B.A. and an M.A. in philosophy. He completed his Ph.D. in philosophy at Yale University, where he taught for a time, subsequently teaching for periods at Wellesley College, Princeton University, the University of Virginia, and finally Stanford University. Among philosophers, Rorty's work was often controversial. He was also one of relatively few contemporary philosophers who wrote and published intellectual works outside the realm of strictly academic philosophy.

Philosophy and the Mirror of Nature is perhaps Rorty's most famous work. In that work, Rorty critiqued analytic philosophy for working—without much result—on apparent philosophical problems that arise from questionable assumptions. These assumptions were representationalism in the philosophy of mind and foundationalism in epistemology; influenced by Wilfrid Sellars (1912–89) and Willard Van Orman Quine (1908–2000), Rorty later rejected them both. To begin with representationalism, in Rorty's account a key assumption in traditional epistemology and philosophy of mind was that mental representations "mirror" the world. Put another way, as a mirror simply reflects back whatever happens to be near enough and appropriately situated to be reflected, the mind represents mentally whatever is in the world; it is in this sense that mind is a mirror of nature. To take a very rough example of this view, when a person sees Pike's Peak, the person's mind represents the mountain, presumably as it actually is. Rorty, however, criticized this view on various grounds. First, he did not think of the mind as simply a thing, like a car or a horse. Second, by Rorty's lights, it is a mistake to think that the world is simply "out there" to be mirrored, and therefore that somehow the mind mirrors it. Of course, Pike's Peak, apples, people, and cats, and so on, do exist, but it is also true that humans apply concepts to them. For example, people regard some things as food—apples and bananas, say—and other things as *not* food, such as doorknobs and mud. Regardless of what we think about them, apples and bananas and doorknobs and mud exist. However, it is not somehow built into reality that apples and bananas are food for humans and doorknobs and mud are not; apples and bananas exist *as food* for humans at least in part because that is how we regard them. To return to the mind as a mirror of nature, then, it is part of our reality—what counts as real—that apples and bananas are food, but this is not because the human mind merely reflects the objective fact that apples and bananas are food; this is not something the mind would mirror. Mental representations do not simply read off from reality what is objectively the case; rather, how we perceive and cognize about the world depends on (among other things) the concepts that we use and decisions that we make. To grasp this point, it might be helpful to remember that different cultures have different ideas of what counts as food. For instance, to many cultures, insects are food, and to others they are not. So, insects really are food for some peoples, but not for others. But there is nothing about the nature of reality—nothing about the nature of insects, say—that dictates that insects would either count as food or not count as food. So when some people react with disgust at the idea of eating ants, for example, this is not because they have mental representations about ants that are simply accurate reflections of what ants actually are.

Rorty also rejected foundationalism. In epistemology, foundationalism is a view about the nature of justification of beliefs. Foundationalism is based on the idea that our beliefs are justified by other beliefs. For example, suppose you believe that your neighbors are moving, and you believe this because you believe you overheard a conversation that indicated they were moving; this second belief is what justifies your belief that your neighbors are moving. Typically, foundationalist views in epistemology hold that, while many beliefs are justified by other beliefs, there are some beliefs that are self-justifying in some way. These beliefs do not require further justification, but they provide justification for all other beliefs; to use a common metaphor, these basic, self-justifying beliefs are rather like the bricks that make up the foundation of a building (all other beliefs rest on them, just like a building rests on its foundation). Rorty rejected foundationalism. On his view, no beliefs provide a foundation for any others, or put another way, no belief (or set of beliefs) has a privileged status relative to that of others.

Similarly and not surprisingly, Rorty rejected the view that language represents the world. So, by his lights, views such as those of the logical atomists and logical positivists—each of whom saw language as picturing the world or being structurally similar to the structure of the world—were mistaken. For Rorty, language does not match up neatly with the world anymore than mental representations match up neatly with the world. Rather, Rorty saw language as a tool for dealing with the world; its purpose is not to picture reality but to help us get along in the world, and he believed that some vocabularies might help us do that better than others.

Rorty's anti-representationalism and anti-foundationalism had important consequences. First, if the notion that the mind mirrors the world is misguided, then it is also misguided to suppose that it is possible to check the accuracy of our beliefs just by trying to match them up against the world, or what is actually the case. For example, one cannot verify the belief that ants are food (or that *ants are food* is true) by investigating ants, quite independent of how we think about them or regard them. Whether ants are food depends to some degree on *us*. So, there is no purely objective way to verify the belief that ants are food. To take another example, it is evident that mammals exist: there really are whales, horses, badgers, and so on. However, on this view, what counts as a mammal depends on us in the sense that humans regard some set of characteristics (giving birth to live young, having hair, being warm-blooded, and so on) are important enough that it makes sense to classify together all the creatures that have those characteristics. But we might have and could classify mammals in other ways; for example, scientists might discover creatures who have all the usual characteristics of mammals except that they are hairless, and in that case find it more useful to decide that it is not necessary to have hair to count as a mammal. For our purposes, the point again is that to check the truth of beliefs (whether mammals must have hair, say, or what kinds of creatures count as mammals) is not simply a matter of reading off what is the case in the world. This is because there is a sense in which what is the case depends on us and, say, what conceptual decisions we make.

A second, related consequence of Rorty's rejections of representationalism and foundationalism is a shift toward what Rorty called "pragmatism." If it is not possible to verify the truth of a claim by seeing whether it matches reality, then we need some other criterion of evaluating a claim. Rorty thought we should hold beliefs that are useful for our community. *Useful* here does not necessarily mean more convenient, or helping us make more money, or get more rest. *Useful* has rather to do with the goals of one's community—such as, for example, to use Rorty's goal, reducing cruelty. Or, in another example, it might be theoretically useful to classify mammals as one way, rather than another. It might do more good—for example, reduce more suffering—by regarding women as having rights equal to those of men, than not. That would be a reason for believing the claim that women have rights equal to those of men. We noted earlier that Rorty's view is that the purpose of language is not to picture reality but to help us get along in the world. It is time now to note that Rorty believed that some vocabularies can help us do that better than others; some ways of talking can better help us achieve our goals than others. The language of science might help us, but for Rorty is not special or privileged; another vocabulary might serve us better. Rorty, then, rejects the view common in analytic philosophy that science is privileged.

An important point here is that, for Rorty, the standards for evaluating claims have not only to do with their usefulness, but also to do with the needs and standards of one's own specific community. There being no objective, external standard by which to evaluate a claim, the only available standards are those of one's community. By making this claim, Rorty advocates ethnocentrism, or privileging one's own community standards over those of others. Many philosophers have found this troubling; one might ask, if there is no objective, external standard by which to evaluate a claim, why would the standards of, say, Nazi communities, not be just as good as those in contemporary, democratic societies? For his part, Rorty often and explicitly denied that he advocated relativism. Relativism, he claimed, is the view that any view is as good as any other; he believed this view is self-defeating. His own view, he said, was not that any view is as good as any other, but rather that one's own view—more accurately, the view of one's community—is better than that of others. There being no external, objective standards, we should aim not for objectivity but for solidarity—the agreement of like-minded individuals, as a community.

One more point is worth noting. Traditionally, philosophers have agreed that it is among the responsibilities of philosophy to give standards and criteria for what counts as truth and knowledge, generally speaking. So, it is up to philosophers, for example, to judge whether the claims of science count as knowledge or merely as belief. In denying that there are objective standard criteria for evaluating the truth of claims, Rorty also rejected this traditional view of philosophy. And in this, at least, he was in agreement with many philosophers working in analytic philosophy.

Concluding Discussion Questions

1. Why did Ludwig Wittgenstein later come to reject his earlier views about language and philosophy?
2. What is the analytic/synthetic distinction and why did W. V. O. Quine reject it?
3. For the sentence *Santa Claus does not exist,* how did Bertrand Russell explain its being true?
4. What did the Logical Positivists mean by the verification principle?
5. What did Gilbert Ryle mean by *category mistake* and how did he relate that to the mind-body problem?
6. What are linguistic performatives? Why can't they be true or false? How can they go wrong?

Further Reading

Ayer, A. J. *Philosophy in the Twentieth Century.* New York: Random House, 1982.

Baillie, James, ed. *Contemporary Analytic Philosophy.* Upper Saddle River, N.J.: Prentice Hall, 1997.

Belshaw, Christopher, and Gary Kemp, eds. *Twelve Modern Philosophers.* Malden, Mass.: Wiley-Blackwell, 2009.

Glock, Hans-Johann. *What Is Analytic Philosophy?* Cambridge: Cambridge University Press, 2008.

Gross, Barry R. *Analytic Philosophy: An Historical Introduction.* New York: Pegasus, 1970.

Hales, Steven D. *Analytic Philosophy: Classic Readings.* Belmont, Calif.: Wadsworth, 2001.

Lindberg, Jordan J. *Analytic Philosophy: Beginnings to the Present.* Mountain View, Calif.: Mayfield Publishing Company, 2001.

Martinich, A. P., and David Sosa, eds. *Analytic Philosophy: An Anthology.* Malden, Mass.: Blackwell, 2001.

Munitz, Milton K. *Contemporary Analytic Philosophy.* New York: Macmillan, 1981.

Soames, Scott. *Philosophical Analysis in the Twentieth Century,* Volume 1: *The Dawn of Analysis;* Volume 2: *The Age of Meaning.* Princeton, N.J.: Princeton University Press, 2003.

Stroll, Avrum. *Twentieth-Century Analytic Philosophy.* Cambridge: Cambridge University Press, 2000.

Weitz, Morris, ed. *Twentieth-Century Philosophy: The Analytic Tradition.* New York: The Free Press, 1966.

Glossary

analytic/synthetic   an analytic statement is a statement that is true or false either by definition or because of the structure of the statement. A synthetic statement is a statement whose truth or falsity does not depend only on definition or the structure of the statement. According to Kant, an analytic statement is a statement that says something already contained in the subject of the sentence, whereas a synthetic statement says more. For instance, *bachelors are unmarried* is analytic because the statement just spells out information already contained in the subject of the sentence (bachelors). By contrast, *bachelors are handsome* is synthetic; it says more than what is contained in *bachelors*.

a priori/a posteriori   a priori is a Latin phrase used to describe what is known or claimed independently of sensory experience (experience via the five senses). For example, mathematical knowledge, such as knowledge that $3 + 2 = 5$, is often considered a priori (it does not seem to be necessary to make observations of the world to come to know mathematical truths). A posteriori is a Latin phrase used to describe what is known or claimed based on sensory experience; much scientific knowledge, for instance, is considered a posteriori knowledge because it is based on observation of the natural world.

category mistake   the error of applying a concept where it does not actually apply. For example, it would be a mistake to ask of the Eiffel Tower, has the building reached puberty yet? Buildings are not the kind of things to which the concept of puberty applies, so asking this question would be a case of committing a category mistake. Gilbert Ryle argued that the mind-body problem was due to a category mistake, that of applying the concept non-physical to mental activity.

counterfactuals   conditional sentences that are contrary to the facts, such as *if Babe Ruth had stayed in Boston, the Red Sox would have won the World Series in 1927.* Because dispositional terms, such as solubility, are often couched in the context of counterfactuals, their analysis is important in understanding laws (for instance, because sugar is soluble in water, *if this sugar cube were in water, it would dissolve* is true even if that sugar cube were never placed in water).

direct realism   also called naïve realism, the view that in perception we directly perceive ordinary objects, such as tables, rocks, and trees, in a world that exists independently of ourselves; opposed to sense data views of perception.

holism   the view that individual sentences have meaning only in the context of larger systems; also, the view that individual sentences cannot be confirmed or falsified on their own, but only in conjunction with other sentences, forming a greater whole.

induction, problem of induction   the problem of knowing whether the future will be like the past—for instance, that kinds of events that have caused other kinds of events in the past will continue to do so in the future; associated with David Hume in particular.

logical atomism   associated with Bertrand Russell and Ludwig Wittgenstein, the view that the world consists of basic constituents (atoms), out of which are built facts or states of affairs; the structure of the world corresponds to the structure of an ideal language.

logical positivism (logical empiricism)   a philosophical movement of the early to mid-20th century, that emphasized the criterion of empirical observation as the basis for meaningfulness and that embraced a sharp division between facts and values (because value statements could not be verified by empirical observation).

logicism   the view that logic is the basis for mathematics (or, all of mathematics can be reduced to logic).

ordinary language philosophy (linguistic philosophy)   an approach to addressing philosophical issues and concerns by means of examining the meanings and uses of language in ordinary (that is, nontechnical) contexts. This approach was especially associated with the work of Ludwig Wittgenstein, Gilbert Ryle, J. L. Austin, and others, all of whom thought that many philosophical problems were linguistic in nature and arose because philosophers neglected, abandoned, or contradicted ordinary language meanings and uses.

performative a type of sentence that performs an action in the context of its utterance beyond merely being an utterance. For example, *I promise to pay you on Monday* is not only to utter words, it is to perform an action (that is, to make a promise) by uttering those words. Performatives themselves are said not to be true or false, although a third-person description of them can be (so, *I suggest you pay attention* is neither true nor false, but *he suggested you pay attention* can be).

rigid designator a term that refers to the same object in all situations, or possible worlds, in which it refers to anything at all. Usually associated with the views of Saul Kripke, proper names are often said to be examples of rigid designators because proper names are said to always refer to the same object (so, *George Washington* always designates George Washington, but, since history might have been different than in fact it was, the phrase *the first president of the United States* might have designated someone other than George Washington, so that phrase is not a rigid designator).

sense/reference two notions of meaning; the reference of a term is whatever is picked out in the world that corresponds to that term (so, *George Washington* picks out, or refers to, a particular historical person and *elm* picks out, or refers to, a particular species of tree), while the sense of a term is the features that something must have in order to be the reference of the term (so, the sense of *elm* is the set of features or properties that something must have for it to be an elm tree). The same reference might have different senses (for example, *the morning star* and *the evening star* are two expressions with different senses, but the same reference, namely, the planet Venus).

tautology a sentence that is always true, either by virtue of the meanings of the words in the sentence (such as *bachelors are unmarried*) or by virtue of its logical structure (such as *if A implies B, then not-B implies not-A*).

Key People

Austin, J. L (1911–1960) *British philosopher in the ordinary language tradition. Austin is best known for introducing the notion of speech acts (that some uses of language perform actions beyond merely being utterances of language). He was renowned for finding and articulating very subtle distinctions in everyday ordinary language, distinctions that he claimed had deep philosophical importance. The passage below is from his book* How to Do Things with Words. *Here he briefly notes that some sentences are performatives, meaning that the utterance of them performs an action.*

> The constative utterance, under the name, so dear to philosophers, of *statement,* has the property of being true or false. The performance utterance, by contrast, can never be either: it has its own special job, it is used to perform an action. To issue such an utterance is to perform the action—an action, perhaps, which one scarcely could perform, at least with so much precision, in any other way. Here are some examples: I name this ship *Liberté;* I apologize; I welcome you; I advise you to do it.
>
> Utterances of this kind are common enough: we find them, for instance, everywhere in what are called in English the "operative" clauses of a legal instrument. Plainly, many of them are not without interest for philosophers: to say "I promise to . . ."—to issue, as we say, this performative utterance—just is the act of making a promise; not, as we see, at all a mysterious act.

[Austin, J. L. *How to Do Things with Words.* Oxford: Oxford University Press, 1962.]

Ayer, A. J. (1910–1989) *British philosopher who was best known for popularizing logical positivism and for detailing the notion of verifiability as a criterion of meaning. His most famous work was* Language, Truth, and Logic, *from which the following selection is taken. In this selection, Ayer states that much of traditional philosophy, in particular,* *metaphysics, is simply nonsense because there is no way to test or verify it empirically.*

> The traditional disputes of philosophers are, for the most part, as unwarranted as they are unfruitful. The surest way to end them is to establish beyond question what should be the purpose and method of philosophical enquiry. And this is by no means so difficult a task as the history of philosophy would lead one to suppose. For if there are any questions which science leaves it to philosophy to answer, a straightforward process of elimination must lead to their discovery.
>
> We may begin by criticizing the metaphysical thesis that philosophy affords us knowledge of a reality transcending the world of science and common sense . . . Our charge against the metaphysician is not that he attempts to employ the understanding in a field where it cannot profitably venture, but that he produces sentences which fail to conform to the conditions under which alone a sentence can be literally significant . . .
>
> The criterion which we use to test the genuineness of apparent statements of fact is the criterion of verifiability.

[Ayer, A. J. *Language, Truth, and Logic,* 2nd edition. New York: Dover, 1946.]

Davidson, Donald (1917–2003) *American philosopher who was noted for his work in the philosophy of language, epistemology, and action theory, among other areas. Among his concerns was the issue of how language hooks up with the world. He challenged (and rejected) the notion that different languages (or, conceptual schemes) are so different that there is no objective basis for comparing them. In the selection below, taken from his article "On the Very Idea of a Conceptual Scheme," he claims that such a relativist view is mistaken.*

> Conceptual relativism is a heady and exotic doctrine, or would be if we could make good sense of it. The trouble is, as so often in philosophy, it is hard to improve intelligibility while retaining the excitement. At any rate that is what I shall argue . . .
>
> The idea is then that something is a language, and associated with a conceptual scheme, whether we can translate it or not, if

it stands in a certain relation (predicting, organizing, facing or fitting) to experience (nature, reality, sensory promptings). The problem is to say what the relation is, and to be clearer about the entities related . . .

Our attempt to characterize languages or conceptual schemes in terms of the notion of fitting some entity has come down, then, to the simple thought that something is an acceptable conceptual scheme or theory if it is true. Perhaps we better say *largely* true in order to allow sharers of a scheme to differ on details. And the criterion of a conceptual scheme different from our own now becomes: largely true but not translatable. The question whether this is a useful criterion is just the question how well we understand the notion of truth, as applied to language, independent of the notion of translation.

[Davidson, Donald. "On the Very Idea of a Conceptual Scheme." In *Inquiries into Truth and Interpretation*. Oxford: Oxford University Press, 1984.]

Frege, Gottlob (1848–1925) *German logician and mathematician who is generally considered one of the founders of modern symbolic logic and of what is called logicism, the view that logic is the foundation of mathematics. He also contributed to the analysis of meaning. In the passage below, he distinguishes between the sense of a term and the reference of a term.*

It is natural, now, to think of there being connected with a sign (name, combination of words, letter), besides that to which the sign refers, which may be called the reference of the sign, also what I should like to call the *sense* of the sign, wherein the mode of presentation is contained. In our example, accordingly, the reference of the expressions "the point of intersection of *a* and *b*" and "the point of intersection of b and c" [in a triangle whose three sides are labeled *a*, *b*, and *c*] would be the same, but not their senses. The reference of "evening star" would be the same as that of "morning star," but not the sense.

[Frege, Gottlob. "On Sense and Reference." In *Analytic Philosophy: An Anthology*. Edited by A. P. Martinich and David Sosa. Malden: Blackwell Publishers, 2001.]

Goodman, Nelson (1906–1998) *American philosopher who formulated the new riddle of induction, in which he claimed that what counts as confirmation for some hypothesis is not simply determined by facts in the world and, indeed, the "same" facts can support different, even contradictory, hypotheses. The passage below is from his book* Fact, Fiction, and Forecast. *In this book he introduces the following problem: If we observe a green emerald, then that observation seems to (help) confirm the hypothesis that all emeralds are green. However, a green emerald also seems to (help) confirm the hypothesis that all emeralds are grue, where* grue *means that something is green if it is examined before some specified time (say, January 1, 3000) and blue if it is examined after that time.*

> The odd cases [such as grue] that we have been considering are clinically pure cases that, though seldom encountered in practice, nevertheless display to the best advantage the symptoms of a widespread and destructive malady.
>
> We have so far neither any answer nor any promising clue to an answer to the question what distinguishes lawlike or confirmable hypotheses from accidental or non-confirmable ones; and what may at first have seemed a minor technical difficulty has taken on the stature of a major obstacle to the development of a satisfactory theory of confirmation. It is this problem that I call the new riddle of induction.

> [Goodman, Nelson. *Fact, Fiction, and Forecast.* Cambridge: Harvard University Press, 1955.]

Kripke, Saul (1940–   ) *American philosopher who provided technical and conceptual advances in modal logic, but who is best known for his work in the philosophy of language, especially for introducing the causal theory of reference, a summary statement of which is given below.*

> A rough statement of a theory [of reference] might be the following: An initial "baptism" takes place. Here the object may be named by ostension, or the reference of the name may be fixed by a description. What the name is "passed from link to link," the receiver of the name must, I think, intend when he learns it to use it with the same reference as the man from whom he

heard it. If I hear the name "Napoleon" and decide it would be a nice name for my pet aardvark, I do not satisfy this condition.

[Kripke, Saul. *Naming and Necessity.* Cambridge, Mass.: Harvard University Press, 1980.]

Moore, G. E. (1873–1958) *British philosopher who is usually credited, along with Bertrand Russell, with rejecting much of late 19th-century philosophy and initiating the analytic approach of the early 20th century. In the passage below, Moore gives his famous proof of the existence of an external world (a world outside ourselves).*

It seems to me that, so far from its being true . . . that there is only one possible proof of the existence of the things outside of us . . . I can now give a large number of different proofs, each of which is a perfectly rigorous proof . . . I can prove now, for instance, that two human hands exist. How? By holding up my two hands, and saying, as I make a certain gesture with the right hand, "Here is one hand," and adding, as I make a certain gesture with the left, "and here is another."

[Moore, G. E. "Proof of An External World." In *Contemporary Analytic and Linguistic Philosophies.* Edited by E. D. Klemke. Amherst, N.Y.: Prometheus Books, 1983.]

Putnam, Hilary (1926–) *American philosopher, very influential in the second half of the 20th century in a wide range of philosophical areas, and, like Quine and Rorty, blending the concerns and methods of analytic philosophy with views derived from pragmatism. The following passage, taken from his book* Reason, Truth, and History, *speaks of internalism, by which he means the view that criteria for truth and meaning are in part dependent upon (or, internal to) conceptual schemes. It is a rejection of both the view of absolute objective realism and of the view of cultural relativism.*

Internalism is not a facile relativism that says, "Anything goes." Denying that it makes sense to ask whether our concepts match something totally uncontaminated by conceptualization is one thing; but to hold that every conceptual system is therefore just as good as every other one would be something else . . . Internalism does not deny that there are experiential *inputs* to knowledge; knowledge is not a story with no constraints except *internal* coherence; but it does deny that there are any inputs *which are not themselves to some extent shaped by our concepts,* by the vocabulary we use to report and describe them, or any inputs *which admit of only one description, independent of all conceptual choices.* Even our description of our own sensations, so dear as a starting point for knowledge to generations of epistemologists, is heavily affected (as are the sensations themselves, for that matter) by a host of conceptual choices. The very inputs upon which our knowledge is based are conceptually contaminated; but contaminated inputs are better than none. If contaminated inputs are all we have, still all we have has proved to be quite a bit.

[Putnam, Hilary. *Reason, Truth, and History.* Cambridge: Cambridge University Press, 1981.]

Quine, Willard Van Orman (1908–2000) *American philosopher, generally considered one of the most prominent and influential 20th-century philosophers. He combined an empiricist view with pragmatism to produce a series of books and articles that were unparalleled throughout the middle of the 1900s. One of his most famous positions was the rejection of the analytic/synthetic distinction, a distinction that had been held by philosophers for centuries. The passage below, from a famous article entitled "Two Dogmas of Empiricism," identifies his rejection of this distinction as well as his rejection of reductionism.*

Modern empiricism has been conditioned . . . by two dogmas. One is a belief in some fundamental cleavage between truths which are analytic . . . and truths which are synthetic . . . The other dogma is reductionism: the belief that each meaningful statement is equivalent to some logical construct upon terms which refer to immediate experience. Both dogmas . . . are ill-founded. One effect of abandoning them is . . . a blurring of the supposed boundary between speculative metaphysics and natural science. Another effect is a shift toward pragmatism.

[Quine, Willard Van Orman. "Two Dogmas of Empiricism." In *From a Logical Point of View.* Cambridge, Mass.: Harvard University Press, 1953.]

Rorty, Richard (1931–2007) *American philosopher, often labeled as a neopragmatist because of his support of many of the doctrines associated with classical American pragmatism (especially the thought of John Dewey) and blending these doctrines with others from both analytic philosophy and European continental philosophy. His book* Philosophy and the Mirror of Nature *was highly influential and controversial. The selection below, in which he criticizes much of 20th-century analytic philosophy, is taken from his 1981 paper "Philosophy in America Today."*

1. Analytic philosophy started off as a way of moving from speculation to science—from philosophy as an historically based discipline to philosophy as a discipline centering around "logical analysis."

2. The notion of "logical analysis" turned upon itself, and committed slow suicide, in Wittgensteinian, "ordinary language," Quinean, Kuhnian, and Sellarsian criticisms of the purportedly "scientific" vocabulary which Reichenbach, e.g., had taken for granted.

3. Analytic philosophy was thus left without a genealogy, a sense of mission, or a metaphilosophy. Training in philosophy turned into a sort of "casebook" procedure, of the sort found in law schools. Students' wits were sharpened by reading preprints of articles by currently fashionable figures, and finding objections to them. The students so trained began to think of themselves neither as continuing a tradition nor as participating in the solution of the "outstanding problems" at the frontiers of a science. Rather, they took their self-image from a style and quality of argumentation. They became quasi-lawyers rather than quasi-scientists—hoping an interesting new case would turn up.

[Rorty, Richard. "Philosophy in America Today." In *Consequences of Pragmatism.* Minneapolis: University of Minnesota Press, 1982.]

Russell, Bertrand (1872–1970) *British philosopher, generally recognized as one of the most influential philosophers of the first half of the 20th century. His three-volume work on the foundations of logic,* Principia Mathematica, *which was cowritten with his mentor Alfred North Whitehead, is still considered one of the most important works in the history of logic. Early in the 20th century, he formulated a view that he called logical atomism, in which (among other things) he claimed that the* *task of philosophy was to engage in logical analysis as the proper means of addressing philosophical issues. The following passage states this view.*

> The business of philosophy, as I conceive it, is essentially that of logical analysis, followed by logical synthesis . . . The most important part, to my mind, consists in criticizing and clarifying notions which are apt to be regarded as fundamental and accepted uncritically. As instances, I might mention: mind, matter, consciousness, knowledge, experience, causality, will, time. I believe all these notions to be inexact and approximate, essentially infected with vagueness . . . logical structures can be built which will have properties sufficiently like those of the above common notions to account for their prevalence, but sufficiently unlike to allow a great deal of error to creep in through their acceptance as fundamental.

> [Russell, Bertrand. "Logical Atomism." In *Contemporary British Philosophers.* Edited by J. H. Muirhead. London: Allen and Unwin, 1924.]

Ryle, Gilbert (1900–1976) *British philosopher, generally considered one of the chief advocates of ordinary language philosophy. Ryle was (and is) best known for his notion of a category mistake, that is, applying certain properties that are relevant to one kind of thing to objects of a totally different kind (for example, asking how happy a mountain is; mountains are not the kinds of things that can be happy or unhappy). He was also known for rejecting the view of the mind as some sort of nonphysical substance (for which he coined the phrase the ghost in the machine). In the passage below, he claims that the proper task of philosophy is to analyze language.*

> [There] is . . . a sense in which we can properly inquire and even say "what it really means to say so and so." For we can ask what is the real form of the fact recorded when this is concealed or disguised and not duly exhibited by the expression in question. And we can often succeed in stating this fact in a new form of words which does exhibit what the other failed to exhibit. And I am for the present inclined to believe that this is what philosophical analysis is, and that this is the sole and whole function of philosophy . . .

But, as confession is good for the soul, I must admit that I do not very much relish the conclusions towards which these conclusions point. I would rather allot to philosophy a sublimer task than the detection of the sources in linguistic idioms of recurrent misconstructions and absurd theories. But that it is at least this I cannot feel any serious doubt.

[Ryle, Gilbert. "Systematically Misleading Expressions." In *Collected Papers*, Volume 2. New York: Barnes and Noble, 1971.]

Vienna Circle (logical positivism)   *a term used to refer to a group of philosophers and other academics who met and worked in Vienna at the beginning of the 20th century; they formed the core of the school of thought called Logical Positivism, advocating the view that philosophy needed to be more scientific and that the only meaningful claims are ones that can be verified. The passage below is from a manifesto authored by three members of the Vienna Circle (Hans Hahn, Rudolf Carnap, and Otto Neurath), in which they state their scientific world conception.*

The scientific world conception is characterized not so much by theses of its own, but rather by its basic attitude, its points of view and direction of research . . . We have characterized the scientific world conception essentially by two features. First it is empiricist and positivist: there is knowledge only from experience, which rests on what is immediately given. This sets the limits for the content of legitimate science. Second, the scientific world conception is marked by application of a certain method, namely logical analysis. The aim of the scientific effort is to reach the goal, unified science, by applying logical analysis to the empirical material. Since the meaning of every statement of science must be statable by a reduction to a statement about the given, likewise the meaning of any concept, whatever branch of science it may belong to, must be statable by step-wise reduction to other concepts, down to the concepts of the lowest level which refer directly to the given.

[Neurath, Otto. *Empiricism and Sociology.* Dordrecht, Netherlands: Kluwer Academic Publishers, 1973.]

Wittgenstein, Ludwig (1889–1951)   *Austrian philosopher who is universally acknowledged as one of the most important and influential philosophers of the 20th century, both inside and outside of the discipline of philosophy. Wittgenstein's early work was important in the movement of logical analysis of language, while his later work (in which he rejected much of his early thought) was important in the movement of ordinary language philosophy. The following selection, taken from his later book* Philosophical Investigations, *presents his view of family resemblance. This view involves a rejection of the assumption that things have essences and that there are necessary and sufficient conditions for the meaning of terms.*

Instead of producing something common to all that we call language, I am saying that these phenomena have no one thing in common which makes us use the same word for all—but that they are *related* to one another in many different ways. And it is because of this relationship, or these relationships, that we call them all "language." I will try to explain this.

Consider for example the proceedings that we call "games." I mean board-games, card-games, ball-games, Olympic games, and so on. What is common to them all?—Don't say: "There *must* be something common, or they would not be called 'games'"—but *look and see* whether there is anything common to all.—For if you look at them you will not see something that is common to *all,* but similarities, relationships, and a whole series of them at that . . . And the result of this examination is: we see a complicated network of similarities, overlapping and criss-crossing: sometime overall similarities, sometimes similarities in details.

I can think of no better expression to characterize these similarities than "family resemblances" . . .

[Wittgenstein, Ludwig. *Philosophical Investigations.* New York: Macmillan, 1953.]

Index